Exploring Philosophy of Religion

An Introductory Anthology

EDITED BY

Steven M. Cahn

The City University of New York Graduate Center

New York Oxford

OXFORD UNIVERSITY PRESS

2009

Oxford University Press, Inc., publishes works that further Oxford University's objective of excellence in research, scholarship, and education.

Oxford New York
Auckland Cape Town Dar es Salaam Hong Kong Karachi
Kuala Lumpur Madrid Melbourne Mexico City Nairobi
New Delhi Shanghai Taipei Toronto

With offices in
Argentina Austria Brazil Chile Czech Republic France Greece
Guatemala Hungary Italy Japan Poland Portugal Singapore
South Korea Switzerland Thailand Turkey Ukraine Vietnam

Published by Oxford University Press, Inc.
198 Madison Avenue, New York, New York 10016
http://www.oup.com

Library of Congress Cataloging-in-Publication Data

Exploring philosophy of religion : an introductory anthology / edited by Steven M. Cahn.
p. cm.
Includes index.
ISBN 978-0-19-534085-3 (pbk. : alk. paper) 1. Religion-Philosophy.
I. Cahn, Steven M.
BL51.E97 2008
210—dc22 2007044608

Printing number: 9 8 7 6 5 4 3 2 1

Printed in the United States of America
on acid-free paper

To the memory of my mother,
Evelyn Baum Cahn

her parents,
Solomon Baum
Victoria Bieber Baum

and her brothers,
Lester Baum
Morton Baum

Contents

PART 3 RELIGIOUS LANGUAGE

PART 4 MIRACLES AND MYSTICISM

PART 5 BELIEF IN GOD

PART 6 RESURRECTION AND IMMORTALITY

PART 7 RELIGIOUS PLURALISM

Preface

Many students approach philosophy of religion with a keen desire to explore issues that have long been of personal concern. The most widely used anthologies, however, contain much material that is daunting in its complexity, thereby undermining the interest of many readers. Furthermore, the ordering of topics is often hard to fathom, and no synthesis is provided.

The guiding principle of this book is that reading clear, recent essays along with the most accessible and influential historical sources offers an inviting avenue to the subject. Many of these materials have been shortened to sharpen their focus and make them easier to understand. Introductions offer guides to the selections, and the bracketed footnotes contain explanatory materials. The appendix provides my own extended, interpretative overview of the field.

I am grateful to my editor, Robert Miller, for his continuing support and advice and also to associate editor Sarah Calabi for her conscientiousness and ingenuity. I also appreciate the thoughtful work of editorial assistant Yelena Bromberg, and the help provided by other staff members of Oxford University Press.

Long ago my interest in this field was initiated by my late father, Rabbi Judah Cahn, who strongly influenced my thinking. More recently I have benefited greatly from numerous discussions over many years with my friend and twice coeditor Professor David Shatz of Yeshiva University. My brother, Victor L. Cahn, playwright, critic, and Professor of English at Skidmore College, offered numerous stylistic suggestions. My wife, Marilyn, provided unwavering encouragement and so much more.

Finally, a few words about the book's dedication. Even as a youngster I was aware of my mother's remarkable family. Her father, who died a decade before I was born, had served as President of the Cantors Association of America; her mother, like my mother herself, exemplified practical wisdom and was devoted to Judaism but shorn of superstition; my mother's eldest brother, Lester, served as a New York State Senator; and her elder brother, Morton, was a distinguished attorney and brilliant pianist, who provided the administrative acumen and creative planning that led to the success of the New York City Center of Music and Drama, including the New York City Opera and the New York City Ballet. The deep appreciation they all felt for their heritage provided me with exemplars of the sort of religious commitment with which I myself am most comfortable.

Introduction

Philosophy of religion is an ancient branch of inquiry that attempts to clarify religious beliefs and subject them to critical scrutiny. Some thinkers have employed the methods of philosophy to support religion, whereas others have used these same methods with quite different aims. All philosophy of religion, however, is concerned with questions that arise when religious doctrines are tested by the canons of reason.

While philosophers of religion take into account doctrines held by adherents of a variety of religions, philosophy of religion is not the same as comparative religion, the historical and sociological study of the growth and influence of various religious traditions. Philosophers focus not on describing beliefs but on analyzing their meaning and assessing their justification.

Some readers may suppose that religious commitment is based on faith, not reason, and so should not be subject to critical evaluation. This concern, however, should be eased by considering the work of such eminent philosophers as St. Augustine (354–430), the greatest of the Church fathers; Moses Maimonides (1135–1204), the preeminent authority on Jewish law; and St. Thomas Aquinas (1225–1274), the Dominican teacher whose voluminous writings were recognized six centuries later by Pope Leo XIII as authoritative for the Catholic church. These great thinkers, along with so many others who were equally committed to testing their religious beliefs by the canons of reason, did not fear critical inquiry but embraced it, even if they concluded on occasion that some of their beliefs rested only on revelation.

But what is the meaning of key religious beliefs? Which of them are defensible by reason and which not? On what basis can we adjudicate among the conflicting revelations of different religions? These complex and intriguing questions lie at the core of the fascinating field of philosophy of religion.

In deciding which proposed answers to these questions are correct, readers are the jury. Just as each juror at a trial needs to make a decision and defend a view after considering all the relevant evidence, so each philosophical inquirer needs to make a decision and defend a view after considering all the relevant arguments. This book makes available in convenient form the materials on which to base your thinking. The challenge and excitement of philosophy, however, is that after taking account of the work others have done, the responsibility for reaching conclusions is your own.

Should you wish to learn more about particular philosophers or specific philosophical issues, an excellent source to consult is Edward Craig, ed., *Encyclopedia of Philosophy* (London: Routledge, 1999). Shorter entries, but informative and reliable, are found in Simon Blackburn, ed., *The Oxford Dictionary of Philosophy*, Second Edition (New York: Oxford University Press, 2007) and Robert Audi, ed., *The Cambridge Dictionary of Philosophy*, Second Edition (Cambridge and New York: Cambridge University Press, 1999). A useful guide to the entire field of philosophy of religion is William Wainwright, ed., *The Oxford Handbook of Philosophy of Religion* (New York: Oxford University Press, 2007).

One other note. Some of the following selections were written when the custom was to use the noun "man" and the pronoun "he" to designate all persons, regardless of sex. Similarly, God was often referred to in masculine terms without necessarily intending to conceptualize the divine as gendered. In the interest of historical accuracy, I have left each author's terminology unchanged. With this proviso, let us embark on exploring philosophy of religion.

PART 1

The Concept of God

God and Goodness

James Rachels

Theism is the belief that God exists. *Atheism* is the belief that God does not exist. *Agnosticism* is the belief that sufficient evidence is not available to decide whether God exists. But what is meant by the term *God?*

Let us adopt a view shared by many theists that the word *God* refers to an all-good, all-powerful, all-knowing, eternal creator of the world. Before proceeding to consider whether God exists, we need to examine how the divine attributes themselves give rise to philosophical perplexities.

Consider the goodness of God. Is God all-good because God always acts in accord with a standard of rightness or because God creates the standard of rightness? In other words, does God choose the standard of rightness, or is God subject to the standard? Either answer raises difficulties, as you will see in our first selection, authored by James Rachels (1941–2003), who was Professor of Philosophy at the University of Alabama at Birmingham.

In both the Jewish and Christian traditions, God is presented as a lawgiver who has created us, and the world we live in, for a purpose. That purpose is not completely understood, but much has been revealed through the prophets, the Holy Scriptures, and the church. These sources teach that, to guide us in righteous living, God has promulgated rules that we are to obey. He does not compel us to obey them. We were created as free agents, so we may choose to accept or to reject his commandments. But if we are to live as we *should* live, we must follow God's laws. This, it is said, is the essence of morality.

This line of thought has been elaborated by some theologians into a theory about the nature of right and wrong, known as the *Divine Command Theory.* Essentially, this theory says that "morally right" means "commanded by God," and "morally wrong" means "forbidden by God."

From a theoretical point of view, this conception has a number of pleasing features. It immediately solves the old problem about the subjectivity/objectivity of ethics. According to this theory, ethics is not merely a matter

---

From James Rachels, *The Elements of Moral Philosophy,* Second Edition. Reprinted by permission of McGraw-Hill.

of personal feelings or social custom. Whether something is right or wrong is a perfectly objective matter: it is right if God commands it, wrong if God forbids it. Moreover, the Divine Command Theory suggests an answer to the perennial question of why anyone should bother with morality. Why not just look out for one's own interests? If immorality is the violation of God's commandments, there is an easy answer: on the day of final reckoning, you will be held accountable.

There are, however, serious problems for the theory. Of course, atheists would not accept it, because they do not believe that God exists. But the problems that arise are not merely problems for atheists. There are difficulties even for believers. The main problem was first noted by Plato, the Greek philosopher who lived 400 years before the birth of Jesus.

Plato's writings were in the form of dialogues, usually between Socrates and one or more interlocutors. In one of these dialogues, the *Euthyphro,* there is a discussion concerning whether "right" can be defined as "that which the gods command." Socrates is skeptical and asks: *Is conduct right because the gods command it, or do the gods command it because it is right?* It is one of the most famous questions in the history of philosophy. The contemporary British philosopher Antony Flew suggests that "one good test of a person's aptitude for philosophy is to discover whether he can grasp its force and point."

The point is this. If we accept the theological conception of right and wrong, we are caught in a dilemma. Socrates's question asks us to clarify what we mean. There are two things we might mean, and both options lead to trouble.

1. First, we might mean that conduct is right *because God commands it.* For example, according to Exodus 20:16, God commands us to be truthful. On this option, the *reason* we should be truthful is simply that God requires it. Apart from the divine command, truth telling is neither good nor bad. It is God's command that *makes* truthfulness right.

But this leads to trouble, for it represents God's commands as arbitrary. It means that God could have given *different* commands just as easily. He could have commanded us to be liars, and then lying, and not truthfulness, would be right. (You may be tempted to reply: "But God would never command us to be liars!" But why not? If he did endorse lying, God would not be commanding us to do wrong, because his command would make lying right.) Remember that on this view, honesty was not right *before* God commanded it. Therefore, he could have had no more reason to command it than its opposite; and so, from a moral point of view, his command is perfectly arbitrary.

Moreover, on this view, the doctrine of the goodness of God is reduced to nonsense. It is important to religious believers that God is not only all-powerful and all-knowing, but that he is also *good;* yet if we accept the idea that good and bad are defined by reference to God's will, this notion is deprived of any meaning. What could it mean to say that God's commands are good? If "X is good" simply means "X is commanded by God," then "God's commands are good" would mean only "God's commands are commanded by God"—an empty truism. In his *Discourse on Metaphysics* (1686) Leibniz put the point very clearly:

> So in saying that things are not good by any rule of goodness, but sheerly by the will of God, it seems to me that one destroys, without realizing it, all the love of God and all his glory. For why praise him for what he has done if he would be equally praiseworthy in doing exactly the contrary?

Thus if we choose the first of Socrates's two options, we are stuck with consequences that even the most religious people must find unacceptable.

2. There is a way to avoid these troublesome consequences. We can take the second of Socrates's options. We need not say that right conduct is right because God commands it. Instead, we may say that God commands right conduct *because it is right*. God, who is infinitely wise, realizes that truthfulness is far better than deceitfulness, and so he commands us to be truthful; he sees that killing is wrong, and so he commands us not to kill; and so on for all the commandments.

If we take this option, we avoid the troublesome consequences that plagued the first alternative. God's commands turn out to be not at all arbitrary; they are the result of his wisdom in knowing what is best. And the doctrine of the goodness of God is preserved: to say that his commands are good means that he commands only what, in perfect wisdom, he sees to be the best. But this option leads to a different problem, which is equally troublesome for the theological conception of right and wrong: indeed, in taking this option, we have virtually *abandoned* the theological conception of right and wrong.

If we say that God commands us to be truthful because truthfulness is right, then we are admitting that there is some standard of right and wrong that is independent of God's will. We are saying that God *sees* or *recognizes* that truthfulness is right: this is very different from his *making* it right. The rightness exists prior to and independent of God's command, and it is the reason for the command. Thus if we want to know why we should be truthful, the reply "Because God commands it" will not take us very far. We may still ask "But why does God command it?" and the answer to *that* question will provide the underlying reasons why truthfulness is a good thing.

All this may be summarized in the following argument:

(1) Suppose God commands us to do what is right. Then *either* (a) the right actions are right because he commands them *or* (b) he commands them because they are right.

(2) If we take option (a), then God's commands are, from a moral point of view, arbitrary; moreover, the doctrine of the goodness of God is rendered meaningless.

(3) If we take option (b), then we have admitted there is a standard of right and wrong that is independent of God's will.
(4) Therefore, we must *either* regard God's commands as arbitrary, and give up the doctrine of the goodness of God, *or* admit that there is a standard of right and wrong that is independent of his will, and give up the theological definitions of right and wrong.
(5) From a religious point of view, it is undesirable to regard God's commands as arbitrary or to give up the doctrine of the goodness of God.
(6) Therefore, even from a religious point of view, a standard of right and wrong that is independent of God's will must be accepted.

Many religious people believe that they should accept a theological conception of right and wrong because it would be impious not to do so. They feel, somehow, that if they believe in God, they *should* think that right and wrong are to be defined ultimately in terms of his will. But this argument suggests otherwise: it suggests that, on the contrary, the Divine Command Theory of right and wrong itself leads to impious results, so that a pious person should *not* accept it. And in fact, some of the greatest theologians, such as St. Thomas Aquinas, rejected the theory for just this reason.

God's Omnipotence

George Mavrodes

Omnipotence or all-powerfulness is another divine attribute that raises philosophical problems. Consider this question: Can God make a stone so heavy that God cannot lift it? If God can make such a stone, then it would seem that God is not omnipotent because the task of lifting the stone is beyond God's power. But if God cannot make such a stone, then it would seem again that God is not omnipotent because a task has been described that God cannot perform. So in either case God is not omnipotent.

Is the argument valid, that is, do the premises imply the conclusion? Is the argument also sound, that is, is it not only valid but does

From *The Philosophical Review* 73 (1964).

it also have true premises? In our next selection, George Mavrodes, who is Professor Emeritus of Philosophy at the University of Michigan, maintains that the argument, although valid, is unsound and therefore does not demonstrate any defect in the doctrine of God's omnipotence.

The doctrine of God's omnipotence appears to claim that God can do anything. Consequently, there have been attempts to refute the doctrine by giving examples of things which God cannot do; for example, He cannot draw a square circle.

Responding to objections of this type, St. Thomas pointed out that "anything" should be here construed to refer only to objects, actions, or states of affairs whose descriptions are not self-contradictory.[1] For it is only such things whose nonexistence might plausibly be attributed to a lack of power in some agent. My failure to draw a circle on the exam may indicate my lack of geometrical skill, but my failure to draw a square circle does not indicate any such lack. Therefore, the fact that it is false (or perhaps meaningless) to say that God could draw one does no damage to the doctrine of His omnipotence.

A more involved problem, however, is posed by this type of question: can God create a stone too heavy for Him to lift? This appears to be stronger than the first problem, for it poses a dilemma. If we say that God can create a stone, then it seems that there might be such a stone. And if there might be a stone too heavy for Him to lift, then He is evidently not omnipotent. But if we deny that God can create such a stone, we seem to have given up His omnipotence already. Both answers lead us to the same conclusion.

Further, this problem does not seem obviously open to St. Thomas' solution. The form "x is able to draw a square circle" seems plainly to involve a contradiction, while "x is able to make a thing too heavy for x to lift" does not. For it may easily be true that I am able to make a boat too heavy for me to lift. So why should it not be possible for God to make a stone too heavy for Him to lift?

Despite this apparent difference, this second puzzle *is* open to essentially the same answer as the first. The dilemma fails because it consists of asking whether God can do a self-contradictory thing. And the reply that He cannot does no damage to the doctrine of omnipotence.

The specious nature of the problem may be seen in this way. God is either omnipotent or not.[2] Let us assume first that He is not. In that case the phrase "a stone too heavy for God to lift" may not be self-contradictory. And then, of course, if we assert either that God is able or that He is not able to create such a stone, we may conclude that He is not omnipotent. But this is no more than the assumption with which we began, meeting us again after our roundabout journey. If this were all that the dilemma could establish it would be trivial. . . .

On the assumption that God is omnipotent, the phrase "a stone too heavy for God to lift" becomes self-contradictory. For it becomes "a stone which cannot be lifted by Him whose power is sufficient for lifting anything." But the "thing" described by a self-contradictory phrase is absolutely impossible and hence has nothing to do with the doctrine of omnipotence. Not being an object of power at all, its failure to exist cannot be the result of some lack in the power of God. And, interestingly, it is the very omnipotence of God which makes the existence of such a stone absolutely impossible, while it is the fact that I am finite in power which makes it possible for me to make a boat too heavy for me to lift.

But suppose that some die-hard objector takes the bit in his teeth and denies that the phrase "a stone too heavy for God to lift" is self-contradictory, even on the assumption that God is omnipotent. In other words, he contends that the description "a stone too heavy for an omnipotent God to lift" is self-coherent and therefore describes an absolutely possible object. Must I then attempt to prove the contradiction which I assume above as intuitively obvious? Not necessarily. Let me reply simply that if the objector is right in this contention, then the answer to the original question is "Yes, God can create such a stone." It may seem that this reply will force us into the original dilemma. But it does not. For now the objector can draw no damaging conclusion from this answer. And the reason is that he has just now contended that such a stone is compatible with the omnipotence of God. Therefore, from the possibility of God's creating such a stone it cannot be concluded that God is not omnipotent. The objector cannot have it both ways. The conclusion which he himself wishes to draw from an affirmative answer to the original question is itself the required proof that the descriptive phrase which appears there is self-contradictory. . . .

Nothing I have said above, of course, goes to prove that God is, in fact, omnipotent. All I have intended to show is that certain arguments intended to prove that He is not omnipotent fail. They fail because they propose, as tests of God's power, putative tasks whose descriptions are self-contradictory. Such pseudo-tasks, not falling within the realm of possibility, are not objects of power at all. Hence the fact that they cannot be performed implies no limit on the power of God, and hence no defect in the doctrine of omnipotence.

NOTES

1. St. Thomas Aquinas, *Summa Theologiae,* la, q. 25, a. 3.
2. I assume, of course, the existence of God, since that is not being brought in question here.

God's Foreknowledge and Free Will

AUGUSTINE

If God is omniscient, then God knows now whether you will perform a specific action at a particular moment in the future. How then can you be held morally responsible for performing that action? You must do what God knows you will do.

Faced with this argument, a theist who believes in free will must either find some error in the reasoning or reinterpret the doctrine of God's omniscience. The former approach was taken by St. Augustine (354–430), the first of the great Christian philosophers, who was born in North Africa, taught rhetoric in Milan, was converted to Christianity, then lived a monastic life and eventually became bishop of Hippo (in what is present-day Algeria).

He rejected any supposed incompatibility between God's omniscience and free will, arguing that what God foreknows is that you will act freely. According to St. Augustine, God knows which choices you will make but does not cause you to make them. Thus even though God is omniscient, His punishment of wrongdoers is just, because they are responsible for their actions.

AUGUSTINE: Surely this is the problem that is disturbing and puzzling you. How is it that these two propositions are not contradictory and inconsistent: (1) God has foreknowledge of everything in the future; and (2) We sin by the will, not by necessity? For, you say, if God foreknows that someone is going to sin, then it is necessary that he sin. But if it is necessary, the will has no choice about whether to sin; there is an inescapable and fixed necessity. And so you fear that this argument forces us into one of two positions: either we draw the heretical conclusion that God does not foreknow everything in the future; or, if we cannot accept this conclusion, we must admit that sin happens by necessity and not by will. Isn't that what is bothering you?

EVODIUS: That's it exactly.

AUGUSTINE: So you think that anything that God foreknows happens by necessity and not by will.

From Augustine, *On Free Choice of the Will*, trans. Thomas Williams.

EVODIUS: Precisely. . . .

AUGUSTINE: Just notice how imperceptive someone would have to be to argue thus: "If God has foreknown my future will, it is necessary that I will what he has foreknown, since nothing can happen otherwise than as he has foreknown it. But if it is necessary, then one must concede that I will it by necessity and not by will." What extraordinary foolishness! If God foreknew a future will that turned out not to be a will at all, things would indeed happen otherwise than as God foreknew them. And I will overlook this objector's equally monstrous statement that "it is necessary that I will," for by assuming necessity he tries to abolish will. For if his willing is necessary, how does he will, since there is no will? . . .

Thus, we believe both that God has foreknowledge of everything in the future and that nonetheless we will whatever we will. Since God foreknows our will, the very will that he foreknows will be what comes about. Therefore, it will be a will, since it is a will that he foreknows. And it could not be a will unless it were in our power. Therefore, he also foreknows this power. It follows, then, that his foreknowledge does not take away my power; in fact, it is all the more certain that I will have that power, since he whose foreknowledge never errs foreknows that I will have it.

EVODIUS: I agree now that it is necessary that whatever God has foreknown will happen, and that he foreknows our sins in such a way that our wills remain free and are within our power.

AUGUSTINE: Then what is troubling you? . . .

EVODIUS: . . . I must admit that I can't quite see how God's foreknowledge of our sins can be consistent with our free choice in sinning. For we must admit that God is just, and that he has foreknowledge. But I would like to know how it can be just to punish sins that happen necessarily, or how things that God foreknows do not happen necessarily. . . .

AUGUSTINE: Why do you think that our free choice is inconsistent with God's foreknowledge? Because it's foreknowledge, or because it's *God's* foreknowledge?

EVODIUS: Because it's God's foreknowledge.

AUGUSTINE: If you knew that someone was going to sin, he wouldn't sin necessarily, would he?

EVODIUS: Indeed he would. Unless I foreknew something with certainty, it wouldn't be foreknowledge at all.

AUGUSTINE: Then it's not *God's* foreknowledge that makes his sin necessary, but any foreknowledge, since if something is not foreknown with certainty, it is not foreknown at all.

EVODIUS: I agree. But where are you headed with this?

AUGUSTINE: Unless I am mistaken, you do not force someone to sin just because you foreknow that he is going to sin. Nor does your foreknowledge force him to sin, even if he is undoubtedly going to sin—since otherwise you would not have genuine foreknowledge. So if your foreknowledge is consistent with his freedom in sinning, so that you foreknow what someone else is going to do by his own will, then God forces no one to sin, even though he foresees those who are going to sin by their own will.

Why then can't our just God punish those things that his foreknowledge does not force to happen? Just as your memory does not force the past to have happened, God's foreknowledge does not force the future to happen. And just as you remember some things that you have done but did not do everything that you remember, God foreknows everything that he causes but does not cause everything that he foreknows. Of such things he is not the evil cause, but the just avenger. Therefore, you must understand that God justly punishes the sins that he foreknows but does not cause. If the fact that God foresees their sins means that he should not punish sinners, then he should also not reward those who act rightly, for he also foresees their righteous actions. Let us rather confess that nothing in the future is hidden from God's foreknowledge, and that no sin is left unpunished by his justice, for sin is committed by the will, not coerced by God's foreknowledge.

God's Omniscience and Contingent Events

Levi Gersonides

Rabbi Levi ben Gershom (1288–1344), known as Gersonides, lived in Province, France. He was renowned not only as an astronomer, mathematician, and Biblical commentator but also as a remarkably acute philosopher, deeply committed to rational inquiry and prepared to interpret all religious beliefs in the light of scientific knowledge.

 The use of brackets within the text indicates insertions by the translator.

In his philosophical masterpiece, *The Wars of the Lord,* he faced the apparent conflict between God's omniscience and free will, and developed a position that has come to be known as the "Principle of Gersonides." He maintained that God is omniscient, knowing all things as they are. God understands the general laws that govern the world but also recognizes that some particular future events, most notably human choices, are contingent, that is, they may occur or may not occur. In short, future events are in some measure up to us. God does not know the choices we shall make, for they are unknowable, but God is nevertheless omniscient because God knows everything that can be known.

God knows particulars in one respect but does not know them in another respect. But what these respects are, would that I knew!

It has been previously shown that these particulars are ordered and determined in one sense, yet contingent in another sense. Accordingly, it is evident that the sense in which God knows these particulars is the sense in which they are ordered and determined. . . . For from this aspect it is possible to have knowledge of them. On the other hand, the sense in which God does not know particulars is the sense in which they are not ordered, i.e., the sense in which they are contingent. For in the latter sense knowledge of them is not possible. However, God does know from this aspect that these events may not occur because of the choice, which He has given man. . . . But He does not know which of the contradictory outcomes will be realized insofar as they are [genuinely] contingent affairs; for if He did, there would not be any contingency at all. [Nevertheless,] the fact that God does not have the knowledge of which possible outcomes will be realized does not imply any defect in God (may He be blessed). For perfect knowledge of something is the knowledge of what that thing is in reality; when the thing is not apprehended as it is, this is error, not knowledge. Hence, God knows these things in the best manner possible, for He knows them insofar as they are ordered in a determinate and certain way, and He knows in addition that these events are contingent, insofar as they fall within the domain of human choice, [and as such knows them] truly as contingent. Thus, God (may He be blessed), by means of the Prophets, commands men who are about to suffer evil fortune that they mend their ways so that they will avert this punishment, as in the case of King Zedekiah who was commanded to make peace with the King of Babylonia.[1] Now this indicates that what God knows of future events is known by Him as not necessarily occurring; however, He knows these events in the sense that they are part of the general order and also as possibly not occurring insofar as they are contingent. . . .

It is now incumbent upon us to show that the theory we have established by philosophical argument is identical with the view of our Torah. It is a fundamental and pivotal belief of the Torah that there are contingent events in the world. Accordingly, the Torah commands us to perform certain things and prohibits other things. It is [also] a fundamental principle implicit in all the Prophets (may they rest in peace) that God informs them of these contingent events before they actually occur, as it is said, "God does nothing without having revealed His purpose to His servants the prophets."[2] Yet it is not necessary that any evil predicted by them must occur, as it is said, "God is gracious . . . [abounding in kindness] and renouncing punishment."[3] These principles are reconcilable only on the hypothesis that [first] these contingent events are in some sense ordered, and it is in this respect that knowledge of them is possible, but in another sense not ordered, and it is in the latter sense that they are contingent; and [second] that God (may He be blessed) knows all future contingent events insofar as they are ordered and [in addition] knows that they are contingent. It is, therefore, clear that the view of our Torah is identical with the theory that philosophical argument has proved with respect to divine knowledge. . . .

Moreover, the Torah maintains that the will of God does not change, as it said, "I am the Lord—I have not changed."[4] And Balaam, when he was a prophet, said: "God is not man to be capricious, or mortal to change His mind."[5] [Yet] in some of the Prophets [it is related that] God does repent of His acts, as it is said, "The Lord renounced the punishment He had planned to bring upon His people";[6] "For God is gracious . . . renouncing punishment."[7] Since this difficulty cannot be removed when it is assumed that God (may He be blessed) knows particulars as particulars but can be easily removed when it is assumed that He knows them as we have argued [i.e., generally], it is proper, according to the Torah, that we should interpret the doctrine of divine knowledge according to our philosophical theory.

That our theory of divine cognition can easily solve this problem can be shown as follows. God's knowledge does not imply that a particular event will occur to a particular man, but that it may occur to *any* man who falls under this [general] ordering of events, insofar as these events are ordered; in addition, God knows that this event may *not* occur because of human choice. But if we were to claim that God knows this affair with respect to this particular man as a definite individual, it would follow that His will would be subject to change.

In short, there is nothing in the words of the Prophets (may they rest in peace) that implies anything incompatible with the theory we have developed by means of philosophy. Hence, it is incumbent upon us to follow philosophy in this matter. For, when the Torah, interpreted literally, seems to conflict with doctrines that have been proved by reason, it is proper to interpret these passages according to philosophical understanding, so long as none of the fundamental principles of the Torah is destroyed.

NOTES

1. ["Then Jeremiah said to Zedekiah, Thus said the LORD, the God of Hosts, the God of Israel: If you surrender to the officers of the king of Babylon, your life will

be spared and this city will not be burned down. You and your household will live. But if you do not surrender to the officers of the king of Babylon, this city will be delivered into the hands of the Chaldeans, who will burn it down, and you will not escape from them." (Jeremiah 38: 17–18.) The translation is from *Tanakh: The Holy Scriptures* (Philadelphia: Jewish Publication Society, 1988). Zedekiah chose not to surrender, and subsequently he was captured and the walls of Jerusalem torn down.]

2. [Amos 3:7.]
3. [Joel 2:13.]
4. [Mal. 3:6.]
5. [Num. 23:19.]
6. [Ex. 32:14.]
7. [Joel 2:13]

Does God Know the Future?

Steven M. Cahn

In the next selection, Steven M. Cahn, editor of this book and Professor of Philosophy at The City University of New York Graduate Center, maintains that if we have free will, God does not know the outcome of our future choices. After defending this view against a series of objections by major philosophers of the past, including St. Augustine, Cahn goes on to defend Gersonides' position that, despite God's not knowing the decisions we shall make, God still might be described appropriately as omniscient.

In the Book of Deuteronomy, God says to the people of Israel, "I have put before you life and death, blessing and curse. Choose life—if you and your offspring would live. . . ."[1] Did God know which option the people would choose? If so, how could their choice have been free? For if God knew they would choose life, then to have chosen death would have confuted God's knowledge—which is impossible. If God knew they would choose death, then to have chosen life would also have confuted God's knowledge. But

From Steven M. Cahn and David Shatz, eds., *Questions About God: Today's Philosophers Ponder the Divine.* Oxford University Press. Reprinted by permission of Steven M. Cahn.

God gave the people a genuine choice. So even God did not know how they would choose.

I find this line of argument persuasive, but many notable thinkers have believed it unsound. In what follows I shall present briefly a sampling of their objections and my replies.

Objection 1. "Just as your memory does not force the past to have happened, God's foreknowledge does not force the future to happen." So argued St. Augustine.[2]

Reply. Admittedly, my remembering that an event occurred does not cause the event's occurrence. And God's foreknowledge that an event will occur does not cause its occurrence. But if I know that an event occurred, then it is not within my power to alter its occurrence. Not only won't I alter it, I can't. Similarly, if God knows that an event will occur, then it is not within God's power to alter its occurrence. Even assuming God is all-powerful, God can only do what is logically possible, for what is logically impossible is incoherent, and an incoherent task is no task at all. Thus if an event will occur, even if God does not cause its occurrence, God is bound by logic to allow its occurrence. In short, knowledge does not cause events, but, given definitive knowledge of events, they are unavoidable.

Objection 2. "[W]e estimate the intimacy of relationship between two persons by the foreknowledge one has of the action of the other, without supposing that in either case the one or the other's freedom has thereby been endangered. So even divine foreknowledge cannot endanger freedom." So said the German theologian Friedrich Schleiermacher.[3]

Reply. We rarely claim more than strong belief about what others will do, for we realize that however likely our prediction, we may be proved wrong. But when we do possess knowledge, it is incompatible with free choice. For example, we know we all shall die. It follows that it is not within anyone's power to remain alive forever. If we knew not only *that* we would die but also when, where, and how we would die, then we could not avoid death in the known time, place, and manner. Strong beliefs can be confuted, but not knowledge.

Objection 3. "It is not true, then, that because God foreknew what would be within the power of our wills, nothing therefore lies within the power of our wills. For when He foreknew this, He did not foreknow nothing. Therefore, if He who foreknew what would lie within the power of our wills did not foreknow nothing, but something, then clearly something lies within in the power of our wills even though God has foreknowledge of it." Again, St. Augustine.[4]

Reply. This line of reasoning begs the question, assuming what is supposed to be proved. If God foreknew our free choices, then they would be free. But can God foreknow our free choices? The argument I presented originally concludes that God cannot foreknow our free choices. Simply assuming the possibility of such foreknowledge carries no weight against the argument and identifies no mistake in it.

Objection 4. "[S]ince God lives in the eternal present, His knowledge transcends all movement of time and abides in the simplicity of its immediate present. It encompasses the infinite sweep of past and future, and regards all things in its simple comprehension as if they were now taking place. Thus if you will think about the foreknowledge by which God distinguishes all things, you will rightly consider it to be not a foreknowledge of future events, but knowledge of a never changing present." So argued the Roman philosopher Boethius.[5]

Reply. We make certain choices before others. Indeed, certain choices presuppose others. For example, the choice to seek a divorce requires a prior choice to marry. Whatever is meant by the assertion that God transcends time (a murky claim), God presumably knows that we make certain choices before others. So God takes account of time. Admittedly, God is supposed to view the future as clearly as we view the present. But appeals to the clarity of God's knowledge only underscore why that knowledge is incompatible with the freedom of choices we are yet to make.

Objection 5. "[T]hough we do not know the true nature of God's knowledge . . . yet we know that . . . nothing of all existing things is hidden from Him and that His knowledge of them does not change their nature, but the possible retains its nature as a possibility. Anything in this enumeration that appears contradictory is so only owing to the structure of our knowledge, which has nothing in common with His knowledge except the name." So wrote the medieval Jewish sage Maimonides.[6]

Reply. If God's knowledge has nothing in common with human knowledge, then God's knowledge, unlike human knowledge, would not imply the truth of what is known. So God's knowledge, whatever its nature, may be compatible with free choice but only in some sense not relevant to the original argument. If we do not understand the meaning of the words we use, we cannot use them to make claims we understand.

Supposing that the argument with which I began can be sustained in the face of all criticisms (and much more can be said on both sides), does it follow that God lacks omniscience? Not if one adopts the view, which some commentators have attributed to Aristotle,[7] that statements about future choices are neither true nor false, but, at present, indeterminate. According to this view, it is not now true you will finish reading this entire book and not true you won't. Until you decide, the matter is indeterminate.

As the medieval Jewish philosopher Gersonides argued, to be omniscient is to know every true statement. Because it is not true you will finish reading the entire book and not true you won't, but true that the matter is indeterminate, an omniscient being does not know you will finish reading and does not know you won't, but does know the whole truth, namely, that the matter is indeterminate and depends on your free choice.

Thus assuming God is omniscient, God knows the entire physical structure of the universe but not the outcome of free choices. As Gersonides wrote, "[T]he fact that God does not have the knowledge of which possible outcome will be realized does not imply any defect in God (may He be blessed). For perfect knowledge of something is the knowledge of what that thing is in reality; when the thing is not apprehended as it is, this is error, not knowledge. Hence, God knows these things in the best manner possible. . . ."[8]

In other words, when God offered the people of Israel both life and death, God, although omniscient, did not know which choice they would make. God knew all that was knowable, the whole truth. But the whole truth was that the choice of life or death rested with the people of Israel. They were responsible for their decision. God awaited, but could not foresee, the outcome of their exercise of freedom.

Some may find this view unsettling, because it implies that God's knowledge, while in a sense complete, does not include within its purview definitive answers to all questions about the future. But, like Gersonides, I find this conclusion consistent with the Holy Scriptures. As Gersonides wrote,

> God (may He be blessed), by means of the Prophets, commands men who are about to suffer evil fortune that they mend their ways so that they will avert this punishment. . . . Now this indicates that what God knows of future events is known by Him as not necessarily occurring.[9]

In short, divine warnings imply uncertain outcomes.

I conclude with an admission. Certain Biblical passages may suggest, contrary to what I have argued, that God knows the future in all its details, including the outcome of future free choices. If such textual evidence were presented, how would I respond? I could echo Gersonides: "If the literal sense of the Torah differs from reason, it is necessary to interpret these passages in accordance with the demands of reason."[10] The task of developing such interpretations, if required, I would leave to others.

NOTES

1. *Tanakh: The Holy Scriptures* (Philadelphia: Jewish Publication Society, 1988), Deuteronomy 30:19.
2. *On Free Choice of the Will,* trans. Thomas Williams (Indianapolis: Hackett Publishing Company, 1993), Book III, sec. 4, p. 78.
3. *The Christian Faith,* eds. H.R. Mackintosh and J.S. Stewart (Edinburgh: T. and T. Clark, 1928), p. 228.
4. *The City of God Against the Pagans,* trans. R.W. Dysen (Cambridge: Cambridge University Press, 1998), Book V, sec. 10, p. 205.
5. *The Consolation of Philosophy,* trans. Richard Green (New York: Library of Liberal Arts, 1962), Book 5, prose 6, p. 116.
6. *The Guide of the Perplexed,* trans. Chaim Rabin (Indianapolis: Hackett Publishing Company, 1995), p. 163.
7. See, for example, Richard Taylor, "The Problem of Future Contingencies," *The Philosophical Review* 66 (1957), pp. 1–28.

8. *The Wars of the Lord*, trans. Seymour Feldman (Philadelphia: Jewish Publication Society, 1987), vol. 2, p. 118.
9. Ibid., p. 118.
10. Ibid., p. 98.

Does God Change?

WILLIAM HASKER

God is described as eternal or existing forever. This concept, however, is not easy to understand. Is God self-contained, existing outside time, or does God interact with us through the changes of time? In other words, is God impassive and unmoved by events, or is God open to the possibility of joy and sorrow, depending on what happens to us?

The doctrine that God acts in time is defended here by William Hasker, who is Professor of Philosophy at Huntington College. He maintains that belief in God's timelessness is neither found in the Bible nor required by philosophical considerations.

The claim that God is timelessly eternal, until recently a majority view among orthodox Christian theists, has suffered massive defections in recent years. Still, the doctrine of divine timelessness continues to enjoy . . . acceptance among philosophers . . . and it may retain even more of its popularity among theologians. So it may be worthwhile to state briefly the reasons for preferring the view that God is temporal—that he lives and interacts with us through the changes of time. First of all, it is clear that the doctrine of divine timelessness is not taught in the Bible and does not reflect the way the biblical writers understood God. In spite of appeals by defenders of the doctrine to texts such as Exodus 3:14, John 8:58 and 2 Peter 3:8, there simply is no trace in the Scripture of the elaborate metaphysical and conceptual apparatus that is required to make sense of divine timelessness. On the positive side, the biblical writers undeniably do present God as living, acting and reacting in time. . . .

In the face of this, the defender of timelessness has to say either that the scriptural texts do not mean what they seem plainly to say or that what they say (and mean) is, strictly speaking, false: what they say may be adequate for the religious needs of simple people, but the truly enlightened must think of God rather in the categories of timeless eternity while still (no doubt) "speaking with the masses" in ordinary religious contexts so as not to give offense to those who are not up to the rigors of proper theology. Now it might possibly be acceptable to say this sort of thing if there were clear and compelling reasons for preferring divine timelessness to taking the Scriptures at face value. But if such reasons are lacking, it seems much better to take the Bible at its word and to understand God as a temporal being.

The other main difficulty about divine timelessness is that it is very hard to make clear logical sense of the doctrine. If God is truly timeless, so that temporal determinations of "before" and "after" do not apply to him, then how can God *act* in time, as the Scriptures say that he does? How can he *know* that is occurring on the changing earthly scene? How can he *respond* when his children turn to him in prayer and obedience? And above all, if God is timeless and incapable of change, how can God be born, grow up, live with and among people, suffer and die, as we believe he did as incarnated in Jesus? Whether there are good answers to these questions, whether the doctrine of divine timelessness is intelligible and logically coherent, and whether it can be reconciled with central Christian beliefs such as the incarnation remain matters of intense controversy.

But even if divine timelessness is not incoherent and not in conflict with other key beliefs, it seems that we have at best only a tenuous grasp on the conception of God as a timeless being. Once again, this might be something we could have to accept, *if* there were compelling reasons forcing us to affirm divine timelessness. But do such reasons exist? I think not. . . .

In the philosophical lineage stretching from Parmenides to Plato to Plotinus, there is a strong metaphysical and valuational preference for permanence over change. True Being, in this tradition, must of necessity be changeless; whatever changes, on the other hand, enjoys a substandard sort of being if any at all—at best it may be, in Plato's lovely phrase, a "moving image of eternity." And this bias against change has been powerfully influential in classical theology, leading to the insistence on an excessively strong doctrine of divine immutability—which, in turn, provides key support for divine timelessness, since timelessness is the most effective way (and perhaps the only way) to rule out, once and for all, the possibility of any change in God.

For us moderns, this preference for permanence over change is scarcely compelling. Indeed, it is arguable that in our intellectual life as well as in our general culture the pendulum has swung too far in the other direction, so that if anything at all remains constant for a while our response is one of boredom and impatience. Be that as it may, the extreme valuational preference for immutability has little hold on our thinking, and the appeal of theological doctrines based on this valuation is weakened accordingly.

Finally, let us consider the doctrine of divine impassibility—the claim that God's perfection requires that God be completely self-contained, not influenced or conditioned in any way by creatures, and in particular incapable of any suffering, distress or negative emotions of any kind. One of the more extreme versions of impassibility appears in Aristotle's claim that God, being perfect, cannot take any notice of lesser beings such as humans; a perfect Thinker must be one that thinks only perfect thoughts, which means that God is eternally engaged in reflecting on his own thoughts: "His thinking is a thinking of thinking." This view is so clearly in conflict with a Christian understanding of God that it has never, to my knowledge, been adopted by Christian thinkers. But in slightly less extreme forms, divine impassibility has left a lasting imprint on Christian theology. Thus, Anselm addresses God as follows: "Thou art both compassionate, because thou dost save the wretched, and spare those who sin against thee; and not compassionate, because thou art affected by no sympathy for wretchedness" (*Proslogium* 7). Plainly stated, this says that God *acts* as we would expect a compassionate person to act—but the *feeling* of compassion forms no part of the divine life and experience.

On this point, also, Nicholas Wolterstorff makes an important contribution when he connects Augustine's doctrine of divine impassibility with Augustine's own reaction at the death of a friend.[1] Augustine was endowed with a nature that was richly emotional as well as intellectually powerful, and he speaks in moving terms of the void left in his life by the departure of his friend. Yet he also severely criticizes this love of his, "a love so intense for a being so fragile that its destruction could cause such grief."[2] Such an excess of "worldly affection," he thought, should have no part in the life of the Christian—and later on, at the death of his mother, Augustine attempted (though without complete success) to restrain himself from any overt expression of grief.

Few of us today share Augustine's view of these matters. Common experience shows us (and is reinforced by psychology) that the suppression of grief is a poor strategy—that the "work of grieving" needs to be done lest one carry the grief unresolved for years to come. And the suggestion that we should not care deeply for our fellow human beings because if we care too much we expose ourselves to suffering causes us to shake our heads sadly and turn away.

But it is hard to avoid the logic of the connection Augustine makes between the ideal of human life and the perfection of God's life. If the majestic and supremely admirable Lord of all is "without passion"—if he views the world and all its sorrows and sufferings with serene, imperturbable bliss—then should not this be our aim as well? Conversely, if it is fitting and good that we humans should care deeply for one another, should love one another in a way that makes us vulnerable to suffering and loss, then should not a love like this be attributed to God also? Perhaps the two ideals, of human and divine love, could be pried apart—but only at the cost of voiding the scriptural injunction to be "imitators of God" (Eph 5:1).

In order to give greater focus to the considerations of this section, it may be helpful to examine in some detail an argument for divine immutability that has been prevalent since the time of Plato. If God were to change, so the argument goes, then he would change either for the better or for the worse. But God cannot change for the better, since he is already perfect. And he cannot change for the worse, for this would mean that he would no longer be perfect. So God cannot change.

A first point to notice is that this argument is an instance of "perfect being" theology. That is, the assumption is made that God is an absolutely perfect being—in Anselm's phrase, "the being than which nothing greater can be conceived"—and then conclusions concerning God's attributes are drawn from this assumption. Clearly, perfect being theology is operative, both explicitly and implicitly, at many, many points in the theological tradition.

I believe the assumption that God is an absolutely perfect being is proper and correct. It does seem to be part of our conception of God that God is deserving of absolute, unreserved and unconditional worship and devotion. But suppose that we were to discover that God was in some significant way deficient and imperfect—suppose, for example, that God's attitude toward humans was a harshly demanding one that took little or no account of our needs and frailties. We might still worship God in spite of this "fault" on God's part—but would our worship not be tinged with disappointment, with regret for what "might have been" had God not suffered from this particular imperfection? But a worship tinged with such regret is not an expression of "absolute, unreserved and unconditional devotion." I think we do well to reject such possibilities and to see in God the sum of all perfections.

The difficulties with perfect being theology do not, in my view, stem from the assumption that God is an absolutely perfect being—that he is "whatever it is better to be than not to be." Rather, difficulties have arisen because people have been too ready to assume that they can determine, easily and with little effort, what perfection *is* in the case of God—that is, what attributes a perfect being must possess. Yet it clearly is no simple matter to say what is the best kind of life for a human being or what are the ideal attributes (or virtues) for a human being to possess. So why should we assume that this is simple in the case of God? I do not think it should be taken as obvious, without long and thoughtful consideration, that it is "better" for God to be temporal *or* timeless, mutable *or* immutable, passible *or* impassible. So if we are going to object to Plato's argument, we need not reject perfect being theology as such; rather, it is the application the argument makes of divine perfection that we must question.

And we can indeed question the application in this case. In fact, Plato's argument is straightforwardly fallacious, because it rests on a false dichotomy.

It rests on the assumption that all change is either for the better or for the worse, an assumption that is simply false. Consider the operation of an extremely accurate watch. A short while ago, it registered the time as five minutes after six o'clock, but now it registers twelve minutes after six. Clearly, this is a change in the watch. (Compare this watch with an "immutable" watch that always registers 10:37, day in and day out.) Is this a change for the better, suggesting a previous state of imperfection? Not at all; the watch when it registered 6:05 was perfectly accurate. Is it then a change for the worse, a decline from perfection? Again, this is clearly not the case: the time now *is* 6:12, and the watch would be inaccurate, run down or broken if it failed to register that time. So there are changes that are neither for the better nor for the worse, and the change in the watch is such a change. It is, in fact, an example of *a change that is consistent with and/or required by a constant state of excellence.*

This is not to say that the changes that occur in God are all like the changes in the watch. There are such changes in God, to be sure: God always knows what time it is. But there are other, more significant changes in God that go far beyond simply "tracking" a changing situation. When I do something wrong, God comes to be in a state of knowing that I am doing something wrong, and this is a change in God. (He could not have known ten minutes ago that I was doing something wrong, because I was not doing wrong ten minutes ago.) God also becomes displeased with me, in a way he was not before, and he may initiate actions toward me designed to remedy the situation. (For instance, the Holy Spirit may begin working in my life in such a way as to bring me to repentance for the wrong I have done.) Turning to a broader context, when God began to create the universe he changed, beginning to do something that previously he had not done. This act of creation, our faith tells us, is not something that was required in order for God to be perfect in every respect; it was sheerly a matter of free choice for God whether to create at all. Such a change, then, is consistent with, though not required by, God's maintaining a constant state of perfection.

But it is time to bring this section to a close. We have reviewed a series of divine attributes with regard to which the theology of divine openness reaches different conclusions from the classical theory of a God who is totally self-contained and unconditioned by his creation. God, we want to say, exists and carries on his life in time; he undergoes changing states. And this means that God changes—not indeed in his essential nature, his love and wisdom and power and faithfulness, but in his thoughts and deeds toward us and the rest of his creation, matching his thoughts toward the creature with the creature's actual state at the time God thinks of it. And finally, God is not impassive and unmoved by his creation; rather, in deciding to create us and love us God has opened himself to the possibility of joy and sorrow, depending on what happens to us and especially on how we respond to his love and grace.

NOTES

1. Nicholas Wolterstorff, "Suffering Love," in *Philosophy and the Christian Faith,* ed. Thomas V. Morris (Notre Dame, Ind.: University of Notre Dame Press, 1988), pp. 196–237.
2. Ibid., p. 196 (the words quoted are Wolterstorff's).

God and Forgiveness

Anne C. Minas

God is often thought to be the prime source of forgiveness. Even if human beings fail to forgive your wrongs, divine forgiveness is supposed to wipe the slate clean. While God's goodness, omnipotence, and omniscience taken together might seem to render God especially capable of forgiveness, in the article that follows, Anne C. Minas, Professor of Philosophy at the University of Waterloo, argues that God's benevolence, power, and knowledge combine to make God's forgiveness logically impossible. Indeed, she maintains that human frailty, not divine perfection, makes forgiveness possible. This article demonstrates how the perfections typically attributed to God sometimes may have unexpected, even counterintuitive, consequences.

To err is human, to forgive, divine. Most of us tend to believe this whether or not we also believe in the actual existence of a divine being. The nonbeliever reasons that if there were such a being he would forgive the wrongdoings of mortals, and insofar as he himself exercises forgiveness his nature approaches that which believers attribute to a deity. There is supposed to be something about being divine that makes a deity especially capable of exercising forgiveness; and, conversely, it is human frailty which prevents us from this exercise on occasions when we ought to forgive.

This belief in a connection between forgiving and being divine I want to show is mistaken, in a radical way. Far from its being the case that divine

From *The Philosophical Quarterly* 25 (1975). Reprinted by permission of Blackwell Publishing Ltd.

nature makes its possessor especially prone to forgive, such a nature makes forgiveness impossible. Such a being logically cannot forgive, since possession of divine attributes logically precludes conditions which are necessary for forgiveness. So, far from its being the case that human frailty makes forgiveness difficult or impossible, it is the possession of distinctly human, nondivine characteristics, that makes forgiveness appropriate for human beings. Only a human being can forgive—a divine being cannot.

In my discussion, I shall be assuming mainly that a divine being (if there is one) is perfect. He has a perfect moral sense, a perfect moral will, perfect knowledge, and perfect benevolence. I shall try not to make too many assumptions about the nature of forgiveness. The definitions given in the *Oxford English Dictionary* [*OED*] and the uses made of the word "forgiveness" are varied enough to rule out any assumption that forgiveness amounts to one kind of thing in all circumstances. So I shall instead take up various kinds of actions forgiveness is, or might be, and show that not one of them is an action that could be performed by a perfect being.

I

The *OED* in some of its definitions of "forgive" directs forgiveness upon actions that are wrong. Part of definition 3 of "forgive" is "to give up resentment or claim to requital for, pardon (an offence)." In this connection it mentions Hobbes' writing on "An Authority to Forgive, or Retain Sins," in *Leviathan* (III xlii 274); and *Isaiah* XXXIII 24, about forgiving iniquities. So let us suppose that forgiveness of one kind involves the forgiver's believing that the person forgiven has done something wrong and that it is this wrong action that the forgiveness is being directed upon.

Forgiveness of this sort may simply be retraction or modification of a previous adverse moral judgment about the act in question. The eloping couple might be forgiven in this way by their parents. The parents, in their shock and dismay when first hearing the news, censure the action harshly. Later, however, they realize that their judgment about the elopement was too severe and so they modify or abandon it, and so forgive the couple.

Now with human beings this reversal or modification of moral judgment is sometimes laudable, sometimes not. It depends on whether the original judgment was correct, or whether the person who made the judgment had good reason to believe it correct. If the parents changed their minds about the elopement, that would probably be laudable, since presumably elopement is not wrong (or not *very* wrong) and the parents had no good reason to think it was. But suppose a son had asked his parents to reverse their censure of his having murdered his sister. There would be no cause to praise them if they somehow deluded themselves into believing that the son had not done anything really wrong. They would then apparently have lost all sense of right and wrong, at least as regards their son, not to mention any special feelings they might have had about this particular victim, their daughter. Forgiveness, in the sense of reversal of moral judgment, is not always in order for human beings.

But when it is a deity considering an action, reversal of moral judgment is never in order. When contradictory judgments are made about the same action, one of them is wrong, and a being with a perfect moral sense cannot (logically cannot) make wrong moral judgments. If he was right in his second appraisal of the situation, he was wrong in his first and vice versa. And this is quite aside from the difficulty of how a being who is not in time can reverse his judgments, having no time in which to do so.

The situation is not appreciably changed if forgiveness, in the sense of reversal of judgment, is granted because new facts have come to light which should affect an assessment of the situation. One human being may be forgiven by another for this reason. "I didn't understand the situation fully," the forgiver says. "At first I could see no reason for your firing Smith. But since then I have learned he has had his hand in the till, and has been malicious towards his subordinates, etc. I now see you were quite right in letting him go." It is fine for a human being to make a new assessment of an action when new facts come to light. It is impossible for an omniscient deity, however, because, being omniscient, he always knows all the facts. For him, there can be no such thing as learning something new. And, of course, for such a being there can be no such thing as a temporary lapse of consciousness where he overlooks, or temporarily fails to remember, a relevant fact. So such things cannot be reasons for reversal of judgment in a deity, although they certainly can be for us. For this reason it is a little hard to see how some one can argue with a deity that he or someone else ought to be forgiven, by trying to bring certain facts to his attention. One of the last things Jesus said was "Father, forgive them, for they know not what they do." But how could Jesus have been trying to draw a certain fact to God's attention when God, being (as we sometimes say) omnipercipient, must have all facts in his attention all the time? He is also supposed to show perfect moral judgment in weighing facts, so it is equally insulting or, more accurately, blasphemous, to try to argue with God that a fact should have a particular moral weight in his consideration.

Sometimes it is thought that people ought to be forgiven for doing wrong for special considerations pertaining to their case. Such considerations include the motives of the agent (he stole the loaf of bread to feed his starving children), or special difficulties in which he found himself (he shot the burglar in self-defence), or any other special characteristics of the action (he went through the red light at 4 A.M. when the streets were virtually deserted). According to the rule (moral, legal, or whatever) he did something wrong, but the wrongness seems to be mitigated by special circumstances. But in cases like these, the fact of the matter is that the rule is too crude, or too general, to take the special circumstances into account. What someone who appeals to mitigating circumstances is arguing is that while the action is wrong according to the rule, it is not wrong (or not as wrong) in a more general, all things considered, sort of way. Forgiveness in this sense is really a kind of moral judgment; a recognition that the rule has only limited application to the assessment and that other factors must also be taken into account.

It is very difficult to see how God could make this kind of judgment, for what would the defective rule be for him? It could hardly be one of his own, one of the rules which he makes to define right and wrong (if this is indeed what he does) for why should he make a defective one? His only motivation, as far as I can see, would be considerations of simplicity and ease of understanding for human beings. This, however, would only function as a reason for giving human beings defective rules, and not for using them himself. Complexities being no problem for a perfectly omniscient being, he would, if he used rules at all to make moral assessments, use ones which had the degree of complexity necessary to take into account *all* morally relevant factors in a situation to be judged. Our rules would only be crude approximations to these perfectly accurate divine rules, and thus while it might appear to us as if God is making an exception to his own rules (not judging an action wrong which is wrong by our crude rules) this appearance would be delusory.

Finally, a human being may *condone* offences by others, meaning, according to *OED*, "to forgive or overlook (an offence) so as to treat it as nonexistent." This is especially appropriate with minor wrongdoings. For I take it that the idea of condoning is that of refusing to form an adverse moral judgment of an action, even though there may be some reason to do so. One overlooks, refuses to take account of, the immoral aspects of an action. Essentially, it is making an exception for a particular case for no reason. If this is a kind of forgiveness, as the definition suggests, it is again difficult to see how it is something a divine being can do. Being omniscient, he knows everything there is to be known, and is not able to overlook it, in the sense of refusing to know it. So in particular, he cannot do this with moral aspects of an action. In addition, condoning may show a certain lack of moral sense and so there is a second reason why a deity cannot do it. This is most clear when the immoral aspects are fairly substantial. Someone who condones mass murders shows a significant moral blindness, to say the least.

II

Reversing moral judgments, exhibiting moral blindness, and making exceptions to moral rules being impossible for perfect beings, it is time to consider other types of actions which might merit the name "forgiveness." In the passage quoted earlier, the *OED* mentioned giving up a claim to requital for an offence. When requital or punishment is remitted or reduced because of a new, more favourable judgment about the moral aspects of the case, then such cases become instances of the kinds discussed in the first part of this paper. This includes cases where special circumstances merit a special kind of judgment about the action. These are simply ways of forming judgments where all relevant circumstances are considered.[1]

But there are also cases where punishment is remitted without reversing or modifying a judgment about the wrongdoing the punishment was supposed to be punishment for. This kind of forgiveness is akin to clemency exercised by a judge in the courts, or pardon by a high official. Someone who is in a position to mete out punishment for a wrongdoing decides to give less punishment than what is called for by the nature of the wrongdoing, or no punishment at all.

It is easy to envisage the deity in the role of a judge who makes decisions about punishments and rewards. For it is he who decides the lots of humans in life after death and these lots are often conceived of as rewards or punishments. People who are good or bad in this life get good or bad lots, respectively, in the afterlife. In addition, it is often thought that virtue is rewarded and vice punished by the deity in this life. Misfortunes, for instance, are sometimes thought of as being sent by God as a punishment for wrongdoing.

What is not so easy to envisage, however, is how a perfectly just God can remit punishment. In the first place, what would be the mechanism by which the punishment was originally assigned which was then remitted by God? With human beings the assignment and remission typically is done by two separate agencies, the remitting agency taking precedence over the assigning one. A judge (the remitter) gives a lighter punishment than that prescribed by law (the assigner). Or a high political official, a governor, say, remits a punishment assigned by the courts. But who or what assigns punishments which God then remits? God himself? He then appears to be something of a practical joker, assigning punishments which he, with perfect foreknowledge, knows he is going to remit, perhaps doing this to scare some virtue into sinners. If not he but his laws assign the original punishment, essentially the same problem arises, namely why God makes laws that he knows he is going to override.

Other problems would appear here as well. One concerns the question of whether the punishment over which the sinner is being forgiven by God was what the sinner justly deserved. If it was, then in remitting him this punishment God is not giving the sinner what he deserves, and thus not behaving in a way consistent with his being a perfectly just being. If, on the other hand, the sinner did not deserve the punishment, then it was an unjust mechanism which assigned such punishment. If this mechanism were God's laws or decrees, then once again he would not be a perfectly just being, although he certainly would be more just in remitting one of his own unjust sentences than in letting it stand. If the mechanism assigning the punishment were, on the other hand, a human one, it is difficult to see why God should pay any attention to it. Ignoring this punishment would be a much more appropriate attitude than remitting it.

Another problem has to do with God's absolving only some sinners from their punishments. For either God forgives everyone or he does not. If he only forgives some people, and not others, then he might be behaving unjustly towards those whose punishment he allows to stand. If he picks out people to forgive for no special reason, then he is acting arbitrarily and immorally. A just God does not play favourites with rewards and punishments.

So is there a reason God might have for remitting punishment in some cases but not in others? We have been assuming that these are all cases where God does not reverse his moral condemnation of the actions, so this cannot be a reason. But one reason that is often cited is repentance on the part of the sinner. This repentance would be an overt expression of the agent's realization of having done wrong, his having the appropriate feelings about his actions, and his resolve not to repeat them. So in asking for forgiveness with this attitude, the penitent is not asking God for a new judgment on his actions—as noted earlier, this smacks of blasphemy—but rather a new and more favourable judgment on *him,* as an agent. He is not the wrongdoer he once was, but has a new, reformed, character.

We, as human beings, revise our judgments about people's characters in the light of evidence that they are repentant about their past misdeeds. But for an omniscient being, such revision would not be possible. In his omniscience, God would be able to foreknow the repentance of the agent; therefore he need not make, and could not have made, a judgment about the agent's character which did not take this act of repentance into account. It is difficult to see, moreover, why God should count the end of the agent's life, the post-repentance period, more heavily than the beginning in his final assessment of the agent's character. Because God is omniscient and outside time, all parts of a human life are known to him in exactly the same way, known to him much as a number series is known to us. We do not attach any special significance to the later numbers in the series just because they are later, nor do we believe they are better representatives of the series. Similarly God should not regard an agent's later character as the best representative of his total character.

We, on the other hand, do attach special significance to an agent's later character, for at least two reasons. One is that it is the man's most recent character with which we are (presently) confronted, and with which we have to deal. And the other is that insofar as we need, or want to make, predictions about his future character, the most recent evidence will tend to be the most reliable. These two reasons have importance in a utilitarian justification of infliction or withholding of punishment. The utilitarian treats punishment as a method for obtaining good results, one of the foremost being improvement of the agent's character, behaviour and motivation. Punishment is only justified to the extent it is effective in these areas. So a utilitarian would not be able to derive this kind of justification when he is considering punishing an already reformed character. The effect already having been gained, the punishment is superfluous as a method, and hence unjustified.

A utilitarian can thus consider withholding or remitting punishment for repentant, reformed agents. Now the question is, can God be such a utilitarian, consistently with his perfection, and thus exercise forgiveness in this particular way? He would be a God who uses threats and bribes to get people to behave themselves, threatening them with punishment if they misbehave, bribing them with forgiveness, remission of punishment, if they decide to behave.

It seems to me that this portrayal of God the manipulator is inconsistent with the image of divine perfection. There must be better, fairer, and more effective ways to instil into human beings a sense of right and wrong and a will to do the right. Moreover, the whole exercise of threats and bribes would presumably become inoperative at the end of an individual's life. Since he has no more opportunities to choose the wrong, there is no longer a utilitarian reason for punishing him as a threat. To condemn him to the eternal flames just as an example to mortals still on earth is not, I think, something that a just God could contemplate, particularly since these mortals seem to have no good way of knowing who has been condemned and who has not. So everyone would have to have his punishment remitted at the end of this life, i.e., everyone would have to be forgiven, a possibility that was mentioned, but not discussed, a little earlier. But then the whole activity of threats and bribes during an individual's life becomes meaningless, a little game God plays with us where everything comes out all right in the end anyway. The juiciest rewards and the most terrible punishments he can mete out would be those in the after-life, and it is just these that he can have no utilitarian reasons for conferring.

Nor, I believe, can God remit punishment for a repentant sinner for non-utilitarian reasons, as has already been noted, although he must take reformed periods of the agent's life into account in making his judgment. But to weigh (in some non-utilitarian way) the amount of punishment, if any, due to a repentant character and give him just that much would be to disregard the pre-repentance period of the agent's life and this, I have argued, a just omniscient god could not do. Far from having the special significance which they are sometimes thought to have, death-bed confessions and pleas for forgiveness would be pretty useless. If the agent spent ten minutes of his life reformed, and seventy years of his life unreformed, the seventy years should count much more heavily when God is considering what kinds of punishment to mete out.

III

The kinds of forgiveness so far considered have been essentially ones involving either a reversal of moral judgment on the actions forgiven or a reversal of judgment about punishing the agent. It may be felt that the discussion so far has missed the most central kinds of forgiveness, those, for instance, fitting this definition in the *OED:* "4. To give up resentment against, pardon (an offender)." Although pardoning an offender may mean remission of punishment, which I have already discussed, giving up resentment seems to be something different. Resentment being a kind of feeling or attitude, to give it up would be to change a feeling or attitude. This would not necessarily involve reversing a judgment. The change may be partly, or even wholly, non-cognitive.

Joseph Butler devotes two sermons to a discussion of resentment and forgiveness, viewing forgiveness as an avoidance of the abuses of resentment. He defines resentment thus: "the natural object or occasion of settled resentment then being injury as distinct from pain or loss . . . but from this [sudden anger], deliberate anger or resentment is essentially distinguished, as the latter is not naturally excited by, or intended to prevent mere harm without the appearance of wrong or injustice."[2] Resentment is a moral feeling or attitude whose object must be an action believed wrong or unjust, and not just any harm. Giving up of resentment might then mean giving up or reversing the belief that the action was wrong, as discussed in Part I of this paper; or it might mean merely giving up part or all of an accompanying feeling or attitude toward the action, while retaining the belief that it was wrong. It is forgiveness of this second sort that I want now to discuss.

Such seems to be the case of the forgiving father of the Prodigal Son. Presumably the father did not reverse his judgment of the son's prodigality, deciding that the son's actions were not so bad after all. Rather, it was in spite of this judgment that he was able to forgive him.

Something of this sort seems to be the kind of forgiveness Butler urges. He does not think we ought to reverse our moral judgments about those who have wronged us (except in instances where the evidence warrants it). Nor does he recommend giving up what he calls "a due, natural sense of the injury." Some moral attitudes and feelings toward a wrongdoing may be appropriate to retain in forgiveness. What has to be given up, according to Butler, seems to be what we might call taking the wrongdoing personally. For to forgive, according to him, is just "to be affected towards the injurious person in the same way any good men, uninterested in the case, would be, if they had the same just sense, which we have supposed the injured person to have, of the fault, after which there will yet remain real goodwill towards the offender."[3] To forgive is just to cease to have any personal interest in the injury. It is to regard it as if it had happened to someone else in whom we have no special interest, other than the general interest we have in all human beings. So the father might forgive his prodigal son by ceasing to take the son's prodigality personally. He regards it no longer as a wasting of *his* money, as something *his* son has done to *him,* but instead as a mere wasting of someone's good money.

How and why can this change in feeling happen? One suggestion is that the personal feelings are gradually forgotten, or wear off in some natural manner. "Forgive and forget" is what is sometimes said, and one possibility is that forgiving is forgetting. It could be argued that personal feelings only last naturally for so long and then wear off, unless the person makes a determined effort to retain or renew them, or as Butler puts it, "resentment has taken possession of the temper and will not quit its hold," suggesting that the mechanism by which this happens is "bare obstinacy."[4]

This may be true of human beings, but it cannot be true of God, and thus this kind of forgiveness is not open to him to exercise. An omniscient being cannot (logically) forget anything, so cannot in particular forget his feelings. And all his feelings are equally alive to him at all times, this being, I think, part of what is meant in calling him omnipercipient. In perceiving situations, he knows them in a way in which they are fully real to him, meaning that he reacts not just by forming judgments, but also with all appropriate feelings. Then, to be omnipercipient is to have all reactions to all situations equally vivid, regardless of when they happened. So the reactions of omnipercipient beings cannot change over time. So even if God were subject to change, and this change could take place in time (even though he is supposed to exist outside time) he would not be able to change in this particular way, since this change involves a dimming of feeling.

Let us then consider a different kind of situation where resentment, in the sense of taking an injury personally, is dispelled, not through forgetting or some other kind of natural erosion, but as a result of conscious effort on the part of the forgiver. What reasons would he have for making this kind of effort?

When an injury is taken personally, the result is a certain breach between the injured person and the person who has injured him. This breach is not wholly due to the nature of the injury, nor to the injured person's reactions by way of judgment or sense of wrongness of the action. Other people could have these same reactions without such a breach occurring. Friends of the father of the Prodigal Son could agree with him in his judgments of the son's behaviour and could react with moral indignation at the son's waste without such reactions causing estrangement from the son. They have not themselves been injured, so there is no reason to take the prodigality personally. And also their relations with the boy are not such as to be affected by resentment in the way the father's are, since he is much more involved with the boy. This involvement, I think, also makes it more important for the father that the breach should be healed.

The father's motivation for forgiveness is thus to heal the breach, and this breach presumably is virtually intolerable because of his relationship with the boy. His involvement in and regard for the relationship require that he should not spoil it by feelings of personal injury.[5] Abandoning his feelings of personal injury is also required by a regard for the injuring party as a human being. Presumably more things should be taken into account in forming an attitude toward him than the injury he has caused. The trouble with a sense of personal injury is that it tends to swamp other considerations in the formation of attitudes. The person tends to be seen just as the agent of the injury and nothing else.

A final reason for trying to get rid of feelings of personal injury as soon as possible is that harbouring such feelings tends to be bad for the person who refuses to forgive. At least, this is what the psychologists tell us—that it is unhealthy to harbour and brood over personal resentments.

A change in attitude becomes particularly appropriate when the offender repents, shows remorse for his wrongdoing.[6] If the remorse is genuine he has dissociated himself from the wrongdoing in the sense that if he had it to do over again he would refrain, and he censures himself for having done it in the same way as if the agent had been someone else. So, since he is no longer the kind of person who would commit such an injury, an attitude that presupposes that he is such a person is inappropriate. And a sense of personal injury is, I think, just such an attitude since it is an attitude toward a person as the agent of a certain deed. Repentance as an overt sign of remorse makes such a difference in forgiveness (as an abandonment of a sense of personal injury) that it is sometimes difficult to see how forgiveness can take place without it. The parent who is willing to forgive a child anything, despite the fact that the child shows absolutely no signs of remorse, can be regarded as indulgent at best, and, at worst, as lacking a certain sense of appropriateness in his/her relations with the child. Too much of a readiness to forgive without repentance indicates a certain lack of awareness of personal injury, which in turn indicates a general lack of awareness in personal relations. Or sometimes the injuries are so great that the person really has no redeeming features which will outbalance them. Take the operators of the furnaces at Buchenwald, for example: if they are unrepentant what possible reasons could we have for forgiving them? In the absence of remorse there may not be any basis for realigning one's attitude toward the offender. The best one can do is just forget about him, taking the method of forgiveness I previously suggested.

Now, how could God figure in this kind of forgiveness? Since it presupposes a sense of taking an injury personally (it is this attitude that is remitted in forgiveness) it is very difficult to see how God could forgive in this way. For I think it is fairly clear that taking an injury personally, as opposed to having a general sense of its wrongness, is a distinctly human failing, an imperfection. Try to imagine a god sulking or brooding, perhaps plotting revenge because someone has, say, made off with the treasure in one of his churches, and you have imagined a less than perfect being. The Olympian gods and goddesses were noted for their pettiness in their relations with each other, with regard to injuries, real or imagined, and this is one good reason why they were not and are not regarded as perfect. A god whose perspective of another god or a person is distorted by a sense of personal injury—I argued earlier that this was an accompaniment of, if not part of, resentment and so was one reason for human forgiveness, getting rid of this attitude—is at the very least not omnipercipient, and probably also not just in his assessment of the human being who committed the injury. Relations with the injuring party are also severed, I maintained, by this attitude, and surely a perfect being could not allow this to happen. And the third reason for our getting rid of feelings of personal injury also serves as a reason for God's not having them at all. They are detrimental to one's psychological well-being, and in extreme cases make a person a candidate for the psychiatrist's couch. This sort of thing obviously cannot (logically) happen to a perfect being.

God, then, cannot forgive personal injuries where what is given up is personal resentment (*OED*—for "forgive"—"1. To give up, cease to harbour [resentment, wrath]") since he cannot have such feelings. But, it is sometimes said, God forgives us before we ask for forgiveness, sometimes even before we do wrong. Such a line of thinking perhaps would mean that God forgives before he resents, gives up the resentment before he has it, thus skipping the resentment phase of the process. More simply, he decides, wills not to harbour resentment. But the problem here is whether it makes any sense to make decisions where there is only one logically possible alternative. It is a little peculiar for me to make a decision about whether I am going to be the number 2, since I have only one alternative which is logically possible, and that is not to be the number 2. God presumably is in the same position with regard to harbouring resentment. Only the alternative of not harbouring it is logically open to him.

It is, however, sometimes maintained that God has all his perfections because he wills to have them, and so has made a meaningful decision in choosing them. If this is true, it would apply to a decision not (ever) to harbour resentment. But I think there are nonetheless good reasons not to count this as real forgiveness, since forgiveness has to be a giving up of something, and no one can give up something he never had. It would be as if I decided as a New Year's resolution to give up gambling, when I had never gambled. Also, repentance and remorse would lose their connection with God's forgiveness. Since he harbours no resentment anyway, there would be no point in setting matters straight by repenting. The only likely function repentance could have, in restoring a relationship with God which had been severed by a misdeed, would be if the injury made some change in the *sinner*'s attitude toward God which had severed the relationship, and if this attitude could be changed back by repentance. This may well happen (although I cannot understand just how the mechanism would work), but it is clearly not a case of God's forgiving, since it is not a case of God's doing anything. Everything that is done is done by the sinner, and it is in him that the changes take place.

IV

It is, moreover, only harm, or supposed harm, to himself that a person can take personally. Even if others are harmed as well, it is only the concomitant, or resultant, harm to oneself that causes feelings of personal resentment. If a son takes insults about his parents personally, for instance, this is because he believes that, when they are insulted, he is as well. Thus, forgiveness as a ceasing to hold personal resentment can only be directed toward actions which have wronged the forgiver (or which he believes have wronged him). And I think this is true of any kind of forgiveness—it is appropriately directed only toward actions which have wronged the forgiver. It would be a bit high-handed of me, for instance, to forgive someone else's husband's excessive drinking and womanizings when his wife felt not the least inclined in that direction—high-handed because I would have to construe his behaviour as wronging me rather than her. Only in certain restricted cases can one person forgive wrongs to another by proxy, as it were. Typically this happens only when the forgiver bears a special relationship to the wronged person and the wronged person is dead. I could, for instance, conceivably forgive a wrong done to one of my dead ancestors if my relationship to him/her were such that if I were not to forgive the action, it would never be forgiven.

The implications here for God are that he can only forgive wrongs, sins, that are injuries to him. If he has universal powers of forgiveness, for all sins, sins must all have this characteristic.

Several problems arise immediately. One is how it is possible to wrong, to injure, a perfect being. His very perfection should make him immune from the kind of injury which makes forgiveness appropriate. The other problem is how even an imperfect being could construe as primarily wrongs to himself actions which seem mainly to harm someone else. On such a construction the person stolen from, raped, injured, killed, enslaved, is not really wronged at all, or at least the injury done him is rather minimal compared to that done to God by breaking his laws, contravening his wishes, or whatever. But this would have to be true if God is to forgive these actions, and especially if he is to forgive them independently of whether they have been forgiven by the ostensible injured party. To give God the first or primary right to forgive is to view him as the primary injured party.

Finally, I want to mention a kind of forgiveness which God alone is supposed to be able to exercise, which is associated with the washing away of one's sins. The idea, as nearly as I have been able to make out, is that before God forgives there are a certain number of wrongs which the person committed. Afterwards there are none. He did the actions all right, but after God's forgiveness, they are no longer wrong.

This is a little like a child's plea that a parent make things all right. The child imagines that rightness and wrongness depend wholly on the parent's say-so. So an action, or anything, might be changed from wrong to right, while remaining otherwise unchanged, because the parent first said it was wrong and then later says it is right. I think we sometimes expect God to set things right in the same way and we call this "forgiveness."

But much as we would like sometimes to retreat into these childhood fancies where God as parent makes things all right by some kind of magic, I think they embody too many confusions to make them worth considering. The first is the idea that the rightness or wrongness of an action can change without anything else about it changing. And another is the dependence of right or wrong on God's say-so. For in a situation like the ones being described it is not as if God gave us general precepts by which to live and they were right because they were expressions of the will of God. Many people have objections to the view that God's will has anything to do with right or wrong. But quite aside from these general objections, there is the problem that a god like the one being described does not impart to his decrees any generality. He literally changes wrong to right from one day to the next. This absence of generality, I think, disqualifies these changeable decrees from being *ethical* precepts. It also gives human beings considerable motivation for disobedience to God's will. If there is no telling how God is going to regard an action from one day to the next, then someone might want to take his chances on disobedience, figuring that what contravenes God's will one day will be favourably regarded the next.

With some actions, a necessary condition for their being wrong is an unfavourable reaction by someone affected by the action. So if the person ceases to show the reaction, the action is no longer wrong. The person to whom a promise is made can make a broken promise cease to be wrong by welcoming the fact that it was broken. The masochist, by welcoming injuries to himself, makes them cease to be injuries. Thus, if (1) all wrongs are injuries to God only and (2) they are the kind of wrongs which God eventually shows a favourable reaction to, God might be able to set all wrongs right.

I have already commented on (1) above, maintaining that it is very difficult to take the point of view that God is always the only one injured in a wrongdoing. (2), I think, is even more absurd. How could a morally sensitive and just God welcome human beings torturing, maiming, killing and causing suffering to one another?

So we cannot without logical and/or moral absurdity say of a fully divine being that it forgives in any sense I have been able to give to "forgive." Whether this is because divine forgiveness is beyond the scope of human understanding is another question, not the concern of this paper. I have only tried to show that divine forgiveness does appear absurd to the human understanding, or at least to mine.

NOTES

1. Alwynne Smart makes essentially this point in connection with mercy ("Mercy," in *The Philosophical Quarterly*, 17 (1967), 345–59). She argues that remission or modification of punishment in the light of special circumstances surrounding the crime is not a genuine exercise of mercy, but making a judgment about the appropriate punishment taking *all* relevant considerations into account.
2. Joseph Butler, *Fifteen Sermons Preached at the Rolls Chapel* (London, 1967), pp. 125 ff.
3. Butler, op. cit., p. 143.
4. Butler, op. cit., p. 129 ff.

5. Thus R. S. Downie argues ("Forgiveness," in *The Philosophical Quarterly*, 15 (1965), 128–34) that an injury severs the relationship of *agape* with the person injured, forgiveness restores it.
6. In fact, Strawson makes repentance, in the sense of repudiation of the injury, a necessary condition for forgiveness (P. F. Strawson, "Freedom and Resentment," in *Studies in the Philosophy of Thought and Action*, ed. Strawson [Oxford, 1968]) since he defines forgiveness thus: "and to forgive is to accept the repudiation and to forswear the resentment." In this paper Strawson makes a number of interesting comments about resentment, too many for me to discuss here.

God and the Concept of Worship

James Rachels

God is commonly conceived as worthy of worship. But does total subservience to God conflict with being a moral agent? In other words, if you are required to do whatever God tells you to do, can you at the same time retain your commitment to do what you think is right? Of course, you may believe that what God tells you to do is right. That decision, however, is one you yourself make and not one God makes for you. In the next selection James Rachels, whose work we read previously, argues that no one, not even God, has an unqualified claim on those who take seriously moral reasoning.

Worship

The concept of worship has received surprisingly little attention from philosophers of religion. When it has been treated, the usual approach is by way of referring to God's awesomeness or mysteriousness: to worship is to "bow down in silent awe" when confronted with a being that is "terrifyingly mysterious."[1] But neither of these notions is of much help in understanding worship. Awe is certainly not the same thing as worship; one can be awed by a performance of *King Lear*, or by witnessing an eclipse of the sun or an

From James Rachels, "God and Human Attitudes," *Religious Studies* 7 (1971).
Reprinted by permission of Cambridge University Press.

earthquake, or by meeting one's favorite film star, without worshiping any of these things. And a great many things are both terrifying and mysterious that we have not the slightest inclination to worship—the Black Death probably fits that description for many people. So we need an account of worship that does not rely on such notions as awesomeness and mysteriousness. . . .

Worship is something that is done; but it is not clear just what is done when one worships. Other actions, such as throwing a ball or insulting one's neighbor, seem transparent enough; but not so with worship. When we celebrate Mass in the Roman Catholic Church, for example, what are we doing (apart from eating a wafer and drinking wine)? Or when we sing hymns in a Protestant church, what are we doing (other than merely singing songs)? What is it that makes these acts of *worship?* One obvious point is that these actions, and others like them, are ritualistic in character; so before we can make any progress in understanding worship, perhaps it will help to ask about the nature of ritual.

First we need to distinguish the ceremonial form of a ritual from what is supposed to be accomplished by it. Consider, for example, the ritual of investiture for an English prince. The prince kneels; the queen (or king) places a crown on his head; and he takes an oath: "I do become your liege man of life and limb and of earthly worship, and faith and trust I will bear unto thee to live and die against all manner of folks." By this ceremony the prince is elevated to his new station, and by this oath he acknowledges the commitments that, as prince, he will owe the queen. In one sense, the ceremonial form of the ritual is unimportant; it is possible that some other procedure might have been laid down, without the point of the ritual being affected in any way. Rather than placing a crown on his head, the queen might break an egg into his palm (that could symbolize all sorts of things). Once this was established as the procedure, it would do as well as the other. It would still be the ritual of investiture, so long as it was understood that by the ceremony a prince is created. The performance of a ritual, then, is in certain respects like the use of language. In speaking, sounds are uttered, and, thanks to the conventions of the language, something is said, or affirmed, or done; and in a ritual performance, a ceremony is enacted, and, thanks to the conventions associated with the ceremony, something is done, or affirmed, or celebrated. . . .

So, once we understand the social system in which there are queens, princes, and subjects, and therefore understand the role assigned to each within that system, we can sum up what is happening in the ritual of investiture in this way: someone is being made a prince, and he is accepting that role with all that it involves. Similar explanations could be given for other rituals, such as the marriage ceremony: two people are being made husband and wife, and they are accepting those roles with all that they involve.

The question to be asked about the ritual of worship is what analogous explanation can be given of it. The ceremonial form of the ritual may vary according to the customs of the religious community; it may involve singing, drinking wine, counting beads, sitting with a solemn expression on one's face, dancing, making a sacrifice, or what have you. But what is the point of it?

[T]he worshiper thinks of himself as inhabiting a world created by an infinitely wise, infinitely powerful, perfectly good God; and it is a world in which he, along with other people, occupies a special place in virtue of God's intentions. This gives him a certain role to play: the role of a "child of God." In worshiping God, one is acknowledging and accepting this role, and that is the point of the ritual of worship. Just as the ritual of investiture derives its significance from its place within the social system of queens, princes, and subjects, the ritual of worship gets its significance from an assumed system of relationships between God and human beings. In the ceremony of investiture, the prince assumes a role with respect to the queen and the citizenry. In marriage, two people assume roles with respect to one another. And in worship, a person accepts and affirms his role with respect to God.

Worship presumes the superior status of the one worshiped. This is reflected in the logical point that there can be no such things as mutual or reciprocal worship, unless one or the other of the parties is mistaken as to his own status. We can very well comprehend people loving one another or respecting one another, but not (unless they are misguided) worshiping one another. This is because the worshiper necessarily assumes his own inferiority; and since inferiority is an asymmetrical relation, so is worship. (The nature of the "superiority" and "inferiority" involved here is of course problematic; but in the account I am presenting, it may be understood on the model of superior and inferior positions within a social system.) This is also why humility is necessary on the part of the worshiper. The role to which he commits himself is that of the humble servant, "not worthy to touch the hem of his garment." Compared to God's gloriousness, "all our righteousnesses are as filthy rags." So in committing oneself to this role, one is acknowledging God's greatness and one's own relative worthlessness. This humble attitude is not a mere embellishment of the ritual: on the contrary, worship, unlike love or respect, requires humility. Pride is a sin, and pride before God is incompatible with worshiping him.

The function of worship as "glorifying" or "praising" God, which is often taken to be primary, may be regarded as derivative from the more fundamental nature of worship as commitment to the role of God's child. "Praising" God is giving him the honor and respect due to one in his position of eminence, just as one shows respect and honor in giving fealty to a king.

In short, the worshiper is in this position: He believes that there is a being, God, who is the perfectly good, perfectly powerful, perfectly wise Creator of the universe; and he views himself as the child of God, made for God's purposes and responsible to God for his conduct. And the ritual of worship, which may have any number of ceremonial forms according to the customs of the religious community, has as its point the acceptance of, and commitment to, this role as God's child, with all that this involves. If this account is accepted, then there is no mystery as to the relation between the act of worship and the worshiper's other activity. Worship will be regarded not as an isolated act taking place on Sunday morning, with no necessary connection to one's behavior the rest of the week, but as a ritualistic expression of, and commitment to, a role that dominates one's whole way of life.[2]

An important feature of roles is that they can be violated: we can act and think consistently with a role, or we can act and think inconsistently with it. The prince can, for example, act inconsistently with his role as prince by giving greater importance to his own interests and welfare than to the queen's; in this case, he is no longer her liege man. And a father who does not attend to the welfare of his children is not acting consistently with his role as a father, and so on. What would count as violating the role to which one is pledged in virtue of worshiping God?

In Genesis two familiar stories, both concerning Abraham, are relevant. The first is the story of the near sacrifice of Isaac. We are told that Abraham was "tempted" by God, who commanded him to offer Isaac as a human sacrifice. Abraham obeyed—he prepared an altar, bound Isaac to it, and was about to kill him until God intervened at the last moment, saying, "Lay not thine hand upon the lad, neither do thou any thing unto him: for now I know that thou fearest God, seeing thou hast not withheld thy son, thine only son from me" (Gen. 22:12). So Abraham passed the test. But how could he have failed? What was his temptation? Obviously, his temptation was to disobey God; God had ordered him to do something contrary both to his wishes and to his sense of what would otherwise have been right. He could have defied God, but he did not—he subordinated himself, his own desires and judgments, to God's command, even when the temptation to do otherwise was strongest.

It is interesting that Abraham's record in this respect was not perfect. We also have the story of him bargaining with God over the conditions for saving Sodom and Gomorrah from destruction. God had said that he would destroy those cities because they were so wicked; but Abraham gets God to agree that if fifty righteous men can be found there, the cities will be spared. Then he persuades God to lower the number to forty-five, then forty, then thirty, then twenty, and finally ten. Here we have a different Abraham, not servile and obedient, but willing to challenge God and bargain with him. However, even as he bargains with God, Abraham realizes that there is something radically inappropriate about it: he says, "Behold now, I have taken upon me to speak unto the Lord, which am but dust and ashes. . . . Oh let not the Lord be angry" (Gen. 18:27, 30).

The fact is that Abraham could not, consistent with his role as God's subject, set his own judgment and will against God's. The author of Genesis was certainly right about this. We cannot recognize any being *as God* and at the same time set ourselves against him. The point is not merely that it would be imprudent to defy God, since we certainly can't get away with it. Rather, there is a stronger, logical point involved—namely, that if we recognize any being as God, then we are committed, in virtue of that recognition, to obeying him.

To see why this is so, we must first notice that "God" is not a proper name like "Richard Nixon" but a title like "president of the United States" or "king."[3] Thus, "Jehovah is God" is a nontautological statement in which the title "God" is assigned to Jehovah, a particular being, just as "Richard Nixon is president of the United States" assigns the title "president of the United States" to a particular man. This permits us to understand how statements like "God is perfectly wise" can be logical truths, which is problematic if "God" is regarded as a proper name. Although it is not a logical truth that any particular being is perfectly wise, it nevertheless is a logical truth that if any being is God (that is, if any being properly holds that title), then that being is perfectly wise. This is exactly analogous to saying that although it is not a logical truth that Richard Nixon has the authority to veto congressional legislation, nevertheless it is a logical truth that if Richard Nixon is president of the United States, then he has that authority.

To bear the title "God," then, a being must have certain qualifications: he must be all-powerful and perfectly good in addition to being perfectly wise. And in the same vein, to apply the title "God" to a being is to recognize him as one to be obeyed. The same is true, to a lesser extent, of "king"; to recognize anyone as king is to acknowledge that he occupies a place of authority and has a claim on one's allegiance as his subject. And to recognize any being as God is to acknowledge that he has unlimited authority and an unlimited claim on one's allegiance. Thus, we might regard Abraham's reluctance to defy Jehovah as grounded not only in his fear of Jehovah's wrath but as a logical consequence of his acceptance of Jehovah as God. Albert Camus was right to think that "from the moment that man submits God to moral judgment, he kills Him his own heart."[4] What a man can "kill" by defying or even questioning God is not the being that (supposedly) *is* God but his own conception of that being as God. That God is not to be judged, challenged, defied, or disobeyed is at bottom a truth of logic. To do any of these things is incompatible with taking him as one to be worshiped. . . .

So the idea that any being could be worthy of worship is much more problematic than we might have at first imagined. In saying that a being is worthy of worship, we would be recognizing him as having an unqualified claim on our obedience. The question, then, is whether there could be such an unqualified claim. It should be noted that the description of a being as all-powerful, all-wise, and so on would not automatically settle the issue; for even while admitting the existence of such an awesome being, we might still question whether we should recognize him as having an unlimited claim on our obedience.

There is a long tradition in moral philosophy, from Plato to Kant, according to which such a recognition could never be made by a moral agent. According to this tradition, to be a moral agent is to be autonomous, or self-directed. Unlike the precepts of law or social custom, moral precepts are imposed by the agent upon himself, and the penalty for their violation is, in Kant's words, "self-contempt and inner abhorrence."[5] The virtuous person is therefore identified with the person of integrity, the person who acts according to precepts that she can, on reflection, conscientiously approve in her own heart.

On this view, to deliver oneself over to a moral authority for directions about what to do is simply incompatible with being a moral agent. To say "I will follow so-and-so's directions no matter what they are and no matter what my own conscience would otherwise direct me to do" is to opt out of moral thinking altogether; it is to abandon one's role as a moral agent. And it does not matter whether "so-and-so" is the law, the customs of one's society, or Jehovah. This does not, of course, preclude one from seeking advice on moral matters and even on occasion following that advice blindly, trusting in the good judgment of the adviser. But this is justified by the details of the particular case—for example, that you cannot form any reasonable judgment of your own because of ignorance or inexperience or lack of time. What is precluded is that a person should, while in possession of his wits, adopt this style of decision making (or perhaps we should say this style of abdicating decision making) as a general strategy of living, or abandon his own best judgment when he can form a judgment of which he is reasonably confident.

We have, then, a conflict between the role of worshiper, which by its very nature commits one to total subservience to God, and the role of moral agent, which necessarily involves autonomous decision making. The role of worshiper takes precedence over every other role the worshiper has; when there is any conflict, the worshiper's commitment to God has priority over everything. But the first commitment of a moral agent is to do what in his own heart he thinks is right.

NOTES

1. These phrases are from John Hick, *Philosophy of Religion* (Englewood Cliffs, N.J.: Prentice-Hall, 1963), 13–14.
2. This account of worship, specified here in terms of what it means to worship God, may easily be adapted to the worship of other beings, such as Satan. The only changes required are (a) that we substitute for beliefs about God analogous beliefs about Satan, and (b) that we understand the ritual of worship as committing the Satan-worshiper to a role as Satan's servant in the same way that worshiping God commits theists to the role of his servant.
3. Cf. Nelson Pike, "Omnipotence and God's Ability to Sin," *American Philosophical Quarterly* 6 (1969): 208–9; and C. B. Martin, *Religious Belief* (Ithaca, N.Y.: Cornell University Press, 1964), chap. 4.
4. Albert Camus, *The Rebel*, trans. Anthony Bower (New York: Vintage, 1956), 62.
5. Immanuel Kant, *Foundations of the Metaphysics of Morals*, trans. Lewis White Beck (Indianapolis: Bobbs-Merrill, 1959), 44.

PART 2

THE EXISTENCE OF GOD

The Ontological Argument

Anselm and Gaunilo

At this point we put aside temporarily questions about the attributes of God and turn to the issue of whether God exists. Throughout the history of philosophy, various arguments have been offered to prove God's existence, but only one, the ontological argument, is a priori, making no appeal to empirical evidence and relying solely on an analysis of the concept of God.

Its classic formulation was provided by Saint Anselm (1033–1109), who was born in a village that is now part of Italy, was educated in a Benedictine monastery, and became Archbishop of Canterbury. He understood God to be the Being greater than which none can be conceived. Anselm reasoned that if God did not exist, then a greater being could be conceived, namely, a being that exists. In that case, the Being greater than which none can be conceived would not be the Being greater than which none can be conceived, which is a contradiction. So the Being greater than which none can be conceived must exist, that is, God must exist. Indeed, Anselm goes on to claim that God cannot even be thought not to exist because a being that *cannot* be thought not to exist is greater than one that *can* be thought not to exist.

The first known response to Anselm's argument was offered by his contemporary Gaunilo, a monk of Marmoutier, France, about whom little is known. Gaunilo maintained that Anselm's line of reasoning could be used to prove the existence of an island greater than which none can be conceived, an absurd conclusion. In reply, Anselm maintained that the argument did not apply to an island because, unlike God, an island has a beginning and end and so can be thought not to exist.

The ontological argument has continued to intrigue thinkers throughout the centuries. While its intricacy may not win many converts to theism, the argument retains the power to fascinate philosophers.

From Brian Davies and G. R. Evans, eds., *Anselm of Canterbury: The Major Works.* Reprinted by permission of Oxford University Press. The words enclosed in brackets have been interpolated by the translator, M. J. Charlesworth, to make the meaning clearer.

Proslogion

2

Well then, Lord, You who give understanding to faith, grant me that I may understand, as much as You see fit, that You exist as we believe You to exist, and that You are what we believe You to be. Now we believe that You are something than which nothing greater can be thought. Or can it be that a thing of such a nature does not exist, since "the Fool has said in his heart, there is no God" [Ps. 13: 1; 52: 1]? But surely, when this same Fool hears what I am speaking about, namely, "something-than-which-nothing-greater-can-be-thought," he understands what he hears, and what he understands is in his mind, even if he does not understand that it actually exists. For it is one thing for an object to exist in the mind, and another thing to understand that an object actually exists. Thus, when a painter plans beforehand what he is going to execute, he has [the picture] in his mind, but he does not yet think that it actually exists because he has not yet executed it. However, when he has actually painted it, then he both has it in his mind and understands that it exists because he has now made it. Even the Fool, then, is forced to agree that something-than-which-nothing-greater-can-be-thought exists in the mind, since he understands this when he hears it, and whatever is understood is in the mind. And surely that-than-which-a-greater-cannot-be-thought cannot exist in the mind alone. For if it exists solely in the mind, it can be thought to exist in reality also, which is greater. If then that-than-which-a-greater-cannot-be-thought exists in the mind alone, this same that-than-which-a-greater-*cannot*-be-thought is that-than-which-a-greater-*can*-be-thought. But this is obviously impossible. Therefore there is absolutely no doubt that something-than-which-a-greater-cannot-be-thought exists both in the mind and in reality.

3

And certainly this being so truly exists that it cannot be even thought not to exist. For something can be thought to exist that cannot be thought not to exist, and this is greater than that which can be thought not to exist. Hence, if that-than-which-a-greater-cannot-be-thought can be thought not to exist, then that-than-which-a-greater-cannot-be-thought is not the same as that-than-which-a-greater-cannot-be-thought, which is absurd. Something-than-which-a-greater-cannot-be-thought exists so truly then, that it cannot be even thought not to exist.

And You, Lord our God, are this being. You exist so truly, Lord my God, that You cannot even be thought not to exist. And this is as it should be, for if some intelligence could think of something better than You, the creature would be above its Creator and would judge its Creator—and that is completely absurd. In fact, everything else there is, except You alone, can be thought of as not existing. You alone, then, of all things most truly exist and therefore of all things possess existence to the highest degree; for anything else does not exist as truly, and so possesses existence to a lesser degree. Why then did 'the Fool say in his heart, there is no God' [Ps. 13: 1; 52: 1] when it is so evident to any rational mind that You of all things exist to the highest degree? Why indeed, unless because he was stupid and a fool?

4

How indeed has he "said in his heart" what he could not think; or how could he not think what he "said in his heart," since to "say in one's heart" and to "think" are the same? But if he really (indeed, since he really) both thought because he "said in his heart" and did not "say in his heart" because he could not think, there is not only one sense in which something is "said in one's heart" or thought. For in one sense a thing is thought when the word signifying it is thought; in another sense when the very object which the thing is is understood. In the first sense, then, God can be thought not to exist, but not at all in the second sense. No one, indeed, understanding what God is can think that God does not exist, even though he may say these words in his heart either without any [objective] signification or with some peculiar signification. For God is that-than-which-nothing-greater-can-be-thought. Whoever really understands this understands clearly that this same being so exists that not even in thought can it not exist. Thus whoever understands that God exists in such a way cannot think of Him as not existing.

I give thanks, good Lord, I give thanks to You, since what I believed before through Your free gift I now so understand through Your illumination, that if I did not want to *believe* that You existed, I should nevertheless be unable not to *understand* it.

On Behalf of the Fool

Gaunilo

1

To one doubting whether there is, or denying that there is, something of such a nature than which nothing greater can be thought, it is said here that its existence is proved, first because the very one who denies or doubts it already has it in his mind, since when he hears it spoken of he understands what is said; and further, because what he understands is necessarily such that it exists not only in the mind but also in reality. And this is proved by the fact that it is greater to exist both in the mind and in reality than in the mind alone. For if this same being exists in the mind alone, anything that existed also in reality would be greater than this being, and thus that which is greater than everything would be less than some thing and would not be greater than everything, which is obviously contradictory. Therefore, it is necessarily the case that that which is greater than everything, being already proved to exist in the mind, should exist not only in the mind but also in reality, since otherwise it would not be greater than everything.

2

But he [the Fool] can perhaps reply that this thing is said already to exist in the mind only in the sense that I understand what is said. For could I not say that all kinds of unreal things, not existing in themselves in any way at all, are equally in the mind since if anyone speaks about them I understand whatever he says? . . .

6

For example: they say that there is in the ocean somewhere an island which, because of the difficulty (or rather the impossibility) of finding that which does not exist, some have called the "Lost Island." And the story goes that it is blessed with all manner of priceless riches and delights in abundance, much more even than the Happy Isles, and, having no owner or inhabitant, it is superior everywhere in abundance of riches to all those other lands that men inhabit. Now, if anyone tell me that it is like this, I shall easily understand what is said, since nothing is difficult about it. But if he should then go on to say, as though it were a logical consequence of this: You cannot any more doubt that this island that is more excellent than all other lands truly exists somewhere in reality than you can doubt that it is in your mind; and since it is more excellent to exist not only in the mind alone but also in reality, therefore it must needs be that it exists. For if it did not exist, any other land existing in reality would be more excellent than it, and so this island, already conceived by you to be more excellent than others, will not be more excellent. If, I say, someone wishes thus to persuade me that this island really exists beyond all doubt, I should either think that he was joking, or I should find it hard to decide which of us I ought to judge the bigger fool—I, if I agreed with him, or he, if he thought that he had proved the existence of this island with any certainty, unless he had first convinced me that its very excellence exists in my mind precisely as a thing existing truly and indubitably and not just as something unreal or doubtfully real.

Reply to Gaunilo

You claim, however, that this is as though someone asserted that it cannot be doubted that a certain island in the ocean (which is more fertile than all other lands and which, because of the difficulty or even the impossibility of discovering what does not exist, is called the "Lost Island") truly exists in reality since anyone easily understands it when it is described in words. Now, I truly promise that if anyone should discover for me something existing either in reality or in the mind alone—except "that-than-which-a-greater-cannot-be-thought"—to which the logic of my argument would apply, then I shall find that Lost Island and give it, never more to be lost, to that person. It has already been clearly seen, however, that "that-than-which-a-greater-cannot-be-thought" cannot be thought not to exist, because it exists as a matter of such certain truth. Otherwise it would not exist at all. In short, if anyone says that he thinks that this being does not exist, I reply that, when he thinks of this, either he thinks of something than which a greater cannot be thought, or he does not think of it. If he does not think of it, then he does not think that what he does not think of does not exist. If, however, he does think of it, then indeed he thinks of something which cannot be even thought not to exist. For if it could be thought not to exist, it could be thought to have a beginning and an end—but this cannot be. Thus, he who thinks of it thinks of something that cannot be thought not to exist; indeed, he who thinks of this does not think of it as not existing, otherwise he would think what cannot be thought. Therefore "that-than-which-a-greater-cannot-be-thought" cannot be thought not to exist.

The Ontological Argument: A Restatement

René Descartes

Another version of the ontological argument was developed by the Frenchman René Descartes (1596–1650), mathematician, scientist, and a key figure in the development of modern philosophy. In his highly influential *Meditations on First Philosophy,* published in Latin, he argues that just as the essence of a triangle contains its three-sidedness, so the essence of God contains God's existence. Because God is a perfect Being and existence is a perfection, it follows that God exists. If God did not exist, then a perfect Being would not be perfect, which is a contradiction.

From *Meditations on First Philosophy,* trans. John Cottingham. Reprinted by permission of Cambridge University Press.

[T]he idea of God, or a supremely perfect being, is one which I find within me just as surely as the idea of any shape or number. And my understanding that it belongs to his nature that he always exists is no less clear and distinct than is the case when I prove of any shape or number that some property belongs to its nature. Hence, even if it turned out that not everything on which I have meditated in these past days is true, I ought still to regard the existence of God as having at least the same level of certainty as I have hitherto attributed to the truths of mathematics.

At first sight, however, this is not transparently clear, but has some appearance of being a sophism. Since I have been accustomed to distinguish between existence and essence in everything else, I find it easy to persuade myself that existence can also be separated from the essence of God, and hence that God can be thought of as not existing. But when I concentrate more carefully, it is quite evident that existence can no more be separated from the essence of God than the fact that its three angles equal two right angles can be separated from the essence of a triangle, or than the idea of a mountain can be separated from the idea of a valley. Hence it is just as much of a contradiction to think of God (that is, a supremely perfect being) lacking existence (that is, lacking a perfection), as it is to think of a mountain without a valley.

However, even granted that I cannot think of God except as existing, just as I cannot think of a mountain without a valley, it certainly does not follow from the fact that I think of a mountain with a valley that there is any mountain in the world; and similarly, it does not seem to follow from the fact that I think of God as existing that he does exist. For my thought does not impose any necessity on things; and just as I may imagine a winged horse even though no horse has wings, so I may be able to attach existence to God even though no God exists.

But there is a sophism concealed here. From the fact that I cannot think of a mountain without a valley, it does not follow that a mountain and valley exist anywhere, but simply that a mountain and a valley, whether they exist or not, are mutually inseparable. But from the fact that I cannot think of God except as existing, it follows that existence is inseparable from God, and hence that he really exists. It is not that my thought makes it so, or imposes any necessity on any thing; on the contrary, it is the necessity of the thing itself, namely the existence of God, which determines my thinking in this respect. For I am not free to think of God without existence (that is, a supremely perfect being without a supreme perfection) as I am free to imagine a horse with or without wings.

And it must not be objected at this point that while it is indeed necessary for me to suppose God exists, once I have made the supposition that he has all perfections (since existence is one of the perfections), nevertheless the original supposition was not necessary. Similarly, the objection would run, it is not necessary for me to think that all quadrilaterals can be inscribed in a circle; but given this supposition, it will be necessary for me to admit that a rhombus can be inscribed in a circle—which is patently false. Now admittedly, it is not necessary that I ever light upon any thought of God; but whenever I do choose to think of the first and supreme being, and bring forth the idea of God from the treasure house of my mind as it were, it is necessary that I attribute all perfections to him, even if I do not at that time enumerate them or attend to them individually. And this necessity plainly guarantees that, when I later realize that existence is a perfection, I am correct in inferring that the first and supreme being exists. In the same way, it is not necessary for me ever to imagine a triangle; but whenever I do wish to consider a rectilinear figure having just three angles, it is necessary that I attribute to it the properties which license the inference that its three angles equal no more than two right angles, even if I do not notice this at the time. By contrast, when I examine what figures can be inscribed in a circle, it is in no way necessary for me to think that this class includes all quadrilaterals. Indeed, I cannot even imagine this, so long as I am willing to admit only what I clearly and distinctly understand. So there is a great difference between this kind of false supposition and the true ideas which are innate in me, of which the first and most important is the idea of God.

The Ontological Argument: A Critique

Immanuel Kant

Immanuel Kant (1724–1804), who lived his entire life in the Prussian town of Königsberg, is a preeminent figure in the history of philosophy. In his monumental *Critique of Pure Reason,* written in German, he argued that the ontological argument in any version fails because it treats existence as though it were a predicate or part of the description of something instead of an indication that the thing is found in the world. To use Kant's example, the concept of a hundred thalers (silver coins) remains the same regardless of whether any thalers exist. Of course, I can spend real thalers and not imaginary ones, but what I believe a thaler to be not does change because I happen to possess one. If existence does not belong to the

From *Critique of Pure Reason,* trans. Norman Kemp Smith. Reprinted by permission of St. Martin's Press.

concept of anything, then it does not belong to the concept of God. Thus a being is no greater or more perfect because it exists, and so the ontological argument does not succeed.

In all ages men have spoken of an *absolutely necessary* being, and in so doing have endeavoured, not so much to understand whether and how a thing of this kind allows even of being thought, but rather to prove its existence. There is, of course, no difficulty in giving a verbal definition of the concept, namely, that it is something the non-existence of which is impossible. But this yields no insight into the conditions which make it necessary to regard the non-existence of a thing as absolutely unthinkable. It is precisely these conditions that we desire to know, in order that we may determine whether or not, in resorting to this concept, we are thinking anything at all. . . .

[T]his concept . . . has been supposed to have its meaning exhibited in a number of examples; and on this account all further enquiry into its intelligibility has seemed to be quite needless. Thus the fact that every geometrical proposition, as, for instance, that a triangle has three angles, is absolutely necessary, has been taken as justifying us in speaking of an object which lies entirely outside the sphere of our understanding as if we understood perfectly what it is that we intend to convey by the concept of that object. . . .

To posit a triangle, and yet to reject its three angles, is self-contradictory; but there is no contradiction in rejecting the triangle together with its three angles. The same holds true of the concept of an absolutely necessary being. If its existence is rejected, we reject the thing itself with all its predicates; and no question of contradiction can then arise. There is nothing outside it that would then be contradicted, since the necessity of the thing is not supposed to be derived from anything external; nor is there anything internal that would be contradicted, since in rejecting the thing itself we have at the same time rejected all its internal properties. "God is omnipotent" is a necessary judgment. The omnipotence cannot be rejected if we posit a Deity, that is, an infinite being; for the two concepts are identical. But if we say, "There is no God," neither the omnipotence nor any other of its predicates is given; they are one and all rejected together with the subject, and there is therefore not the least contradiction in such a judgment. . . .

"*Being*" is obviously not a real predicate; that is, it is not a concept of something which could be added to the concept of a thing. It is merely the positing of a thing, or of certain determinations, as existing in themselves. . . .

A hundred real thalers do not contain the least coin more than a hundred possible thalers. For as the latter signify the concept, and the former the object and the positing of the object, should the former contain more than the latter, my concept would not, in that case, express the whole object, and would not therefore be an adequate concept of it. My financial position is, however, affected very differently by a hundred real thalers than it is by the mere concept of them (that is, of their possibility). . . .

By whatever and by however many predicates we may think a thing—even if we completely determine it—we do not make the least addition to the thing when we further declare that this thing *is*. Otherwise, it would not be exactly the same thing that exists, but something more than we had thought in the concept; and we could not, therefore, say that the exact object of my concept exists. If we think in a thing every feature of reality except one, the missing reality is not added by my saying that this defective thing exists. On the contrary, it exists with the same defect with which I have thought it, since otherwise what exists would be something different from what I thought. When, therefore, I think a being as the supreme reality, without any defect, the question still remains whether it exists or not. . . .

The attempt to establish the existence of a supreme being by means of the famous ontological argument of Descartes is therefore merely so much labour and effort lost; we can no more extend our stock of [theoretical] insight by mere ideas, than a merchant can better his position by adding a few noughts to his cash account.

The Ontological Argument: An Assessment

John H. Hick

John H. Hick is Danforth Professor Emeritus of the Philosophy of Religion at Claremont Graduate University and H. G. Wood Professor of Theology Emeritus at the University of Birmingham. In the following selection he reviews the history of the ontological argument and explains how work done by Bertrand Russell (1872–1970), the illustrious English philosopher and mathematician, helped clarify the Kantian claim that existence is not a predicate.

The ontological argument for the existence of God was first developed by Anselm, one of the Christian Church's most original thinkers and the greatest theologian ever to have been archbishop of Canterbury.

Anselm begins by concentrating the monotheistic concept of God into the formula: *"a being than which nothing greater can be conceived."* It is clear that by "greater" Anselm means more perfect, rather than spatially bigger. It is important to notice that the idea of the most perfect conceivable being is different from the idea of the most perfect being that there is. The ontological argument could not be founded upon this latter notion, for although it is true by definition that the most perfect being that there is exists, there is no guarantee that this being is what Anselm means by God. Consequently, instead of describing God as the most perfect being that there is, Anselm describes God as the being who is so perfect that no more perfect can even be conceived.

First Form of the Argument

In the next and crucial stage of his argument Anselm distinguishes between something, *x*, existing in the mind only and its existing in reality as well. If the most perfect conceivable being existed only in the mind, we should then have the contradiction that it is possible to conceive of a yet more perfect being, namely, the same being existing in reality as well as in the mind. Therefore, the most perfect conceivable being must exist in reality as well as in the mind. Anselm's own formulation of this classic piece of philosophical reasoning is found in the second chapter of the *Proslogion*. . . .

Second Form of the Argument

In his third chapter Anselm states the argument again, directing it now not merely to God's existence but to His uniquely *necessary* existence. God is defined in such a way that it is impossible to conceive of God's not existing. The core of this notion of necessary being is self-existence *(aseity)*. Since God as infinitely perfect is not limited in or by time, the twin possibilities of God's having ever come to exist or ever ceasing to exist are alike excluded and God's nonexistence is rendered impossible. . . .

Criticisms of the Argument

In introducing the ontological argument, Anselm refers to the psalmist's "fool" who says in his heart, "There is no God." Even such a person, he says, possesses the idea of God as the greatest conceivable being; and when we unpack the implications of this idea we see that such a being must actually exist. The first important critic of the argument, Gaunilo, a monk at Marmoutiers in France and a contemporary of Anselm's, accordingly entitled his reply *In Behalf of the Fool.* He claims that Anselm's reasoning would lead to absurd conclusions if applied in other fields, and he sets up a supposedly parallel ontological argument for the most perfect island. Gaunilo spoke of the most perfect of islands rather than (as he should have done) of the most perfect conceivable island; but his argument could be rephrased in terms of the latter idea. Given the idea of such an island, by using Anselm's principle we can argue that unless it exists in reality it cannot be the most perfect conceivable island!

Anselm's reply, emphasizing the uniqueness of the idea of God to show that his ontological reasoning applies only to it, is based upon the second form of the argument. The element in the idea of God which is lacking in the notion of the most perfect island is *necessary* existence. An island (or any other material object) is by definition a part of the contingent world. The most perfect island, so long as it is genuinely an island—"a piece of land surrounded by water" and thus part of the physical globe—is by definition a dependent reality, which can without contradiction be thought not to exist; and therefore Anselm's principle does not apply to it. It applies only to the most perfect conceivable being, which is defined as having eternal and independent (i.e., necessary) existence. Thus far, then, it would seem that the second form of his argument is able to withstand criticism.

Can Anselm's argument in its *first* form, however, be defended against Gaunilo's criticism? This depends upon whether the idea of the most perfect conceivable island is a coherent and consistent idea. Is it possible, even in theory, to specify the characteristics of the most perfect conceivable island? This is a question for the reader to consider.

A second phase of the debate was opened when René Descartes, often called the father of modern philosophy, reformulated the argument and thereby attracted widespread attention to it. Descartes brought to the fore the point upon which most of the modern discussions of the ontological argument have centered, namely, the assumption that existence is a property or predicate. He explicitly treats existence as a characteristic, the possession or lack of which by a given *x* is properly open to inquiry. The essence or defining nature of each kind of thing includes certain predicates, and Descartes's ontological argument claims that existence must be among the defining predicates of God. Just as the fact that its internal angles are equal to two right angles is a necessary characteristic of a triangle, so existence is a necessary characteristic of a supremely perfect being. A triangle without its defining properties would not be a triangle, and God without existence would not be God. The all-important difference is that in the case of the triangle we cannot infer that any triangles exist, since existence is not of the essence of triangularity. However, in the case of a supremely perfect being we can infer existence, for existence is an essential attribute without which no being would be unlimitedly perfect.

This Cartesian version of the ontological argument was later challenged at two levels by the great German philosopher, Immanuel Kant.

At one level he accepted Descartes's claim that the idea of existence belongs analytically to the concept of God, as the idea of having three angles belongs analytically to that of a three-sided plane figure. In each case the predicate is necessarily linked with the subject. But, Kant replied, it does not follow from this that the subject, with its predicates, actually exists. What is analytically true is that *if* there is a triangle, it must have three angles, and *if* there is an infinitely perfect being, that being must have existence. . . .

At a deeper level, however, Kant rejected the basic assumption upon which Descartes's argument rested, the assumption that existence, like triangularity, is a predicate that something can either have or lack, and that may in some cases be analytically connected with a subject. He points out . . . that the idea of existence does not add anything to the concept of a particular thing or kind of thing. An imaginary hundred dollars, for example, consists of the same number of dollars as a real hundred dollars. When we affirm that the dollars are real, or exist, we are saying that the concept is instantiated in the world. Thus to say of *x* that it exists is not to say that in addition to its various other attributes it has the attribute of existing, but is to say that there is an *x* in the real world.

Essentially the same point has more recently been made by Bertrand Russell in his analysis of the word "exists."[1] He has shown that although "exists" is grammatically a predicate, logically it performs a different function, which can be brought out by the following translation: "Cows exist" means "There are *x*'s such that '*x* is a cow' is true." This translation makes it clear that to say that cows exist is not to attribute a certain quality (namely existence) to cows, but is to assert that there are objects in the world to which the description summarized in the word "cow" applies. Similarly "Unicorns do not exist" is the equivalent of "There are no *x*'s such that '*x* is a unicorn' is true." This way of construing negative existential statements—statements that deny that some particular kind of thing exists—avoids the ancient puzzle about the status of the "something" of which we assert that it does not exist. Since we can talk about unicorns, for example, it is easy to think that unicorns must in some sense be or subsist or, perhaps, that they inhabit a paradoxical realm of nonbeing or potential being. Russell's analysis, however, makes it clear that "unicorns do not exist" is not a statement about unicorns but about the concept or description "unicorn" and is the assertion that this concept has no instances.

The bearing of this upon the ontological argument is evident. If existence is, as Anselm and Descartes assumed, an attribute or predicate that can be included in a definition and that, as a desirable attribute, must be included in the definition of God, then the ontological argument is valid. For it would be self-contradictory to say that the most perfect conceivable being lacks the attribute of existence. But if existence, although it appears grammatically in the role of a predicate, has the quite different logical function of asserting that a description applies to something in reality, then the ontological argument, considered as a proof of God's existence, fails. For if existence is not a predicate, it cannot be a defining predicate of God, and the question whether anything in reality corresponds to the concept of the most perfect conceivable being remains open to inquiry. A definition of God describes one's concept of God but cannot prove the actual existence of any such being.

NOTE

1. This aspect of the theory of descriptions is summarized by Russell in his *History of Western Philosophy* (London: George Allen & Unwin Ltd., 1946, and New York: Simon & Schuster), pp. 859–60. For a more technical discussion, see his *Introduction to Mathematical Philosophy* (1919), chap. 16.

The Five Ways

Thomas Aquinas

St. Thomas Aquinas (1225–1274), born near Naples, was the most influential philosopher of the medieval period. He joined the Dominican order and taught at the University of Paris. In his vast writings, composed in Latin, he sought to demonstrate that all Christian doctrines were consistent with reason, even if some transcended reason and were believed on faith, for example, that the world did not always exist but was created at a particular time.

Aquinas's greatest work was the *Summa Theologiae,* and its most famous passage, reprinted here, is the five ways to prove the existence of God. These arguments are a posteriori, relying on empirical evidence.

The first way depends on observing that in the world some things are in motion, leading to the conclusion that God, the first mover, exists. The second way depends on observing that in the world each thing that exists is caused to exist by something other than itself, leading to the conclusion that God, the first cause, exists. The third way depends on observing that some things that exist in the world might possibly not exist, leading to the conclusion that God, whose nonexistence is not possible, exists. The fourth way depends on observing that in the world some things are more or less good, leading to the conclusion that God, the greatest good and the cause of all other goodness, exists. The fifth way depends on observing that things in the world act together to achieve a good

From Anton C. Pegis, ed., *Basic Writings of Saint Thomas Aquinas.* Reprinted by permission of Hackett Publishing Company, Inc end, leading to the conclusion that God, who directs all things to their end, exists.

How do these five arguments fit together? In the words of the distinguished historian of philosophy Father F. C. Copleston (1907–1994), the arguments "are mutually complementary in the sense that in each argument things are considered from a different point of view or under a different aspect. They are so many different approaches to God."

The existence of God can be proved in five ways.

The first and more manifest way is the argument from motion. It is certain, and evident to our senses, that in the world some things are in motion. Now whatever is moved is moved by another, for nothing can be moved except it is in potentiality to that towards which it is moved; whereas a thing moves inasmuch as it is in act. For motion is nothing else than the reduction of something from potentiality to actuality. But nothing can be reduced from potentiality to actuality, except by something in a state of actuality. Thus that which is actually hot, as fire, makes wood, which is potentially hot, to be actually hot, and thereby moves and changes it. Now it is not possible that the same thing should be at once in actuality and potentiality in the same respect, but only in different respects. For what is actually hot cannot simultaneously be potentially hot; but it is simultaneously potentially cold. It is therefore impossible that in the same respect and in the same way a thing should be both mover and moved, i.e., that it should move itself. Therefore, whatever is moved must be moved by another. If that by which it is moved be itself moved, then this also must needs be moved by another, and that by another again. But this cannot go on to infinity, because then there would be no first mover, and, consequently, no other mover, seeing that subsequent movers move only inasmuch as they are moved by the first mover; as the staff moves only because it is moved by the hand. Therefore it is necessary to arrive at a first mover, moved by no other; and this everyone understands to be God.

The second way is from the nature of efficient cause. In the world of sensible things we find there is an order of efficient causes. There is no case known (neither is it, indeed, possible) in which a thing is found to be the efficient cause of itself; for so it would be prior to itself, which is impossible. Now in efficient causes it is not possible to go on to infinity, because in all efficient causes following in order, the first is the cause of the intermediate cause, and the intermediate is the cause of the ultimate cause, whether the intermediate cause be several, or one only. Now to take away the cause is to take away the effect. Therefore, if there be no first cause among efficient causes, there will be no ultimate, nor any intermediate, cause. But if in efficient causes it is possible to go on to infinity, there will be no first efficient cause, neither will there be an ultimate effect, nor any intermediate efficient causes; all of which is plainly false. Therefore it is necessary to admit a first efficient cause, to which everyone gives the name of God.

The third way is taken from possibility and necessity, and runs thus. We find in nature things that are possible to be and not to be, since they are found to be generated, and to be corrupted, and consequently, it is possible for them to be and not to be. But it is impossible for these always to exist, for that which can not-be at some time is not. Therefore, if everything can not-be, then at one time there was nothing in existence. Now if this were true, even now there would be nothing in existence, because that which does not exist begins to exist only through something already existing. Therefore, if at one time nothing was in existence, it would have been impossible for anything to have begun to exist; and thus even now nothing would be in existence—which is absurd. Therefore, not all beings are merely possible, but there must exist something the existence of which is necessary. But every necessary thing either has its necessity caused by another, or not. Now it is impossible to go on to infinity in necessary things which have their necessity caused by another, as has been already proved in regard to efficient causes. Therefore we cannot but admit the existence of some being having of itself its own necessity, and not receiving it from another, but rather causing in others their necessity. This all men speak of as God.

The fourth way is taken from the gradation to be found in things. Among beings there are some more and some less good, true, noble, and the like. But *more* and *less* are predicated of different things according as they resemble in their different ways something which is the maximum, as a thing is said to be hotter according as it more nearly resembles that which is hottest; so that there is something which is truest, something best, something noblest, and, consequently, something which is most being, for those things that are greatest in truth are greatest in being, as it is written in *Metaph.* ii.[1] Now the maximum in any genus is the cause of all in that genus, as fire, which is the maximum of heat, is the cause of all hot things, as is said in the same book. Therefore there must also be something which is to all beings the cause of their being, goodness, and every other perfection; and this we call God.

The fifth way is taken from the governance of the world. We see that things which lack knowledge, such as natural bodies, act for an end, and this is evident from their acting always, or nearly always, in the same way, so as to obtain the best result. Hence it is plain that they achieve their end, not fortuitously, but designedly. Now whatever lacks knowledge cannot move towards an end, unless it be directed by some being endowed with knowledge and intelligence; as the arrow is directed by the archer. Therefore some intelligent being exists by whom all natural things are directed to their end; and this being we call God.

Reply Obj. 1. As Augustine says: *Since God is the highest good, He would not allow any evil to exist in His works, unless His omnipotence and goodness were such as to bring good even out of evil.* This is part of the infinite goodness of God, that He should allow evil to exist, and out of it produce good.

Reply Obj. 2. Since nature works for a determinate end under the direction of a higher agent, whatever is done by nature must be traced back to God as to its first cause. So likewise whatever is done voluntarily must be traced back to some higher cause other than human reason and will, since these can change and fail; for all things that are changeable and capable of defect must be traced back to an immovable and self-necessary first principle, as has been shown.

NOTE

1. The reference is to Aristotle's *Metaphysics.*

The Cosmological Argument

RICHARD TAYLOR

Arguments of the sort St. Thomas Aquinas presented are commonly referred to as "cosmological" because they are based on a variety of fundamental principles about the structure of the world. A contemporary version of the cosmological argument is presented in our next selection by Richard Taylor (1919–2003), who was Professor of Philosophy at the University of Rochester. He argues that the existence of the world requires an explanation, and that the most plausible one points to God as the Being on whom the world depends for its existence.

The Principle of Sufficient Reason

Suppose you were strolling in the woods and, in addition to the sticks, stones, and other accustomed litter of the forest floor, you one day came upon some quite unaccustomed object, something not quite like what you had ever seen before and would never expect to find in such a place. Suppose, for example, that it is a large ball, about your own height, perfectly smooth and translucent. You would deem this puzzling and mysterious, certainly, but if one considers the matter, it is no more inherently mysterious that such a thing should exist than that anything else should exist. If you were quite accustomed to finding such objects of various sizes around you most of the time, but had never seen an ordinary rock, then upon finding a large rock in the woods one day you would be just as puzzled and mystified. This illustrates the fact that something that is mysterious ceases to seem so simply by its accustomed presence. It is strange indeed, for example, that a world such as ours should exist; yet few people are very often struck by this strangeness but simply take it for granted.

Suppose, then, that you have found this translucent ball and are mystified by it. Now whatever else you might wonder about it, there is one thing you would hardly question; namely, that it did not appear there all by itself, that it owes its existence to something. You might not have the remotest idea whence and how it came to be there, but you would hardly doubt that there was an explanation. The idea that it might have come from nothing at all, that it might exist without there being any explanation of its existence, is one that few people would consider worthy of entertaining.

This illustrates a metaphysical belief that seems to be almost a part of reason itself, even though few ever think upon it; the belief, namely, that there is some explanation for the existence of anything whatever, some reason why it should exist rather than not. The sheer nonexistence of anything, which is not to be confused with the passing out of existence of something, never requires a reason; but existence does. That there should never have been any such ball in the forest does not require any explanation or reason, but that there should ever be such a ball does. If one were to look upon a barren plain and ask why there is not and never has been any large translucent ball there, the natural response would be to ask why there should be; but if one finds such a ball, and wonders why it is there, it is not quite so natural to ask why it should *not* be—as though existence should simply be taken for granted. That anything should not exist, then, and that, for instance, no such ball should exist in the forest, or that there should be no forest for it to occupy, or no continent containing a forest, or no Earth, nor any world at all, do not seem to be things for which there needs to be any explanation or reason; but that such things should be *does* seem to require a reason.

The principle involved here has been called the principle of sufficient reason. Actually, it is a very general principle, and it is best expressed by saying that, in the case of any positive truth, there is some sufficient reason for it, something that, in this sense, makes it true—in short, that there is some sort of explanation, known or unknown, for everything.

Now, some truths depend on something else, and are accordingly called *contingent,* while others depend only upon themselves, that is, are true by their very natures and are accordingly called *necessary.* There is, for example, a reason why the stone on my window sill is warm; namely, that the sun is shining upon it. This happens to be true, but not by its very nature. Hence, it is contingent, and depends upon something other than itself. It is also true that all the points of a circle are equidistant from the center, but this truth depends upon nothing but itself. No matter what happens, nothing can make it false. Similarly, it is a truth, and a necessary one, that if the stone on my window sill is a body, as it is, then it has a form, because this fact depends upon nothing but itself for its confirmation. Untruths are also, of course, either contingent or necessary, it being contingently false, for example, that the stone on my window sill is cold, and necessarily false that it is both a body and formless, because this is by its very nature impossible.

The principle of sufficient reason can be illustrated in various ways, as we have done, and if one thinks about it, he is apt to find that he presupposes it in his thinking about reality, but it cannot be proved. It does not appear to be itself a necessary truth, and at the same time it would be most odd to say it is contingent. If one were to try proving it, he would sooner or later have to appeal to considerations that are less plausible than the principle itself. Indeed, it is hard to see how one could even make an argument for it without already assuming it. For this reason it might properly be called a presupposition of reason itself. One can deny that it is true, without embarrassment or fear of refutation, but one is then apt to find that what he is denying is not really what the principle asserts. We shall, then, treat it here as a datum—not something that is provably true, but as something that people, whether they ever reflect upon it or not, seem more or less to presuppose.

The Existence of a World

It happens to be true that something exists, that there is, for example, a world, and although no one ever seriously supposes that this might not be so, that there might exist nothing at all, there still seems to be nothing the least necessary in this, considering it just by itself. That no world should ever exist at all is perfectly comprehensible and seems to express not the slightest absurdity. Considering any particular item in the world it seems not at all necessary that the totality of these things, or any totality of things, should ever exist.

From the principle of sufficient reason it follows, of course, that there must be a reason not only for the existence of everything in the world but for the world itself, meaning by "the world" simply everything that ever does exist, except God, in case there is a god. This principle does not imply that there must be some purpose or goal for everything, or for the totality of all things; for explanations need not be, and in fact seldom are, teleological or purposeful. All the principle requires is that there be some sort of reason for everything. And it would certainly be odd to maintain that everything in the world owes its existence to something, that nothing in the world is either purely accidental, or such that it just bestows its own being upon itself, and then to deny this of the world itself. One can indeed *say* that the world is in some sense a pure accident, that there simply is no reason at all why this or any world should exist, and one can equally say that the world exists by its very nature, or is an inherently necessary being. But it is at least very odd and arbitrary to deny of this existing world the need for any sufficient reason, whether independent of itself or not, while presupposing that there is a reason for every other thing that ever exists.

Consider again the strange ball that we imagine has been found in the forest. Now, we can hardly doubt that there must be an explanation for the existence of such a thing, though we may have no notion what that explanation is. It is not, moreover, the fact of its having been found in the forest rather than elsewhere that renders an explanation necessary. It matters not in the least where it happens to be, for our question is not how it happens to be *there* but how it happens to be at all. If we in our imagination annihilate the forest, leaving only this ball in an open field, our conviction that it is a contingent thing and owes its existence to something other than itself is not reduced in the least. If we now imagine the field to be annihilated, and in fact everything else as well to vanish into nothingness, leaving only this ball to constitute the entire physical universe, then we cannot for a moment suppose that its existence has thereby been explained, or the need for any explanation eliminated, or that its existence is suddenly rendered self-explanatory. If we now carry this thought one step further and suppose that no other reality ever has existed or ever will exist, that this ball forever constitutes the entire physical universe, then we must still insist on there being some reason independent of itself why it should exist rather than not. If there must be a reason for the existence of any particular thing, then the necessity of such a reason is not eliminated by the mere supposition that certain other things do *not* exist. And again, it matters not at all what the thing in question is, whether it be large and complex, such as the world we actually find ourselves in, or whether it be something small, simple, and insignificant, such as a ball, a bacterium, or the merest grain of sand. We do not avoid the necessity of a reason for the existence of something merely by describing it in this way or that. And it would, in any event, seem quite plainly absurd to say that if the world were composed entirely of a single ball about six feet in diameter, or of a single grain of sand, then it would be contingent and there would have to be some explanation other than itself why such a thing exists, but that, since the actual world is vastly more complex than this, there is no need for an explanation of its existence, independent of itself.

Beginningless Existence

It should now be noted that it is no answer to the question, why a thing exists, to state *how long* it has existed. A geologist does not suppose that she has explained why there should be rivers and mountains merely by pointing out that they are old. Similarly, if one were to ask, concerning the ball of which we have spoken, for some sufficient reason for its being, he would not receive any answer upon being told that it had been there since yesterday. Nor would it be any better answer to say that it had existed since before anyone could remember, or even that it had always existed; for the question was not one concerning its age but its existence. If, to be sure, one were to ask where a given thing came from, or how it came into being, then upon learning that it had always existed he would learn that it never really *came* into being at all; but he could still reasonably wonder why it should exist at all. If, accordingly, the world—that is, the totality of all things excepting God, in case there is a god—had really no beginning at all, but has always existed in some form or other, then there is clearly no answer to the question, where it came from and when; it did not, on this supposition, *come* from anything at all, at any time. But still, it can be asked why there is a world, why indeed there is a beginningless world, why there should have perhaps always been something rather than nothing. And, if the principle of sufficient reason is a good principle, there must be an answer to that question, an answer that is by no means supplied by giving the world an age, or even an infinite age.

Creation

This brings out an important point with respect to the concept of creation that is often misunderstood, particularly by those whose thinking has been influenced by Christian ideas. People tend to think that creation—for example, the creation of the world by God—*means* creation *in time,* from which it of course logically follows that if the world had no beginning in time, then it cannot be the creation of God. This, however, is erroneous, for creation means essentially *dependence,* even in Christian theology. If one thing is the creation of another, then it depends for its existence on that other, and this is perfectly consistent with saying that both are eternal, that neither ever came into being and hence, that neither was ever created at any point of time. Perhaps an analogy will help convey this point. Consider, then, a flame that is casting beams of light. Now, there seems to be a clear sense in which the beams of light are dependent for their existence upon the flame, which is their source, while the flame, on the other hand, is not similarly dependent for its existence upon them. The beams of light arise from the flame, but the flame does not arise from them. In this sense, they are the creation of the flame; they derive their existence from it. And none of this has any reference to time; the relationship of dependence in such a case would not be altered in the slightest if we supposed that the flame, and with it the beams of light, had always existed, that neither had ever *come* into being.

Now if the world is the creation of God, its relationship to God should be thought of in this fashion; namely, that the world depends for its existence upon God, and could not exist independently of God. If God is eternal, as those who believe in God generally assume, then the world may (though it need not) be eternal too, without that altering in the least its dependence upon God for its existence, and hence without altering its being the creation of God. The supposition of God's eternality, on the other hand, does not by itself imply that the world is eternal too; for there is not the least reason why something of finite duration might not depend for its existence upon something of infinite duration—though the reverse is, of course, impossible.

God

If we think of God as "the creator of heaven and earth," and if we consider heaven and earth to include everything that exists except God, then we appear to have, in the foregoing considerations, fairly strong reasons for asserting that God, as so conceived, exists. Now of course most people have much more in mind than this when they think of God, for religions have ascribed to God ever so many attributes that are not at all implied by describing him merely as the creator of the world; but that is not relevant here. Most religious persons do, in any case, think of God as being at least the creator, as that being upon which everything ultimately depends, no matter what else they may say about Him in addition. It is, in fact, the first item in the creeds of Christianity that God is the "creator of heaven and earth." And, it seems, there are good metaphysical reasons, as distinguished from the persuasions of faith, for thinking that such a creative being exists.

If, as seems clearly implied by the principle of sufficient reason, there must be a reason for the existence of heaven and earth—i.e., for the world—then that reason must be found either in the world itself, or outside it, in something that is literally supranatural, or outside heaven and earth. Now if we suppose that the world—i.e., the totality of all things except God—contains within itself the reason for its existence, we are supposing that it exists by its very nature, that is, that it is a necessary being. In that case there would, of course, be no reason for saying that it must depend upon God or anything else for its existence; for if it exists by its very nature, then it depends upon nothing but itself, much as the sun depends upon nothing but itself for its heat. This, however, is implausible, for we find nothing about the world or anything in it to suggest that it exists by its own nature, and we do find, on the contrary, ever so many things to suggest that it does not. For in the first place, anything that exists by its very nature must necessarily be eternal and indestructible. It would be a self-contradiction to say of anything that it exists by its own nature, or is a necessarily existing thing, and at the same time to say that it comes into being or passes away, or that it ever could come into being or pass away. Nothing about the world seems at all like this, for concerning anything in the world, we can perfectly easily think of it as being annihilated, or as never having existed in the first place, without there being the slightest hint of any absurdity in such a supposition. Some of the things in the universe are, to be sure, very old; the moon, for example, or the stars and the planets. It is even possible to imagine that they have always existed. Yet it seems quite impossible to suppose that they owe their existence to nothing but themselves, that they bestow existence upon themselves by their very natures, or that they are in themselves things of such nature that it would be impossible for them not to exist. Even if we suppose that something, such as the sun, for instance, has existed forever, and will never cease, still we cannot conclude just from this that it exists by its own nature. If, as is of course very doubtful, the sun has existed forever and will never cease, then it is possible that its heat and light have also existed forever and will never cease; but that would not show that the heat and light of the sun exist by their own natures. They are obviously contingent and depend on the sun for their existence, whether they are beginningless and everlasting or not.

There seems to be nothing in the world, then, concerning which it is at all plausible to suppose that it exists by its own nature, or contains within itself the reason for its existence. In fact, everything in the world appears to be quite plainly the opposite, namely, something that not only need not exist, but at some time or other, past or future or both, does not in fact exist. Everything in the world seems to have a finite duration, whether long or short. Most things, such as ourselves, exist only for a short while; they come into being, then soon cease. Other things, like the heavenly bodies, last longer, but they are still corruptible, and from all that we can gather about them, they too seem destined eventually to perish. We arrive at the conclusion, then, that although the world may contain some things that have always existed and are destined never to perish, it is nevertheless doubtful that it contains any such thing, and, in any case, everything in the world is capable of perishing, and nothing in it, however long it may already have existed and however long it may yet remain, exists by its own nature but depends instead upon something else.

Although this might be true of everything in the world, is it necessarily true of the world itself? That is, if we grant, as we seem forced to, that nothing in the world exists by its own nature, that everything in the world is contingent and perishable, must we also say that the world itself, or the totality of all these perishable things, is also contingent and perishable? Logically, we are not forced to, for it is logically possible that the totality of all perishable things might itself be imperishable, and hence, that the world might exist by its own nature, even though it is composed exclusively of things that are contingent. It is not logically necessary that a totality should share the defects of its members. For example, even though every person is mortal, it does not follow from this that the human race, or the totality of all people, is also mortal; for it is possible that there will always be human beings, even though there are no human beings who will always exist. Similarly, it is possible that the world is in itself a necessary thing, even though it is composed entirely of things that are contingent.

This is logically possible, but it is not plausible. For we find nothing whatever about the world, any more than in its parts, to suggest that it exists by its own nature. Concerning anything in the world, we have not the slightest difficulty in supposing that it should perish, or even that it should never have existed in the first place. We have almost as little difficulty in supposing this of the world itself. It might be somewhat hard to think of everything as utterly perishing and leaving no trace whatever of its ever having been, but there seems to be not the slightest difficulty in imagining that the world should never have existed in the first place. We can, for instance, perfectly easily suppose that nothing in the world had ever existed except, let us suppose, a single grain of sand, and we can thus suppose that this grain of sand has forever constituted the whole universe. Now if we consider just this grain of sand, it is quite impossible for us to suppose that it exists by its very nature and could never have failed to exist. It clearly depends for its existence upon something other than itself, if it depends on anything at all. The same will be true if we consider the world to consist not of one grain of sand but of two, or of a million, or, as we in fact find, of a vast number of stars and planets and all their minuter parts.

It would seem, then, that the world, in case it happens to exist at all—and this is quite beyond doubt—is contingent and thus dependent upon something other than itself for its existence, if it depends upon anything at all. And it must depend upon something, for otherwise there could be no reason why it exists in the first place. Now, that upon which the world depends must be something that either exists by its own nature or does not. If it does not exist by its own nature, then it, in turn, depends for its existence upon something else, and so on. Now then, we can say either of two things; namely, (1) that the world depends for its existence upon something else, which in turn depends on still another thing, this depending upon still another, ad infinitum; or (2) that the world derives its existence from something that exists by its own nature and that is accordingly eternal and imperishable, and is the creator of heaven and earth. The first of these alternatives, however, is impossible, for it does not render a sufficient reason why anything should exist in the first place. Instead of supplying a reason why any world should exist, it repeatedly begs off giving a reason. It explains what is dependent and perishable in terms of what is itself dependent and perishable, leaving us still without a reason why perishable things should exist at all, which is what we are seeking. Ultimately, then, it would seem that the world, or the totality of contingent or perishable things, in case it exists at all, must depend upon something that is necessary and imperishable, and that accordingly exists, not in dependence upon something else, but by its own nature.

"Self-Caused"

What has been said thus far gives some intimation of what meaning should be attached to the concept of a self-caused being; a concept that is quite generally misunderstood, sometimes even by scholars. To say that something—God, for example—is self-caused, or is the cause of its own existence, does not mean that this being brings itself into existence, which is a perfectly absurd idea. Nothing can *bring* itself into existence. To say that something is self-caused (*causa sui*) means only that it exists, not contingently or in dependence upon something else but by its own nature, which is only to say that it is a being which is such that it can neither come into being nor perish. Now, whether in fact such a being exists or not, there is in any case no absurdity in the idea. We have found, in fact, that the principle of sufficient reason seems to point to the existence of such a being, as that upon which the world, with everything in it, must ultimately depend for its existence.

"Necessary Being"

A being that depends for its existence upon nothing but itself and is in this sense self-caused, can equally be described as a necessary being; that is to say, a being that is not contingent, and hence not perishable. For in the case of anything that exists by its own nature and is dependent upon nothing else, it is impossible that it should not exist, which is equivalent to saying that it is necessary. Many persons have professed to find the gravest difficulties in this concept, too, but that is partly because it has been confused with other notions. If it makes sense to speak of anything as an *impossible* being, or something that by its very nature does not exist, then it is hard to see why the idea of a necessary being, or something that in its very nature exists, should not be just as comprehensible. And of course, we have not the slightest difficulty in speaking of something, such as a square circle or a formless body, as an impossible being. And if it makes sense to speak of something as being perishable, contingent, and dependent upon something other than itself for its existence, as it surely does, then there seems to be no difficulty in thinking of something as imperishable and dependent upon nothing other than itself for its existence.

"First Cause"

From these considerations we can see also what is properly meant by a "first cause," an appellative that has often been applied to God by theologians and that many persons have deemed an absurdity. It is a common criticism of this notion to say that there need not be any first cause, because the series of causes and effects that constitute the history of the universe might be infinite or beginningless and must, in fact, be infinite in case the universe itself had no beginning in time. This criticism, however, reflects a total misconception of what is meant by a first cause. *First* here does not mean first in time, and when God is spoken of as a first cause He is not being described as a being that, at some time in the remote past, *started* everything. To describe God as a first cause is only to say that He is literally a *primary* rather than a secondary cause, an *ultimate* rather than a derived cause, or a being upon which all other things, heaven and earth, ultimately depend for their existence. It is, in short, only to say that God is the creator, in the sense of creation previously explained. Now this, of course, is perfectly consistent with saying that the world is eternal or beginningless. As we have seen, one gives no reason for the existence of a world merely by giving it an age, even if it is supposed to have an infinite age. To use a helpful analogy, we can say that the sun is the first cause of daylight and, for that matter, of the moonlight of the night as well, which means only that daylight and moonlight ultimately depend upon the sun for their existence. The moon, on the other hand, is only a secondary or derivative cause of its light. This light would be no less dependent upon the sun if we affirmed that it had no beginning, for an ageless and beginningless light requires a source no less than an ephemeral one. If we supposed that the sun has always existed, and with it its light, then we would have to say that the sun has always been the first—i.e., the primary or ultimate—cause of its light. Such is precisely the manner in which God should be thought of, and is by theologians often thought of, as the first cause of heaven and earth.

The Cosmological Argument: An Assessment

John H. Hick

In the following selection John H. Hick, the contemporary British philosopher and minister whose work we read previously, explains why he believes that no version of the cosmological argument, whether of a sort Aquinas or Taylor presents, offers a compelling reason to believe in the existence of God.

Thomas Aquinas . . . offers five ways of proving divine existence. Unlike the ontological argument, which focuses attention upon the *idea* of God and proceeds to unfold its inner implications, Aquinas's proofs start from some general feature of the world around us and argue that there could not be a world with this particular characteristic unless there were also the ultimate reality which we call God. The first Way argues from the fact of change to a Prime Mover; the second from causation to a First Cause; the third from contingent beings to a Necessary Being; the fourth from degrees of value to Absolute Value; and the fifth from evidences of purposiveness in nature to a Divine Designer.

We may concentrate upon Aquinas's second and third proofs. His second proof, known as *the First-Cause argument*, is presented as follows: everything that happens has a cause, and this cause in turn has a cause, and so on in a series that must either be infinite or have its starting point in a first cause. Aquinas excludes the possibility of an infinite regress of causes and so concludes that there must be a First Cause, which we call God. (His first proof, which infers a First Mover from the fact of motion, is basically similar.)

The weakness of the argument as Aquinas states it lies in the difficulty . . . of excluding as impossible an endless regress of events, requiring no first state.

However, some contemporary Thomists (i.e., thinkers who in general follow Thomas Aquinas) have reformulated the argument in order to avoid this difficulty. They interpret the endless series that it excludes, not as a regress of events back in time, but as an endless and therefore eternally inconclusive regress of explanations. If fact A is made intelligible by its relation to facts B, C, and D (which may be antecedent to or contemporary with A), and if each of these is in turn rendered intelligible by other facts, at the back of the complex there must be a reality which is self-explanatory, whose existence constitutes the ultimate explanation of the whole. If no such reality exists, the universe is a mere unintelligible brute fact.

However, this reinterpretation still leaves the argument open to two major difficulties. First, how do we know that the universe is not "a mere unintelligible brute fact"? Apart from the emotional coloring suggested by the phrase, this is precisely what the skeptic believes it to be; and to exclude this possibility at the outset is merely to beg the question at issue. The argument in effect presents the dilemma: either there is a First Cause or the universe is ultimately unintelligible; but it does not compel us to accept one horn of the dilemma rather than the other.

Second (although there is only space to suggest this difficulty, leaving the reader to develop it), the argument still depends upon a view of causality that can be, and has been, questioned. The assumption of the reformulated argument is that to indicate the causal conditions of an event is thereby to render that event intelligible. Although this assumption is true on the basis of some theories of the nature of causality, it is not true on the basis of others. For example, if (as much contemporary science assumes) causal laws state statistical probabilities . . . , the Thomist argument fails.

Aquinas's third Way, known as the argument from the contingency of the world, and often monopolizing the name *the cosmological argument,* runs as follows. Everything in the world about us is contingent—that is, it is true of each item that it might not have existed at all or might have existed differently. The proof of this is that there was a time when it did not exist. The existence of this printed page is contingent upon the prior activities of trees, lumber-jacks, transport workers, paper manufacturers, publishers, printers, author, and others, as well as upon the contemporary operation of a great number of chemical and physical laws; and each of these in turn depends upon other factors. Everything points beyond itself to other things. Saint Thomas argues that if everything were contingent, there would have been a time when nothing existed. In this case, nothing could ever have come to exist, for there would have been no causal agency. Since there are things in existence, there must therefore be something that is not contingent, and this we call God.

Aquinas's reference to a hypothetical time when nothing existed seems to weaken rather than strengthen his argument, for there might be an infinite series of finite contingent events overlapping in the time sequence so that no moment occurs that is not occupied by any of them. . . . If we remove the reference to time, we have an argument based upon the logical connection between a contingent world (even if this should consist of an infinite series of events) and its noncontingent ground. One writer points as an analogy to the workings of a watch. The movement of each separate wheel and cog is accounted for by the way in which it meshes with an adjacent wheel. Nevertheless, the operation of the whole system remains inexplicable until we refer to something else outside it, namely, the spring. In order for there to be a set of interlocking wheels in movement, there must be a spring; and in order for there to be a world of contingent realities, there must be a noncontingent ground for their existence. Only a self-existent reality, containing in itself the source of its own being, can constitute an ultimate ground of the existence of anything else. Such an ultimate ground is the "necessary being" that we call God. . . .

There remains, however, an important objection to the cosmological argument, parallel to one of those applying to the First-Cause argument. The force of the cosmological form of reasoning resides in the dilemma: *either* there is a necessary being *or* the universe is ultimately unintelligible. Clearly such an argument is cogent only if the second alternative has been ruled out. Far from being ruled out, however, it represents the skeptic's position. This inability to exclude the possibility of an unintelligible universe prevents the cosmological argument from operating for the skeptic as a proof of God's existence—and the skeptic is, after all, the only person who needs such a proof.

The Argument to Design

William Paley

William Paley (1743–1805) was an English theologian and moral philosopher. He gave a classic presentation of another argument for the existence of God, the so-called teleological argument or argument to design. This argument proceeds from the premise of the world's magnificent order to the conclusion that the world must be the work of a Supreme Mind responsible for this order.

Chapter I: The State of the Argument

In crossing a heath, suppose I pitched my foot against a stone and were asked how the stone came to be there. I might possibly answer that for anything I knew to the contrary it had lain there forever; nor would it, perhaps, be very easy to show the absurdity of this answer. But suppose I had found a watch upon the ground, and it should be inquired how the watch happened to be in that place. I should hardly think of the answer which I had before given, that for anything I knew the watch might have always been there. Yet why should not this answer serve for the watch as well as for the stone? Why is it not as admissible in the second case as in the first? For this reason, and for no other, namely, that when we come to inspect the watch, we perceive—what we could not discover in the stone—that its several parts are framed and put together for a purpose, e.g., that they are so formed and adjusted as to produce motion, and that motion so regulated as to point out the hour of the day; that if the different parts had been differently shaped from what they are, of a different size from what they are, or placed after any other manner or in any other order than that in which they are placed, either no motion at all would have been carried on in the machine, or none which would have answered the use that is now served by it. To reckon up a few of the plainest of these parts and of their offices, all tending to one result; we see a cylindrical box containing a coiled elastic spring, which, by its endeavor to relax itself, turns round the box. We next observe a flexible chain—artificially wrought for the sake of flexure—communicating the

---

From William Paley, *Natural Theology*.

action of the spring from the box to the fusee. We then find a series of wheels, the teeth of which catch in and apply to each other, conducting the motion from the fusee to the balance and from the balance to the pointer, and at the same time, by the size and shape of those wheels, so regulating that motion as to terminate in causing an index, by an equable and measured progression, to pass over a given space in a given time. We take notice that the wheels are made of brass, in order to keep them from rust; the springs of steel, no other metal being so elastic; that over the face of the watch there is placed a glass, a material employed in no other part of the work, but in the room of which, if there had been any other than a transparent substance, the hour could not be seen without opening the case. This mechanism being observed—it requires indeed an examination of the instrument, and perhaps some previous knowledge of the subject, to perceive and understand it; but being once, as we have said, observed and understood—the inference we think is inevitable, that the watch must have had a maker—that there must have existed, at some time and at some place or other, an artificer or artificers who formed it for the purpose which we find it actually to answer, who comprehended its construction and designed its use.

I. Nor would it, I apprehend, weaken the conclusion, that we had never seen a watch made—that we had never known an artist capable of making one—that we were altogether incapable of executing such a piece of workmanship ourselves, or of understanding in what manner it was performed; all this being no more than what is true of some exquisite remains of ancient art, of some lost arts, and, to the generality of mankind, of the more curious productions of modern manufacture. Does one man in a million know how oval frames are turned? Ignorance of this kind exalts our opinion of the unseen and unknown artist's skill, if he be unseen and unknown, but raises no doubt in our minds of the existence and agency of such an artist, at some former time and in some place or other. Nor can I perceive that it varies at all the inference, whether the question arise concerning a human agent or concerning an agent of a different species, or an agent possessing in some respects a different nature.

II. Neither, secondly, would it invalidate our conclusion, that the watch sometimes went wrong or that it seldom went exactly right. The purpose of the machinery, the design, and the designer might be evident, and in the case supposed, would be evident, in whatever way we accounted for the irregularity of the movement, or whether we could account for it or not. It is not necessary that a machine be perfect in order to show with what design it was made: still less necessary, where the only question is whether it were made with any design at all.

III. Nor, thirdly, would it bring any uncertainty into the argument, if there were a few parts of the watch, concerning which we could not discover or had not yet discovered in what manner they conduced to the general effect; or even some parts, concerning which we could not ascertain whether they conduced to that effect in any manner whatever. For, as to the first branch of the case, if by the loss, or disorder, or decay of the parts in question, the movement of the watch were found in fact to be stopped, or disturbed, or retarded, no doubt would remain in our minds as to the utility or intention of these parts, although we should be unable to investigate the manner according to which, or the connection by which, the ultimate effect depended upon their action or assistance; and the more complex is the machine, the more likely is this obscurity to arise. Then, as to the second thing supposed, namely, that there were parts which might be spared without prejudice to the movement of the watch, and that we had proved this by experiment, these superfluous parts, even if we were completely assured that they were such, would not vacate the reasoning which we had instituted concerning other parts. The indication of contrivance remained, with respect to them, nearly as it was before.

IV. Nor, fourthly, would any man in his senses think the existence of the watch with its various machinery accounted for, by being told that it was one out of possible combinations of material forms; that whatever he had found in the place where he found the watch, must have contained some internal configuration or other; and that this configuration might be the structure now exhibited, namely, of the works of a watch, as well as a different structure.

V. Nor, fifthly, would it yield his inquiry more satisfaction, to be answered that there existed in things a principle of order, which had disposed the parts of the watch into their present form and situation. He never knew a watch made by the principle of order; nor can he even form to himself an idea of what is meant by a principle of order distinct from the intelligence of the watchmaker.

VI. Sixthly, he would be surprised to hear that the mechanism of the watch was no proof of contrivance, only a motive to induce the mind to think so:

VII. And not less surprised to be informed that the watch in his hand was nothing more than the result of the laws of *metallic* nature. It is a perversion of language to assign any law as the efficient, operative cause of any thing. A law presupposes an agent, for it is only the mode according to which an agent proceeds; it implies a power, for it is the order according to which that power acts. Without this agent, without this power, which are both distinct from itself, the *law* does nothing, is nothing. The expression, "the law of metallic nature," may sound strange and harsh to a philosophic ear; but it seems quite as justifiable as some others which are more familiar to him, such as "the law of vegetable nature," "the law of animal nature," or, indeed, as "the law of nature" in general, when assigned as the cause of phenomena, in exclusion of agency and power, or when it is substituted into the place of these.

VIII. Neither, lastly, would our observer be driven out of his conclusion or from his confidence in its truth by being told that he knew nothing at all about the matter. He knows enough for his argument; he knows the utility of the end; he knows the subserviency and adaptation of the means to the end. These points being known, his ignorance of other points, his doubts concerning other points affect not the certainty of his reasoning. The consciousness of knowing little need not beget a distrust of that which he does know. . . .

Chapter III: Application of the Argument

. . . Every indication of contrivance, every manifestation of design, which existed in the watch, exists in the works of nature; with the difference, on the side of nature, of being greater and more, and that in a degree which exceeds all computation. I mean that the contrivances of nature surpass the contrivances of art in the complexity, subtility, and curiosity of the mechanism; and still more, if possible, do they go beyond them in number and variety; yet, in a multitude of cases, are not less evidently mechanical, not less evidently contrivances, not less evidently accommodated to their end, or suited to their office, than are the most perfect productions of human ingenuity. . . .

I know no better method of introducing so large a subject, than that of comparing a single thing with a single thing; an eye, for example, with a telescope. As far as the examination of the instrument goes, there is precisely the same proof that the eye was made for vision, as there is that the telescope was made for assisting it. They are made upon the same principles; both being adjusted to the laws by which the transmission and reflection of rays of light are regulated. I speak not of the origin of the laws themselves; but such laws being fixed, the construction, in both cases, is adapted to them. For instance, these laws require, in order to produce the same effect, that the rays of light, in passing from water into the eye, should be refracted by a more convex surface than when it passes out of air into the eye. Accordingly we find, that the eye of a fish, in that part of it called the crystalline lens, is much rounder than the eye of terrestrial animals. What plainer manifestation of design can there be than this difference? What could a mathematical instrument-maker have done more, to show his knowledge of his principle, his application of that knowledge, his suiting of his means to his end; I will not say to display the compass or excellence of his skill and art, for in these all comparison is indecorous, but to testify counsel, choice, consideration, purpose?

The Argument to Design and the Problem of Evil

David Hume

The Scotsman David Hume (1711–1776) was a widely read essayist, distinguished historian, and one of the most influential of all philosophers. His extraordinarily powerful *Dialogues Concerning Natural Religion* is one of the most important books in the philosophy of religion. During his lifetime, his friends, fearful of public disapproval, had dissuaded him from publishing the manuscript, but he took great pains to ensure that the work would not be lost, and it appeared in print three years after his death, although without any publisher's name attached.

"Natural religion" was the term used by eighteenth-century writers to refer to theological tenets that are provable by reason without appeal to revelation. The three participants in the *Dialogues* are distinguished by their views concerning the scope and limits of reason. Cleanthes claims that he can present arguments that demonstrate the truth of traditional Christian theology. Demea is committed to that theology but does not believe empirical evidence can provide any defense for his faith. Philo doubts that reason yields conclusive results in any field of inquiry and is especially critical of theological dogmatism.

In the sections of the book reprinted here, the argument to design is subjected to trenchant criticism. In addition, Hume develops in detail what is probably the strongest argument against the existence of God, namely, the problem of evil: How can evil exist in a world created by an all-good, all-powerful God?

Part II

. . . Not to lose any time in circumlocutions, said Cleanthes, . . . I shall briefly explain how I conceive this matter. Look round the world, contemplate the whole and every part of it: you will find it to be nothing but one great

From David Hume, *Dialogues Concerning Natural Religion.*

machine, subdivided into an infinite number of lesser machines, which again admit of subdivisions to a degree beyond what human senses and faculties can trace and explain. All these various machines, and even their most minute parts, are adjusted to each other with an accuracy which ravishes into admiration all men who have ever contemplated them. The curious adapting of means to ends, throughout all nature, resembles exactly, though it much exceeds, the productions of human contrivance—of human design, thought, wisdom, and intelligence. Since therefore the effects resemble each other, we are led to infer, by all the rules of analogy, that the causes also resemble, and that the Author of nature is somewhat similar to the mind of man, though possessed of much larger faculties, proportioned to the grandeur of the work which he has executed. By this argument a posteriori, and by this argument alone, do we prove at once the existence of a Deity and his similarity to human mind and intelligence.

I shall be so free, Cleanthes, said Demea, as to tell you that from the beginning I could not approve of your conclusion concerning the similarity of the Deity to men, still less can I approve of the mediums by which you endeavour to establish it. What! No demonstration of the Being of God! No abstract arguments! No proofs a priori! Are these which have hitherto been so much insisted on by philosophers all fallacy, all sophism? Can we reach no farther in this subject than experience and probability? I will not say that this is betraying the cause of a Deity; but surely, by this affected candour, you give advantages to atheists which they never could obtain by the mere dint of argument and reasoning.

What I chiefly scruple in this subject, said Philo, is not so much that all religious arguments are by Cleanthes reduced to experience, as that they appear not to be even the most certain and irrefragable of that inferior kind. That a stone will fall, that fire will burn, that the earth has solidity, we have observed a thousand and a thousand times; and when any new instance of this nature is presented, we draw without hesitation the accustomed inference. The exact similarity of the cases gives us a perfect assurance of a similar event, and a stronger evidence is never desired nor sought after. But wherever you depart, in the least, from the similarity of the cases, you diminish proportionably the evidence, and may at last bring it to a very weak *analogy,* which is confessedly liable to error and uncertainty. After having experienced the circulation of the blood in human creatures, we make no doubt that it takes place in Titius and Maevius,[1] but from its circulation in frogs and fishes it is only a presumption, though a strong one, from analogy that it takes place in men and other animals. The analogical reasoning is much weaker when we infer the circulation of the sap in vegetables from our experience that the blood circulates in animals; and those who hastily followed that imperfect analogy are found, by more accurate experiments, to have been mistaken.

If we see a house, Cleanthes, we conclude, with the greatest certainty, that it had an architect or builder because this is precisely that species of effect which we have experienced to proceed from that species of cause. But surely you will not affirm that the universe bears such a resemblance to a house that we can with the same certainty infer a similar cause, or that the analogy is here entire and perfect. The dissimilitude is so striking that the utmost you can here pretend to is a guess, conjecture, a presumption concerning a similar cause; and how that pretension will be received in the world, I leave you to consider.

It would surely be very ill received, replied Cleanthes; and I should be deservedly blamed and detested did I allow that the proofs of Deity amounted to no more than a guess or conjecture. But is the whole adjustment of means to ends in a house and in the universe so slight a resemblance? the economy of final causes? the order, proportion, and arrangement of every part? Steps of a stair are plainly contrived that human legs may use them in mounting; and this inference is certain and infallible. Human legs are also contrived for walking and mounting; and this inference, I allow, is not altogether so certain because of the dissimilarity which you remark; but does it, therefore, deserve the name only of presumption or conjecture?

Good God! cried Demea, interrupting him, where are we? Zealous defenders of religion allow that the proofs of a Deity fall short of perfect evidence! And you, Philo, on whose assistance I depended in proving the adorable mysteriousness of the Divine Nature, do you assent to all these extravagant opinions of Cleanthes? For what other name can I give them? or, why spare my censure when such principles are advanced, supported by such an authority, before so young a man as Pamphilus?

You seem not to apprehend, replied Philo, that I argue with Cleanthes in his own way, and, by showing him the dangerous consequences of his tenets, hope at last to reduce him to our opinion. But what sticks most with you, I observe, is the representation which Cleanthes has made of the argument a posteriori; and, finding that the argument is likely to escape your hold and vanish into air, you think it so disguised that you can scarcely believe it to be set in its true light. Now, however much I may dissent, in other respects, from the dangerous principle of Cleanthes, I must allow that he has fairly represented that argument, and I shall endeavour so to state the matter to you that you will entertain no further scruples with regard to it.

Were a man to abstract from everything which he knows or has seen, he would be altogether incapable, merely from his own ideas, to determine what kind of scene the universe must be, or to give the preference to one state or situation of things above another. For as nothing which he clearly conceives could be esteemed impossible or implying a contradiction, every chimera of his fancy would be upon an equal footing; nor could he assign any just reason why he adheres to one idea or system, and rejects the others which are equally possible.

Again, after he opens his eyes and contemplates the world as it really is, it would be impossible for him at first to assign the cause of any one event, much less of the whole of things, or of the universe. He might set his fancy a rambling, and she might bring him in an infinite variety of reports and representations. These would all be possible, but, being all equally possible, he would never of himself give a satisfactory account for his preferring one of them to the rest. Experience alone can point out to him the true cause of any phenomenon.

Now, according to this method of reasoning, Demea, it follows (and is, indeed, tacitly allowed by Cleanthes himself) that order, arrangement, or the adjustment of final causes, is not of itself any proof of design, but only so far as it has been experienced to proceed from that principle. For aught we can know a priori, matter may contain the source or spring of order originally within itself, as well as mind does; and there is no more difficulty in conceiving that the several elements, from an internal unknown cause, may fall into the most exquisite arrangement, than to conceive that their ideas, in the great universal mind, from a like internal unknown cause, fall into that arrangement. The equal possibility of both these suppositions is allowed. But, by experience, we find (according to Cleanthes) that there is a difference between them. Throw several pieces of steel together, without shape or form, they will never arrange themselves so as to compose a watch. Stone and mortar and wood, without an architect, never erect a house. But the ideas in a human mind, we see, by an unknown, inexplicable economy, arrange themselves so as to form the plan of a watch or house. Experience, therefore, proves that there is an original principle of order in mind, not in matter. From similar effects we infer similar causes. The adjustment of means to ends is alike in the universe, as in a machine of human contrivance. The causes, therefore, must be resembling.

I was from the beginning scandalized, I must own, with this resemblance which is asserted between the Deity and human creatures, and must conceive it to imply such a degradation of the Supreme Being as no sound theist could endure. With your assistance, therefore, Demea, I shall endeavour to defend what you justly call the adorable mysteriousness of the Divine Nature, and shall refute this reasoning of Cleanthes, provided he allows that I have made a fair representation of it.

When Cleanthes had assented, Philo, after a short pause, proceeded in the following manner.

That all inferences, Cleanthes, concerning fact are founded on experience, and that all experimental reasonings are founded on the supposition that similar causes prove similar effects, and similar effects similar causes, I shall not at present much dispute with you. But observe, I entreat you, with what extreme caution all just reasoners proceed in the transferring of experiments to similar cases. Unless the cases be exactly similar, they repose no perfect confidence in applying their past observation to any particular phenomenon. Every alteration of circumstances occasions a doubt concerning the event; and it requires new experiments to prove certainly that the new circumstances are of no moment or importance. A change in bulk, situation, arrangement, age, disposition of the air, or surrounding bodies—any of these particulars may be attended with the most unexpected consequences. And unless the objects be quite familiar to us, it is the highest temerity to expect with assurance, after any of these changes, an event similar to that which before fell under our observation. The slow and deliberate steps of philosophers here, if anywhere, are distinguished from the precipitate march of the vulgar, who, hurried on by the smallest similitude, are incapable of all discernment or consideration.

But can you think, Cleanthes, that your usual phlegm and philosophy have been preserved in so wide a step as you have taken when you compared to the universe houses, ships, furniture, machines, and, from their similarity in some circumstances, inferred a similarity in their causes? Thought, design, intelligence, such as we discover in men and other animals, is no more than one of the springs and principles of the universe, as well as heat or cold, attraction or repulsion, and a hundred others which fall under daily observation. It is an active cause by which some particular parts of nature, we find, produce alterations on other parts. But can a conclusion, with any propriety, be transferred from parts to the whole? Does not the great disproportion bar all comparison and inference? From observing the growth of a hair, can we learn anything concerning the generation of a man? Would the manner of a leaf's blowing, even though perfectly known, afford us any instruction concerning the vegetation of a tree?

But allowing that we were to take the *operations* of one part of nature upon another for the foundation of our judgment concerning the *origin* of the whole (which never can be admitted), yet why select so minute, so weak, so bounded a principle as the reason and design of animals is found to be upon this planet? What peculiar privilege has this little agitation of the brain which we call *thought,* that we must thus make it the model of the whole universe? Our partiality in our own favour does indeed present it on all occasions, but sound philosophy ought carefully to guard against so natural an illusion.

So far from admitting, continued Philo, that the operations of a part can afford us any just conclusion concerning the origin of the whole, I will not allow any one part to form a rule for another part if the latter be very remote from the former. Is there any reasonable ground to conclude that the inhabitants of other planets possess thought, intelligence, reason, or anything similar to these faculties in men? When nature has so extremely diversified her manner of operation in this small globe, can we imagine that she incessantly copies herself throughout so immense a universe? And if thought, as we may well suppose, be confined merely to this narrow corner and has even there so limited a sphere of action, with what propriety can we assign it for the original cause of all things? The narrow views of a peasant who makes his domestic economy the rule for the government of kingdoms is in comparison a pardonable sophism.

But were we ever so much assured that a thought and reason resembling the human were to be found throughout the whole universe, and were its activity elsewhere vastly greater and more commanding than it appears in this globe, yet I cannot see why the operations of a world constituted, arranged, adjusted, can with any propriety be extended to a world which is in its embryo state, and is advancing towards that constitution and arrangement. By observation we know somewhat of the economy, action, and nourishment of a finished animal, but we must transfer with great caution that observation to the growth of a fetus in the womb, and still more to the formation of an animalcule in the loins of its male parent. Nature, we find, even from our limited experience, possesses an infinite number of springs and principles which incessantly discover themselves on every change of her position and situation. And what new and unknown principles would actuate her in so new and unknown a situation as that of the formation of a universe, we cannot, without the utmost temerity, pretend to determine.

A very small part of this great system, during a very short time, is very imperfectly discovered to us; and do we thence pronounce decisively concerning the origin of the whole?

Admirable conclusion! Stone, wood, brick, iron, brass, have not, at this time, in this minute globe of earth, an order or arrangement without human art and contrivance; therefore, the universe could not originally attain its order and arrangement without something similar to human art. But is a part of nature a rule for another part very wide of the former? Is it a rule for the whole? Is a very small part a rule for the universe? Is nature in one situation a certain rule for nature in another situation vastly different from the former?

And can you blame me, Cleanthes, if I here imitate the prudent reserve of Simonides, who, according to the noted story, being asked by Hiero, *What God was?* desired a day to think of it, and then two days more; and after that manner continually prolonged the term, without ever bringing in his definition or description? Could you even blame me if I had answered, at first, *that I did not know,* and was sensible that this subject lay vastly beyond the reach of my faculties? You might cry out sceptic and raillier, as much as you pleased; but, having found in so many other subjects much more familiar the imperfections and even contradictions of human reason, I never should expect any success from its feeble conjectures in a subject so sublime and so remote from the sphere of our observation. When two *species* of objects have always been observed to be conjoined together, I can *infer,* by custom, the existence of one wherever I *see* the existence of the other; and this I call an argument from experience. But how this argument can have place where the objects, as in the present case, are single, individual, without parallel or specific resemblance, may be difficult to explain. And will any man tell me with a serious countenance that an orderly universe must arise from some thought and art like the human because we have experience of it? To ascertain this reasoning it were requisite that we had experience of the origin of worlds; and it is not sufficient, surely, that we have seen ships and cities arise from human art and contrivance. . . .

Part V

But to show you still more inconveniences, continued Philo, in your anthropomorphism, please to take a new survey of your principles. *Like effects prove like causes.* This is the experimental argument, and this, you say too, is the sole theological argument. Now it is certain that the liker the effects are which are seen and the liker the causes which are inferred, the stronger is the argument. Every departure on either side diminishes the probability and renders the experiment less conclusive. You cannot doubt of the principle; neither ought you to reject its consequences.

All the new discoveries in astronomy which prove the immense grandeur and magnificence of the works of nature are so many additional arguments for a Deity, according to the true system of theism; but, according to your hypothesis of experimental theism, they become so many objections, by removing the effect still farther from all resemblance to the effects of human art and contrivance. . . .

If this argument, I say, had any force in former ages, how much greater must it have at present when the bounds of Nature are so infinitely enlarged and such a magnificent scene is opened to us? It is still more unreasonable to form our idea of so unlimited a cause from our experience of the narrow productions of human design and invention.

The discoveries by microscopes, as they open a new universe in miniature, are still objections, according to you, arguments, according to me. The further we push our researches of this kind, we are still led to infer the universal cause of all to be vastly different from mankind, or from any object of human experience and observation.

And what say you to the discoveries in anatomy, chemistry, botany? . . . These surely are no objections, replied Cleanthes; they only discover new instances of art and contrivance, it is still the image of mind reflected on us from innumerable objects. Add a mind *like the human,* said Philo. I know of no other, replied Cleanthes. And the liker, the better, insisted Philo. To be sure, said Cleanthes.

Now, Cleanthes, said Philo, with an air of alacrity and triumph, mark the consequences. *First,* by this method of reasoning you renounce all claim to infinity in any of the attributes of the Deity. For, as the cause ought only to be proportioned to the effect, and the effect, so far as it falls under our cognizance, is not infinite, what pretensions have we, upon your suppositions, to ascribe that attribute to the Divine Being? You will still insist that, by removing him so much from all similarity to human creatures, we give in to the most arbitrary hypothesis, and at the same time weaken all proofs of his existence.

Secondly, you have no reason, on your theory, for ascribing perfection to the Deity, even in his finite capacity, or for supposing him free from every error, mistake, or incoherence, in his undertakings. There are many inexplicable difficulties in the works of nature which, if we allow a perfect author to be proved a priori, are easily solved, and become only seeming difficulties from the narrow capacity of man, who cannot trace infinite relations. But according to your method of reasoning, these difficulties become all real, and, perhaps, will be insisted on as new instances of likeness to human art and contrivance. At least, you must acknowledge that it is impossible for us to tell, from our limited views, whether this system contains any great faults or deserves any considerable praise if compared to other possible and even real systems. Could a peasant, if the *Aeneid* were read to him, pronounce that poem to be absolutely faultless, or even assign to it its proper rank among the productions of human wit, he who had never seen any other production?

But were this world ever so perfect a production, it must still remain uncertain whether all the excellences of the work can justly be ascribed to the workman. If we survey a ship, what an exalted idea must we form of the ingenuity of the carpenter who framed so complicated, useful, and beautiful a machine? And what surprise must we feel when we find him a stupid mechanic who imitated others, and copied an art which, through a long succession of ages, after multiplied trials, mistakes, corrections, deliberations, and controversies, had been gradually improving? Many worlds might have been botched and bungled, throughout an eternity, ere this system was struck out; much labour lost, many fruitless trials made, and a slow but continued improvement carried on during infinite ages in the art of world-making. In such subjects, who can determine where the truth, nay, who can conjecture where the probability lies, amidst a great number of hypotheses which may be proposed, and a still greater which may be imagined?

And what shadow of an argument, continued Philo, can you produce from your hypothesis to prove the unity of the Deity? A great number of men join in building a house or ship, in rearing a city, in framing a commonwealth; why may not several deities combine in contriving and framing a world? This is only so much greater similarity to human affairs. By sharing the work among several, we may so much further limit the attributes of each, and get rid of that extensive power and knowledge which must be supposed in one deity, and which, according to you, can only serve to weaken the proof of his existence. And if such foolish, such vicious creatures as man can yet often unite in framing and executing one plan, how much more those deities or demons, whom we may suppose several degrees more perfect!

To multiply causes without necessity is indeed contrary to true philosophy, but this principle applies not to the present case. Were one deity antecedently proved by your theory who were possessed of every attribute requisite to the production of the universe, it would be needless, I own (though not absurd) to suppose any other deity existent. But while it is still a question whether all these attributes are united in one subject or dispersed among several independent beings, by what phenomena in nature can we pretend to decide the controversy? Where we see a body raised in a scale, we are sure that there is in the opposite scale, however concealed from sight, some counterpoising weight equal to it; but it is still allowed to doubt whether that weight be an aggregate of several distinct bodies or one uniform united mass. And if the weight requisite very much exceeds anything which we have ever seen conjoined in any single body, the former supposition becomes still more probable and natural. An intelligent being of such vast power and capacity as is necessary to produce the universe, or, to speak in the language of ancient philosophy, so prodigious an animal exceeds all analogy and even comprehension.

But further, Cleanthes: Men are mortal, and renew their species by generation; and this is common to all living creatures. The two great sexes of male and female, says Milton, animate the world. Why must this circumstance, so universal, so essential, be excluded from those numerous and limited deities? Behold, then, the theogeny of ancient times brought back upon us.

And why not become a perfect anthropomorphite? Why not assert the deity or deities to be corporeal, and to have eyes, a nose, mouth, ears, etc.? Epicurus maintained that no man had ever seen reason but in a human figure; therefore, the gods must have a human figure. And this argument, which is deservedly so much ridiculed by Cicero, becomes, according to you, solid and philosophical.

In a word, Cleanthes, a man who follows your hypothesis is able, perhaps, to assert or conjecture that the universe sometime arose from something like design; but beyond that position he cannot ascertain one single circumstance, and is left afterwards to fix every point of his theology by the utmost license of fancy and hypothesis. This world, for aught he knows, is very faulty and imperfect, compared to a superior standard, and was only the first rude essay of some infant deity who afterwards abandoned it, ashamed of his lame performance; it is the work only of some dependent, inferior deity, and is the object of derision to his superiors; it is the production of old age and dotage in some superannuated deity, and ever since his death has run on at adventures, from the first impulse and active force which it received from him. You justly give signs of horror, Demea, at these strange suppositions; but these, and a thousand more of the same kind, are Cleanthes' suppositions, not mine. From the moment the attributes of the Deity are supposed finite, all these have place. And I cannot, for my part, think that so wild and unsettled a system of theology is, in any respect, preferable to none at all.

These suppositions I absolutely disown, cried Cleanthes: they strike me, however, with no horror, especially when proposed in that rambling way in which they drop from you. On the contrary, they give me pleasure when I see that, by the utmost indulgence of your imagination, you never get rid of the hypothesis of design in the universe, but are obliged at every turn to have recourse to it. To this concession I adhere steadily; and this I regard as a sufficient foundation for religion.

Part VI

It must be a slight fabric, indeed, said Demea, which can be erected on so tottering a foundation. While we are uncertain whether there is one deity or many, whether the deity or deities, to whom we owe our existence, be perfect or imperfect, subordinate or supreme, dead or alive, what trust or confidence can we repose in them? What devotion or worship address to them? What veneration or obedience pay them? To all the purposes of life the theory of religion becomes altogether useless; and even with regard to speculative consequences its uncertainty, according to you, must render it totally precarious and unsatisfactory.

To render it still more unsatisfactory, said Philo, there occurs to me another hypothesis which must acquire an air of probability from the method of reasoning so much insisted on by Cleanthes. That like effects arise from like causes—this principle he supposes the foundation of all religion. But there is another principle of the same kind, no less certain and derived from the same source of experience, that, where several known circumstances are observed to be similar, the unknown will also be found similar. Thus, if we see the limbs of a human body, we conclude that it is also attended with a human head, though hid from us. Thus, if we see, through a chink in a wall, a small part of the sun, we conclude that were the wall removed we should see the whole body. In short, this method of reasoning is so obvious and familiar that no scruple can ever be made with regard to its solidity.

Now, if we survey the universe, so far as it falls under our knowledge, it bears a great resemblance to an animal or organized body, and seems actuated with a like principle of life and motion. A continual circulation of matter in it produces no disorder; a continual waste in every part is incessantly repaired; the closest sympathy is perceived throughout the entire system; and each part or member, in performing its proper offices, operates both to its own preservation and to that of the whole. The world, therefore, I infer, is an animal; and the Deity is the *soul* of the world, actuating it, and actuated by it. . . .

This theory, I own, replied Cleanthes, has never before occurred to me, though a pretty natural one; and I cannot readily, upon so short an examination and reflection, deliver any opinion with regard to it. You are very scrupulous, indeed, said Philo; were I to examine any system of yours, I should not have acted with half that caution and reserve, in starting objections and difficulties to it. However, if anything occur to you, you will oblige us by proposing it.

Why then, replied Cleanthes, it seems to me that, though the world does, in many circumstances, resemble an animal body, yet is the analogy also defective in many circumstances the most material: no organs of sense, no seat of thought or reason; no one precise origin of motion and action. In short, it seems to bear a stronger resemblance to a vegetable than to an animal, and your inference would be so far inconclusive in favor of the soul of the world. . . .

Part VII

But here, continued Philo, in examining the ancient system of the soul of the world there strikes me, all of a sudden, a new idea which, if just, must go near to subvert all your reasoning, and destroy even your first inferences on which you repose such confidence. If the universe bears a greater likeness to animal bodies and to vegetables than to the works of human art, it is more probable that its cause resembles the cause of the former than that of the latter, and its origin ought rather to be abscribed to generation or vegetation than to reason or design. Your conclusion, even according to your own principles, is therefore lame and defective.

Pray open up this argument a little further, said Demea, for I do not rightly apprehend it in that concise manner in which you have expressed it.

Our friend Cleanthes, replied Philo, as you have heard, asserts that since no question of fact can be proved otherwise than by experience, the existence of a Deity admits not of proof from any other medium. The world, says he, resembles the works of human contrivance; therefore its cause must also resemble that of the other. Here we may remark that the operation of one very small part of nature, to wit, man, upon another very small part, to wit, that inanimate matter lying within his reach, is the rule by which Cleanthes judges of the origin of the whole; and he measures objects, so widely disproportioned, by the same individual standard. But to waive all objections drawn from this topic, I affirm that there are other parts of the universe (besides the machines of human invention) which bear still a greater resemblance to the fabric of the world, and which, therefore, afford a better conjecture concerning the universal origin of this system. These parts are animals and vegetables. The world plainly resembles more an animal or a vegetable than it does a watch or a knitting loom. Its cause, therefore, it is more probable, resembles the cause of the former. The cause of the former is generation or vegetation. The cause, therefore, of the world we may infer to be something similar or analogous to generation or vegetation.

But how is it conceivable, said Demea, that the world can arise from anything similar to vegetation or generation?

Very easily, replied Philo. In like manner as a tree sheds its seed into the neighboring fields and produces other trees; so the great vegetable, the world, or this planetary system, produces within itself certain seeds which, being scattered into the surrounding chaos, vegetate into new worlds. A comet, for instance, is the seed of a world; and after it has been fully ripened, by passing from sun to sun, and star to star, it is at last tossed into the unformed elements which everywhere surround this universe, and immediately sprouts up into a new system.

Or if, for the sake of variety (for I see no other advantage) we should suppose this world to be an animal; a comet is the egg of this animal; and in like manner as an ostrich lays its egg in the sand, which, without any further care, hatches the egg and produces a new animal, so . . . I understand you, says Demea: But what wild, arbitrary suppositions are these? What *data* have you for such extraordinary conclusions? And is the slight, imaginary resemblance of the world to a vegetable or an animal sufficient to establish the same inference with regard to both? Objects which are in general so widely different; ought they to be a standard for each other?

Right, cries Philo: This is the topic on which I have all along insisted. I have still asserted that we have no *data* to establish any system of cosmogony. Our experience, so imperfect in itself and so limited both in extent and duration, can afford us no probable conjecture concerning the whole of things. But if we must needs fix on some hypothesis, by what rule, pray, ought we to determine our choice? Is there any other rule than the great similarity of the objects compared? And does not a plant or an animal, which springs from vegetation or generation, bear a stronger resemblance to the world than does any artificial machine, which arises from reason and design?

But what is this vegetation and generation of which you talk? said Demea. Can you explain their operations, and anatomize that fine internal structure on which they depend?

As much, at least, replied Philo, as Cleanthes can explain the operations of reason, or anatomize that internal structure on which *it* depends. But without any such elaborate disquisitions, when I see an animal, I infer that it sprang from generation; and that with as great certainty as you conclude a house to have been reared by design. These words *generation, reason* mark only certain powers and energies in nature whose effects are known, but whose essence is incomprehensible; and one of these principles, more than the other, has no privilege for being made a standard to the whole of nature.

In reality, Demea, it may reasonably be expected that the larger the views are which we take of things, the better will they conduct us in our conclusions concerning such extraordinary and such magnificent subjects. In this little corner of the world alone, there are four principles, *reason, instinct, generation, vegetation,* which are similar to each other, and are the causes of similar effects. What a number of other principles may we naturally suppose in the immense extent and variety of the universe could we travel from planet to planet, and from system to system, in order to examine each part of this mighty fabric? Any one of these four principles above mentioned (and a hundred others which lie open to our conjecture) may afford us a theory by which to judge of the origin of the world; and it is a palpable and egregious partiality to confine our view entirely to that principle by which our own minds operate. Were this principle more intelligible on that account, such a partiality might be somewhat excusable; but reason, in its internal fabric and structure, is really as little known to us as instinct or vegetation; and, perhaps, even that vague, undeterminate word *nature* to which the vulgar refer everything is not at the bottom more inexplicable. The effects of these principles are all known to us from experience; but the principles themselves and their manner of operation are totally unknown; nor is it less intelligible or less conformable to experience to say that the world arose by vegetation, from a seed shed by another world, than to say that it arose from a divine reason or contrivance, according to the sense in which Cleanthes understands it.

But methinks, said Demea, if the world had a vegetative quality and could sow the seeds of new worlds into the infinite chaos, this power would be still an additional argument for design in its author. For whence could arise so wonderful a faculty but from design? Or how can order spring from anything which perceives not that order which it bestows?

You need only look around you, replied Philo, to satisfy yourself with regard to this question. A tree bestows order and organization on that tree which springs from it, without knowing the order; an animal in the same manner on its offspring; a bird on its nest; and instances of this kind are even more frequent in the world than those of order which arise from reason and contrivance. To say that all this order in animals and vegetables proceeds ultimately from design is begging the question; nor can that great point be ascertained otherwise than by proving, a priori, both that order is, from its nature, inseparably attached to thought, and that it can never of itself or from original unknown principles belong to matter. . . .

Part X

It is my opinion, I own, replied Demea, that each man feels, in a manner, the truth of religion within his own breast, and, from a consciousness of his imbecility and misery rather than from any reasoning, is led to seek protection from that Being on whom he and all nature is dependent. So anxious or so tedious are even the best scenes of life that futurity is still the object of all our hopes and fears. We incessantly look forward and endeavour, by prayers, adoration, and sacrifice, to appease those unknown powers whom we find, by experience, so able to afflict and oppress us. Wretched creatures that we are! What resource for us amidst the innumerable ills of life did not religion suggest some methods of atonement, and appease those terrors with which we are incessantly agitated and tormented?

I am indeed persuaded, said Philo, that the best and indeed the only method of bringing everyone to a due sense of religion is by just representations of the misery and wickedness of men. And for that purpose a talent of eloquence and strong imagery is more requisite than that of reasoning and argument. For is it necessary to prove what everyone feels within himself? It is only necessary to make us feel it, if possible, more intimately and sensibly.

The people, indeed, replied Demea, are sufficiently convinced of this great and melancholy truth. The miseries of life, the unhappiness of man, the general corruptions of our nature, the unsatisfactory enjoyment of pleasures, riches, honours—these phrases have become almost proverbial in all languages. And who can doubt of what all men declare from their own immediate feeling and experience?

In this point, said Philo, the learned are perfectly agreed with the vulgar; and in all letters, *sacred* and *profane,* the topic of human misery has been insisted on with the most pathetic eloquence that sorrow and melancholy could inspire. The poets, who speak from sentiment, without a system, and whose testimony has therefore the more authority, abound in images of this nature. From Homer down to Dr. Young, the whole inspired tribe have ever been sensible that no other representation of things would suit the feeling and observation of each individual.

As to authorities, replied Demea, you need not seek them. Look round this library of Cleanthes. I shall venture to affirm that, except authors of particular sciences, such as chemistry or botany, who have no occasion to treat of human life, there is scarce one of those innumerable writers from whom the sense of human misery has not, in some passage or other, extorted a complaint and confession of it. At least, the chance is entirely on that side; and no one author has ever, so far as I can recollect, been so extravagant as to deny it.

There you must excuse me, said Philo: Leibniz has denied it, and is perhaps the first who ventured upon so bold and paradoxical an opinion; at least, the first who made it essential to his philosophical system.

And by being the first, replied Demea, might he not have been sensible of his error? For is this a subject in which philosophers can propose to make discoveries especially in so late an age? And can any man hope by a simple denial (for the subject scarcely admits of reasoning) to bear down the united testimony of mankind, founded on sense and consciousness?

And why should man, added he, pretend to an exemption from the lot of all other animals? The whole earth, believe me, Philo, is cursed and polluted. A perpetual war is kindled amongst all living creatures. Necessity, hunger, want stimulate the strong and courageous; fear, anxiety, terror agitate the weak and infirm. The first entrance into life gives anguish to the new-born infant and to its wretched parent; weakness, impotence, distress attend each stage of that life, and it is, at last finished in agony and horror.

Observe, too, says Philo, the curious artifices of nature in order to embitter the life of every living being. The stronger prey upon the weaker and keep them in perpetual terror and anxiety. The weaker, too, in their turn, often prey upon the stronger, and vex and molest them without relaxation. Consider that innumerable race of insects, which either are bred on the body of each animal or, flying about, infix their stings in him. These insects have others still less than themselves which torment them. And thus on each hand, before and behind, above and below, every animal is surrounded with enemies which incessantly seek his misery and destruction.

Man alone, said Demea, seems to be, in part, an exception to this rule. For by combination in society he can easily master lions, tigers, and bears, whose greater strength and agility naturally enable them to prey upon him.

On the contrary, it is here chiefly, cried Philo, that the uniform and equal maxims of nature are most apparent. Man, it is true, can, by combination, surmount all his *real* enemies and become master of the whole animal creation; but does he not immediately raise up to himself *imaginary* enemies, the demons of his fancy, who haunt him with superstitious terrors and blast every enjoyment of life? His pleasure, as he imagines, becomes in their eyes a crime; his food and repose give them umbrage and offence; his very sleep and dreams furnish new materials to anxious fear; and even death, his refuge from every other ill, presents only the dread of endless and innumerable woes. Nor does the wolf molest more the timid flock than superstition does the anxious breast of wretched mortals.

Besides, consider, Demea: This very society by which we surmount those wild beasts, our natural enemies, what new enemies does it not raise to us? What woe and misery does it not occasion? Man is the greatest enemy of man. Oppression, injustice, contempt, contumely, violence, sedition, war, calumny, treachery, fraud—by these they mutually torment each other, and they would soon dissolve that society which they had formed were it not for the dread of still greater ills which must attend their separation.

But though these external insults, said Demea, from animals, from men, from all the elements, which assault us from a frightful catalogue of woes, they are nothing in comparison of those which arise within ourselves, from the distempered condition of our mind and body. How many lie under the lingering torment of diseases? . . .

The disorders of the mind, continued Demea, though more secret, are not perhaps less dismal and vexatious. Remorse, shame, anguish, rage, disappointment, anxiety, fear, dejection, despair—who has ever passed through life without cruel inroads from these tormentors? How many have scarcely ever felt any better sensations? Labour and poverty, so abhorred by everyone, are the certain lot of the far greater number; and those few privileged persons who enjoy ease and opulence never reach contentment or true felicity. All the goods of life united would not make a very happy man, but all the ills united would make a wretch indeed, and any one of them almost (and who can be free from every one?), nay, often the absence of one good (and who can possess all?) is sufficient to render life ineligible.

Were a stranger to drop on a sudden into this world, I would show him, as a specimen of its ills, an hospital full of diseases, a prison crowded with malefactors and debtors, a field of battle strewed with carcases, a fleet floundering in the ocean, a nation languishing under tyranny, famine, or pestilence. To turn the gay side of life to him and give him a notion of its pleasures—whither should I conduct him? To a ball, to an opera, to court? He might justly think that I was only showing him a diversity of distress and sorrow.

There is no evading such striking instances, said Philo, but by apologies which still further aggravate the charge. Why have all men, I ask, in all ages, complained incessantly of the miseries of life? . . . They have no just reason, says one: these complaints proceed only from their discontented, repining, anxious disposition. . . . And can there possibly, I reply, be a more certain foundation of misery than such a wretched temper?

But if they were really as unhappy as they pretend, says my antagonist, why do they remain in life? . . .

Not satisfied with life, afraid of death—

This is the secret chain, say I, that holds us. We are terrified, not bribed to the continuance of our existence.

It is only a false delicacy, he may insist, which a few refined spirits indulge, and which has spread these complaints among the whole race of mankind. . . . And what is this delicacy, I ask, which you blame? Is it anything but a greater sensibility to all the pleasures and pains of life? And if the man of a delicate, refined temper, by being so much more alive than the rest of the world, is only so much more unhappy, what judgment must we form in general of human life?

Let men remain at rest, says our adversary, and they will be easy. They are willing artificers of their own misery. . . . No! reply I: an anxious languor follows their repose: disappointment, vexation, trouble, their activity and ambition.

I can observe something like what you mention in some others, replied Cleanthes, but I confess I feel little or nothing of it in myself, and hope that it is not so common as you represent it.

If you feel not human misery yourself, cried Demea, I congratulate you on so happy a singularity. Others, seemingly the most prosperous, have not been ashamed to vent their complaints in the most melancholy strains. Let us attend to the great, the fortunate emperor, Charles V, when tired with human grandeur, he resigned all his extensive dominions into the hands of his son. In the last harangue which he made on that memorable occasion, he publicly avowed *that the greatest prosperities which he had ever enjoyed had been mixed with so many adversities that he might truly say he had never enjoyed any satisfaction or contentment.* But did the retired life in which he sought for shelter afford him any greater happiness? If we may credit his son's account, his repentance commenced the very day of his resignation.

Cicero's fortune, from small beginnings, rose to the greatest luster and renown; yet what pathetic complaints of the ills of life do his familiar letters, as well as philosophical discourses, contain? And suitably to his own experience, he introduces Cato, the great, the fortunate Cato protesting in his old age that had he a new life in his offer he would reject the present.

Ask yourself, ask any of your acquaintance, whether they would live over again the last ten or twenty years of their life. No! but the next twenty, they say, will be better. . . .

Thus, at last, they find (such is the greatness of human misery, it reconciles even contradictions) that they complain at once of the shortness of life and of its vanity and sorrow.

And is it possible, Cleanthes, said Philo, that after all these reflections, and infinitely more which might be suggested, you can still perservere in your anthropomorphism, and assert the moral attributes of the Deity, his justice, benevolence, mercy, and rectitude, to be of the same nature with these virtues in human creatures? His power, we allow, is infinite; whatever he wills is executed; but neither man nor any other animal is happy; therefore, he does not will their happiness. His wisdom is infinite; he is never mistaken in choosing the means to any end; but the course of nature tends not to human or animal felicity; therefore, it is not established for that purpose. Through the whole compass of human knowledge there are no inferences more certain and infallible than these. In what respect, then, do his benevolence and mercy resemble the benevolence and mercy of men?

Epicurus' old questions are yet unanswered.

Is he willing to prevent evil, but not able? then is he impotent. Is he able, but not willing? then is he malevolent. Is he both able and willing? whence then is evil?

You ascribe, Cleanthes (and I believe justly), a purpose and intention to nature. But what, I beseech you, is the object of that curious artifice and machinery which she has displayed in all animals—the preservation alone of individuals, and propagation of the species? It seems enough for her purpose, if such a rank be barely upheld in the universe, without any care or concern for the happiness of the members that compose it. No resource for this purpose: no machinery in order merely to give pleasure or ease; no fund of pure joy and contentment; no indulgence without some want or necessity accompanying it. At least, the few phenomena of this nature are over-balanced by opposite phenomena of still greater importance.

Our sense of music, harmony, and indeed beauty of all kinds, gives satisfaction, without being absolutely necessary to the preservation and propagation of the species. But what racking pains, on the other hand, arise from gouts, gravels, megrims, toothaches, rheumatisms, where the injury to the animal machinery is either small or incurable? Mirth, laughter, play, frolic seem gratuitous satisfactions which have no further tendency; spleen, melancholy, discontent, superstition are pains of the same nature. How then does the Divine benevolence display itself, in the sense of you anthropomorphites? None but we mystics, as you were pleased to call us, can account for this strange mixture of phenomena, by deriving it from attributes infinitely perfect but incomprehensible.

And have you, at last, said Cleanthes smiling, betrayed your intentions, Philo? Your long agreement with Demea did indeed a little surprise me, but I find you were all the while erecting a concealed battery against me. And I must confess that you have now fallen upon a subject worthy of your noble spirit of opposition and controversy. If you can make out the present point, and prove mankind to be unhappy or corrupted, there is an end at once of all religion. For to what purpose establish the natural attributes of the Deity, while the moral are still doubtful and uncertain?

You take umbrage very easily, replied Demea, at opinions the most innocent and the most generally received, even amongst the religious and devout themselves; and nothing can be more surprising than to find a topic like this—concerning the wickedness and misery of man—charged with no less than atheism and profaneness. Have not all pious divines and preachers who have indulged their rhetoric on so fertile a subject, have they not easily,

I say, given a solution of any difficulties which may attend it? This world is but a point in comparison of the universe, this life but a moment in comparison of eternity. The present evil phenomena, therefore, are rectified in other regions, and in some future period of existence. And the eyes of men, being then opened to larger views of things, see the whole connection of general laws, and trace, with adoration, the benevolence and rectitude of the Deity through all the mazes and intricacies of his providence.

No! replied Cleanthes, no! These arbitrary suppositions can never be admitted, contrary to matter of fact, visible and uncontroverted. Whence can any cause be known but from its known effects? Whence can any hypothesis be proved but from the apparent phenomena? To establish one hypothesis upon another is building entirely in the air; and the utmost we ever attain by these conjectures and fictions is to ascertain the bare possibility of our opinion, but never can we, upon such terms, establish its reality.

The only method of supporting Divine benevolence—and it is what I willingly embrace—is to deny absolutely the misery and wickedness of man. Your representations are exaggerated; your melancholy views mostly fictitious; your inferences contrary to fact and experience. Health is more common than sickness; pleasure than pain; happiness than misery. And for one vexation which we meet with, we attain, upon computation, a hundred enjoyments.

Admitting your position, replied Philo, which yet is extremely doubtful, you must at the same time allow that, if pain be less frequent than pleasure, it is infinitely more violent and durable. One hour of it is often able to outweigh a day, a week, a month of our common insipid enjoyments; and how many days, weeks, and months are passed by several in the most acute torments? Pleasure, scarcely in one instance, is ever able to reach ecstasy and rapture; and in no one instance can it continue for any time at its highest pitch and altitude. The spirits evaporate, the nerves relax, the fabric is disordered, and the enjoyment quickly degenerates into fatigue and uneasiness. But pain often, good God, how often! rises to torture and agony; and the longer it continues, it becomes still more genuine agony and torture. Patience is exhausted, courage languishes, melancholy seizes us, and nothing terminates our misery but the removal of its cause or another event which is the sole cure of all evil, but which, from our natural folly, we regard with still greater horror and consternation.

But not to insist upon these topics, continued Philo, though most obvious, certain, and important, I must use the freedom to admonish you, Cleanthes, that you have put the controversy upon a most dangerous issue, and are unawares introducing a total scepticism into the most essential articles of natural and revealed theology. What! no method of fixing a just foundation for religion unless we allow the happiness of human life, and maintain a continued existence even in this world, with all our present pains, infirmities, vexations, and follies, to be eligible and desirable! But this is contrary to everyone's feeling and experience; it is contrary to an authority so established as nothing can subvert. No decisive proofs can ever be produced against this authority; nor is it possible for you to compute, estimate, and compare all the pains and all the pleasures in the lives of all men and of all animals; and thus, by your resting the whole system of religion on a point which, from its very nature, must for ever be uncertain, you tacitly confess that that system is equally uncertain.

But allowing you what never will be believed, at least, what you never possibly can prove, that animal or, at least, human happiness in this life exceeds its misery, you have yet done nothing; for this is not, by any means, what we expect from infinite power, infinite wisdom, and infinite goodness. Why is there any misery at all in the world? Not by chance, surely. From some cause then. Is it from the intention of the Deity? But he is perfectly benevolent. Is it contrary to his intention? But he is almighty. Nothing can shake the solidity of this reasoning, so short, so clear, so decisive, except we assert that these subjects exceed all human capacity, and that our common measures of truth and falsehood are not applicable to them—a topic which I have all along insisted on, but which you have, from the beginning, rejected with scorn and indignation.

But I will be contented to retire still from this entrenchment, for I deny that you can ever force me in it. I will allow that pain or misery in man is *compatible* with infinite power and goodness in the Deity, even in your sense of these attributes: what are you advanced by all these concessions? A mere possible compatibility is not sufficient. You must *prove* these pure, unmixed, and uncontrollable attributes from the present mixed and confused phenomena, and from these alone. A hopeful undertaking! Were the phenomena ever so pure and unmixed, yet, being finite, they would be insufficient for that purpose. How much more, where they are also so jarring and discordant!

Here, Cleanthes, I find myself at ease in my argument. Here I triumph. Formerly, when we argued concerning the natural attributes of intelligence and design, I needed all my sceptical and metaphysical subtlety to elude your grasp. In many views of the universe and of its parts, particularly the latter, the beauty and fitness of final causes strike us with such irresistible force that all objections appear (what I believe they really are) mere cavils and sophisms; nor can we then imagine how it was ever possible for us to repose any weight on them. But there is no view of human life or of the condition of mankind from which, without the greatest violence, we can infer the moral attributes or learn that infinite benevolence, conjoined with infinite power and infinite wisdom, which we must discover by the eyes of faith alone. It is your turn now to tug the labouring oar, and to support your philosophical subtleties against the dictates of plain reason and experience.

NOTE

1. [Conventional names of ordinary persons, such as Smith and Jones.]

The Problem of Evil

John H. Hick

In the next selection John H. Hick, whose work we read previously, develops from a Christian perspective one of the best-known answers to the problem of evil. He views moral evils, those for which people are responsible, as tied inextricably to the exercise of our free will so that one is not possible without the other. He views physical evils, those for which people are not responsible, as providing the opportunity for "soul making," the development of the best qualities of the human personality. He admits, however, that his theodicy, that is, his defense of God's goodness and omnipotence in the face of evil, requires life after death to justify all the world's pains and sorrows.

To many, the most powerful positive objection to belief in God is the fact of evil. Probably for most agnostics it is the appalling depth and extent of human suffering, more than anything else, that makes the idea of a loving Creator seem so implausible and disposes them toward one or another of the various naturalistic theories of religion.

As a challenge to theism, the problem of evil has traditionally been posed in the form of a dilemma: if God is perfectly loving, he must wish to abolish evil; and if he is all-powerful, he must be able to abolish evil. But evil exists; therefore God cannot be both omnipotent and perfectly loving.

Certain solutions, which at once suggest themselves, have to be ruled out so far as the Judaic Christian faith is concerned.

To say, for example (with contemporary Christian Science), that evil is an illusion of the human mind, is impossible within a religion based upon the stark realism of the Bible. Its pages faithfully reflect the characteristic mixture of good and evil in human experience. They record every kind of sorrow and suffering, every mode of man's inhumanity to man and of his painfully insecure existence in the world. There is no attempt to regard evil as anything but dark, menacingly ugly, heart-rending, and crushing. In the Christian scriptures, the climax of this history of evil is the crucifixion of Jesus, which is presented not only as a case of utterly unjust suffering, but as the violent and murderous rejection of God's Messiah. There can be no

---

doubt, then, that for biblical faith evil is unambiguously evil and stands in direct opposition to God's will.

Again, to solve the problem of evil by means of the theory . . . of a finite deity who does the best he can with a material, intractable and coeternal with himself, is to have abandoned the basic premise of Hebrew-Christian monotheism; for the theory amounts to rejecting belief in the infinity and sovereignty of God.

Indeed, any theory that would avoid the problem of the origin of evil by depicting it as an ultimate constituent of the universe, co-ordinate with good, has been repudiated in advance by the classic Christian teaching, first developed by Augustine, that evil represents the going wrong of something that in itself is good.[1] Augustine holds firmly to the Hebrew-Christian conviction that the universe is *good*—that is to say, it is the creation of a good God for a good purpose. He completely rejects the ancient prejudice that matter is evil. There are, according to Augustine, higher and lower, greater and lesser goods in immense abundance and variety; but everything that has being is good in its own way and degree, except in so far as it may have become spoiled or corrupted. Evil—whether it be an evil will, an instance of pain, or some disorder or decay in nature—has not been set there by God, but represents the distortion of something that is inherently valuable. Whatever exists is, as such, and in its proper place, good; evil is essentially parasitic upon good, being disorder and perversion in a fundamentally good creation. This understanding of evil as something negative means that it is not willed and created by God; but it does not mean (as some have supposed) that evil is unreal and can be disregarded. On the contrary, the first effect of this doctrine is to accentuate even more the question of the origin of evil.

Theodicy,[2] as many modern Christian thinkers see it, is a modest enterprise, negative rather than positive in its conclusions. It does not claim to explain, nor to explain away, every instance of evil in human experience, but only to point to certain considerations that prevent the fact of evil (largely incomprehensible though it remains) from constituting a final and insuperable bar to rational belief in God.

In indicating these considerations it will be useful to follow the traditional division of the subject. There is the problem of *moral evil* or wickedness: why does an all-good and all-powerful God permit this? And there is the problem of the *nonmoral evil* of suffering or pain, both physical and mental: why has an all-good and all-powerful God created a world in which this occurs?

Christian thought has always considered moral evil in its relation to human freedom and responsibility. To be a person is to be a finite center of freedom, a (relatively) free and self-directing agent responsible for one's own decisions. This involves being free to act wrongly as well as to act rightly. The idea of a person who can be infallibly guaranteed always to act rightly is self-contradictory. There can be no certainty in advance that a genuinely free moral agent will never choose amiss. Consequently, the possibility of wrongdoing or sin is logically inseparable from the creation of finite persons, and to say that God should not have created beings who might sin amounts to saying that he should not have created people.

This thesis has been challenged in some recent philosophical discussions of the problem of evil, in which it is claimed that no contradiction is involved in saying that God might have made people who would be genuinely free but who could at the same time be guaranteed always to act rightly. A quote from one of these discussions follows:

> If there is no logical impossibility in a man's freely choosing the good on one, or on several occasions, there cannot be a logical impossibility in his freely choosing the good on every occasion. God was not, then, faced with a choice between making innocent automata and making beings who, in acting freely, would sometimes go wrong: there was open to him the obviously better possibility of making beings who would act freely but always go right. Clearly, his failure to avail himself of this possibility is inconsistent with his being both omnipotent and wholly good.[3]

A reply to this argument is indirectly suggested in another recent contribution to the discussion.[4] If by a free action we mean an action that is not externally compelled but that flows from the nature of the agent as he reacts to the circumstances in which he finds himself, there is indeed no contradiction between our being free and our actions being "caused" (by our own nature) and therefore being in principle predictable. There is a contradiction, however, in saying that God is the cause of our acting as we do but that we are free beings *in relation to God.* There is, in other words, a contradiction in saying that God has made us so that we shall of necessity act in a certain way, and that we are genuinely independent persons in relation to him. If all our thoughts and actions are divinely predestined, however free and morally responsible we may seem to be to ourselves, we cannot be free and morally responsible in the sight of God but must instead be his helpless puppets. Such "freedom" is like that of a patient acting out a series of posthypnotic suggestions: he appears, even to himself, to be free, but his volitions have actually been predetermined by another will, that of the hypnotist, in relation to whom the patient is not a free agent.

A different objector might raise the question of whether or not we deny God's omnipotence if we admit that he is unable to create persons who are free from the risks inherent in personal freedom. The answer that has always been given is that to create such beings is logically impossible. It is no limitation upon God's power that he cannot accomplish the logically impossible, since there is nothing here to accomplish, but only a meaningless conjunction of words[5]—in this case "person who is not a person." God is able to create beings of any and every conceivable kind; but creatures who lack moral freedom, however superior they might be to human beings in other respects, would not be what we mean by persons. They would constitute a different form of life that God might have brought into existence instead of persons.

When we ask why God did not create such beings in place of persons the traditional answer is that only persons could, in any meaningful sense, become "children of God," capable of entering into a personal relationship with their Creator by a free and uncompelled response to his love.

When we turn from the possibility of moral evil as a correlate of man's personal freedom to its actuality, we face something that must remain inexplicable even when it can be seen to be possible. For we can never provide a complete causal explanation of a free act; if we could, it would not be a free act. The origin of moral evil lies forever concealed within the mystery of human freedom.

The necessary connection between moral freedom and the possibility, now actualized, of sin throws light upon a great deal of the suffering that afflicts mankind. For an enormous amount of human pain arises either from the inhumanity or the culpable incompetence of mankind. This includes such major scourges as poverty, oppression and persecution, war, and all the injustice, indignity, and inequity that occur even in the most advanced societies. These evils are manifestations of human sin. Even disease is fostered to an extent, the limits of which have not yet been determined by psychosomatic medicine, by emotional and moral factors seated both in the individual and in his social environment. To the extent that all of these evils stem from human failures and wrong decisions, their possibility is inherent in the creation of free persons inhabiting a world that presents them with real choices followed by real consequences.

We may now turn more directly to the problem of suffering. Even though the major bulk of actual human pain is traceable to man's misused freedom as a sole or part cause, there remain other sources of pain that are entirely independent of the human will, for example, earthquake, hurricane, storm, flood, drought, and blight. In practice, it is often impossible to trace a boundary between the suffering that results from human wickedness and folly and that which falls upon mankind from without; both kinds of suffering are inextricably mingled together in human experience. For our present purpose, however, it is important to note that the latter category does exist and that it seems to be built into the very structure of our world. In response to it, theodicy, if it is wisely conducted, follows a negative path. It is not possible to show positively that each item of human pain serves a divine purpose of good; but, on the other hand, it does seem possible to show that the divine purpose as it is understood in Judaism and Christianity could not be forwarded in a world that was designed as a permanent hedonistic paradise.[6]

An essential premise of this argument concerns the nature of the divine purpose in creating the world. The skeptic's assumption is that man is to be viewed as a completed creation and that God's purpose in making the world was to provide a suitable dwelling-place for this fully formed creature. Since God is good and loving, the environment that he has created for human life to inhabit will naturally be as pleasant and comfortable as possible. The problem is essentially similar to that of a man who builds a cage for some pet animal. Since our world, in fact, contains sources of hardship, inconvenience and danger of innumerable kinds, the conclusion follows that this world cannot have been created by a perfectly benevolent and all-powerful deity.

Christianity, however, has never supposed that God's purpose in the creation of the world was to construct a paradise whose inhabitants would experience a maximum of pleasure and a minimum of pain. The world is seen, instead, as a place of "soul making" or person making in which free beings, grappling with the tasks and challenges of their existence in a common environment, may become "children of God" and "heirs of eternal life." A way of thinking theologically of God's continuing creative purpose for man was suggested by some of the early Hellenistic Fathers of the Christian Church, especially Irenaeus. Following hints from Saint Paul, Irenaeus taught that man has been made as a person in the image of God but has not yet been brought as a free and responsible agent into the finite likeness of God, which is revealed in Christ.[7] Our world, with all its rough edges, is the sphere in which this second and harder stage of the creative process is taking place.

This conception of the world (whether or not set in Irenaeus's theological framework) can be supported by the method of negative theodicy. Suppose, contrary to fact, that this world were a paradise from which all possibility of pain and suffering where excluded. The consequences would be very far-reaching. For example, no one could ever injure anyone else: the murderer's knife would turn to paper or his bullets to thin air; the bank safe, robbed of a million dollars, would miraculously become filled with another million dollars (without this device, on however large a scale, proving inflationary); fraud, deceit, conspiracy, and treason would somehow always leave the fabric of society undamaged. Again, no one would ever be injured by accident: the mountain climber, steeplejack, or playing child falling from a height would float unharmed to the ground; the reckless driver would never meet with disaster. There would be no need to work, since no harm could result from avoiding work; there would be no call to be concerned for others in time of need or danger, for in such a world there could be no real needs or dangers.

To make possible this continual series of individual adjustments, nature would have to work by "special providences" instead of running according to general laws that men must learn to respect on penalty of pain or death. The laws of nature would have to be extremely flexible: sometimes gravity would operate, sometimes not; sometimes an object would be hard and solid, sometimes soft. There could be no science, for there would be no enduring world structure to investigate. In eliminating the problems and hardships of an objective environment, with its own laws, life would become like a dream in which, delightfully but aimlessly, we would float and drift at ease.

One can at least begin to imagine such a world. It is evident that our present ethical concepts would have no meaning in it. If, for example, the notion of harming someone is an essential element in the concept of a wrong action, in our hedonistic paradise there could be no wrong actions—nor any right actions in distinction from wrong. Courage and fortitude would have no point in an environment in which there is, by definition, no danger or difficulty. Generosity, kindness, the *agape* aspect of love, prudence, unselfishness, and all other ethical notions which presuppose life in an objective environment could not even be formed. Consequently, such a world, however well it might promote pleasure, would be very ill adapted for the development of the moral qualities of human personality. In relation to this purpose it might be the worst of all possible worlds!

It would seem, then, that an environment intended to make possible the growth in free beings of the finest characteristics of personal life must have a good deal in common with our present world. It must operate according to general and dependable laws; and it must involve real dangers, difficulties, problems, obstacles, and possibilities of pain, failure, sorrow, frustration, and defeat. If it did not contain the particular trials and perils that—subtracting man's own very considerable contribution—our world contains, it would have to contain others instead.

To realize this is not, by any means, to be in possession of a detailed theodicy. It is to understand that this world, with all its "heartaches and the thousand natural shocks that flesh is heir to," an environment so manifestly not designed for the maximization of human pleasure and the minimization of human pain, may nevertheless be rather well adapted to the quite different purpose of "soul making."

These considerations are related to theism as such. Specifically Christian theism goes further in the light of the death of Christ, which is seen paradoxically both (as the murder of the divine Son) as the worst thing that has ever happened and (as the occasion of man's salvation) as the best thing that has ever happened. As the supreme evil turned to supreme good, it provides the paradigm for the distinctively Christian reaction to evil. Viewed from the standpoint of Christian faith, evils do not cease to be evils; and certainly, in view of Christ's healing work, they cannot be said to have been sent by God. Yet, it has been the persistent claim of those seriously and wholeheartedly committed to Christian discipleship that tragedy, though truly tragic, may nevertheless be turned, through a man's reaction to it, from a cause of despair and alienation from God to a stage in the fulfillment of God's loving purpose for that individual. As the greatest of all evils, the crucifixion of Christ, was made the occasion of man's redemption, so good can be won from other evils. As Jesus saw his execution by the Romans as an experience which God desired him to accept, an experience which was to be brought within the sphere of the divine purpose and made to serve the divine ends, so the Christian response to calamity is to accept the adversities, pains, and afflictions which life brings, in order that they can be turned to a positive spiritual use.

At this point, theodicy points forward in two ways to the subject of life after death . . .

First, although there are many striking instances of good being triumphantly brought out of evil through a man's or a woman's reaction to it, there are many other cases in which the opposite has happened. Sometimes obstacles breed strength of character, dangers evoke courage and unselfishness, and calamities produce patience and moral steadfastness. But sometimes they lead, instead, to resentment, fear, grasping selfishness, and disintegration of character. Therefore, it would seem that any divine purpose of soul making that is at work in earthly history must continue beyond this life if it is ever to achieve more than a very partial and fragmentary success.

Second, if we ask whether the business of soul making is worth all the toil and sorrow of human life, the Christian answer must be in terms of a future good great enough to justify all that has happened on the way to it.

NOTES

1. See Augustine's *Confessions,* Book VII, Chap. 12; *City of God,* Book XII, Chap. 3; *Enchiridion,* Chap. 4.
2. The word "theodicy," from the Greek *theos* (God) and *dike* (righteous), means the justification of God's goodness in the face of the fact of evil.
3. J. L. Mackie, "Evil and Omnipotence," *Mind* (April, 1955), p. 209. A similar point is made by Antony Flew in "Divine Omnipotence and Human Freedom," *New Essays in Philosophical Theology.* An important critical comment on these arguments is offered by Ninian Smart in "Omnipotence, Evil, and Supermen," *Philosophy* (April, 1961), with replies by Flew (January, 1962) and Mackie (April, 1962).
4. Flew, in *New Essays in Philosophical Theology.*
5. As Aquinas said, ". . . nothing that implies a contradiction falls under the scope of God's omnipotence." *Summa Theologica,* Part I, Question 25, Art. 4.
6. From the Greek *hedone,* pleasure.
7. See Irenaeus's *Against Heresies,* Book IV, Chaps. 37 and 38.

A Defense of Atheism

ERNEST NAGEL

In the next selection, Ernest Nagel (1902–1985), who was Professor of Philosophy at Columbia University, exposes what he considers flaws in the cosmological, ontological, and teleological arguments

From Ernest Nagel, "Philosophical Concepts of Atheism," in J. E. Fairchild, ed., *Basic Beliefs: The Religious Philosophies of Mankind* (Dobbs Ferry, NY: Sheridan House, Inc., 1959, 1987). Reprinted by permission.

for the existence of God. He then explains why he finds unacceptable the arguments theists have offered to explain the presence of evil in a world supposedly created by an all-good, all-powerful God.

1

I want now to discuss three classical arguments for the existence of God, arguments which have constituted at least a partial basis for theistic commitments. As long as theism is defended simply as a dogma, asserted as a matter of direct revelation or as the deliverance of authority, belief in the dogma is impregnable to rational argument. In fact, however, reasons are frequently advanced in support of the theistic creed, and these reasons have been the subject of acute philosophical critiques.

One of the oldest intellectual defenses of theism is the cosmological argument, also known as the argument from a first cause. Briefly put, the argument runs as follows. Every event must have a cause. Hence an event A must have as cause some event B, which in turn must have a cause C, and so on. But if there is no end to this backward progression of causes, the progression will be infinite; and in the opinion of those who use this argument, an infinite series of actual events is unintelligible and absurd. Hence there must be a first cause, and this first cause is God, the initiator of all change in the universe.

The argument is an ancient one, and . . . it has impressed many generations of exceptionally keen minds. The argument is nonetheless a weak reed on which to rest the theistic thesis. Let us waive any question concerning the validity of the principle that every event has a cause, for though the question is important, its discussion would lead us far afield. However, if the principle is assumed, it is surely incongruous to postulate a first cause as a way of escaping from the coils of an infinite series. For if everything must have a cause, why does not God require one for His own existence? The standard answer is that He does not need any, because He is self-caused. But if God can be self-caused, why cannot the world itself be self-caused? Why do we require a God transcending the world to bring the world into existence and to initiate changes in it? On the other hand, the supposed inconceivability and absurdity of an infinite series of regressive causes will be admitted by no one who has competent familiarity with the modern mathematical analysis of infinity. The cosmological argument does not stand up under scrutiny.

The second "proof" of God's existence is usually called the ontological argument. It too has a long history going back to early Christian days, though it acquired great prominence only in medieval times. The argument can be stated in several ways, one of which is the following. Since God is conceived to be omnipotent, he is a perfect being. A perfect being is defined as one whose essence or nature lacks no attributes (or properties) whatsoever, one whose nature is complete in every respect. But it is evident that we have an idea of a perfect being, for we have just defined the idea; and since this is so, the argument continues, God who is the perfect being must exist. Why must he? Because his existence follows from his defined nature. For if God lacked the attribute of existence, he would be lacking at least one attribute, and would therefore not be perfect. To sum up, since we have an idea of God as a perfect being, God must exist.

There are several ways of approaching this argument, but I shall consider only one. The argument was exploded by the eighteenth century philosopher Immanuel Kant. The substance of Kant's criticism is that it is just a confusion to say that existence is an attribute, and that though the *word* "existence" may occur as the grammatical predicate in a sentence, no attribute is being predicated of a thing when we say that the thing exists or has existence. Thus, to use Kant's example, when we think of $100 we are thinking of the nature of this sum of money; but the nature of $100 remains the same whether we have $100 in our pockets or not. Accordingly, we are confounding grammar with logic if we suppose that some characteristic is being attributed to the nature of $100 when we say that a hundred dollar bill exists in someone's pocket.

To make the point clearer, consider another example. When we say that a lion has a tawny color, we are predicating a certain attribute of the animal, and similarly when we say that the lion is fierce or is hungry. But when we say the lion exists, all that we are saying is that something is (or has the nature of) a lion; we are not specifying an attribute which belongs to the nature of anything that is a lion. In short, the word "existence" does not signify any attribute, and in consequence no attribute that belongs to the nature of anything. Accordingly, it does not follow from the assumption that we have an idea of a perfect being that such a being exists. For the idea of a perfect being does not involve the attribute of existence as a constituent of that idea, since there is no such attribute. The ontological argument thus has a serious leak, and it can hold no water.

2

The two arguments discussed thus far are purely dialectical, and attempt to establish God's existence without any appeal to empirical data. The next argument, called the argument from design, is different in character, for it is based on what purports to be empirical evidence. I wish to examine two forms of this argument.

One variant of it calls attention to the remarkable way in which different things and processes in the world are integrated with each other, and concludes that this mutual "fitness" of things can be explained only by the assumption of a divine architect who planned the world and everything in it.

For example, living organisms can maintain themselves in a variety of environments, and do so in virtue of their delicate mechanisms which adapt the organisms to all sorts of environmental changes. There is thus an intricate pattern of means and ends throughout the animate world. But the existence of this pattern is unintelligible, so the argument runs, except on the hypothesis that the pattern has been deliberately instituted by a Supreme Designer. If we find a watch in some deserted spot, we do not think it came into existence by chance, and we do not hesitate to conclude that an intelligent creature designed and made it. But the world and all its contents exhibit mechanisms and mutual adjustments that are far more complicated and subtle than are those of a watch. Must we not therefore conclude that these things too have a Creator?

The conclusion of this argument is based on an inference from analogy: the watch and the world are alike in possessing a congruence of parts and an adjustment of means to ends; the watch has a watch-maker; hence the world has a world-maker. But is the analogy a good one? Let us once more waive some important issues, in particular the issue whether the universe is the unified system such as the watch admittedly is. And let us concentrate on the question what is the ground for our assurance that watches do not come into existence except through the operations of intelligent manufacturers. The answer is plain. We have never run across a watch which has not been deliberately made by someone. But the situation is nothing like this in the case of the innumerable animate and inanimate systems with which we are familiar. Even in the case of living organisms, though they are generated by their parent organisms, the parents do not "make" their progeny in the same sense in which watch-makers make watches. And once this point is clear, the inference from the existence of living organisms to the existence of a supreme designer no longer appears credible.

Moreover, the argument loses all its force if the facts which the hypothesis of a divine desigher is supposed to explain can be understood on the basis of a better supported assumption. And indeed, such an alternative explanation is one of the achievements of Darwinian biology. For Darwin showed that one can account for the variety of biological species, as well as for their adaptations to their environments, without invoking a divine creator and acts of special creation. The Darwinian theory explains the diversity of biological species in terms of chance variations in the structure of organisms, and of a mechanism of selection which retains those variant forms that possess some advantages for survival. The evidence for these assumptions is considerable, and developments subsequent to Darwin have only strengthened the case for a thoroughly naturalistic explanation of the facts of biological adaptation. In any event, this version of the argument from design has nothing to recommend it.

A second form of this argument has been recently revived in the speculations of some modern physicists. No one who is familiar with the facts can fail to be impressed by the success with which the use of mathematical methods has enabled us to obtain intellectual mastery of many parts of nature. But some thinkers have therefore concluded that since the book of nature is ostensibly written in mathematical language, nature must be the creation of a divine mathematician. However, the argument is most dubious. For it rests, among other things, on the assumption that mathematical tools can be successfully used only if the events of nature exhibit some *special* kind of order, and on the further assumption that if the structure of things were different from what they are, mathematical language would be inadequate for describing such structure. But it can be shown that no matter what the world were like—even if it impressed us as being utterly chaotic—it would still possess some order, and would in principle be amenable to a mathematical description. In point of fact, it makes no sense to say that there is absolutely *no* pattern in any conceivable subject matter. To be sure, there are differences in complexities of structure, and if the patterns of events were sufficiently complex, we might not be able to unravel them. But however that may be, the success of mathematical physics in giving us some understanding of the world around us does not yield the conclusion that only a mathematician could have devised the patterns of order we have discovered in nature.

3

Thus far the discussion has been concerned with noting inadequacies in various arguments widely used to support theism. However, much atheistic criticism is also directed toward exposing incoherencies in the very thesis of theism. I want therefore to consider this aspect of the atheistic critique, though I will restrict myself to the central difficulty in the theistic position which arises from the simultaneous attribution of omnipotence, omniscience, and omnibenevolence to the Deity. The difficulty is that of reconciling these attributes with the occurrence of evil in the world. Accordingly, the question to which I now turn is whether, despite the existence of evil, it is possible to construct a theodicy which will justify the ways of an infinitely powerful and just God to man.

Two main types of solutions have been proposed for this problem. One way that is frequently used is to maintain that what is commonly called evil is only an illusion, or at worst only the "privation" or absence of good. Accordingly, evil is not "really real," it is only the "negative" side of God's beneficence, it is only the product of our limited intelligence which fails to plumb the true character of God's creative bounty. A sufficient comment on this proposed solution is that facts are not altered or abolished by rebaptizing them. Evil may indeed be only an appearance and not genuine. But this does not eliminate from the realm of appearance the tragedies, the sufferings, and the iniquities which men so frequently endure. And it raises once more, though on another level, the problem of reconciling the fact that there is evil in the realm of appearance with God's alleged omnibenevolence. In any event, it is small comfort to anyone suffering a cruel misfortune for which he is in no way responsible, to be told that what he is undergoing is only the absence of good. It is a gratuitous insult to mankind, a symptom of insensitivity and indifference to human suffering, to be assured that all the miseries and agonies men experience are only illusory.

Another gambit often played in attempting to justify the ways of God to man is to argue that the things called evil are evil only because they are viewed in isolation; they are not evil when viewed in proper perspective and in relation to the rest of creation. Thus, if one attends to but a single instrument in an orchestra, the sounds issuing from it may indeed be harsh and discordant. But if one is placed at a proper distance from the whole orchestra, the sounds of that single instrument will mingle with the sounds issuing from the other players to produce a marvellous bit of symphonic music. Analogously, experiences we call painful undoubtedly occur and are real enough. But the pain is judged to be an evil only because it is experienced in a limited perspective—the pain is there for the sake of a more inclusive good, whose reality eludes us because our intelligences are too weak to apprehend things in their entirety.

It is an appropriate retort to this argument that of course we judge things to be evil in a human perspective, but that since we are not God this is the only proper perspective in which to judge them. It may indeed be the case that what is evil for us is not evil for some other part of creation. However, we are not this other part of creation, and it is irrelevant to argue that were we something other than what we are, our evaluations of what is good and bad would be different. Moreover, the worthlessness of the argument becomes even more evident if we remind ourselves that it is unsupported speculation to suppose that whatever is evil in a finite perspective is good from the purported perspective of the totality of things. For the argument can be turned around: what we judge to be a good is a good only because it is viewed in isolation; when it is viewed in proper perspective, and in relation to the entire scheme of things, it is an evil. This is in fact a standard form of the argument for a universal pessimism. Is it any worse than the similar argument for a universal optimism? The very raising of this question is a *reductio ad absurdum* of the proposed solution to the ancient problem of evil.

I do not believe it is possible to reconcile the alleged omnipotence and omnibenevolence of God with the unvarnished facts of human existence. In point of fact, many theologians have concurred in this conclusion; for in order to escape from the difficulty which the traditional attributes of God present, they have assumed that God is not all powerful, and that there are limits as to what He can do in his efforts to establish a righteous order in the universe. But whether such a modified theology is better off is doubtful; and in any event, the question still remains whether the facts of human life support the claim that an omnibenevolent Deity, though limited in power, is revealed in the ordering of human history. It is pertinent to note in this connection that though there have been many historians who have made the effort, no historian has yet succeeded in showing to the satisfaction of his professional colleagues that the hypothesis of a Divine Providence is capable of explaining anything which cannot be explained just as well without this hypothesis.

Why God Allows Evil

Richard Swinburne

Theists continue to seek the most persuasive possible reply to the problem of evil. Here is a recent attempt to defuse the issue written by Richard Swinburne, who is Nolloth Professor of the Philosophy of the Christian Religion at the University of Oxford. He argues that the world, although it contains much evil, exhibits God's goodness. Whether Swinburne's arguments are persuasive I leave for you to decide.

The world . . . contains much evil. An omnipotent God could have prevented this evil, and surely a perfectly good and omnipotent God would have done so. So why is there this evil? Is not its existence strong evidence against the existence of God? It would be unless we can construct what is known as a theodicy, an explanation of why God would allow such evil to occur. I believe that that can be done, and I shall outline a theodicy. . . . I emphasize that . . . in writing that God would do this or that, I am not taking for granted the existence of God, but merely claiming that, if there is a God, it is to be expected that he would do certain things, including allowing the occurrence of certain evils; and so, I am claiming, their occurrence is not evidence against his existence.

It is inevitable that any attempt by myself or anyone else to construct a theodicy will sound callous, indeed totally insensitive to human suffering. Many theists, as well as atheists, have felt that any attempt to construct a theodicy evinces an immoral approach to suffering. I can only ask the reader to believe that I am not totally insensitive to human suffering, and that

---

From Richard Swinburne, *Is There a God?* Reprinted by permission of Oxford University Press.

I do mind about the agony of poisoning, child abuse, bereavement, solitary imprisonment, and marital infidelity as much as anyone else. True, I would not in most cases recommend that a pastor give this chapter to victims of sudden distress at their worst moment to read for consolation. But this is not because its arguments are unsound; it is simply that most people in deep distress need comfort, not argument. Yet there is a problem about why God allows evil, and, if the theist does not have (in a cool moment) a satisfactory answer to it, then his belief in God is less than rational, and there is no reason why the atheist should share it. To appreciate the argument of this chapter, each of us needs to stand back a bit from the particular situation of his or her own life and that of close relatives and friends (which can so easily seem the only important thing in the world), and ask very generally what good things would a generous and everlasting God give to human beings in the course of a short earthly life. Of course thrills of pleasure and periods of contentment are good things, and—other things being equal—God would certainly seek to provide plenty of those. But a generous God will seek to give deeper good things than these. He will seek to give us great responsibility for ourselves, each other, and the world, and thus a share in his own creative activity of determining what sort of world it is to be. And he will seek to make our lives valuable, of great use to ourselves and each other. The problem is that God cannot give us these goods in full measure without allowing much evil on the way. . . .

[T]here are plenty of evils, positive bad states, which God could if he chose remove. I divide these into moral evils and natural evils. I understand by "natural evil" all evil which is not deliberately produced by human beings and which is not allowed by human beings to occur as a result of their negligence. Natural evil includes both physical suffering and mental suffering, of animals as well as humans; all the trial of suffering which disease, natural disasters, and accidents unpredictable by humans bring in their train. "Moral evil" I understand as including all evil caused deliberately by humans doing what they ought not to do (or allowed to occur by humans negligently failing to do what they ought to do) *and* also the evil constituted by such deliberate actions or negligent failure. It includes the sensory pain of the blow inflicted by the bad parent on his child, the mental pain of the parent depriving the child of love, the starvation allowed to occur in Africa because of negligence by members of foreign governments who could have prevented it, and also the evil of the parent or politician deliberately bringing about the pain or not trying to prevent the starvation.

Moral Evil

The central core of any theodicy must, I believe, be the "free-will defence," which deals—to start with—with moral evil, but can be extended to deal with much natural evil as well. The free-will defence claims that it is a great good that humans have a certain sort of free will which I shall call free and responsible choice, but that, if they do, then necessarily there will be the natural possibility of moral evil. (By the "natural possibility" I mean that it will not be determined in advance whether or not the evil will occur.) A God who gives humans such free will necessarily brings about the possibility, and puts outside his own control whether or not that evil occurs. It is not logically possible—that is, it would be self-contradictory to suppose—that God could give us such free will and yet ensure that we always use it in the right way.

Free and responsible choice is not just free will in the narrow sense of being able to choose between alternative actions, without our choice being causally necessitated by some prior cause. . . . [H]umans could have that kind of free will merely in virtue of being able to choose freely between two equally good and unimportant alternatives. Free and responsible choice is rather free will (of the kind discussed) to make significant choices between good and evil, which make a big difference to the agent, to others, and to the world.

Given that we have free will, we certainly have free and responsible choice. Let us remind ourselves of the difference that humans can make to themselves, others, and the world. Humans have opportunities to give themselves and others pleasurable sensations, and to pursue worthwhile activities—to play tennis or the piano, to acquire knowledge of history and science and philosophy, and to help others to do so, and thereby to build deep personal relations founded upon such sensations and activities. And humans are so made that they can form their characters. Aristotle famously remarked: "we become just by doing just acts, prudent by doing prudent acts, brave by doing brave acts." That is, by doing a just act when it is difficult—when it goes against our natural inclinations (which is what I understand by desires)—we make it easier to do a just act next time. We can gradually change our desires, so that—for example—doing just acts becomes natural. Thereby we can free ourselves from the power of the less good desires to which we are subject. And, by choosing to acquire knowledge and to use it to build machines of various sorts, humans can extend the range of the differences they can make to the world—they can build universities to last for centuries, or save energy for the next generation; and by cooperative effort over many decades they can eliminate poverty. The possibilities for free and responsible choice are enormous.

It is good that the free choices of humans should include *genuine* responsibility for other humans, and that involves the opportunity to benefit *or* harm them. God has the power to benefit or to harm humans. If other agents are to be given a share in his creative work, it is good that they have that power too (although perhaps to a lesser degree). A world in which agents can benefit each other but not do each other harm is one where they have only very limited responsibility for each other. If my responsibility for you is limited to whether or not to give you a camcorder, but I cannot cause you pain, stunt your growth, or limit your education, then I do not have a great deal of responsibility for you. A God who gave agents only such limited responsibilities for their fellows would not have given much. God would have reserved for himself the all-important choice of the kind of world it was to be, while simply allowing humans the minor choice of filling in the details. He would be like a father asking his elder son to look after the younger son, and adding that he would be watching the elder son's every move and would intervene the moment the elder son did a thing wrong. The elder son might justly retort that, while he would be happy to share his father's work, he could really do so only if he were left to make his own judgements as to what to do within a significant range of the options available to the father. A good God, like a good father, will delegate responsibility. In order to allow creatures a share in creation, he will allow them the choice of hurting and maiming, of frustrating the divine plan. Our world is one where creatures have just such deep responsibility for each other. I cannot only benefit my children, but harm them. One way in which I can harm them is that I can inflict physical pain on them. But there are much more damaging things which I can do to them. Above all I can stop them growing into creatures with significant knowledge, power, and freedom; I can determine whether they come to have the kind of free and responsible choice which I have. The possibility of humans bringing about significant evil is a logical consequence of their having this free and responsible choice. Not even God could give us this choice without the possibility of resulting evil.

Now . . . an action would not be intentional unless it was done for a reason—that is, seen as in some way a good thing (either in itself or because of its consequences). And, if reasons alone influence actions, that regarded by the subject as most important will determine what is done; an agent under the influence of reason alone will inevitably do the action which he regards as overall the best. If an agent does not do the action which he regards as overall the best, he must have allowed factors other than reason to exert an influence on him. In other words, he must have allowed desires for what he regards as good only in a certain respect, but not overall, to influence his conduct. So, in order to have a choice between good and evil, agents need already a certain depravity, in the sense of a system of desires for what they correctly believe to be evil. I need to *want* to overeat, get more than my fair share of money or power, indulge my sexual appetites even by deceiving my spouse or partner, want to see you hurt, if I am to have choice between good and evil. This depravity is itself an evil which is a necessary condition of a greater good. It makes possible a choice made seriously and deliberately, because made in the face of a genuine alternative. I stress that, according to the free-will defence, it is the natural possibility of moral evil which is the necessary condition of the great good, not the actual evil itself. Whether that occurs is (through God's choice) outside God's control and up to us.

Note further and crucially that, if I suffer in consequence of your freely chosen bad action, that is not by any means pure loss for me. In a certain respect it is a good for *me*. My suffering would be pure loss for me if the only good thing in life was sensory pleasure, and the only bad thing sensory pain; and it is because the modern world tends to think in those terms that the problem of evil seems so acute. If these were the only good and bad things, the occurrence of suffering would indeed be a conclusive objection to the existence of God. But we have already noted the great good of freely choosing and influencing our future, that of our fellows, and that of the world. And now note another great good—the good of our life serving a purpose, of being of use to ourselves and others. Recall the words of Christ, "it is more blessed to give than to receive" (as quoted by St. Paul (Acts 20: 35)). We tend to think, when the beggar appears on our doorstep and we feel obliged to give and do give, that that was lucky for him but not for us who happened to be at home. That is not what Christ's words say. They say that *we* are the lucky ones, not just because we have a lot, out of which we can give a little, but because we are privileged to contribute to the beggar's happiness—and that privilege is worth a lot more than money. And, just as it is a great good freely to choose to do good, so it is also a good to be used by someone else for a worthy purpose (so long, that is, that he or she has the right, the authority, to use us in this way). Being allowed to suffer to make possible a great good is a privilege, even if the privilege is forced upon you. Those who are allowed to die for their country and thereby save their country from foreign oppression are privileged. Cultures less obsessed than our own by the evil of purely physical pain have always recognized that. And they have recognized that it is still a blessing, even if the one who died had been conscripted to fight.

And even twentieth-century man can begin to see that—sometimes—when he seeks to help prisoners, not by giving them more comfortable quarters, but by letting them help the handicapped; or when he pities rather than envies the "poor little rich girl" who has everything and does nothing for anyone else. And one phenomenon prevalent in end-of-century Britain draws this especially to our attention—the evil of unemployment. Because of our system of Social Security, the unemployed on the whole have enough money to live without too much discomfort; certainly they are a lot better off than are many employed in Africa or Asia or Victorian Britain. What is evil about unemployment is not so much any resulting poverty but the uselessness of the unemployed. They often report feeling unvalued by society, of no use, "on the scrap heap." They rightly think it would be a good for them to contribute; but they cannot. Many of them would welcome a system where they were obliged to do useful work in preference to one where society has no use for them.

It follows from that fact that being of use is a benefit for him who is of use, and that those who suffer at the hands of others, and thereby make possible the good of those others who have free and responsible choice, are themselves benefited in this respect. I am fortunate if the natural possibility of my suffering if you choose to hurt me is the vehicle which makes your choice really matter. My vulnerability, my openness to suffering (which necessarily involves my actually suffering if you make the wrong choice), means that you are not just like a pilot in a simulator, where it does not matter if mistakes are made. That our choices matter tremendously, that we can make great differences to things for good or ill, is one of the greatest gifts a creator can give us. And if my suffering is the means by which he can give you that choice, I too am in this respect fortunate. Though of course suffering is in itself a bad thing, my good fortune is that the suffering is not random, pointless suffering. It is suffering which is a consequence of my vulnerability which makes me of such use.

Someone may object that the only good thing is not *being* of use (dying for one's country or being vulnerable to suffering at your hands), but *believing* that one is of use—believing that one is dying for one's country and that this is of use; the "feel-good" experience. But that cannot be correct. Having comforting beliefs is only a good thing if they are true beliefs. It is not a good thing to believe that things are going well when they are not, or that your life is of use when it is not. Getting pleasure out of a comforting falsehood is a cheat. But if I get pleasure out of a true belief, it must be that I regard the state of things which I believe to hold to be a good thing. If I get pleasure out of the true belief that my daughter is doing well at school, it must be that I regard it as a good thing that my daughter does well at school (whether or not I believe that she is doing well). If I did not think the latter, I would not get any pleasure out of believing that she is doing well. Likewise, the belief that I am vulnerable to suffering at your hands, and that that is a good thing, can only be a good thing if being vulnerable to suffering at your hands is itself a good thing (independently of whether I believe it or not). Certainly, when my life is of use and that is a good for me, it is even better if I believe it and get comfort therefrom; but it can only be even better if it is already a good for me whether I believe it or not.

But though suffering may in these ways serve good purposes, does God have the right to allow me to suffer for your benefit, without asking my permission? For surely, an objector will say, no one has the right to allow one person A to suffer for the benefit of another one B without A's consent. We judge that doctors who use patients as involuntary objects of experimentation in medical experiments which they hope will produce results which can be used to benefit others are doing something wrong. After all, if my arguments about the utility of suffering are sound, ought we not all to be causing suffering to others in order that those others may have the opportunity to react in the right way?

There are, however, crucial differences between God and the doctors. The first is that God as the author of our being has certain rights, a certain authority over us, which we do not have over our fellow humans. He is the cause of our existence at each moment of our existence and sustains the laws of nature which give us everything we are and have. To allow someone to suffer for his own good or that of others, one has to stand in some kind of parental relationship towards him. I do not have the right to let some stranger suffer for the sake of some good, when I could easily prevent this, but I do have *some* right of this kind in respect of my own children. I may let the younger son suffer *somewhat* for his own good or that of his brother. I have this right because in small part I am responsible for the younger son's existence, his beginning and continuance. If I have begotten him, nourished, and educated him, I have some limited rights over him in return; to a *very limited* extent I can use him for some worthy purpose. If this is correct, then a God who is so much more the author of our being than are our parents has so much more right in this respect. Doctors do have over us even the rights of parents.

But secondly and all-importantly, the doctors *could* have asked the patients for permission; and the patients, being free agents of some power and knowledge, could have made an informed choice of whether or not to allow themselves to be used. By contrast, God's choice is not about how to use already existing agents, but about the sort of agents to make and the sort of world into which to put them. In God's situation there are no agents to be asked. I am arguing that it is good that one agent A should have deep responsibility for another B (who in turn could have deep responsibility for another C). It is not logically possible for God to have asked B if he wanted things thus, for, if A is to be responsible for B's growth in freedom, knowledge, and power, there will not be a B with enough freedom and knowledge to make any choice, before God has to choose whether or not to give A responsibility for him. One cannot ask a baby into which sort of world he or she wishes to be born. The creator has to make the choice independently of his creatures. He will seek on balance to benefit them—all of them. And, in giving them the gift of life—whatever suffering goes with it—that is a substantial benefit. But when one suffers at the hands of another, often perhaps it is not enough of a benefit to outweigh the suffering. Here is the point to recall that it is an additional benefit to the sufferer that his suffering is the means whereby the one who hurt him had the opportunity to make a significant choice between good and evil which otherwise he would not have had.

Although for these reasons, as I have been urging, God has the right to allow humans to cause each other to suffer, there must be a limit to the amount of suffering which he has the right to allow a human being to suffer for the sake of a great good. A parent may allow an elder child to have the power to do some harm to a younger child for the sake of the responsibility given to the elder child; but there are limits. And there are limits even to the moral right of God, our creator and sustainer, to use free sentient beings as pawns in a greater game. Yet, if these limits were too narrow, God would be unable to give humans much real responsibility; he would be able to allow them only to play a toy game. Still, limits there must be to God's rights to allow humans to hurt each other; and limits there are in the world to the extent to which they can hurt each other, provided above all by the short finite life enjoyed by humans and other creatures—one human can hurt another for no more than eighty years or so. And there are a number of other safety-devices in-built into our physiology and psychology, limiting the amount of pain we can suffer. But the primary safety limit is that provided by the shortness of our finite life. Unending, unchosen suffering would indeed to my mind provide a very strong argument against the existence of God. But that is not the human situation.

So then God, without asking humans, has to choose for them between the kinds of world in which they can live—basically either a world in which there is very little opportunity for humans to benefit or harm each other, or a world in which there is considerable opportunity. How shall he choose? There are clearly reasons for both choices. But it seems to me (just, on balance) that his choosing to create the world in which we have considerable opportunity to benefit or harm each other is to bring about a good at least as great as the evil which he thereby allows to occur. *Of course* the suffering he allows is a bad thing; and, other things being equal, to be avoided. But having the natural possibility of causing suffering makes possible a greater good. God, in creating humans who (of logical necessity) cannot choose for themselves the kind of world into which they are to come, plausibly exhibits his goodness in making for them the heroic choice that they come into a risky world where they may have to suffer for the good of others.

Natural Evil

Natural evil is not to be accounted for along the same lines as moral evil. Its main role rather, I suggest, is to make it possible for humans to have the kind of choice which the free-will defence extols, and to make available to humans specially worthwhile kinds of choice.

There are two ways in which natural evil operates to give humans those choices. First, the operation of natural laws producing evils gives humans knowledge (if they choose to seek it) of how to bring about such evils themselves. Observing you catch some disease by the operation of natural processes gives me the power either to use those processes to give that disease to other people, or through negligence to allow others to catch it, or to take measures to prevent others from catching the disease. Study of the mechanisms of nature producing various evils (and goods) opens up for humans a wide range of choice. This is the way in which in fact we learn how to bring about (good and) evil. But could not God give us the requisite knowledge (of how to bring about good or evil) which we need in order to have free and responsible choice by a less costly means? Could he not just whisper in our ears from time to time what are the different consequences of different actions of ours? Yes. But anyone who believed that an action of his would have some effect because he believed that God had told him so would see all his actions as done under the all-watchful eye of God. He would not merely believe strongly that there was a God, but would know it with real certainty. That knowledge would greatly inhibit his freedom of choice, would make it very difficult for him to choose to do evil. This is because we all have a natural inclination to wish to be thought well of by everyone, and above all by an all-good God; that we have such an inclination is a very good feature of humans, without which we would be less than human. Also, if we were directly informed of the consequences of our actions, we would be deprived of the choice whether to seek to discover what the consequences were through experiment and hard cooperative work. Knowledge would be available on tap. Natural processes alone give humans knowledge of the effects of their actions without inhibiting their freedom, and if evil is to be a possibility for them they must know how to allow it to occur.

The other way in which natural evil operates to give humans their freedom is that it makes possible certain kinds of action towards it between which agents can choose. It increases the range of significant choice. A particular natural evil, such as physical pain, gives to the sufferer a choice—whether to endure it with patience, or to bemoan his lot. His friend can choose whether to show compassion towards the sufferer, or to be callous. The pain makes possible these choices, which would not otherwise exist. There is no guarantee that our actions in response to the pain will be good ones, but the pain gives us the opportunity to perform good actions. The good or bad actions which we perform in the face of natural evil themselves provide opportunities for further choice—of good or evil stances towards the former actions. If I am patient with my suffering, you can choose whether to encourage or laugh at my patience; if I bemoan my lot, you can teach me by word and example what a good thing patience is. If you are sympathetic, I have then the opportunity to show gratitude for the sympathy; or to be so self-involved that I ignore it. If you are callous, I can choose whether to ignore this or to resent it for life. And so on. I do not think that there can be much doubt that natural evil, such as physical pain, makes available these sorts of choice. The actions which natural evil makes possible are ones which allow us to perform at our best and interact with our fellows at the deepest level.

It may, however, be suggested that adequate opportunity for these great good actions would be provided by the occurrence of moral evil without any need for suffering to be caused by natural processes. You can show courage when threatened by a gunman, as well as when threatened by cancer; and show sympathy to those likely to be killed by gunmen as well as to those likely to die of cancer. But just imagine all the suffering of mind and body caused by disease, earthquake, and accident unpreventable by humans removed at a stroke from our society. No sickness, no bereavement in consequence of the untimely death of the young. Many of us would then have such an easy life that we simply would not have much opportunity to show courage or, indeed, manifest much in the way of great goodness at all. We need those insidious processes of decay and dissolution which money and strength cannot ward off for long to give us the opportunities, so easy otherwise to avoid, to become heroes.

God has the right to allow natural evils to occur (for the same reason as he has the right to allow moral evils to occur)—up to a limit. It would, of course, be crazy for God to multiply evils more and more in order to give endless opportunity for heroism, but to have *some* significant opportunity for real heroism and consequent character formation is a benefit for the person to whom it is given. Natural evils give to us the knowledge to make a range of choices between good and evil, and the opportunity to perform actions of especially valuable kinds.

There is, however, no reason to suppose that animals have free will. So what about their suffering? Animals had been suffering for a long time before humans appeared on this planet—just how long depends on which animals are conscious beings. The first thing to take into account here is that, while the higher animals, at any rate the vertebrates, suffer, it is most unlikely that they suffer nearly as much as humans do. Given that suffering depends directly on brain events (in turn caused by events in other parts of the body), then, since the lower animals do not suffer at all and humans suffer a lot, animals of intermediate complexity (it is reasonable to suppose) suffer only a moderate amount. So, while one does need a theodicy to account for why God allows animals to suffer, one does not need as powerful a theodicy as one does in respect of humans. One only needs reasons adequate to account for God allowing an amount of suffering much less than that of humans. That said, there is, I believe, available for animals parts of the theodicy which I have outlined above for humans.

The good of animals, like that of humans, does not consist solely in thrills of pleasure. For animals, too, there are more worthwhile things, and in particular intentional actions, and among them serious significant intentional actions. The life of animals involves many serious significant intentional actions. Animals look for a mate, despite being tired and failing to find one. They take great trouble to build nests and feed their young, to decoy predators and explore. But all this inevitably involves pain (going on despite being tired) and danger. An animal cannot intentionally avoid forest fires, or take trouble to rescue its offspring from forest fires, unless there exists a serious danger of getting caught in a forest fire. The action of rescuing despite danger simply cannot be done unless the danger exists—and the danger will not exist unless there is a significant natural probability of being caught in the fire. Animals do not choose freely to do such actions, but the actions are nevertheless worthwhile. It is great that animals feed their young, not just themselves; that animals explore when they know it to be dangerous; that animals save each other from predators, and so on. These are the things that give the lives of animals their value. But they do often involve some suffering to some creature.

To return to the central case of humans—the reader will agree with me to the extent to which he or she values responsibility, free choice, and being of use very much more than thrills of pleasure or absence of pain. There is no other way to get the evils of this world into the right perspective, except to reflect at length on innumerable very detailed thought experiments (in addition to actual experiences of life) in which we postulate very different sorts of worlds from our own, and then ask ourselves whether the perfect goodness of God would require him to create one of these (or no world at all) rather than our own. But I conclude with a very small thought experiment, which may help to begin this process. Suppose that you exist in another world before your birth in this one, and are given a choice as to the sort of life you are to have in this one. You are told that you are to have only a short life, maybe of only a few minutes, although it will be an adult life in the sense that you will have the richness of sensation and belief characteristic of adults. You have a choice as to the sort of life you will have. You can have either a few minutes of very considerable pleasure, of the kind produced by some drug such as heroin, which you will experience by yourself and which will have no effects at all in the world (for example, no one else will know about it); or you can have a few minutes of considerable pain, such as the pain of childbirth, which will have (unknown to you at the time of pain) considerable good effects on others over a few years. You are told that, if you do not make the second choice, those others will never exist—and so you are under no moral obligation to make the second choice. But you seek to make the choice which will make *your* own life the best life for *you* to have led. How will you choose? The choice is, I hope, obvious. You should choose the second alternative.

For someone who remains unconvinced by my claims about the relative strengths of the good and evils involved—holding that, great though the goods are, they do not justify the evils which they involve—there is a fall-back position. My arguments may have convinced you of the greatness of the goods involved sufficiently for you to allow that a perfectly good God would be justified in bringing about the evils for the sake of the good which they make possible, if and only if God also provided compensation in the form of happiness after death to the victims whose sufferings make possible the goods. . . . While believing that God does provide at any rate for many humans such life after death, I have expounded a theodicy without relying on this assumption. But I can understand someone thinking that the assumption is needed, especially when we are considering the worst evils. (This compensatory afterlife need not necessarily be the everlasting life of Heaven.)

It remains the case, however, that evil is evil, and there is a substantial price to pay for the goods of our world which it makes possible. God would not be less than perfectly good if he created instead a world without pain and suffering, and so without the particular goods which those evils make possible. Christian, Islamic, and much Jewish tradition claims that God has created worlds of both kinds—our world, and the Heaven of the blessed. The latter is a marvellous world with a vast range of possible deep goods, but it lacks a few goods which our world contains, including the good of being able to reject the good. A generous God might well choose to give some of us the choice of rejecting the good in a world like ours before giving to those who embrace it a wonderful world in which the former possibility no longer exists.

Suffering and Evil

George N. Schlesinger

A different approach to the problem of evil is taken by George Schlesinger, Professor Emeritus of Philosophy at the University of North Carolina at Chapel Hill. He draws a distinction between happiness, the fulfillment of one's wants, and the more important state of desirability, a function not only of happiness but also of one's potential for satisfaction. For example, a highly creative person may not be as happy as others yet have the potential to achieve higher satisfaction. Because such satisfaction has no maximum, God is not to be blamed for whatever our state of desirability it could always be raised.

In order to gain real insight into the nature of Divine benevolence, we have to start from the beginning and ask: is there indeed evil in the world? Suffering unquestionably exists, but can this be construed as the existence of evil? Before one can answer this question one must assess the moral status of divine acts. It is generally agreed that divine acts are assessed by the same criterion as human acts; otherwise the notions of "good" and "bad" would not retain their normal meanings. What then are evil human acts? As a rule they are acts which contravene moral obligations. This brings us to the question which must be answered first: what are my obligations toward my fellow man? On the surface, it may seem that my obligation toward another is to make him as happy as I can, provided this does not interfere with the welfare of others. Upon reflection, however, this appears inadequate.

From Steven M. Cahn and David Shatz, eds., *Questions About God: Today's Philosophers Ponder the Divine*, Oxford University Press. Reprinted by permission of the publisher.

Suppose I have under my care a child of very low intelligence but of very happy disposition. Provided his basic bodily needs are minimally taken care of, he enjoys lying on his back all day long and staring into the air. A minor operation, I am assured by the best medical authorities, would spectacularly raise his intelligence and render him capable of creative achievements as well as the appreciation of music, art, literature, and science. Naturally, if his intelligence were raised he would be vulnerable to the frustrations, disappointments, and anxieties most of us are subject to from time to time. Nevertheless, I believe it will be agreed that I should be reprehensible if I refrained from letting the child have the operation, even if I insured to the best of my ability that his physical needs would always be taken care of.

But why is it not good enough that I am keeping him in a state of maximum happiness? Apparently, the degree of desirability of a state is not a simple function of a single factor—namely, the degree to which one's wants are satisfied—but is also dependent on the kind of being one is. The somewhat less happy but intelligent child is ultimately better off than the happy idiot because, although the amount of happiness is less in his case, he is more than compensated for this by having become a preferable kind of person.

Thus, my moral obligations do not consist simply in having to endeavor to raise the amount of happiness a certain being is granted to enjoy. These obligations are somewhat more complex and consist in my having to raise the degree of desirability of his state, a two-valued function depending both on the potentials of the individual and the extent to which his needs are being taken care of. The idea may be illustrated as follows. In recent years much has been heard about machines that electrically stimulate the pleasure centers of one's brain. Once a person's brain is connected to the machine, he becomes completely captivated by the experience it provides and desires absolutely nothing but the passive enjoyment of the sublime pleasures it induces. But I believe that most would condemn me if, without prior consultation, I hooked up *A*, a normal person, to this machine and thus caused him to become addicted to it for the rest of his life. This would be so even if I provided an attendant to look after *A*'s vital physical needs. I should, I believe, be severely condemned, even though *A*'s addiction has no ill aftereffects. But *A*, previously a normal person, has had his usual ups and downs, while now he is in a continual state of "bliss." Shouldn't I be praised for having eliminated the large gap between his potential and actual amounts of happiness by having satiated him with pleasure?

The answer, I believe, is no, and not merely because I have rendered *A* a less useful member of society. Even if the needs of others are not taken into account, it will be agreed by most that by inducing in *A* a permanent state of euphoria I have not done a good thing to him. This is so because I have reduced the desirability of *A*'s state. The latter is not solely a function of how satiated *A* is with pleasure but also of the kind of being he is. *A* was, prior to my interference, capable of a great variety of response, of interaction with others, of creativity and self-improvement, while now he is reduced to a completely inactive, vegetable-like existence. The great increase in the factor of happiness is insufficient to make up for the great loss in the second factor, *A*'s being lowered from the state of a normal human being to the state of an inferior quasi-hibernating inert existence.

The general ethical view I am trying to explain, and which is quite widely accepted, is well-reflected in the famous dictum, "Better Socrates dissatisfied than the fool satisfied; better the fool dissatisfied than the pig satisfied." It suggests that given two different creatures *A* and *B*, with different capacities and appetites and different potentials for suffering and happiness, it may turn out that although *A* is satisfied with his lot while *B* is complaining, *B* is in a more desirable state than *A*. Accordingly, one of the universal rules of ethics is not, "if everything else is equal increase the state of happiness of *A*," but rather, "if everything is equal increase the degree of desirability of the state of *A* by as much as possible." It may be pointed out that generally I have far more opportunities to affect *A*'s happiness than to affect the other factor which determines the degree of desirability of his state. It should also be noted that it is by no means always clear how much increase in one factor makes up for a given decrease in the other factor.

Now I take it that conceptually there is no limit to the degree which the desirability of state may reach. One can easily conceive a super-Socrates who has a much higher intelligence and many more than five senses through which to enjoy the world and who stands to Socrates as the latter stands to the pig. And there is the possibility of a super-super-Socrates and so on ad infinitum. Given this last supposition about an infinite hierarchy of possible beings and hence the limitlessness of the possible increase in the degree of desirability of state, how does the aforementioned universal ethical rule, ". . . increase the degree of desirability of state as much as possible," apply to God? After all, no matter to what degree it is increased it is always logically possible to increase it further. A mortal's possibilities are physically limited, hence in his case there is a natural limit to the principle; but there is no limit to what God can do. It is therefore logically impossible for Him to fulfill the ethical principle, i.e., to do enough to discharge His obligation to do more and further increase the degree of desirability of state. But what is logically impossible to do cannot be done by an omnipotent being either, and it is agreed by practically all philosophers that God's inability to do what is logically impossible does not diminish His omnipotence. Just as it is logically impossible to name the highest integer, it is impossible to grant a creature a degree of desirability of state higher than which is inconceivable; thus it is logically impossible for God to fulfill what is required by the universal ethical principle, and therefore He cannot fulfill it, and so is not obliged to fulfill it. There is no room for complaint, seeing that God has not fulfilled the ethical principle which mortals are bound by and has left His creatures in various low states of desirability. Thus the problem of evil vanishes.

A Reply to Schlesinger

Jeremy Gwiazda

According to Jeremy Gwiazda, a doctoral candidate at The City University of New York Graduate Center, Schlesinger's reply to the problem of evil fails. Gwiazda argues that regardless of our state of desirability, God is obliged to make us as happy as possible and has failed to do so. Whether Schlesinger or Gwiazda has the better of this dispute is for the reader to decide.

In developing his theodicy, George Schlesinger appeals to the case of a happy child of low intelligence who spends all day staring into space. By means of an operation, the youngster could be rendered far more intelligent but, as a result, would be vulnerable to frustrations and disappointments. Nevertheless, Schlesinger presumes all would agree that the operation should be performed because the decrease in happiness would be more than offset by an increase in potential.

To explain this situation, Schlesinger introduces the concept of "the degree of desirability of a state [DDS]," a two-valued function that depends on both an individual's potential (Potential) and the degree to which that person's needs are being met (Happiness). He claims that morality does not require us to increase Happiness but, instead, to increase as much as possible DDS.

Schlesinger then argues that "there is no limit to the degree which the [DDS] may reach," since Potential is limitless, for "there is the possibility of super-super-Socrates and so on ad infinitum." So God cannot fulfill the ethical rule to maximize DDS, but His failure to do so implies no moral shortcoming, as maximizing DDS is logically impossible. Because Happiness is part of DDS, God is not obligated to maximize Happiness, and thus the presence of evil is consistent with the existence of an omnipotent, omnibenevolent God.

To help clarify Schlesinger's strategy, let me introduce some terminology. If an obligation can reach a maximum level, let us call it "maximizable." If it can't, call it, "unmaximizable." Thus, Happiness is maximizable because all a person's needs can be met, but Potential is unmaximizable because it is unlimited.

Now in order to see the weakness in Schlesinger's argument, consider the following parallel piece of reasoning. Imagine a residence, call it "The

Published here for the first time. An extended version of this essay will appear in a forthcoming issue of *Religious Studies*.

Celestial Hotel," where God provides rooms. One day you check in and find your room dirty. When you complain, God's philosopher-in-residence replies that people prefer a slightly dirty but palatial room to a clean but small one. God's obligation, therefore, is not to maximize Cleanliness which is maximizable, but rather to maximize the two-valued function based on both Cleanliness and Size, call it "DCS" (degree of Cleanliness and Size). Because size has no maximum, DCS is not maximizable, and thus God is not blameworthy for giving you a dirty room.

This argument is parallel to Schlesinger's, substituting Cleanliness, Size, and DCS for Happiness, Potential, and DDS. Clearly, however, God does not avoid the obligation to provide you with a clean room just because of the unlimited size of rooms. Similarly, in Schlesinger's argument, God does not avoid the obligation to make you happy just because your Potential is unlimited.

In short, whatever our degree of Potential, God is obliged to make us as happy as possible, but He has not done so. Schlesinger's theodicy fails, therefore, and the evils we endure continue to provide strong reason for us to believe that God does not exist.

Theism and Modern Science

Nicholas Everitt

Nicholas Everitt is Senior Lecturer in Philosophy at the University of East Anglia in England. He argues that what we now know about the size and nature of the universe suggests it was not created in accord with the intentions of a divine being. After all, throughout virtually the entire history of the earth, human beings were not even present. In fact, the dominant forms of life have been bacteria.

Traditional theism presents us with a certain picture of God and of his intentions in creating the universe at large, and in creating human beings in particular. In general, if someone hypothesises that there is an agent with a certain nature and a certain set of intentions, then we can form some idea of what the agent is likely to do—in what respect things will be different just in virtue of the hypothesised agent's having that nature, those beliefs, and that intention. If we then discover that the world is not as we have predicted, then we have evidence that the initial hypothesis that there was such an agent is mistaken. The argument thus has the form:

(1) If there is an agent with nature N, beliefs B, and intention I, then he will produce change C in the world.
(2) The world does not display C. So:
(3) There is evidence against the hypothesis that there is an agent with N and I and B.

As an example of the argument at work in an uncontroversial context, consider an updated Robinson Crusoe. Suppose he considers the hypothesis that elsewhere on the island with him is another survivor of the shipwreck similar to Crusoe himself in his physical and mental capacities, including his beliefs, and with the intention of making contact with any other survivors, such as Crusoe. Even given as vague and impoverished a hypothesis as this, Crusoe can make *some* predictions about what the hypothetical survivor will do. He can formulate in his mind a range of what he might call apt behaviour, and a range of inapt behaviour, which the survivor might display—apt and inapt relative to the intention with which Crusoe has tentatively credited him. It would be apt if, for example, the survivor left visible signs of his presence on the island (marks on trees, scratchings on rocks, carefully arranged pieces of wood or stone). It would be apt if he emitted characteristically human noises (whistling, singing, shouting, etc.). It would be apt if he lit a fire and tried to send smoke signals. These would be apt pieces of behaviour because they are just the sorts of things which a Crusoe-like survivor would do if he were trying to let other possible survivors know of his existence on the island. By contrast, it would not be apt if the hypothetical survivor, for example, found some deep undergrowth and lay in it, quiet and still, for the greater part of each day. It would not be apt if after being in any location on the island, he carefully removed all signs of his presence (footprints, ashes from fires, etc.). And so on. These are not apt ways of realising the intention of making your presence known to another human who might be in the vicinity. They are not the kind of actions which it would be reasonable for Crusoe to expect another survivor to pursue, given the intentions and beliefs with which Crusoe is crediting him.

So, even before starting his empirical investigation of the island, Crusoe can formulate to himself a description of what evidence would help to confirm his initial hypothesis, and what evidence would help to disconfirm it. If he looks hard and carefully for evidence of what we have called apt behaviour, and finds none, that constitutes some evidence against his initial hypothesis that there is another survivor. It is evidence for saying that either there is no actual survivor, or if there is one, the initial hypothesis was wrong about either his capacities or his intentions. In saying that some kinds of behaviour by the hypothetical survivor would be "inapt," we do not mean that it *absolutely disproves* the initial hypothesis about the survivor's capacities and intentions, but rather that it constitutes *evidence against* the hypothesis. The evidence is defeasible in that it is possible that there is some factor of which Crusoe is unaware which would explain away its initial anti-hypothesis import. (Perhaps the survivor is injured or even unconscious.) But if he does not discover any such factor, he would be justified in concluding that the initial hypothesis is to some degree disconfirmed.

Let us see now how considerations of this kind can be applied on a cosmic scale, and how the nature of the universe as revealed by modern science gives us reason to reject traditional theism.

Consider, first, the account of God's nature and purposes with which theism presents us. Theism tells us that God is a being who is omnipotent and omniscient, wholly self-sufficient, with no needs, or lacks, or deficiencies of any kind. For reasons that are not entirely clear, God decides to create a universe in which human beings will be the jewel. Although he will have a care for the whole of his creation, God will have an especial care for human beings. He will give these creatures the power of free choice. Exactly what this power is, no one can agree. Some think that it is a capacity the possession of which is incompatible with the truth of determinism; others think that it is a kind of freedom which is compatible with determinism, and which perhaps even requires determinism. Because humans are the jewel of creation, the rest of the universe will be at least not unremittingly hostile or even indifferent to human flourishing. Even if the universe will not make such flourishing immediately and easily and painlessly accessible, it will make it at least accessible in principle for humanity at large. The question then to ask is: given this much information about God and his nature and his purposes, what sort of a universe would you expect to find? Which of all the possible worlds that God could create would you expect him to create, given this much knowledge of his nature and of his overall plan?

As with our example of Robinson Crusoe, it is difficult to answer this question in any great detail. The description of God is so sketchy, and in particular the theistic hypothesis gives us so little information about his aims, that a large number of possible worlds are left equally likely. But among the more likely scenarios is a universe somewhat like the one presented to us in the story of Genesis. In particular, traditional theism would lead you to expect human beings to appear fairly soon after the start of the universe. For, given the central role of humanity, what would be the point of a universe which came into existence and then existed for unimaginable aeons without the presence of the very species that supplied its rationale? You would expect humans to appear after a great many animals, since the animals are subordinate species available for human utilisation, and there would be no point in having humans arrive on the scene needing animals (e.g., as a source of food, or clothing, or companionship) only for them to discover that animals had not yet been created. But equally, you would not expect humans to arrive *very* long after the animals, for what would be the point of a universe existing for aeons full of animals created for humanity's delectation, in the absence of any humans? Further, you would expect the earth to be fairly near the centre of the universe if it had one, or at some similarly significant location if it did not have an actual centre. You would expect the total universe to be not many orders of magnitude greater than the size of the earth. The universe would be on a *human* scale. You would expect that even if there are regions of the created world which are hostile to human life, and which perhaps are incompatible with it, the greater part of the universe would be accessible to human exploration. If this were not so, what would the point be of God creating it?

These expectations are largely what we find in the Genesis story (or strictly, stories) of creation. There is, then, a logic to the picture of the universe with which the Genesis story presents us: given the initial assumptions about God, his nature, and his intentions, the Genesis universe is pretty much how it would be reasonable for God to proceed. Given the hypothesis of theism and no scientific knowledge, and then asked to construct a picture of the universe and its creation, it is not surprising that the author(s) of Genesis came up with the account which they did. It is not that God would have *had* to proceed in the Genesis way (just as there is not just one kind of behaviour which a possible island survivor would need to produce to confirm Crusoe's initial hypothesis), and it is not that *every* non-Genesis way would be extremely puzzling. There is in fact a wide range of possible universes which God could have created and about which there would not be a puzzle of the form "But how could a universe like *that* be an expression of a set of intentions like *those?*" Nevertheless, we can still draw a distinction between universes which would be apt, given the initial hypothesis, and universes which would be inapt. The Genesis universe is clearly an apt one, given the theistic hypothesis; but a universe in which (say) most humans could survive only by leading lives of great and endless pain would be a surprising one for God to choose, given the other assumptions we make about him.

The question now to raise is "Is the universe as it is revealed to us by modern science roughly the sort of universe which we would antecedently expect a God of traditional theism to create? Is it an apt universe, given the admittedly sketchy conception we have of his nature and his intentions?"

The short answer to this is "No." In almost every respect, the universe as it is revealed to us by modern science is *hugely* unlike the sort of universe which the traditional thesis would lead us to expect. Although the bare quantitative facts will be familiar to many readers, it is worth repeating them. First, in terms of age: our best estimates are that the universe itself is very roughly 15 billion years, and the Earth is roughly 5 billion years old. How long humans have existed will depend partly on what we take a human to be. But if we take humans to be homo sapiens, and if we take them to be creatures with some sort of language and some sort of social culture, then realistic estimates would allow that they have existed for no more than 100,000 years. So if we imagine the history of the universe represented by a line which is roughly 24 miles long, human life would occupy only the last inch. Or if we imagine this history of the universe represented by a single year, humanity would emerge only in the last few seconds of the last minute of the last hour of the last day of the year. So for something more than 99.999 percent of the history of the universe, the very creatures which are meant to be the jewel of creation have been absent from it. The question that at once arises is "What, given the hypothesis of theism, was the point of this huge discrepancy between the age of the universe and the age of humanity?" How very inapt a creation of that kind must strike us.

The same story recurs if we turn to the size of the universe. Suppose we take the size of our solar system to be within the expectable parameters of the theistic hypothesis. (This might seem over-generous to theism: why would God need a solar system as big as ours to achieve any of his purposes? Why does he need a sun that is 93 *million* miles from earth? Why wouldn't 93 thousand miles have been enough? Of course the laws of physics would then have had to be different if the sun were to make earth habitable—but as an omnipotent being, God could easily have adjusted the laws of physics. However, let us overlook this and allow that a distance of 93 million miles counts as intelligible—it is intelligible, that is, that a God with the nature and intentions ascribed by traditional theism should create a universe that big.) But of course, we know now that the universe is staggeringly larger than any such intelligible size. The sun is about 8 light minutes from us, the next nearest star is about 4.3 light years, the next nearest galaxy to the Milky Way is scores of light years away. Current findings indicate that the furthest star visible from earth is about 3 billion light years away. In other words, the most distant star is very roughly some 200,000,000,000,000,000 times (two hundred thousand trillion times) as far from us as the sun. This sort of scale to the universe makes no conceivable sense on the theistic hypothesis. Nor should we assume that the most distant visible star is the most distant detectable entity. The furthest galaxy, detectable only by radio telescopes, is reckoned to be about three times further away—9 billion light years. The possible limits of the universe lie further away still. If the Big Bang occurred about 15 billion years ago, and if the expansion had occurred at the speed of light, the limits of the universe would be about 30 billion light years. Assuming that the expansion was at less than the speed of light, that still leaves the possibility of a universe whose overall size is between 10 and 30 billion light years across (i.e., up to two million trillion miles). Why would a God make it that big?

Further, astronomers tell us that there are about 100 trillion galaxies, each with a billion stars (giving us something of the order of 100,000,000,000,000,000,000,000 stars).[1] It could count as apt if a creator created a universe with one star or perhaps a few dozen or even a few hundred, so that the night sky were as beautiful as we now find it. But what could be the point of the huge superabundance of celestial matter, especially given the fact that the very great majority of humanity will never be aware of most of it? Again, given the theistic hypothesis, it is strikingly inapt.

If we confine our attention to the earth, the same extraordinary inaptness confronts us. The Genesis story presents God's actions as apt in relation to the non-human creatures who share the planet with humans: they all emerge at about the same time; and all the creatures which surround humanity in that story share a human scale—none are so tiny that it is impossible to detect them by the senses, and none are so huge (e.g., thousands or millions of times larger than humans) as to be unrecognisable as organisms at all. But again, modern science reveals this to be deeply wrong—not just in points of detail, but in almost every major respect. Life has existed on the planet for something like 3 to 3.5 billion years. For roughly half of that time, it has been solely bacterial in form. Given that humans have emerged only in the last 100,000 years, that means that for 99.99 percent of the history of life on earth, there have been no humans. How very bizarre, given the theistic hypothesis! Further, from a biological point of view "On any possible or reasonable or fair criterion, bacteria are—and always have been the dominant forms of life on earth"[2] In terms of their numbers, their longevity, their ability to exploit the widest variety of habitats, their degree of genetic variation, and even (amazingly, given how tiny they are individually) their total biomass, they outstrip every other kind of life. If God had intended any species to flourish, the obvious candidate for divine favour would be bacteria, not humans.

In short, then, everything that modern science tells us about the size and scale and nature of the universe around us reveals it to be strikingly inapt as an expression of a set of divine intentions of the kind that theism postulates. Let us emphasise that the claim here is not that there is a logical incompatibility between these modern scientific findings and traditional theism. It is not that the findings *disprove* theism. The claim is weaker than that. The claim is only that the findings of modern science *significantly reduce the probability* that theism is true, because the universe is turning out to be very unlike the sort of universe which we would have expected, had theism been true.

NOTES

1. Sarah Woodward, "Things to Come," *Cambridge Alumni Magazine* 30 (2000), p. 25.
2. Stephen Jay Gould, *Life's Grandeur* (London: Jonathan Cape, 1996), p. 176.

PART 3

Religious Language

Negative Attributes

Moses Maimonides

In Hume's *Dialogues Concerning Natural Religion,* Demea refers to "the adorable mysteriousness of the Divine Nature." Granting Demea's description, can we use our ordinary language to describe something so extraordinarily mysterious as God?

A famous answer was provided by Rabbi Moses ben Maimon (1135–1204), known as Maimonides, who was the most influential Jewish philosopher of the medieval period and has been called "the most significant Jewish philosopher of all time." He was born in Cordova, Spain, became a court physician in Cairo, Egypt, where he was the leader of the Jewish community, and wrote monumental works on Jewish law as well as his philosophical masterpiece, *The Guide of the Perplexed.* In his view, God is beyond the power of human conceptualization.

According to Maimonides, the only way to describe God is to use negative attributes. Thus one speaks of God not as existing but rather as not nonexistent, not as powerful but rather as not non-powerful, not as knowing but rather as not not-knowing. Even using ordinary words to try to describe God is misleading because, as Maimonides said, we might as well "say of a wall that it does not see." His point was that just as a wall neither sees nor is blind, so God neither knows nor is ignorant, neither possesses power nor is powerless. In short, when we try to express the essence of God, words fail us.

It is the negative attributes which we must employ to guide our mind . . . to the utmost limit of what man can apprehend of God. For instance, it has been proved to us that something must exist apart from those objects which our senses apprehend and which our reason can encompass with its knowledge. We say about this thing that it exists, meaning that it is absurd to say that He does not exist. Then we apprehend that its existence is not like the existence of, say, the elements, which are lifeless bodies, and consequently say that He lives, meaning that God is not subject to death. Then we apprehend that this being is also not like the existence of heaven, which is a living

---

body, and consequently we say that He is not a body. Then we apprehend that this being is not like the existence of an Intelligence, which is neither a body nor subject to death, but is due to a cause, and consequently say that God is eternal, meaning that there is no cause which called Him into being. Then we apprehend that the existence of this Being, which is its essence, is not only sufficient for that Being itself to exist, but many existences emanate from it. It is, however, not like the emanation of heat from the fire or the automatic connection between light and the sun, but it is an emanation which He perpetually keeps going, giving it a constant flow arranged according to a wise plan. . . . We shall say on account of these arrangements that He is omnipotent, omniscient, and possessed of will. By these attributes we mean to say that He is neither powerless nor ignorant nor distracted or disinterested. When we say He is not powerless, we mean that His existence is sufficient to bring into existence things other than Himself. When we say He is not ignorant, we mean that He apprehends, i.e., lives, for whatever apprehends lives. When we say He is not distracted or disinterested, we mean that all those existing things run along an ordered and planned course, not without supervision and coming into being just by chance, just like anything which a person possessed of will plans with purpose and will. Then we apprehend that there is no other being like this one. When we, therefore, say He is One, we mean thereby to deny any plurality.

Thus it becomes clear that every attribute with which we describe Him . . . has the purport of negating its own absence if our intention thereby is to apprehend His essence rather than His works. These negative terms are also not used absolutely of God, but only in the manner mentioned before, that one denies of a thing something that by the nature of things could not exist in it, as when we say of a wall that it does not see. . . .

We can only apprehend that He is; that there exists a Being unlike any other being which He brought into existence, having nothing whatsoever in common with them, who has no plurality in Him, and is not powerless to bring into existence things other than He himself, and that His relation to the world is that of the captain to the ship. This also is not a true relation, and not even remotely resembles the real one, but it serves to guide the mind to the idea that God governs the universe, meaning that He supports it and keeps its order as it should be. . . .

Praise be to Him who is such that when our minds try to visualize His essence, their power of apprehending becomes imbecility; when they study the connection between His works and His will, their knowledge becomes ignorance; and when our tongues desire to declare His greatness by descriptive terms, all eloquence becomes impotence and imbecility.

The Use of Analogy

THOMAS AQUINAS

Our next selection is another excerpt from the *Summa Theologiae* of Thomas Aquinas. Here he considers the view of Moses Maimonides, whom Aquinas refers to as "Rabbi Moses," that when we use words to describe God they do not have the same meaning as when we use them ordinarily. In Aquinas's terminology, the issue is whether when names are applied to God and to creatures the terms are "predicated univocally," that is, with the same meaning, or "in a purely equivocal sense," that is, with different meanings.

Aquinas's conclusion is that the terms are used neither univocally nor equivocally but analogously. For example, the term "healthy" can be applied to an animal and by analogy to a related medicine, such as one that causes health in the animal. Similarly, the term "wise" can be applied to a human being and by analogy to God.

[A]s regards names of God said absolutely and affirmatively, as *good, wise,* and the like, various and many opinions have been held. For some have said that all such names, although they are applied to God affirmatively, nevertheless have been brought into use more to remove something from God than to posit something in Him. Hence they assert that when we say that God lives, we mean that God is not like an inanimate thing; and the same in like manner applies to other names. This was taught by Rabbi Moses. Others say that these names applied to God signify His relationship towards creatures: thus in the words, *God is good,* we mean, God is the cause of goodness in things; and the same interpretation applies to other names.

Both of these opinions, however, seem to be untrue . . . because in neither of them could a reason be assigned why some names more than others should be applied to God. For He is assuredly the cause of bodies in the same way as He is the cause of good things; therefore if the words *God is good* signified no more than, *God is the cause of good things,* it might in like manner be said that God is a body, inasmuch as He is the cause of bodies. . . .

[W]hen any name expressing perfection is applied to a creature, it signifies that perfection as distinct from the others according to the nature of its definition; as, for instance, by this term *wise* applied to a man, we signify some perfection distinct from a man's essence, and distinct from his power

---

From Anton C. Pegis, ed., *Basic Writings of Saint Thomas Aquinas.* Reprinted by permission of the Hackett Publishing Company, Inc.

and his being, and from all similar things. But when we apply *wise* to God, we do not mean to signify anything distinct from His essence or power or being. And thus when this term *wise* is applied to man, in some degree it circumscribes and comprehends the thing signified; whereas this is not the case when it is applied to God, but it leaves the thing signified as uncomprehended and as exceeding the signification of the name. Hence it is evident that this term *wise* is not applied in the same way to God and to man. The same applies to other terms. Hence, no name is predicated univocally of God and of creatures.

Neither, on the other hand, are names applied to God and creatures in a purely equivocal sense, as some have said. Because if that were so, it follows that from creatures nothing at all could be known or demonstrated about God; for the reasoning would always be exposed to the fallacy of equivocation. . . . Therefore it must be said that these names are said of God and creatures in an *analogous* sense, that is, according to proportion.

This can happen in two ways: either according as many things are proportioned to one (thus, for example *healthy* is predicated of medicine and urine in relation and in proportion to health of body, of which the latter is the sign and the former the cause), or according as one thing is proportioned to another (thus, *healthy* is said of medicine and an animal, since medicine is the cause of health in the animal body). And in this way some things are said of God and creatures analogically, and not in a purely equivocal nor in a purely univocal sense. . . . For in analogies, the idea is not, as it is in univocals, one and the same; yet it is not totally diverse as in equivocals; but the name which is thus used in a multiple sense signifies various proportions to some one thing, *e.g., healthy,* applied to urine, signifies the sign of animal health; but applied to medicine, it signifies the cause of the same health. . . .

The arguments adduced . . . prove indeed that . . . names are not predicated univocally of God and creatures; yet they do not prove that they are predicated equivocally.

The Inadequacy of Analogy

F. C. Copleston

To help in assessing Thomas Aquinas's theory of how God can be described using language analogically, we turn to the work of Father

From F. C. Copleston, *Aquinas: An Introduction to the Life and Work of the Great Medieval Thinker.*

F. C. Copleston (1907–1994), mentioned in my introduction to Aquinas, who was Professor of Metaphysics at the Gregorian University in Rome.

He admits, as he believes Aquinas would, that staying within the sphere of analogy does not make possible an adequate understanding of God, but Copleston maintains that Aquinas's approach does yield at least some knowledge of the divine nature. A key question that remains for readers to consider is whether an inadequate understanding of God differs significantly from no understanding at all.

Aquinas points out that when we predicate of God negative terms like "immutable" or "incorporeal" we remove, as it were, something from God, mutability or corporeity; that is, we deny the applicability to God of terms like "mutable" or "corporeal." We are concerned primarily with denying something of God rather than with affirming something positively of the divine substance. But there are other terms, like "wise" and "good" which are predicated of God positively and affirmatively; and it is in regard to the meaning of these terms that a special difficulty arises. Exclusive adherence to the negative way would lead to agnosticism about the divine nature; for a mere addition of negations would not result in positive knowledge. On the other hand, the use of the affirmative way, that is, affirming of God positive predicates, gives rise to a difficult problem. Some terms are predicated of God only metaphorically, as when God is called a "rock." But . . . [w]hen it is said that God is "wise" or "good" the terms are not used merely metaphorically: it is said that God is "really," and not merely metaphorically, wise and good. But at once we seem to be faced with a dilemma. If we mean that God is wise in precisely the same sense that a human being is or can be wise, we make God a kind of superman, and we are involved in anthropomorphism. If on the other hand the term is used purely equivocally, if, that is, its meaning when predicated of God is entirely different from its meaning when predicated of a human being, . . . its meaning is evacuated, without any other meaning being substituted. . . .

Aquinas' answer to the problem is that when terms like "wise" or "good" are predicated of God they are predicated neither univocally nor equivocally but in an analogical sense. . . . To say that certain terms are predicated analogically of God does not mean, of course, that we have an adequate positive idea of what is objectively signified by the term when it is predicated of God. Our knowledge of perfections is derived from creatures, and this origin necessarily colours our concepts of those perfections. We necessarily think and speak of God in terms which, from the linguistic point of view, refer primarily to creatures, and we can only approximate towards, while never reaching, an adequate understanding of what is meant by saying that God is "wise" or "good" or "intelligent" or "living". . . .

In Aquinas' account of our natural knowledge of the divine nature there is, then, a certain agnosticism. When we say that God is wise we affirm of God a positive attribute; but we are not able to give any adequate description of what is objectively signified by the term when it is predicated of God. If we are asked what we mean when we say that God is wise, we may answer that we mean that God possesses wisdom in an infinitely higher degree than human beings. But we cannot provide any adequate description of the content, so to speak, of this infinitely higher degree; we can only approximate towards it by employing the way of negation. What is affirmed is positive, but the positive content of the concept in our minds is determined by our experience of creaturely wisdom, and we can only attempt to purify it or correct its inadequacies by means of negations. Obviously enough, this process will never lead to an adequate positive understanding of the objective meaning of (that is, of what is objectively signified by) the terms predicated of God. But Aquinas never claimed that it would. On the contrary, he did not hesitate to draw the logical conclusion. "The first cause surpasses human understanding and speech. He knows God best who acknowledges that whatever he thinks and says falls short of what God really is." Aquinas would have been quite unmoved by the accusation that he could not give the exact significance of the terms predicated of God; for he never pretended to be able to give it.

Now, it is clear that predicating intelligence of God is not exactly like predicating intelligence of a dog. If I call a dog "intelligent," I use the word analogically; but if I am asked what I mean by it I can point to some of the dog's activities. Human beings and their intelligent activities, dogs and their activities, all the terms of the analogy fall within the range of experience. But we cannot observe God or point to God. The question therefore arises whether there is any objective justification for predicating certain terms of God rather than other terms. Or the question can be put in this way. Although no sensible man would demand an adequate account of the positive meaning of the word "intelligent" as used of God, how do we know that the word denotes a reality when it is predicated of God? . . .

It may be said, of course, that there is in fact some resemblance between the case of calling a dog "intelligent" and that of calling God "intelligent." For though I cannot point to God acting in the same way that I can point to the dog acting, I can draw attention to effects of God's activity which fall within the field of our experience. Does not Aquinas himself do this in his fifth proof of God's existence? . . . Can I not therefore by pointing to the perfections of creatures indicate the meaning of the terms which I predicate of God?

This is true. But the meaning which I indicate in this way is, as Aquinas was well aware, the meaning which the term has for me in my own mind, and it by no means follows that this is adequate to the objective reality connoted by the term when predicated of God. This can be shown by an example. Suppose that my one and only reason for calling God "intelligent" is that I consider that there is an intelligible world-system and that this is the creation of a transcendent being whom I name "God." In this case when I think of God as intelligent I think of Him as the sort of being capable of creating this world-system. And if I am asked to explain what I mean by calling God "intelligent," I mention the world-system. But it does not follow that I can give an adequate positive explanation of what the divine intelligence is in itself. The divine intelligence is identical with the divine being, and God transcends all His effects. There must, of course, be some control of analogical predication in the context. That is to say, if analogical predication about God is not to be wild talk, there must be some assignable reason for using one term rather than another. And these reasons will colour the meaning of the terms in my mind. But the explanation of the meaning of the terms which I can give is not adequate, and cannot be adequate, to the objective reality connoted by the terms. As Aquinas saw clearly, a certain measure of "agnosticism" is inevitable. It could be avoided only by relapsing into anthropomorphism on the one hand or on the other by holding that all statements about God are so many myths which may have some useful function, perhaps as a stimulus to moral conduct and certain affective attitudes, but which are not put forward as being true. And Aquinas was not prepared to accept either an anthropomorphic view of God or an interpretation of theological propositions as so many myths.

Aquinas' "agnosticism," then, is not agnosticism in the modern sense. He has no doubt about the existence of God, and he is far from saying that we can know nothing about the divine nature or that we can make only negative statements about it. At the same time he is acutely conscious of the empirical foundation of all human knowledge and of the consequences of this in natural theology. We cannot help thinking and speaking of God in terms which, linguistically speaking, refer primarily to the finite objects of our experience, and we move always within the sphere of analogy. This means that our knowledge of God is necessarily imperfect and inadequate.

Positive Attributes

Levi Gersonides

Can we refer to God using words in their ordinary sense? Maimonides thought not, and Aquinas believed we could use familiar words only in an analogous sense. In this additional excerpt from *The Wars of the Lord,* Gersonides in his typically bold fashion maintained that in describing God, we can use words straightforwardly while recognizing that they refer to God "primarily," describing God's essence, and to human beings "secondarily," describing characteristics that emanate from God. God's knowledge, for example, far exceeds our own, but "we say that God has knowledge because of the knowledge we find in us." As is his style, Gersonides offers one forceful argument after another, as he defends the view that we can reason about God using terms we understand.

[T]he first thing to do is to examine whether the term "knowledge" is equivocal with respect to divine and human knowledge, such that the difference between them is as Maimonides thought. . . . It seems to us that Maimonides' position on this question of divine cognition is not implied by any philosophical principles; indeed, reason denies this view, as I will show. It seems rather that theological considerations have forced him to this view.

That philosophical argument rules out Maimonides' position on this topic will be demonstrated as follows. It would seem that God's knowledge is equivocal with respect to our knowledge in the sense of prior and posterior predication, that is, the term "knowledge" is predicated of God (may He be blessed) *primarily* and of others *secondarily.* For in God knowledge is identical with His essence, whereas in anyone else knowledge is the effect of God's knowledge. In such a case the term is applied to God in a prior sense and to other things in a posterior sense. The same is true with respect to such terms as "exists," "one," "essence," and the like, i.e., they are predicated of God primarily and of other things secondarily. For His existence, unity, and essence belong to Him essentially, whereas the existence, unity, and essence of every [other] existent thing emanate from Him. Now when something is of this kind, the predicate applies to it in a prior sense, whereas the predicate applies in a posterior sense to the other things that are called by it insofar as they are given this property directly by the substance that has the property in the prior sense. . . . Hence, it seems that the difference between divine and human cognition is a difference in terms of greater perfection, for this is what is implied by prior and posterior predication. Now if what we have said is true, and since it is obvious that the most perfect knowledge is more true with respect to specificity and determinateness, it would follow that God's knowledge is more true with respect to specificity and determinateness. Hence, it cannot be that what is considered knowledge with respect to God can be called "belief," "error," or "confusion" with respect to man.

We can show in another way that the difference between divine and human cognition is not as Maimonides thought. It is evident that we proceed to affirm attributes of God from that with which we are familiar. That is, we say that God knows because of the knowledge found in us. For example, since we apprehend that the knowledge belonging to our intellect is a perfection of our intellect—without which it could not be an intellect in act [i.e., perfect]—we predicate of God that He knows by virtue of the fact, which we have demonstrated concerning Him, that God (may He be blessed) is indubitably an intellect in act. It is self-evident that when a predicate is affirmed of some object because it is true of some other thing, it is not predicated of both things in an absolutely equivocal sense, for between things that are absolutely equivocal there is no analogy. . . . Hence, it is clear that the term "knowledge" is not completely equivocal when applied to God (may He be blessed) and man. Since this term cannot be applied univocally with respect to God and man, it must be predicated in the sense of priority and posteriority. The same holds for other attributes that are predicated of both God (may He be blessed) and man. Thus, the difference between divine and human knowledge is one of greater perfection, albeit exceedingly so, and this type of knowledge is more precise and clear. . . .

The inadequacy of Maimonides' contention about the [absolute] difference between our knowledge and God's knowledge can be shown in another way. With respect to those attributes concerning which we want to know whether or not they can be predicated of God, it is evident that such predicates have one meaning regardless whether we affirm or deny them. For example, if we want to know whether God is corporeal or incorporeal, the term "corporeal" has the same meaning in some sense in either case. For if the term "body" has a completely different connotation in the negation from the meaning it has in the affirmation, these statements would not be considered genuine contradictions, as is obvious. . . . Hence, since it is clear when we deny attributes of God that are found in us that such attributes are not completely equivocal with respect to God (may He be blessed) and us, the same is true when we affirm of God predicates that are true of us. For example, we say that God is immovable, since if He were movable He would be a body, for all movable objects [are bodies]. Now it is evident that in this proposition the term "movable" is not completely equivocal with respect to the term "movable" when it is applied to nondivine things. For if it were, there would be no proof that God is not movable, since the movable object that must be a body is that which is movable in the domain of human phenomena, whereas the term "movable" (in the completely equivocal sense) would not imply that it is a body. Hence, since it is evident that the predicates we deny of God are not absolutely equivocal, neither are the terms that we affirm of Him. For at first we were uncertain whether to affirm or deny such predicates of God (may He be blessed). Then when the inquiry was completed, we were able to affirm or deny such predicates of Him. In general, if the terms used in affirming predicates of Him were absolutely equivocal, there would be no term applicable to things in our world that would be more appropriate to deny than to affirm of God or [more appropriate] to affirm than to deny to Him. For example, someone could say "God is a body" but not mean by the term "body," "a magnitude"; rather he would mean something that is completely equivocal with the term "body" as we usually use it. Similarly, someone could say "God does not have knowledge," since the term "knowledge" would not [on this view] have the same meaning for him in this statement as it does for us. It will not do to object that we indeed deny corporeality of God because it is an imperfection for us, whereas we affirm knowledge of Him because it is a perfection for us. For the *term* "corporeality" is not [itself] an imperfection, and it is the term that we deny of Him, but the content of the term is the imperfection. Similarly, the *term* "knowledge" is not [itself] a perfection; its content is. The proof of this is as follows. If by the term "corporeality" we were to connote what the term "knowledge" connotes, and conversely, corporeality would be a perfection for us and knowledge an imperfection. Moreover, we do not affirm or deny anything of God except by determining at the outset whether it is proper or improper for *Him;* we do not ask whether or not it is a perfection for *us.* Thus, it is clear that reason shows that the term "knowledge" is not completely equivocal with respect to God (may He be blessed) and man. . . .

On the basis of this entire discussion, it is now evident that reason shows that the term "knowledge" is predicated of God (may He be blessed) primarily and of creatures secondarily, not absolutely equivocally, and that the principles [of religious language] adopted by Maimonides in order to remove the objections of the philosophers concerning the problem of divine knowledge are not acceptable.

Experience and Metaphor

Janet Martin Soskice

Janet Martin Soskice, who is Reader in Modern Theology and Philosophical Theology at the University of Cambridge, offers a different way to understand descriptions of God. She focuses on the role of metaphor in language and believes the meaning of metaphors that apply to God can be found in religious experience and tradition.

According to Soskice, to say God's presence is like that of a wind is to draw on a series of "stumbling approximations" used by

---

Janet Martin Soskice, *Metaphor and Religious Language.* Reprinted by permission of Oxford University Press.

those who believe they experienced God and understandable by means of Christian sacred texts and accepted modes of interpretation. Whether this approach provides understanding of the divine is for readers to consider.

The descriptive vocabulary which any individual uses is . . . dependent on the community of interest and investigation in which he finds himself, and the descriptive vocabulary which a community has at its disposal is embedded in particular traditions of investigation and conviction; for example, the geneticist will assume that it is a biochemical mechanism which is responsible for trait inheritance and not magical spells or curses. His descriptive language is forged in a particular context of investigation where there is agreement on matters such as what constitutes evidence, what are genuine arguments, what counts as a fact, and so on . . .

Corresponding to the scientific communities of interest, there are religious communities of interest (Christians, for example) which are bound by shared assumptions, interests, and traditions of interpretation, and share a descriptive vocabulary.

The Christian, too, makes claims on the basis of experience which, although different from the kind on which scientific judgements are based, is experience nonetheless. It is important to clarify what we mean by "experience" in this context; it is a portmanteau term to cover two sorts, the first being the dramatic or pointed religious experiences of the kind which might prompt one to say, "whatever appeared to me on the mountain was God," or "whatever caused me to change my life was God." The second are the diffuse experiences which form the subject of subsequent metaphysical reflection, the kind on which Aquinas based his proofs for the existence of God; for example, the experience of contingency which prompts us to postulate the non-contingent, the experience of cause which prompts us to postulate the uncaused, the experience of order which prompts us to postulate an ordering agent, and so on. On this view, even the abstractions of natural theology are based, in the long run, on experience—although of a diffuse kind. When an individual, or the wider religious community, decides upon a particular model or image as a means of elucidating experience, pointed or diffuse, they do so as heirs to an established tradition of explanation and a common descriptive vocabulary. . . . The religious teacher is not always privileged with experiences denied to the common run; he may equally be someone with the gift of putting into words what others have sensed. He may have the ability to find metaphors and choose models which illuminate the experience of others, for example, be the first to say that God's presence is like that of a powerful wind. The great divine and the great poet have this in common: both use metaphor to say that which can be said in no other way but which, once said, can be recognized by many. . . .

But it is not necessary to believe that, at one moment in the history of Israel, the model of God as spirit was given, by cosmic disclosure, in a fully elaborated state and immediately embraced by everyone. It is more likely that this was one of many stumbling approximations used to articulate experiences judged to be of God and that, over the years, this particular model was preferred to others by those attempting to describe similar experiences, that it was enriched by the association of wind with breath and gradually became so much a part of the community's descriptive vocabulary that to speak of God as "spirit" became an accustomed manner of speech. In this way, over time, there comes into being a rich assortment of models whose sources may be unknown but which have been gradually selected out by the faithful as being especially adequate to their experience. This accumulation of favoured models, embellished by the glosses of generations, gives the context for Christian reflection and provides the matrix for the descriptive vocabulary which Christians continue to employ in attempts to describe their experience. . . .

So, to explain what it means to Christians to say that God is a fountain of living water, or a vine-keeper, or a rock, or fortress, or king requires an account not merely of fountains, rocks, vines, and kings but of a whole tradition of experiences and of the literary tradition which records and interprets them.

This, incidentally, is an answer to the frequently put question, "on what basis are some of the Christian's models given priority over others?" Choice is not unconditioned; we do not choose the model of God as shepherd over that of God as poultry keeper or cattleman at random. A favoured model continues to be so in virtue of its own applicability certainly, but also because the history of its application makes it already freighted with meaning. To say that God is "king" recalls a whole history of kingship and insubordination recorded in the biblical texts. . . .

From the literary observation we return to the philosophical one, for the touchstone of these chronicles of faith is experience, experiences pointed or diffuse, the experience of individuals and of communities which are believed to be experiences of the activity of a transcendent God. The language used to account for them is metaphorical and qualified, it stands within a tradition of use and is theory-laden, yet in so far as it is grounded on experience it is referential, and it is the theological realist's conviction that that to which it refers, the source of these experiences, is God who is the source and cause of all that is. . . .

It is a commonplace that in the twentieth century we have lost the living sense of the biblical metaphors which our forefathers had. Sometimes it is suggested that this is a consequence of urban life where few have any contact with shepherds and sheep, kings, and vines. This simple view fails to see that the distinctively Christian reading of the metaphors of God as shepherd, or king, or vine-keeper could never be had simply by knowing about sheep, kings, and vines, and forgets that the Scottish crofter of a previous generation who had no experience of grape vines or Temples had no trouble construing Jesus's claim to be the true vine or Temple. Other times, it is said that we have lost this living sense because we no longer read the Bible and there is much in this, yet it is not difficult to imagine that there are some Christians (extreme fundamentalists) who know the text word for word, yet for whom, precisely because they regard it as simply a book of historical fact, much of its allusive significance is lost. If it is true that biblical imagery is lifeless to modern man (and it is not obvious that this is so), this is more likely to be the legacy of historical criticism, of the search for the historical Jesus, and of attempts made by Christians both liberal and conservative to salvage his exact words and acts from the dross of allusion and interpretation with which the gospel writers surrounded them. It is the legacy of a literalism which equates religious truth with historical facts, whatever these might be. Christianity is indeed a religion of the book, but not of a book of this sort of fact. Its sacred texts are chronicles of experience, armouries of metaphor, and purveyors of an interpretive tradition. The sacred literature thus both records the experiences of the past and provides the descriptive language by which any new experience may be interpreted. If this is so, then experience, customarily regarded as the foundation of natural theology, is also the touchstone of the revealed. All the metaphors which we use to speak of God arise from experiences of that which cannot adequately be described, of that which Jews and Christians believe to be "He Who Is." . . .

Though thou with clouds of anger do disguise
Thy face; yet through that maske I know those eyes,
Which, though they turne away sometimes,
They never will despise.

God, in Donne's poem, is beloved and dreaded, horribly absent and compellingly present. This is the beginning and end of theology.

Metaphors Without Meaning

Paul Edwards

To assert that a word is being used metaphorically neither explains its meaning nor ensures that it has any meaning at all. In the next selection, Paul Edwards (1923–2004), who was Professor of Philosophy at Brooklyn College of the City University of New York, distinguishes what he terms "reducible metaphors" from those that are not. He describes a reducible metaphor as one whose meaning can be expressed in literal terms.

From Paul Edwards, "Professor Tillich's Confusions," *Mind* 74 (1965). Reprinted by permission of Oxford University Press.

According to Edwards, only reducible metaphors can be used to make genuine assertions. Thus he believes that descriptions of God using nonreducible metaphors lack meaning.

The concession by an author that he is using a certain word metaphorically is tantamount to admitting that, in a very important sense . . . he does not mean what he says. It does not automatically tell us what he does mean or whether in fact he means anything at all. . . .

Often indeed when words are used metaphorically, the context or certain special conventions make it clear what is asserted. Thus, when a certain historian wrote that "the Monroe Doctrine has always rested on the broad back of the British navy," it would have been pedantic and foolish to comment "what on earth does he mean—doesn't he know that navies don't have backs?" Or if a man, who has been involved in a scandal and is advised to flee his country, rejects the advice and says, "No, I think I'll stay and face the music," it would be absurd to object to his statement on the ground that it is not exactly music that he is going to hear. In these cases we know perfectly well what the authors mean although they are using certain words metaphorically. But we know this because we can eliminate the metaphorical expression, because we can specify the content of the assertion in non-metaphorical language, because we can supply the literal equivalent.

The examples just cited are what I shall call "reducible metaphors." . . . [I]n calling a metaphor "reducible" all I mean is that the truth-claims made by the sentence in which it occurs can be reproduced by one or more sentences all of whose components are used in literal senses. . . .

[M]any . . . fail to notice the difference between metaphors which are reducible in the sense just explained and those which are not. When a sentence contains an irreducible metaphor, it follows at once that the sentence . . . fails to make a genuine assertion. For what has happened is that the sentence has been deprived of the referent it would have had . . . if the expression in question had been used in its literal sense. To say that the metaphor is irreducible is to say in effect that no new referent can be supplied. . . .

It may be said that I have not been fair to . . . [those] who defend themselves by insisting that they are using certain expressions metaphorically or analogously. It may be said that I have emphasized the negative implications of this admission—that the words in question are not used in their literal senses—without doing justice to its positive implications. For, it may be argued, when it is said that a certain word is used "analogously," it *is* implied that the term has a referent, namely a referent which is in some important respect similar to the referent it has when used literally. . . .

But . . . merely saying that a sentence, or any part of it, has meaning does not by itself give it meaning. Such a claim does not assure us that the sentence is intelligible. Similarly the claim that a sentence has an "analogous" referent is a claim and no more—it may be false. If I say, to use an example given by Sidney Hook,[1] that the sea is angry, the word "angry" really has a referent which is analogous to its referent when used literally. I can in this case specify the features of the sea to which I am referring when I call it angry and I can also specify the similarities between these features and the anger of human beings. If, however, I say that Being-itself is angry, I could not independently identify the features of Being-itself to which I am supposedly referring. Nor of course could I specify the similarities between the anger of human beings and the putative anger of Being-itself. My claim that "angry" is used analogously in this sentence in a sense in which this implies that it has a referent would be false or at any rate baseless.

NOTE

1. "The Quest for Being," *The Journal of Philosophy*, 1953, p. 715.

PART 4

MIRACLES AND MYSTICISM

Of Miracles

David Hume

Even if we find no persuasive arguments that prove the existence of God and cannot use words in ordinary ways to describe the attributes of God, can we nevertheless come to some understanding of God through the study of God's works as revealed in miracles?

David Hume, some of whose writings we read previously, thought not. He argued that believing an event to be a miracle, that is, a deity's transgression of a law of nature, is almost surely unreasonable, for the human testimony on which such beliefs are based is highly improbable compared with the evidence in support of the regularity of the world's order. Furthermore, reports are invariably suspect because the witnesses are likely to exhibit foolishness or dishonesty.

In reading this essay, keep in mind that while Hume is best known today as a philosopher, in his own day he was celebrated as a historian, the author of a six-volume *History of England.* His expertise in both fields is evident in this discussion of miracles.

Part I

I flatter myself that I have discovered an argument . . . , which, if just, will, with the wise and learned, be an everlasting check to all kinds of superstitious delusion, and consequently will be useful as long as the world endures. For so long, I presume, will the accounts of miracles and prodigies be found in all history, sacred and profane.

Though experience be our only guide in reasoning concerning matters of fact, it must be acknowledged that this guide is not altogether infallible, but in some cases is apt to lead us into errors. One who in our climate should expect better weather in any week of June than in one of December, would reason justly, and conformably to experience; but it is certain that he may happen, in the event, to find himself mistaken. However, we may observe that, in such a case, he would have no cause to complain of experience, because it commonly informs us beforehand of the uncertainty, by that contrariety of events, which we may learn from a diligent observation. All effects follow not with like certainty from their supposed causes. Some events are found, in all countries and all ages, to have been constantly conjoined together. Other are

From David Hume, *An Enquiry Concerning Human Understanding.*

found to have been more variable, and sometimes to disappoint our expectations; so that, in our reasonings concerning matter of fact, there are all imaginable degrees of assurance, from the highest certainty to the lowest species of moral evidence. . . .

A wise man, therefore, proportions his belief to the evidence. In such conclusions as are founded on an infallible experience, he expects the event with the last degree of assurance, and regards his past experience as a full *proof* of the future existence of that event. In other cases, he proceeds with more caution: He weighs the opposite experiments; he considers which side is supported by the greater number of experiments; to that side he inclines, with doubt and hesitation; and when at last he fixes his judgement, the evidence exceeds not what we properly call *probability*. All probability, then, supposes an opposition of experiments and observations, where the one side is found to overbalance the other, and to produce a degree of evidence, proportioned to the superiority. A hundred instances or experiments on one side, and fifty on another, afford a doubtful expectation of any event; though a hundred uniform experiments, with only one that is contradictory, reasonably beget a pretty strong degree of assurance. In all cases, we must balance the opposite experiments, where they are opposite, and deduct the smaller number from the greater, in order to know the exact force of the superior evidence. . . .

A miracle is a violation of the laws of nature; and as a firm and unalterable experience has established these laws, the proof against a miracle, from the very nature of the fact, is as entire as any argument from experience can possibly be imagined. Why is it more than probable that all men must die; that lead cannot, of itself, remain suspended in the air; that fire consumes wood, and is extinguished by water; unless it be that these events are found agreeable to the laws of nature, and there is required a violation of these laws, or in other words a miracle to prevent them? Nothing is esteemed a miracle if it ever happen in the common course of nature. It is no miracle that a man, seemingly in good health, should die on a sudden: because such a kind of death, though more unusual than any other, has yet been frequently observed to happen. But it is a miracle that a dead man should come to life, because that has never been observed, in any age or country. There must, therefore, be a uniform experience against every miraculous event, otherwise the event would not merit that appellation. And as an uniform experience amounts to a proof, there is here a direct and full *proof*, from the nature of the fact, against the existence of any miracle; nor can such a proof be destroyed, or the miracle rendered credible, but by an opposite proof, which is superior.[1]

The plain consequence is (and it is a general maxim worthy of our attention), "That no testimony is sufficient to establish a miracle, unless the testimony be of such a kind that its falsehood would be more miraculous than the fact which it endeavours to establish: and even in that case there is a mutual destruction of arguments, and the superior only gives us an assurance suitable to that degree of force, which remains, after deducting the inferior." When any one tells me that he saw a dead man restored to life, I immediately consider with myself, whether it be more probable that this person should either deceive or be deceived, or that the fact which he relates should really have happened. I weigh the one miracle against the other; and according to the superiority which I discover, I pronounce my decision, and always reject the greater miracle. If the falsehood of his testimony would be more miraculous than the event which he relates; then, and not till then, can he pretend to command my belief or opinion.

Part II

In the foregoing reasoning we have supposed that the testimony, upon which a miracle is founded, may possibly amount to an entire proof, and that the falsehood of that testimony would be a real prodigy: But it is easy to show, that we have been a great deal too liberal in our concession, and that there never was a miraculous event established on so full an evidence.

For *first,* there is not to be found, in all history, any miracle attested by a sufficient number of men, of such unquestioned good-sense, education, and learning as to secure us against all delusion in themselves; of such undoubted integrity as to place them beyond all suspicion of any design to deceive others; of such credit and reputation in the eyes of mankind as to have a great deal to lose in case of their being detected in any falsehood; and at the same time attesting facts, performed in such a public manner and in so celebrated a part of the world, as to render the detection unavoidable: All which circumstances are requisite to give us a full assurance in the testimony of men.

Secondly. We may observe in human nature a principle, which, if strictly examined, will be found to diminish extremely the assurance which we might, from human testimony, have in any kind of prodigy. The maxim, by which we commonly conduct ourselves in our reasonings, is that the objects of which we have no experience resemble those of which we have; that what we have found to be most usual is always most probable; and that where there is an opposition of arguments, we ought to give the preference to such as are founded on the greatest number of past observations. But though, in proceeding by this rule, we readily reject any fact which is unusual and incredible in an ordinary degree; yet in advancing farther, the mind observes not always the same rule; but when anything is affirmed utterly absurd and miraculous, it rather the more readily admits of such a fact, upon account of that very circumstance which ought to destroy all its authority. The passion of *surprise* and *wonder* arising from miracles, being an agreeable emotion, gives a sensible tendency towards the belief of those events from which it is derived. And this goes so far that even those who cannot enjoy this pleasure immediately, nor can believe those miraculous events of which they are informed, yet love to partake of the satisfaction at second-hand or by rebound, and place a pride and delight in exciting the admiration of others. . . .

The many instances of forged miracles, and prophecies, and supernatural events, which in all ages have either been detected by contrary evidence, or which detect themselves by their absurdity, prove sufficiently the strong propensity of mankind to the extraordinary and the marvellous, and ought reasonably to beget a suspicion against all relations of this kind. This is our natural way of thinking, even with regard to the most common and most credible events. For instance: There is no kind of report which rises so easily, and spreads so quickly, especially in country places and provincial towns, as those concerning marriages; insomuch that two young persons of equal condition never see each other twice, but the whole neighbourhood immediately join them together. The pleasure of telling a piece of news so interesting, of propagating it, and of being the first reporters of it, spreads the intelligence. And this is so well known that no man of sense gives attention to these reports till he find them confirmed by some greater evidence. Do not the same passions, and others still stronger, incline the generality of mankind to believe and report, with the greatest vehemence and assurance, all religious miracles?

Thirdly. It forms a strong presumption against all supernatural and miraculous relations, that they are observed chiefly to abound among ignorant and barbarous nations; or if a civilized people has ever given admission to any of them, that people will be found to have received them from ignorant and barbarous ancestors, who transmitted them with that inviolable sanction and authority, which always attend received opinions. When we peruse the first histories of all nations, we are apt to imagine ourselves transported into some new world, where the whole frame of nature is disjointed, and every element performs its operations in a different manner from what it does at present. Battles, revolutions, pestilence, famine, and death are never the effect of those natural causes which we experience. Prodigies, omens, oracles, judgments quite obscure the few natural events that are intermingled with them. But as the former grow thinner every page, in proportion as we advance nearer the enlightened ages, we soon learn that there is nothing mysterious or supernatural in the case, but that all proceeds from the usual propensity of mankind towards the marvellous, and that, though this inclination may at intervals receive a check from sense and learning, it can never be thoroughly extirpated from human nature. . . .

I may add as a *fourth* reason which diminishes the authority of prodigies, that there is no testimony for any, even those which have not been expressly detected, that is not opposed by an infinite number of witnesses; so that not only the miracle destroys the credit of testimony, but the testimony destroys itself. To make this the better understood, let us consider that, in matters of religion, whatever is different is contrary; and that it is impossible the religions of ancient Rome, of Turkey, of Siam, and of China should, all of them, be established on any solid foundation. Every miracle, therefore, pretended to have been wrought in any of these religions (and all of them abound in miracles), as its direct scope is to establish the particular system to which it is attributed, so has it the same force, though more indirectly, to overthrow every other system. In destroying a rival system, it likewise destroys the credit of those miracles on which that system was established; so that all the prodigies of different religions are to be regarded as contrary facts, and the evidences of these prodigies, whether weak or strong, as opposite to each other. . . .

Upon the whole, then, it appears that no testimony for any kind of miracle has ever amounted to a probability, much less to a proof; and that, even supposing it amounted to a proof, it would be opposed by another proof, derived from the very nature of the fact which it would endeavour to establish. It is experience only which gives authority to human testimony; and it is the same experience which assures us of the laws of nature. When, therefore, these two kinds of experience are contrary, we have nothing to do but subtract the one from the other, and embrace an opinion, either on one side or the other, with that assurance which arises from the reminder. But according to the principle here explained, this subtraction, with regard to all popular religions, amounts to an entire annihilation; and therefore we may establish it as a maxim that no human testimony can have such force as to prove a miracle, and make it a just foundation for any such system of religion.

I beg the limitations here made may be remarked, when I say that a miracle can never be proved, so as to be the foundation of a system of religion. For I own that otherwise there may possibly be miracles, or violations of the usual course of nature, of such a kind as to admit of proof from human testimony; though perhaps it will be impossible to find any such in all the records of history. Thus, suppose, all authors, in all languages agree that from the first of January 1600 there was a total darkness over the whole earth for eight days: Suppose that the tradition of this extraordinary event is still strong and lively among the people: That all travellers, who return from foreign countries, bring us accounts of the same tradition, without the least variation or contradiction. It is evident that our present philosophers, instead of doubting the fact, ought to receive it as certain, and ought to search for the causes whence it might be derived. The decay, corruption, and dissolution of nature, is an event rendered probable by so many analogies, that any phenomenon which seems to have a tendency towards that catastrophe comes within the reach of human testimony, if that testimony be very extensive and uniform.

But suppose that all the historians who treat of England should agree that, on the first of January 1600, Queen Elizabeth died; that both before and after her death she was seen by her physicians and the whole court, as is usual with persons of her rank; that her successor was acknowledged and proclaimed by the parliament; and that, after being interred a month, she again appeared, resumed the throne, and governed England for three years. I must confess that I should be surprised at the concurrence of so many odd circumstances, but should not have the least inclination to believe so miraculous an event. I should not doubt of her pretended death, and of those other public circumstances that followed it: I should only assert it to have been pretended, and that it neither was, nor possibly could be real. You would in vain object to me the difficulty, and almost impossibility of deceiving the world in an affair of such consequence; the wisdom and solid judgement of that renowned queen; with the little or no advantage which she could reap from so poor an artifice: all this might astonish me; but I would still reply that the knavery and folly of men are such common phenomena, that I should rather believe the most extraordinary events to arise from their concurrence, than admit of so signal a violation of the laws of nature.

But should this miracle be ascribed to any new system of religion; men in all ages have been so much imposed on by ridiculous stories of that kind, that this very circumstance would be a full proof of a cheat, and sufficient, with all men of sense, not only to make them reject the fact, but even reject it without farther examination. Though the Being to whom the miracle is ascribed be, in this case, Almighty, it does not upon that account become a whit more probable; since it is impossible for us to know the attributes or actions of such a Being, otherwise than from the experience which we have of his productions in the usual course of nature. This still reduces us to past observation, and obliges us to compare the instances of the violation of truth in the testimony of men, with those of the violation of the laws of nature by miracles, in order to judge which of them is most likely and probable. As the violations of truth are more common in the testimony concerning religious miracles than in that concerning any other matter of fact, this must diminish very much the authority of the former testimony, and make us form a general resolution never to lend any attention to it, with whatever specious pretence it may be covered. . . .

I am the better pleased with the method of reasoning here delivered, as I think it may serve to confound those dangerous friends or disguised enemies to the *Christian Religion,* who have undertaken to defend it by the principles of human reason. Our most holy religion is founded on *Faith,* not on reason; and it is a sure method of exposing it to put it to such a trial as it is by no means fitted to endure. . . .

[T]he *Christian Religion* not only was at first attended with miracles, but even at this day cannot be believed by any reasonable person without one. Mere reason is insufficient to convince us of its veracity: and whoever is moved by *Faith* to assent to it is conscious of a continued miracle in his own person, which subverts all the principles of his understanding, and gives him a determination to believe what is most contrary to custom and experience.

NOTE

1. Sometimes an event may not, *in itself, seem* to be contrary to the laws of nature, and yet, if it were real, it might, by reason of some circumstances, be denominated a miracle; because, in *fact,* it is contrary to these laws. Thus if a person, claiming a divine authority, should command a sick person to be well, a healthful man to fall down dead, the clouds to pour rain, the winds to blow, in short, should order

many natural events, which immediately follow upon his command; these might justly be esteemed miracles, because they are really, in this case, contrary to the laws of nature. For if any suspicion remain, that the event and command concurred by accident, there is no miracle, and a transgression of these laws; because nothing can be more contrary to nature than that the voice or command of a man should have such an influence. A miracle may be accurately defined, *a transgression of a law of nature by a particular volition of the Deity, or by the interposition of some invisible agent.* A miracle may either be discoverable by men or not. This alters not its nature and essence. The raising of a house or ship into the air is a visible miracle. The raising of a feather, when the wind wants ever so little of a force requisite for that purpose, is as real a miracle, though not so sensible with regard to us.

On Miracles

Paul J. Dietl

Paul J. Dietl (1932–1972) was Associate Professor of Philosophy at Syracuse University. In response to Hume's claim that the evidence for a miracle is invariably insufficient, Dietl constructs what he takes to be a counterexample and defends it against possible objections. Whether his attempt to undermine Hume's position succeeds is for you to judge.

Miracle claims, it is generally believed, could not be true because of the very nature of the concept of a miracle. . . . The crucial issue is whether conditions could ever obtain which would justify one in applying "miracle" in any way resembling its standard historical use. I shall argue that there could be such conditions, that we could very well recognize them, so that we do know what miracles are, and therefore that miracle claims are at worst false.

Here as elsewhere Hume anticipated much later opinion, so it is reasonable to begin with his contribution. The difficulty is that in much of what he wrote on the subject Hume seemed to be arguing that the event which is supposed to have been an exception to a law of nature could not happen. The laws themselves are based on "a firm and unalterable experience" and "as a uniform experience amounts to a proof, there is here a direct and full proof,

From *American Philosophical Quarterly* 5 (1968). Reprinted by permission of the journal.

from the nature of the fact, against the existence of any miracle. . . ." In at least one place, though, Hume does admit that bizarre events could occur.

> Suppose all authors, in all languages, agree that from the first of January, 1600, there was total darkness over the whole earth for eight days; suppose that the tradition of this extraordinary event is still strong and lively among the people; that all travelers who return from foreign countries, bring us accounts of the same tradition without the least variation or contradiction—it is evident that our present philosophers, instead of doubting the fact, ought to receive it as certain and ought to search for the causes from whence it might be derived.

Apparently the bizarre cannot be ruled out on the grounds that it is bizarre. Indeed, given the right circumstances, even the second-hand *reports* of bizarre events are immune to the criticism that the claim must be false on the grounds that it goes against laws of nature. Nevertheless, even though it is possible that exceptions to established laws should occur, apparently we are never justified in describing the events as miraculous. One looks in vain for Hume's reasons for this latter thesis. . . .

Before I construct what I think is a counterexample to [the] thesis, I want to call attention to two features of miracles. The first is simply that there is nothing amiss in one person having several miracles he can perform. In the Book of Exodus, for example, Moses is given more than a dozen miracles with which he attempts to melt the Pharaoh's heart. He brings on several miraculous catastrophes and then stops them. The Pharaoh's heart remains hard, and so Moses brings about several more. The second feature of historical accounts to which I wish to call attention is the rather elaborate circumstances in which they may take place. The people who wrote the Old Testament quite obviously had some notion of how to tell the real thing from a fake. Take the story about Elijah at Carmel (I Kings 18). Controversy had arisen whether prayer should be directed to the Lord God of the Jews or to Baal. Elijah took the people to Mr. Carmel and said: "Let them . . . give us two bullocks; and let them choose one bullock for themselves, and cut it to pieces, and lay it on wood." The ministers of Baal took the meat from one animal and made a pile, and Elijah called upon the ministers of Baal to ask Baal to cook their meat. "But there was no voice, nor any that answered. And they leaped upon the altar which was made. And it came to pass at noon, that Elijah mocked them, and said, Cry aloud; for he is a god; either he is talking, or he is pursuing, or he is on a journey, or peradventure he sleepeth, and must be awakened. And they cried aloud, and cut themselves after their manner with knives and lances, till the blood gushed out upon them." But all this to no avail. Then Elijah stepped up and said: "Fill four barrels with water, and pour it on the burnt sacrifice, and on the wood." And he said, Do it the second time. And they did it the second time. And he said, Do it the third time. And they did it the third time. And the water ran round about the altar; and he filled the trench also with water. Then he called on God for fire and "Then the fire of the Lord fell, and consumed the burnt sacrifice, and the wood, and the stones, and the dust, and licked up the water that was in the trench."

We are given here, first of all, about as artificial a setting as any laboratory affords. The account also involves a random sampling of the material to be set on fire, a prediction that one pile will burn up and one will not, a prediction when the fire will start, and twelve barrels of precaution against earthly independent variables. There is obviously nothing wrong with applying somewhat sophisticated experimental design to miracles.

Now for the example. Its essential ingredients are simply a bundle of miracles no larger than Moses had and a randomizing technique just a little more complicated than Elijah's. Let us assume that a local prophet opens, or appears with the help of God to open, the mighty Schuylkill River. Two possibilities arise. The first is that the prophet does not figure causally in the natural explanation but that he notices a cue in the physical situation which indicates natural sufficient conditions. This is especially tempting because he might not be consciously aware of the cue and so might himself honestly believe in the miracle. This sort of explanation can be ruled out, however, if he is required to do miracles at random. Say he allows non-believers to pick twelve miracles and number them. Which one he will do will be determined by the roll of a pair of unloaded dice, and the hour of the day at which it will occur will be determined by a second roll. Rolling the dice without his prediction could establish that the dice had no efficacy and using the dice to randomize the predictions proves that the prophet does not predict on the basis of a natural cue.

This randomizing also establishes that there is a cause at work other than would have operated if the prophet had not been there. But perhaps there is still some law covering the events. To see how vastly different this would be from an ordinary scientific law, however, one has only to realize that there would be no new scientific department on a par with, say, physics or chemistry, which included such laws. This would be a department which dealt with all the other sciences and had no laws of its own, except that when this prophet spoke, all laws, or any one of an indefinitely large number, are broken.

Odd, you might say, but not yet miraculous. Such a prophet might require a new metascientific department, but we still have not been forced to admit supernatural explanation. But this is so only because we have not yet looked at the *explanans* in these supposed scientific explanations. What could possibly be the natural conditions which this new department will ascertain to be necessary and sufficient for the unexpected events?

If the prophet prayed we might think that the prayer was connected in some curious way with the exceptions. But what if he does not pray? What if he just requests? Could it be the sounds of his words which have the extraordinary effect? Then let him predict in different languages. Might we mention language-independent brain processes as the sufficient conditions? Let him predict what will happen later when he is asleep—even drugged, or dead.

But surely it has become obvious that there is nothing which could be pinned down as the independent variable in a scientific explanation; for no conceivable candidate is necessary. The prophet asks God to do miracle No. 4 at midnight and then goes to sleep. Or he asks God to do whatever miracle turns up at whatever hour turns up and then dies. We are dealing with requests and answers—that is, thoughts, and thoughts not as psychological occurrences but as understood.

No natural law will do because only vehicles of thought could function as the natural *explanans* and no such vehicle is necessary. There would have to be one law connecting the acoustics of English with general law-breaking, another for French, and so on indefinitely—and when the prophet asks that whatever miracle turns upon the dice be performed and then goes to sleep before the dice are thrown, there just is not anything left except his request as understood.

What is needed here is not a law but an understanding which can grasp the request and then bring it about that a physical law be broken. But an understanding physical-law breaker is a supernatural being, and that is why if a new department is set up it will not be with the science faculties at all. It will be a department of religion.

I should like here to attempt to forestall some foreseeable objections. The first one is that even if what I have said is all true, that still does not prove that there ever has been a miracle. Of course I agree with this objection. The sophistication of the experimental design of the Elijah account may be the progressive result of centuries of anxious parents trying to convince doubting children of false stories. The point is that the concept of miracle allowed such sophistication. What they *meant* to say was ascertainable, or at least they meant to *say* that it was ascertainable, in principle. Whether or not their claims were actually true is another question.

A second criticism shows a hankering after a simple a priori disproof. Believing in miracles, it will be said, inevitably involves believing in the suspension of some physical law. We can always avoid this by doubting the data. Hallucinations do not rest on the suspension of such laws. The trouble with this sort of objection to the miraculous is that it can quickly be pushed to the point at which the very distinction between hallucinatory and veridical experiences breaks down. Faith, it has been said, can move mountains. Suppose that someone moved the Poconos to northern Minnesota. Thousands saw them flying through the air. Old maps showed them in Pennsylvania where we all remembered them to have been, and a thriving ski industry grows up where there had only been the exhausted open mines of the Mesabi Range. If that is a hallucination then everything is.

A third criticism is that the account of physical laws in this paper is hopelessly over-simple and crude. I agree. One must show, however, that the crudity and simplicity make a difference to the general thesis about miracles. As far as I can see, the introduction of statistics and probability, or the ideal nature of some or all laws, or of accounts of laws as models or inference tickets or as the designation of patterns we find intelligible, makes no difference. . . .

A fourth rejoinder to my arguments might be that even if I have proved that there could be conditions which, if you experienced them, would justify your belief in a miracle, and even though we might have reason to believe second-hand reports of bizarre phenomena, we could still never have better reasons to believe a second-hand miracle claim than to doubt the veracity of the man reporting it; and surely this is really all that Hume . . . set out to prove. In answer let me say first that if you had good reason to believe that what the report describes as happening really did happen—and happened as the reports describe, viz., with randomizing and predictions—then it seems to me that you have good reasons to believe in supernatural intervention as an explanation of the events. But in any case remember Exodus once more. Moses had brought several miraculous plagues, then called them off, then brought down a new batch. Now say that you happened into Egypt during the second batch of catastrophes. Could you rule out a priori the possibility that there had been an earlier set? I think not.

Fifthly, one might object that even if I have shown that there could be evidence for miracles and even in the sense in which "miracle" implies supernatural intervention, this is still of no religious significance unless "miracle" also implies *divine* intervention. Miracles, as defined here, in short, do not tend to prove the existence of God. My only answer is that to prove the existence of a being who deserves some of the predicates which "God" normally gets would be to go some way toward proving the existence of *God.* The question whether the comprehensibility of miracle claims strengthens the position of the theologians or whether the paucity of latter-day evidence has the opposite effect, I leave to the theologians and more militant atheists. . . .

I conclude that "miracle" is perfectly meaningful. To call an event a miracle is to claim that it is the result of supernatural intervention into the natural course of events. We could know that the supernatural agent was intelligent, but little else (though when and for whom he did miracles would be evidence about his character).

Mysticism

WILLIAM JAMES

Another possible avenue to understanding God lies through mystical experiences in which persons report direct contact with the divine.

The best-known treatment of mysticism is found in Willliam James's book *The Varieties of Religious Experience.* James, who earned a medical degree but never practiced and was the brother of the novelist Henry James, became Professor of Philosophy and Psychology at Harvard University. He relied on his knowledge of both philosophy and psychology in his detailed survey and analysis of mystical experiences. He concluded that they were authoritative for the individuals who underwent them but not for others. Nevertheless, he believed that these experiences offered valuable insights into the range of human consciousness.

Lectures XVI and XVII

Mysticism

Over and over again in these lectures I have raised points and left them open and unfinished until we should have come to the subject of Mysticism. Some of you, I fear, may have smiled as you noted my reiterated postponements. But now the hour has come when mysticism must be faced in good earnest, and those broken threads wound up together. One may say truly, I think, that personal religious experience has its root and centre in mystical states of consciousness; so for us, who in these lectures are treating personal experience as the exclusive subject of our study, such states of consciousness ought to form the vital chapter from which the other chapters get their light. Whether my treatment of mystical states will shed more light or darkness, I do not know, for my own constitution shuts me out from their enjoyment almost entirely, and I can speak of them only at second hand. But though forced to look upon the subject so externally, I will be as objective and receptive as I can; and I think I shall at least succeed in convincing you of the reality of the states in question, and of the paramount importance of their function.

From *The Varieties of Religious Experience.*

First of all, then, I ask, What does the expression "mystical states of consciousness" mean? How do we part off mystical states from other states?

The words "mysticism" and "mystical" are often used as terms of mere reproach, to throw at any opinion which we regard as vague and vast and sentimental, and without a base in either facts or logic. For some writers a "mystic" is any person who believes in thought-transference, or spirit-return. Employed in this way the word has little value: there are too many less ambiguous synonyms. So, to keep it useful by restricting it, I will . . . simply propose to you four marks which, when an experience has them, may justify us in calling it mystical for the purpose of the present lectures. In this way we shall save verbal disputation, and the recriminations that generally go therewith.

1. *Ineffability.*—The handiest of the marks by which I classify a state of mind as mystical is negative. The subject of it immediately says that it defies expression, that no adequate report of its contents can be given in words. It follows from this that its quality must be directly experienced; it cannot be imparted or transferred to others. In this peculiarity mystical states are more like states of feeling than like states of intellect. No one can make clear to another who has never had a certain feeling, in what the quality or worth of it consists. One must have musical ears to know the value of a symphony; one must have been in love one's self to understand a lover's state of mind. Lacking the heart or ear, we cannot interpret the musician or the lover justly, and are even likely to consider him weak-minded or absurd. The mystic finds that most of us accord to his experiences an equally incompetent treatment.
2. *Noetic quality.*—Although so similar to states of feeling, mystical states seem to those who experience them to be also states of knowledge. They are states of insight into depths of truth unplumbed by the discursive intellect. They are illuminations, revelations, full of significance and importance, all inarticulate though they remain; and as a rule they carry with them a curious sense of authority for after-time.

   These two characters will entitle any state to be called mystical, in the sense in which I use the word. Two other qualities are less sharply marked, but are usually found. These are:
3. *Transiency.*—Mystical states cannot be sustained for long. Except in rare instances, half an hour, or at most an hour or two, seems to be the limit beyond which they fade into the light of common day. Often, when faded, their quality can but imperfectly be reproduced in memory; but when they recur it is recognized; and from one recurrence to another it is susceptible of continuous development in what is felt as inner richness and importance.
4. *Passivity.*—Although the oncoming of mystical states may be facilitated by preliminary voluntary operations, as by fixing the attention, or going through certain bodily performances, or in other ways which

> manuals of mysticism prescribe; yet when the characteristic sort of consciousness once has set in, the mystic feels as if his own will were in abeyance, and indeed sometimes as if he were grasped and held by a superior power. This latter peculiarity connects mystical states with certain definite phenomena of secondary or alternative personality, such as prophetic speech, automatic writing, or the mediumistic trance. When these latter conditions are well pronounced, however, there may be no recollection whatever of the phenomenon, and it may have no significance for the subject's usual inner life, to which, as it were, it makes a mere interruption. Mystical states, strictly so called, are never merely interruptive. Some memory of their content always remains, and a profound sense of their importance. They modify the inner life of the subject between the times of their recurrence. Sharp divisions in this region are, however, difficult to make, and we find all sorts of gradations and mixtures.

These four characteristics are sufficient to mark out a group of states of consciousness peculiar enough to deserve a special name and to call for careful study. . . .

In the Christian church there have always been mystics. Although many of them have been viewed with suspicion, some have gained favor in the eyes of the authorities. The experiences of these have been treated as precedents, and a codified system of mystical theology has been based upon them, in which everything legitimate finds its place. The basis of the system is "orison" or meditation, the methodical elevation of the soul towards God. . . .

The first thing to be aimed at in orison is the mind's detachment from outer sensations, for these interfere with its concentration upon ideal things. Such manuals as Saint Ignatius's *Spiritual Exercises* recommend the disciple to expel sensation by a graduated series of efforts to imagine holy scenes. The acme of this kind of discipline would be a semi-hallucinatory monoideism—an imaginary figure of Christ, for example, coming fully to occupy the mind. Sensorial images of this sort, whether literal or symbolic, play an enormous part in mysticism. But in certain cases imagery may fall away entirely, and in the very highest raptures it tends to do so. The state of consciousness becomes then insusceptible of any verbal description. Mystical teachers are unanimous as to this. Saint John of the Cross, for instance, one of the best of them, thus describes the condition called the "union of love," which, he says, is reached by "dark contemplation." In this the Deity compenetrates the soul, but in such a hidden way that the soul

> finds no terms, no means, no comparison whereby to render the sublimity of the wisdom and the delicacy of the spiritual feeling with which she is filled. . . . We receive this mystical knowledge of God clothed in none of the kinds of images, in none of the sensible representations, which our mind makes use of in other circumstances. Accordingly in this knowledge,

since the senses and the imagination are not employed, we get neither form nor impression, nor can we give any account or furnish any likeness, although the mysterious and sweet-tasting wisdom comes home so clearly to the inmost parts of our soul. Fancy a man seeing a certain kind of thing for the first time in his life. He can understand it, use and enjoy it, but he cannot apply a name to it, nor communicate any idea of it, even though all the while it be a mere thing of sense. How much greater will be his powerlessness when it goes beyond the senses! This is the peculiarity of the divine language. The more infused, intimate, spiritual, and supersensible it is, the more does it exceed the senses, both inner and outer, and impose silence upon them. . . . The soul then feels as if placed in a vast and profound solitude, to which no created thing has access, in an immense and boundless desert, desert the more delicious the more solitary it is. There, in this abyss of wisdom, the soul grows by what it drinks in from the well-springs of the comprehension of love, . . . and recognizes, however sublime and learned may be the terms we employ, how utterly vile, insignificant, and improper they are, when we seek to discourse of divine things by their means.[1]

I cannot pretend to detail to you the sundry stages of the Christian mystical life. Our time would not suffice, for one thing; and moreover, I confess that the subdivisions and names which we find in the Catholic books seem to me to represent nothing objectively distinct. So many men, so many minds: I imagine that these experiences can be as infinitely varied as are the idiosyncrasies of individuals.

The cognitive aspects of them, their value in the way of revelation, is what we are directly concerned with, and it is easy to show by citation how strong an impression they leave of being revelations of new depths of truth. Saint Teresa is the expert of experts in describing such conditions, so I will turn immediately to what she says of one of the highest of them, the "orison of union."

"In the orison of union," says Saint Teresa, "the soul is fully awake as regards God, but wholly asleep as regards things of this world and in respect of herself. During the short time the union lasts, she is as it were deprived of every feeling, and even if she would, she could not think of any single thing. Thus she needs to employ no artifice in order to arrest the use of her understanding: it remains so stricken with inactivity that she neither knows what she loves, nor in what manner she loves, nor what she wills. In short, she is utterly dead to the things of the world and lives solely in God. . . . I do not even know whether in this state she has enough life left to breathe. It seems to me she has not; or at least that if she does breathe, she is unaware of it. Her intellect would fain understand something of what is going on within her, but it has so little force now that it can act in no way whatsoever. So a person who falls into a deep faint appears as if dead. . . .

"Thus does God, when he raises a soul to union with himself, suspend the natural action of all her faculties. She neither sees, hears, nor understands, so long as she is united with God. But this time is always short, and it seems even shorter than it is. God establishes himself in the interior of this soul in such a way, that when she returns to herself, it is wholly impossible for her to doubt that she has been in God, and God in her. This truth remains so strongly impressed on her that, even though many years should pass without the condition returning, she can neither forget the favor she received, nor doubt of its reality. If you, nevertheless, ask how it is possible that the soul can see and understand that she has been in God, since during the union she has neither sight nor understanding, I reply that she does not see it then, but that she sees it clearly later, after she has returned to herself, not by any vision, but by a certitude which abides with her and which God alone can give her. I knew a person who was ignorant of the truth that God's mode of being in everything must be either by presence, by power, or by essence, but who, after having received the grace of which I am speaking, believed this truth in the most unshakable manner. So much so that, having consulted a half-learned man who was as ignorant on this point as she had been before she was enlightened, when he replied that God is in us only by 'grace,' she disbelieved his reply, so sure she was of the true answer; and when she came to ask wiser doctors, they confirmed her in her belief, which much consoled her. . . .

"But how, you will repeat, *can* one have such certainty in respect to what one does not see? This question, I am powerless to answer. These are secrets of God's omnipotence which it does not appertain to me to penetrate. All that I know is that I tell the truth; and I shall never believe that any soul who does not possess this certainty has ever been really united to God."[2]

The kinds of truth communicable in mystical ways, whether these be sensible or supersensible, are various. Some of them relate to this world—visions of the future, the reading of hearts, the sudden understanding of texts, the knowledge of distant events, for example; but the most important revelations are theological or metaphysical.

Saint Ignatius confessed one day to Father Laynez that a single hour of meditation at Manresa had taught him more truths about heavenly things than all the teachings of all the doctors put together could have taught him. . . . One day in orison, on the steps of the choir of the Dominican church, he saw in a distinct manner the plan of divine wisdom in the creation of the world. On another occasion, during a procession, his spirit was ravished in God, and it was given him to contemplate, in a form and images fitted to the weak understanding of a dweller on the earth, the deep mystery of the holy Trinity. This last vision flooded his heart with such sweetness, that the mere memory of it in after times made him shed abundant tears.[3]

Similarly with Saint Teresa. "One day, being in orison," she writes, "it was granted me to perceive in one instant how all things are seen and contained

> in God. I did not perceive them in their proper form, and nevertheless the view I had of them was of a sovereign clearness, and has remained vividly impressed upon my soul. It is one of the most signal of all the graces which the Lord has granted me. . . . The view was so subtile and delicate that the understanding cannot grasp it."[4]

She goes on to tell how it was as if the Deity were an enormous and sovereignly limpid diamond, in which all our actions were contained in such a way that their full sinfulness appeared evident as never before. On another day, she relates, while she was reciting the Athanasian Creed,

> Our Lord made me comprehend in what way it is that one God can be in three Persons. He made me see it so clearly that I remained as extremely surprised as I was comforted, . . . and now, when I think of the holy Trinity, or hear It spoken of, I understand how the three adorable Persons form only one God and I experience an unspeakable happiness.

On still another occasion, it was given to Saint Teresa to see and understand in what wise the Mother of God had been assumed into her place in Heaven.[5]

The deliciousness of some of these states seems to be beyond anything known in ordinary consciousness. It evidently involves organic sensibilities, for it is spoken of as something too extreme to be borne, and as verging on bodily pain.[6] But it is too subtle and piercing a delight for ordinary words to denote. God's touches, the wounds of his spear, references to ebriety and to nuptial union have to figure in the phraseology by which it is shadowed forth. Intellect and senses both swoon away in these highest states of ecstasy. "If our understanding comprehends," says Saint Teresa, "it is in a mode which remains unknown to it, and it can understand nothing of what it comprehends. For my own part, I do not believe that it does comprehend, because, as I said, it does not understand itself to do so. I confess that it is all a mystery in which I am lost."[7] In the condition called *raptus* or ravishment by theologians, breathing and circulation are so depressed that it is a question among the doctors whether the soul be or be not temporarily dissevered from the body. One must read Saint Teresa's descriptions and the very exact distinctions which she makes, to persuade one's self that one is dealing, not with imaginary experiences, but with phenomena which, however rare, follow perfectly definite psychological types.

To the medical mind these ecstasies signify nothing but suggested and imitated hypnoid states, on an intellectual basis of superstition, and a corporeal one of degeneration and hysteria. Undoubtedly these pathological conditions have existed in many and possibly in all the cases, but that fact tells us nothing about the value for knowledge of the consciousness which they induce. To pass a spiritual judgment upon these states, we must not content ourselves with superficial medical talk, but inquire into their fruits for life.

Their fruits appear to have been various. Stupefaction, for one thing, seems not to have been altogether absent as a result. You may remember the helplessness in the kitchen and schoolroom of poor Margaret Mary Alacoque. Many other ecstatics would have perished but for the care taken of them by admiring followers. The "other-worldliness" encouraged by the mystical consciousness makes this over-abstraction from practical life peculiarly liable to befall mystics in whom the character is naturally passive and the intellect feeble; but in natively strong minds and characters we find quite opposite results. The great Spanish mystics, who carried the habit of ecstasy as far as it has often been carried, appear for the most part to have shown indomitable spirit and energy, and all the more so for the trances in which they indulged.

Saint Ignatius was a mystic, but his mysticism made him assuredly one of the most powerfully practical human engines that ever lived. Saint John of the Cross, writing of the intuitions and "touches" by which God reaches the substance of the soul, tells us that

> They enrich it marvelously. A single one of them may be sufficient to abolish at a stroke certain imperfections of which the soul during its whole life had vainly tried to rid itself, and to leave it adorned with virtues and loaded with supernatural gifts. A single one of these intoxicating consolations may reward it for all the labors undergone in its life—even were they numberless. Invested with an invincible courage, filled with an impassioned desire to suffer for its God, the soul then is seized with a strange torment—that of not being allowed to suffer enough.[8]

Saint Teresa is as emphatic, and much more detailed. . . . Where in literature is a more evidently veracious account of the formation of a new centre of spiritual energy, than is given in her description of the effects of certain ecstasies which in departing leave the soul upon a higher level of emotional excitement?

> Often, infirm and wrought upon with dreadful pains before the ecstasy, the soul emerges from it full of health and admirably disposed for action . . . as if God had willed that the body itself, already obedient to the soul's desires, should share in the soul's happiness. . . . The soul after such a favor is animated with a degree of courage so great that if at that moment its body should be torn to pieces for the cause of God, it would feel nothing but the liveliest comfort. Then it is that promises and heroic resolutions spring up in profusion in us, soaring desires, horror of the world, and the clear perception of our proper nothingness. . . . What empire is comparable to that of a soul who, from this sublime summit to which God has raised her, sees all the things of earth beneath her feet, and is captivated by no one of them? How ashamed she is of her former attachments! How amazed at her blindness! What lively pity she feels for those whom she recognizes still shrouded in

> the darkness! . . . She groans at having ever been sensitive to points of honor, at the illusion that made her ever see as honor what the world calls by that name. Now she sees in this name nothing more than an immense lie of which the world remains a victim. She discovers, in the new light from above, that in genuine honor there is nothing spurious, that to be faithful to this honor is to give our respect to what deserves to be respected really, and to consider as nothing, or as less than nothing, whatsoever perishes and is not agreeable to God. . . . She laughs when she sees grave persons, persons of orison, caring for points of honor for which she now feels profoundest contempt. It is suitable to the dignity of their rank to act thus, they pretend, and it makes them more useful to others. But she knows that in despising the dignity of their rank for the pure love of God they would do more good in a single day than they would effect in ten years by preserving it. . . . She laughs at herself that there should ever have been a time in her life when she made any case of money, when she ever desired it. . . . Oh! if human beings might only agree together to regard it as so much useless mud, what harmony would then reign in the world! . . . With what friendship we would all treat each other if our interest in honor and in money could but disappear from earth! For my own part, I feel as if it would be a remedy for all our ills.[9]

Mystical conditions may, therefore, render the soul more energetic in the lines which their inspiration favors. But this could be reckoned an advantage only in case the inspiration were a true one. If the inspiration were erroneous, the energy would be all the more mistaken and misbegotten. . . . Do mystical states establish the truth of those theological affections in which the saintly life has its root?

In spite of their repudiation of articulate self-description, mystical states in general assert a pretty distinct theoretic drift. It is possible to give the outcome of the majority of them in terms that point in definite philosophical directions. One of these directions is optimism, and the other is monism. We pass into mystical states from out of ordinary consciousness as from a less into a more, as from a smallness into a vastness, and at the same time as from an unrest to a rest. We feel them as reconciling, unifying states. They appeal to the yes-function more than to the no-function in us. In them the unlimited absorbs the limits and peacefully closes the account. Their very denial of every adjective you may propose as applicable to the ultimate truth—He, the Self, the Atman, is to be described by "No! no!" only, say the Upanishads—though it seems on the surface to be a no-function, is a denial made on behalf of a deeper yes. Whoso calls the Absolute anything in particular, or says that it is *this,* seems implicitly to shut it off from being *that*—it is as if he lessened it. So we deny the "this," negating the negation which it seems to us to imply, in the interests of the higher affirmative attitude by which we are possessed. . . .

I have now sketched with extreme brevity and insufficiency, but as fairly as I am able in the time allowed, the general traits of the mystic range of consciousness. *It is on the whole pantheistic and optimistic, or at least the opposite of pessimistic. It is anti-naturalistic, and harmonizes best with twice-bornness and so-called other-worldly states of mind.*

My next task is to inquire whether we can invoke it as authoritative. Does it furnish any *warrant for the truth* of the twice-bornness and supernaturality and pantheism which it favors? I must give my answer to this question as concisely as I can.

In brief my answer is this—and I will divide it into three parts:

(1) Mystical states, when well developed, usually are, and have the right to be, absolutely authoritative over the individuals to whom they come.
(2) No authority emanates from them which should make it a duty for those who stand outside of them to accept their revelations uncritically.
(3) They break down the authority of the non-mystical or rationalistic consciousness, based upon the understanding and the senses alone. They show it to be only one kind of consciousness. They open out the possibility of other orders of truth, in which, so far as anything in us vitally responds to them, we may freely continue to have faith.

I will take up these points one by one.

1

As a matter of psychological fact, mystical states of a well-pronounced and emphatic sort *are* usually authoritative over those who have them. They have been "there," and know. It is vain for rationalism to grumble about this. If the mystical truth that comes to a man proves to be a force that he can live by, what mandate have we of the majority to order him to live in another way? We can throw him into a prison or a madhouse, but we cannot change his mind—we commonly attach it only the more stubbornly to its beliefs. It mocks our utmost efforts, as a matter of fact, and in point of logic it absolutely escapes our jurisdiction. Our own more "rational" beliefs are based on evidence exactly similar in nature to that which mystics quote for theirs. Our senses, namely, have assured us of certain states of fact; but mystical experiences are as direct perceptions of fact for those who have them as any sensations ever were for us. The records show that even though the five senses be in abeyance in them, they are absolutely sensational in their epistemological quality, if I may be pardoned the barbarous expression—that is, they are face to face presentations of what seems immediately to exist.

The mystic is, in short, *invulnerable*, and must be left, whether we relish it or not, in undisturbed enjoyment of his creed. Faith, says Tolstoy, is that by which men live. And faith-state and mystic state are practically convertible terms.

2

But I now proceed to add that mystics have no right to claim that we ought to accept the deliverance of their peculiar experiences, if we are ourselves outsiders and feel no private call thereto. The utmost they can ever ask of us in this life is to admit that they establish a presumption. They form a consensus and have an unequivocal outcome; and it would be odd, mystics might say, if such a unanimous type of experience should prove to be altogether wrong. At bottom, however, this would only be an appeal to numbers, like the appeal of rationalism the other way; and the appeal to numbers has no logical force. If we acknowledge it, it is for "suggestive," not for logical reasons: we follow the majority because to do so suits our life.

But even this presumption from the unanimity of mystics is far from being strong. In characterizing mystic states as pantheistic, optimistic, etc., I am afraid I over-simplified the truth. I did so for expository reasons, and to keep the closer to the classic mystical tradition. The classic religious mysticism, it now must be confessed, is only a "privileged case." It is an *extract,* kept true to type by the selection of the fittest specimens and their preservation in "schools." It is carved out from a much larger mass; and if we take the larger mass as seriously as religious mysticism has historically taken itself, we find that the supposed unanimity largely disappears. To begin with, even religious mysticism itself, the kind that accumulates traditions and makes schools, is much less unanimous than I have allowed. It has been both ascetic and antinomianly self-indulgent within the Christian church. It is dualistic in Sankhya, and monistic in Vedanta philosophy. I called it pantheistic; but the great Spanish mystics are anything but pantheists. They are with few exceptions non-metaphysical minds, for whom "the category of personality" is absolute. The "union" of man with God is for them much more like an occasional miracle than like an original identity. How different again, apart from the happiness common to all, is the mysticism of Walt Whitman . . . and other naturalistic pantheists, from the more distinctively Christian sort. The fact is that the mystical feeling of enlargement, union, and emancipation has no specific intellectual content whatever of its own. It is capable of forming matrimonial alliances with material furnished by the most diverse philosophies and theologies, provided only they can find a place in their framework for its peculiar emotional mood. We have no right, therefore, to invoke its prestige as distinctively in favor of any special belief, such as that in absolute idealism, or in the absolute monistic identity, or in the absolute goodness, of the world. It is only relatively in favor of all these things—it passes out of common human consciousness in the direction in which they lie.

So much for religious mysticism proper. But more remains to be told, for religious mysticism is only one half of mysticism. The other half has no accumulated traditions except those which the textbooks on insanity supply.

Open any one of these, and you will find abundant cases in which "mystical ideas" are cited as characteristic symptoms of enfeebled or deluded states of mind. In delusional insanity, paranoia, as they sometimes call it, we may have a *diabolical* mysticism, a sort of religious mysticism turned upside down. The same sense of ineffable importance in the smallest events, the same texts and words coming with new meanings, the same voices and visions and leadings and missions, the same controlling by extraneous powers; only this time the emotion is pessimistic: instead of consolations we have desolations; the meanings are dreadful; and the powers are enemies to life. It is evident that from the point of view of their psychological mechanism, the classic mysticism and these lower mysticisms spring from the same mental level, from that great subliminal or transmarginal region of which science is beginning to admit the existence, but of which so little is really known. That region contains every kind of matter: "seraph and snake" abide there side by side. To come from thence is no infallible credential. What comes must be sifted and tested, and run the gauntlet of confrontation with the total context of experience, just like what comes from the outer world of sense. Its value must be ascertained by empirical methods, so long as we are not mystics ourselves.

Once more, then, I repeat that non-mystics are under no obligation to acknowledge in mystical states a superior authority conferred on them by their intrinsic nature.

3

Yet, I repeat once more, the existence of mystical states absolutely overthrows the pretension of non-mystical states to be the sole and ultimate dictators of what we may believe. As a rule, mystical states merely add a supersensuous meaning to the ordinary outward data of consciousness. They are excitements like the emotions of love or ambition, gifts to our spirit by means of which facts already objectively before us fall into a new expressiveness and make a new connexion with our active life. They do not contradict these facts as such, or deny anything that our senses have immediately seized. It is the rationalistic critic rather who plays the part of denier in the controversy, and his denials have no strength, for there never can be a state of facts to which new meaning may not truthfully be added, provided the mind ascend to a more enveloping point of view. It must always remain an open question whether mystical states may not possibly be such superior points of view, windows through which the mind looks out upon a more extensive and inclusive world. The difference of the views seen from the different mystical windows need not prevent us from entertaining this supposition. The wider world would in that case prove to have a mixed constitution like that of this world, that is all. It would have its celestial and its infernal regions, its tempting and its saving moments, its valid experiences and its counterfeit ones, just as our world has them; but it would be a wider world all the same. We should have to use its experiences by selecting and subordinating and substituting just as is our custom in this ordinary naturalistic world; we should be liable to error just as we are now; yet the counting in of that wider world of meanings, and the serious dealing with it, might, in spite of all the perplexity, be indispensable stages in our approach to the final fullness of the truth.

In this shape, I think, we have to leave the subject. Mystical states indeed wield no authority due simply to their being mystical states. But the higher ones among them point in directions to which the religious sentiments even of non-mystical men incline. They tell of the supremacy of the ideal, of vastness, of union, of safety, and of rest. They offer us *hypotheses,* hypotheses which we may voluntarily ignore, but which as thinkers we cannot possibly upset. The supernaturalism and optimism to which they would persuade us may, interpreted in one way or another, be after all the truest of insights into the meaning of this life.

NOTES

1. Saint John of the Cross: *The Dark Night of the Soul,* book ii, ch. xvii, in *Vie et Oeuvres,* 3me édition, Paris, 1893, iii, 428–432. Chapter xi of book ii of Saint John's *Ascent of Carmel* is devoted to showing the harmfulness for the mystical life of the use of sensible imagery.
2. *The Interior Castle,* Fifth Abode, ch. i, in *Oeuvres,* translated by Bouix, iii, 421–424.
3. Bartoli-Michel: *Histoire de S. Ignace de Loyola,* i. 34–36. . . .
4. *Vie,* pp. 581, 582.
5. Loc. cit., p. 574.
6. Saint Teresa discriminates between pain in which the body has a part and pure spiritual pain (*Interior Castle,* 6th Abode, ch. xi). As for the bodily part in these celestial joys, she speaks of it as "penetrating to the marrow of the bones, whilst earthly pleasures affect only the surface of the senses. I think," she adds, "that this is a just description, and I cannot make it better." Ibid., 5th Abode, ch. i.
7. *Vie,* p. 198.
8. *Oeuvres,* ii, 320.
9. *Vie,* pp. 229, 200, 232, 233–234, 243.

Perceiving God

William Alston

William Alston is Professor Emeritus of Philosophy at Syracuse University. He views mystical experience as a form of perception that, assuming God exists, enables us to interact with God. Does such experience offer knowledge of God? Alston concludes that, as in the case of perceptual claims, we should accept them unless we have sufficient reason to the contrary.

I

I pick out what I am calling "experience of God" by the fact that the subject takes the experience (or would take it if the question arose) to be a direct awareness of God. Here is a clear example cited in William James's *The Varieties of Religious Experience.*

> (1) . . . all at once I . . . felt the presence of God—I tell of the thing just as I was conscious of it—as if his goodness and his power were penetrating me altogether. Then, slowly, the ecstasy left my heart; that is, I felt that God had withdrawn the communion which he had granted. . . . I asked myself if it were possible that Moses on Sinai could have had a more intimate communication with God. I think it well to add that in this ecstasy of mine God had neither form, color, odor, nor taste; moreover, that the feeling of his presence was accompanied by no determinate localization. . . . But the more I seek words to express this intimate intercourse, the more I feel the impossibility of describing the thing by any of our usual images. At bottom the expression most apt to render what I felt is this: God was present, though invisible; he fell under no one of my senses, yet my consciousness perceived him.

Note that I do not restrict "experience of God" to cases in which it is really God of whom the subject is aware. The term, as I use it, ranges over all experiences that the subject *takes* to have this status. Thus the general category would be more exactly termed "*supposed* experience of God," where calling it "supposed" does not prejudice the question of whether it is genuine or not. However, I will generally omit this qualification. Note too that my category

Reprinted by permission of the author.

of "experience of God" is much narrower than "religious experience," which covers a diverse and ill-defined multitude of experiences.

In restricting myself to *direct* awareness of God I exclude cases in which one takes oneself to be aware of God through the beauties of nature, the words of the Bible or of a sermon, or other natural phenomena. For example:

> (2) I feel him [God] in the sunshine or rain; and awe mingled with a delicious restfulness most nearly describes my feelings.

My reason for concentrating on direct experience of God, where there is no other object of experience in or through which God is experienced, is that these experiences are the ones that are most plausibly regarded as *presentations* of God to the individual, in somewhat the way in which physical objects are presented to sense perception, as I will shortly make explicit.

Within this territory I will range over both lay and professional examples, both ordinary people living in the world and monastics who more or less devote their lives to attaining union with God. The category also embraces both focal and background experiences; though in order to discern the structure of the phenomenon we are well advised to concentrate on its more intense forms.

There is also the distinction between experiences with and without sensory content. In (1) the subject explicitly denies that the experience was sensory in character. Here is an example that does involve sensory content.

> (3) During the night . . . I awoke and looking out of my window saw what I took to be a luminous star which gradually came nearer, and appeared as a soft slightly blurred white light. I was seized with violent trembling, but had no fear. I knew that what I felt was great awe. This was followed by a sense of overwhelming love coming to me, and going out from me, then of great compassion from this Outer Presence. (Cited in T. Beardsworth, *A Sense of Presence.*)

In this discussion I will concentrate on nonsensory experiences. The main reason for this choice is that since God is purely spiritual, a nonsensory experience has a greater chance of presenting Him as He is than any sensory experience. If God appears to us as bearing a certain shape or as speaking in a certain tone of voice, that is a long way from representing Him as He is in Himself. I shall refer to nonsensory experience of God as "mystical experience," and the form of perception of God that involves that experience as "mystical perception." I use these terms with trepidation, for I do not want them to carry connotations of the merging of the individual subject into the One, or any of the other salient features of what we may term "classical mystical experience." (See William James.) They are to be understood simply as shorthand for "supposed nonsensory experience (perception) of God."

Many people find it incredible, unintelligible, or incoherent to suppose that there could be something that counts as *presentation,* that contrasts with abstract thought in the way sense perception does, but is devoid of sensory content. However, so far as I see, this simply evinces lack of speculative imagination or perhaps a mindless parochialism. Why should we suppose that the possibilities of experiential givenness, for human beings or otherwise, are exhausted by the powers of *our* five senses? Surely it is possible, to start with the most obvious point, that other creatures should possess a sensitivity to other physical stimuli that play a role in their functioning analogous to that played by our five senses in our lives. And, to push the matter a bit further, why can't we also envisage presentations that do not stem from the activity of any physical sense organs, as is apparently the case with mystical perception?

II

As the title indicates, I will be advocating a "perceptual model" of mystical experience. To explain what I mean by that, I must first say something about sense perception, since even if we suppose, as I do, that perception is not restricted to its sensory form, still that is the form with which we are far and away most familiar, and it is by generalizing from sense perception that we acquire a wider concept of perception.

As I see the matter, at the heart of perception (sensory or otherwise) is a phenomenon variously termed *presentation, appearance,* or *givenness.* Something is presented to one's experience (awareness) *as* so-and-so, as blue, as acrid, as a house, as Susie's house, or whatever. I take this phenomenon of *presentation,* to be essentially independent of conceptualization, belief, or judgment. It is possible, in principle, for this book to visually present itself to me as blue even if I do not *take* it to be blue, *think* of it as blue, *conceptualize* it as blue, *judge* it to be blue, or anything else of the sort. No doubt, in mature human perception presentation is intimately intertwined with conceptualization and belief, but presentation does not consist in anything like that. The best way to see this is to contrast actually seeing the book with thinking about the book, or making judgments about it, in its absence. What is involved in the former case but not in the latter that makes the difference? It can't be anything of a conceptual or judgmental order, for anything of that sort can be present in the latter case when the book is not seen. Reflection on this question leads me to conclude that what makes the difference is that when I see the book it is *presented* to my awareness; it occupies a place in my visual field. This crucial notion of presentation cannot be analyzed; it can be conveyed only by helping another to identify instances of it in experience, as I have just done.

On the view of perception I favor, the "Theory of Appearing," perceiving X simply consists in X's appearing to one, or being presented to one, as so-and-so. That's all there is to it, as far as what perception is, in contrast to its causes and effects. Where X is an external physical object like a book, to perceive the book is just for the book to appear to one in a certain way.

In saying that a direct awareness that does not essentially involve conceptualization and judgment is at the heart of perception, I am *not* denying that a person's conceptual scheme, beliefs, cognitive readinesses, and so on, can affect the *way* an object presents itself to the subject, what it presents itself *as.* Things do look and sound differently to us after we are familiar with them, have the details sorted out, can smoothly put everything in its place without effort. My house presents a different appearance to me now after long habituation than it did the first time I walked in. Whereas Stravinsky's *The Rite of Spring* sounded like a formless cacophony the first time I heard it, it now presents itself to me as a complex interweaving of themes. In saying this I am not going back on my assertion that X's presenting itself to one's awareness as P is not the same as S's *taking* S to be P. The latter involves the application of the concept of P to X, but the former does not, even though the character of the presentation can be influenced by one's conceptual repertoire and one's beliefs. But though my conceptual capacities and tendencies can affect the *way* objects appear to me, they have no power over *what object it is* that looks (sounds . . .) that way. When I look at my living room, the same objects present themselves to my visual awareness as when I first saw it. It is essential not to confuse *what* appears with what it appears *as.*

Even if to perceive X is simply for X to appear to one in a certain way, there can be further necessary conditions for someone to perceive X, for there can be further conditions for X's appearing to one. First, and this is just spelling out one thing that is involved in X's appearing to one, X must exist. I can't (really) perceive a tree unless the tree is there to be perceived. Second, it seems to be necessary for X's appearing to me (for my perceiving X) that X make an important *causal* contribution to my current experience. If there is a thick concrete wall between me and a certain house, thereby preventing light reflected from the house from striking my retina, then it couldn't be that that house is visually presented to me. I will assume such a causal condition in this discussion. Third, I will also assume a doxastic condition, that perceiving X at least tends to give rise to beliefs about X. This is much more questionable than the causal condition, but in any event we are concerned here with cases in which perception does give rise to beliefs about what is perceived.

III

Now we are ready to turn to the application of the perceptual model to mystical experience. In this essay I will not try to show that mystical experience (even sometimes) constitutes (genuine) perception of God. Remembering the necessary conditions of perception just mentioned, this would involve showing that God exists and that He makes the right kind of causal contribution to the experiences in question. What I will undertake here is the following. (1) I will argue that mystical experience is the right sort of experience to constitute a genuine perception of God if the other requirements are met. (2) I will argue that there is no bar in principle to these other requirements being satisfied if God does exist. This adds up to a defence of the thesis that it is quite possible that human beings do sometimes perceive God if God is "there" to be perceived. In other words, the thesis defended is that if God exists, then mystical experience is quite properly thought of as mystical perception.

If mystical experience is not construed perceptually, how can it be understood? The most common alternative is to think of it as made up of purely subjective feelings and sensations, to which is added an *explanation* according to which the experience is due to God. A recent example of this approach is the important book, *Religious Experience,* by Wayne Proudfoot. Proudfoot goes so far as to identify the "noetic" quality that James and many others have noted in mystical experience with the supposition by the subject that the experience must be given a theological rather than a naturalistic explanation.

It is not difficult to show that the people I have quoted and countless others take their mystical experiences to be perceptual, to involve what I have been calling a direct presentation of God to their awareness, though they do not typically use this terminology. They take their experience to contrast with thinking about God, calling up mental images, entertaining propositions, reasoning, or remembering something about God, just as seeing a tree contrasts with these other cognitive relations to it. They take it that God has been *presented* or *given* to their consciousness in generically the same way as that in which objects in the environment are *presented* to one's consciousness in sense perception. They emphasize the difference between presence to consciousness and absence. Saint Teresa says that God "presents Himself to the soul by a knowledge brighter than the sun." Again she contrasts a "consciousness of the presence of God" with "spiritual feelings and effects of great love and faith of which we become conscious," and with "the fresh resolutions which we make with such deep emotion." Although she takes it that the latter is a "great favour" that "comes from God," still it does not amount to God's actually being present. Another writer who clearly makes this distinction is Angela of Foligno.

> (4) At times God comes into the soul without being called; and He instills into her fire, love, and sometimes sweetness; and the soul believes this comes from God, and delights therein. But she does not yet know, or see, that He dwells in her; she perceives His grace, in which she delights. . . . And beyond this the soul receives the gift of seeing God. God says to her "Behold Me!" and the soul sees Him dwelling within her. She sees Him more clearly than one man sees another. For the eyes of the soul behold a plenitude of

> which I cannot speak: a plenitude which is not bodily but spiritual, of which I can say nothing. And the soul rejoices in that sight with an ineffable joy; and this is the manifest and certain sign that God indeed dwells in her.

Thus it is quite clear that the people cited, who are representative of a vast throng, take their experiences to be structured the way, on my view, perception generally is structured. In fact, it may be thought that it is too easy to show this, too much like shooting fish in a barrel. For haven't I chosen my cases on the basis of the subjects' taking themselves to be directly aware of God? They are tailor-made for my purpose. I must plead guilty to picking cases that conform to my construal. But the significant point is that it is so easy to find such cases and that they are so numerous, given the fact that most mystical experiences are not reported at all. As pointed out earlier, I do not wish to deny that there are other forms of "religious experience" and even other forms of experience of God, such as the indirect experiences of God mentioned earlier. My contention is that there is a large body of experiences of God that are perceptual in character, and that they have played a prominent role in Christianity and other religions.

I don't know what could be said against this position except to claim that people who report such experiences are all confused about the character of their experience. Let's consider the following charge.

> These people were all having strongly affective experiences that, because of their theological assumptions and preoccupations, they confused with a direct experience of God. Thus (1) was in an unusual state of exaltation that he interpreted as the power and goodness of God penetrating him. In (4) the "ineffable joy" that Angela says to be "the manifest and certain sign that God indeed dwells in her" is simply a state of feeling that her theological convictions lead her to *interpret* as an awareness of the presence of God. Another possibility is that the person is suddenly seized with an extremely strong conviction of the presence of God, together with sensations and feelings that seem to confirm it. Thus Teresa says that she "had a most distinct feeling that He was always on my right hand, a witness of all I did."

It is conceivable that one should suppose that a purely affective experience or a strongly held conviction should involve the experiential presentation of God when it doesn't, especially if there is a strong need or longing for the latter. But, even if an individual's account of the character of his/her own experience is not infallible, it must certainly be taken seriously. Who is in a better position to determine whether S is having an experience as of something's presenting itself to S as divine than S? We would need strong reasons to override the subject's confident report of the character of her experience. And where could we find such reasons? I suspect that most people who put forward these alternative diagnoses do so because they have general philosophical reasons for supposing either that God does not exist or that no human being could perceive Him, and they fail to recognize the difference between a *phenomenological* account of object presentation, and the occurrence of veridical perception. In any event, once we get straight about all this, I cannot see any reason for doubting the subjects' account of the character of their experience, whatever reasons there may be for doubting that God Himself does in fact appear to them.

If these cases are to conform to our account of perceptual consciousness, they must seem to involve God's appearing to the person as being and/or doing so-and-so. And our subjects do tell us this. God is experienced as good, powerful, loving, compassionate, and as exhibiting "plenitude." He is experienced as speaking, forgiving, comforting, and strengthening. And yet how can these be ways in which God presents Himself to experience? Power and goodness are complex dispositional properties or bases thereof, dispositions to act in various ways in various situations. And to forgive or to strengthen someone is to carry out a certain intention. None of this can be read off the phenomenal surface of experience. This is quite different from something's presenting itself to one's sensory consciousness as red, round, sweet, loud, or pungent. Isn't it rather that the subject is *interpreting*, or *taking*, what she is aware of as being good or powerful, as forgiving or strengthening? But then what is God *experienced* as being or doing? We seem to still lack an answer.

But that charge misconstrues the situation. The basic point is that we have different sorts of concepts for specifying how something looks, sounds, tastes, or otherwise perceptually appears. There are *phenomenal* concepts that specify the felt qualities that objects present themselves as bearing—round, red, acrid, etc. But there are also *comparative* concepts that specify a mode of appearance in terms of the sort of objective thing that typically appears in that way. In reporting sensory appearances we typically use comparative concepts whenever the appearances involve something more complex than one or two basic sensory qualities. Thus we say, "She looks like Susie," "It tastes like a pineapple," "It sounds like Bach." In these cases there undoubtedly is some complex pattern of simple sensory qualities, but it is beyond our powers to analyze the appearance into its simple components. We are thrown back on the use of comparative concepts to report how something looks, sounds, or tastes. And so it is in our religious cases. Our subjects tell us that God presented Himself to their experience as a good, powerful, compassionate, forgiving being could be expected to appear. In reporting modes of divine appearance in this way, they are proceeding just as we typically do in reporting modes of sensory appearance.

IV

Now for the task of showing that if God exists there is no bar to the (not infrequent) satisfaction of the causal and doxastic conditions by the subject of mystical experience. First consider the doxastic condition. It is clear that mystical experience typically gives rise to beliefs about God. To be sure, those who perceive God as loving, powerful, and so on, usually believed that God is that way long before they had that experience. But the same is true of sense perception. My 50,000th look at my house doesn't generate any important new beliefs. I knew just what my house looks like long before that 50,000th look. That is why I put the doxastic condition in terms of a "tendency" to engender beliefs about what is perceived. However, in both sensory and mystical cases some kinds of new beliefs will almost always be produced. Even if I don't see anything new about my house on that umpteenth look, I at least learn that it is blue and tall *today.* When what we perceive is a person the new beliefs will be more interesting. On my 50,000th look at my wife I not only learn that she is still beautiful today, but I learn what she is doing right now. And similarly with God. One who perceives God will thereby come to learn that God is strengthening her or comforting her *then,* or telling her so-and-so *then.* There is, if anything, even less of a problem with the doxastic condition here.

The causal condition calls for a bit more discussion. First, there is no reason to think it impossible that God, if He exists, does causally contribute to the occurrence of mystical experiences. Quite the contrary. If God exists and things are as supposed by classical theism, God causally contributes to everything that occurs. That follows just from the fact that nothing would exist without the creative and sustaining activity of God. And with respect to many things, including mystical experiences, God's causality presumably extends farther than that, though the precise story will vary from one theology to another. To fix our thoughts let us say that it is possible (and remember that we are concerned here only with whether this causal condition *can* be satisfied) that at least some of these experiences occur only because God intentionally presents Himself to the subject's awareness as so-and-so.

It may well be pointed out that not every causal contributor to an experience is perceived via that experience. When I see a house, light waves and goings on in my nervous system form parts of the causal chain leading to the visual experience, but I don't see them. Thus it is not enough that God figures somehow or other in the causes of the experience; He would have to make the right kind of causal contribution. But what is the right kind? There is no one answer to this question for all perceptual modalities. The causal contribution a seen object makes to the production of visual experience (transmitting light to the retina) is different from the causal contribution a felt object makes to tactile experience, and different from the causal contribution a heard object makes to aural experience. And how do we tell, for each modality, what the crucial causal contribution is? We have no a priori insight into this. We cannot abstract from everything we have learned from perception and still ascertain how an object must be causally related to a visual experience in order to be what is seen in that experience. Quite the contrary. We learn this by first determining in many cases what is *seen,* felt, or heard in those cases, and then looking for some causal contribution that is distinctive of the object perceived. That is, we have first to be able to determine *what is seen;* then on the basis of that we determine how an entity has to be causally related to the visual experience to be seen therein. We have no resources for doing it the other way around, first determining the specific causal requirement and then picking out objects seen on the basis of what satisfies that requirement.

The application of this to divine perception is as follows. We will have a chance of determining how God has to be causally related to an experience in order to be perceived only if we can first determine in a number of cases that it is God who is being perceived. And since that is so, we can't rule out the possibility of perceiving God on the grounds that God can't be related to the relevant experience in the right way. For unless we do sometimes perceive God we are unable to determine what the right way is. Hence, so long as God does make some causal contribution to the relevant experiences, we can't rule out God's being perceived in those experiences on the grounds that He isn't causally related to them in the right way. To be sure, by the same token we cannot show that we do perceive God by showing that God is causally related to the experiences in the right way. But showing that is no part of our purpose here. It will be sufficient to show that, so far as we can see, there is no reason to doubt that it is possible that God should satisfy an appropriate causal requirement for being perceived in at least some of the cases in which people take themselves to be directly aware of Him.

V

If my arguments have been sound, we are justified in thinking of the experience of God as a mode of perception in the same generic sense of the term as sense perception. And if God exists, there is no reason to suppose that this perception is not sometimes veridical rather than delusory. I will conclude by mentioning a couple of respects in which this conclusion is of importance.

First, the main function of the experience of God in theistic religion is that it constitutes a mode, an avenue of communion between God and us. It makes it possible for us to enter into personal interaction with God. And if it involves our directly perceiving God in a sense generically the same as that in which we perceive each other, this can be personal intercourse in a literal sense, rather than some stripped down, analogical or symbolic reconception thereof. We can have the real thing, not a metaphorical substitute.

Second, there are bearings on the cognitive significance of this mode of experience. If it is perceptual in character, and if it is possible that the other requirements should be satisfied for it to be a genuine perception of God, then the question of whether it is genuine is just a question of whether it is what it seems to its subject to be. Thus the question of genuineness arises here in just the same way as for sense perception, making possible a uniform treatment of the epistemology of the two modes of experience. This is not to beg the question of the genuineness of mystical perception. It could still be true that sense perception is the real thing, whereas mystical perception is not. And it could still be true that sense perception provides knowledge about its objects, whereas mystical perception yields no such results. The point is only that the *problems,* both as to the status of the perception and as to the epistemic status of perceptual beliefs, arise in the same form for both. This contrasts with the situation on the widespread view that "experience of God" is to be construed as purely subjective feelings and sensations to which supernaturalistic causal hypotheses are added. On that view the issues concerning the two modes of experience will look very different, unless one is misguided enough to treat sense perception in the same fashion. For on this subjectivist construal the subject is faced with the task of justifying a causal hypothesis before he can warrantedly claim to be perceiving God. Whereas if the experience is given a perceptual construal from the start, we will at least have to take seriously the view that a claim to be perceiving God is prima facie acceptable on its own merits, pending any sufficient reasons to the contrary.[1]

NOTE

1. See my *Perceiving God* (Cornell University Press, 1991) for a development of this last idea.

Perceiving God: A Critique

William L. Rowe

William Alston contends that we should accept the reports of those who claim to perceive God unless we have sufficient reason to the contrary. William L. Rowe, Professor Emeritus of Philosophy at Purdue University, disagrees. He argues that we do not know what would count as a sufficient reason for deciding that someone's religious experiences are delusive because God's ways are not understandable. Furthermore, such experiences are embedded in a plurality of religious traditions. How can we accept all these conflicting reports of different divine presences?

From *Philosophy of Religion: An Introduction,* Second Edition, by Rowe, 1993.

Experiences in which one senses the immediate presence of a divine being may include some visual and auditory content. . . . But other experiences of the divine do not contain sensory content. Here is a report of one such experience.

> all at once I . . . felt the presence of God—I tell of the thing just as I was conscious of it—as if his goodness and his power were penetrating me altogether. . . . Then, slowly, the ecstasy left my heart; that is, I felt that God had withdrawn the communion which he had granted, . . . I think it well to add that in this ecstasy of mine God had neither form, color, odor, nor taste; moreover, that the feeling of his presence was accompanied with no determinate localization. . . . At bottom the expression most apt to render what I felt is this: God was present, though invisible; he fell under no one of my senses, yet my consciousness perceived him.[1]

The question before us is whether the existence of such experiences as these provide us (or at least those who have them) with a *good reason* to believe that God (or some sort of divine being) exists. Initially, one might be tempted to think that they do not on the grounds that reports of religious experiences may be nothing more than reports of certain *feelings* (joy, ecstasy, etc.) that now and then come over some people who already believe in God and are perhaps all too eager to feel themselves singled out for a special appearance by the divine. Against such an objection, however, we should note that a number of those who report having ordinary religious experiences are keenly aware of the difference between experiences of one's own feelings (joy, sadness, peacefulness, etc.) and experiences that involve a sense of the presence of some other being. They are also aware of the fact that wanting a certain experience may lead one to mistake some other experience for it. Unless we have some very strong reason not to, we should take their reports as sincere, careful efforts to express the contents of their experiences. And those reports are not primarily reports of subjective psychological states; they are reports of encounters with what is taken to be an independently existing divine being.

But still, even if we acknowledge that the experiences cannot fairly be described as reports of nothing more than one's feelings, why should we think they are veridical perceptions of what they seem to be? Macbeth's experience of a dagger isn't fairly described as Macbeth having a certain feeling; it is an experience which purports to be of some object apart from himself. But the experience was a hallucination. Why shouldn't we think that experiences in which one senses the immediate presence of God (or some divine figure) are all hallucinatory? The answer given by those who think religious experiences constitute a good reason to believe God exists is that we should dismiss them as delusory only if we have some special reason to think that they are delusory. And in the absence of such special reasons, the rational thing to do is to view them as probably veridical. It will help us to look at this line of argument in some detail.

If a person has an experience which he or she takes to be of some particular object, is the fact that he or she has that experience a *good reason* to think that particular object exists? Our first reaction is to say no. We are inclined to say no because we all can think of experiences which seem to be of some particular object, when in fact no such object exists. Consider two examples. You walk into a room and have a visual experience that you take to be a perception of a red wall. Unknown to you there are red lights shining on the white wall you are looking at, thus making it appear red. Here you are experiencing an actually existing wall that happens to be white, but there is no red wall for you to perceive. How then can the fact that you have an experience which clearly seems to be a perception of a red wall be a good reason for thinking that there actually is a red wall? Again, unknown to you someone puts a powerful hallucinogenic drug in your coffee resulting in your having an experience which you take to be a perception of a large, coiled snake in front of the chair in which you are sitting. Unlike our first example (there is a wall, it's just not red), there is no snake at all that you are seeing. Others in the room who have no reason to deceive you assure you that there is no snake in the room. Your experience of the snake is entirely delusory. So, how can the fact that you have an experience which clearly seems to be a perception of a coiled snake be a good reason for thinking that the coiled snake exists?

For an experience to be a good reason for believing a claim to be true is for that experience to rationally justify you in believing that claim *provided that you have no reasons for thinking otherwise.* Reasons for thinking otherwise are either (a) reasons for thinking that claim to be false or (b) reasons for thinking that, given the circumstances in which it occurs, the experience is not sufficiently indicative of the truth of the claim. Consider again our second example. Since we know that actually existing physical things (including snakes) would be seen by the other people in the room if they are really there, you come to have a Type A reason for thinking otherwise. That is, when others who are in a position to see it say there is no snake, you come to have some reason for thinking that the snake does not actually exist. In our first example, if we suppose that all you come to know is that red lights are shining on the wall and that such lights would make the wall appear red even if it is white, then our reason to think otherwise is not itself a reason to think that there is no red wall. It is a Type B reason. What it tells us is that, whether the wall is red or not, in the circumstances that exist (red lights are shining on the wall) your experience is not sufficiently indicative of its being true that the wall is red. For you now know that you could be having that experience even if the wall is white.

What we've seen is that we must distinguish an experience being a good reason for a claim from that experience justifying that claim *no matter what else we know.* Those who think that having an experience that one takes to be of some particular object is a *good reason* to think that particular object exists recognize that we may know or come to know Type A or Type B reasons to think otherwise. All they insist is that in the *absence* of such defeating reasons, one who has such an experience is rationally justified in believing that the particular object exists. One prominent philosopher has argued that what is at stake here is a basic principle of rationality, a principle he calls the Principle of Credulity.[2] According to this principle, if a person has an experience which seems to be of x, then, unless there is some reason to think otherwise, it is rational to believe that x exists. If we grant this principle, it would seem arbitrary to refuse to apply it to religious experiences, experiences in which one senses the immediate presence of the divine. So, unless we have some reason to question these experiences, it would seem rational to believe that God or some divine being exists. . . .

[W]e should note two difficulties in the view that the Principle of Credulity renders it rational for us to accept ordinary religious experiences as veridical. The first difficulty is that the Principle of Credulity presupposes that we have some understanding of what reasons there might be for questioning our experiences and some way of telling whether or not these reasons are present. Consider again our example of your experience which you take to be a perception of a large, coiled snake. Like other physical objects that make up the world we perceive by our five senses, snakes are public objects that are observable by others who satisfy certain conditions. That is, we can predict that people with good eyesight will see a snake (if one is there) provided there is good light and they look in the right direction. It is because physical objects are subject to such predictions that we can understand what reasons there might be for questioning an experience which seems to be a perception of a snake and can often tell whether such reasons are present. In the case of divine beings, however, matters are quite different. Presumably, it is entirely up to God whether to reveal his presence to some human being. If God does so, he may or may not disclose himself to others who are in a similar situation. What this means is that it is quite difficult to discover reasons for thinking that someone's ordinary religious experience is delusive. But since the Principle of Credulity supposes that we understand what reasons there might be to question an experience, some doubt exists as to whether the principle can be fairly applied to experiences whose subjects take them to be perceptions of the presence of a divine being. Of course, since God is a perfectly good being, we can from that fact alone discover some reason for thinking an experience that purports to be of God is delusive. For suppose someone reports an experience which he takes to be a perception of God commanding him to kill all those who sincerely seek to live a moral and holy life. We can be confident that God did not reveal that message and thus have a reason for thinking the experience to be delusive. Some doubt remains, however, whether there is an adequate range of reasons for questioning religious experiences to warrant much confidence in the application of the Principle of Credulity to them. Thus, once we come to learn that a presumption of the Principle of Credulity is not adequately satisfied by religious experiences, it is at least doubtful that the principle justifies us in holding religious experiences to be genuine perceptions of reality.

Suppose someone who has not had religious experiences examines various reports of those who have enjoyed them. One salient feature of these experiences is that most of them are embedded in one or another of a plurality of religious traditions, traditions that cannot all be true. For example, Saul's experience on the road to Damascus is embedded in Christianity as an experience of Jesus as a divine being. No such experience is a part of Judaism or Islam. Indeed, within these religious traditions Jesus is not a divine being at all. Experiences of Allah in Islam or God in Judaism are not experiences of a divine being who is a trinity of persons, as is the Christian God. In Hinduism one may have an experience of Krishna, but not Jesus, as a divine being. Moreover, Hinduism also includes a strain in which the divine presence, Brahman, is experienced as something other than a person. It seems unlikely that all of these religious experiences can be veridical perceptions of a divine presence. These experiences are embedded in and support rival religious traditions that contradict one another. Realizing this, what view should be held by a person who has not had any religious experiences? If the Principle of Credulity works for any, it will work equally well for all. But they can hardly all be veridical perceptions of a divine presence. Faced with this situation, it would appear that the rational thing for this person to do is not to accept any one of these religious experiences as veridical. So, even if we agree to continue applying the Principle of Credulity to religious experiences, it may well be that the person who has not had a religious experience is rationally justified in not accepting such experiences as veridical perceptions of reality. For the fact that these experiences are embedded in and support conflicting religious traditions may provide that person with a reason for not accepting any particular religious experience as veridical.

NOTES

1. Quoted in William James, *The Varieties of Religious Experience* (New York: The Modern Library, 1936), pp. 67–68.
2. Richard Swinburne, *The Existence of God* (Oxford: The Clarendon Press, 1979), p. 254.

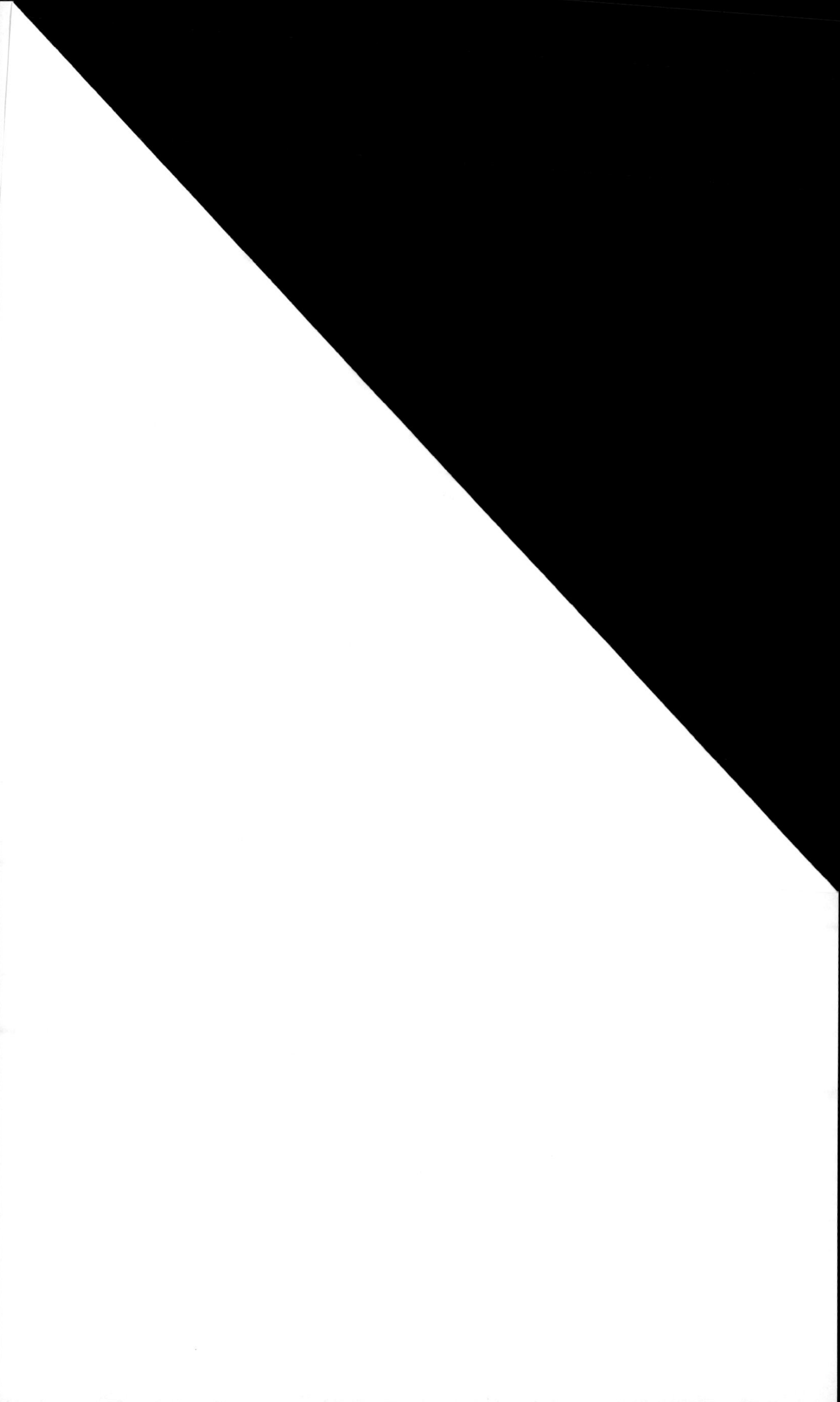

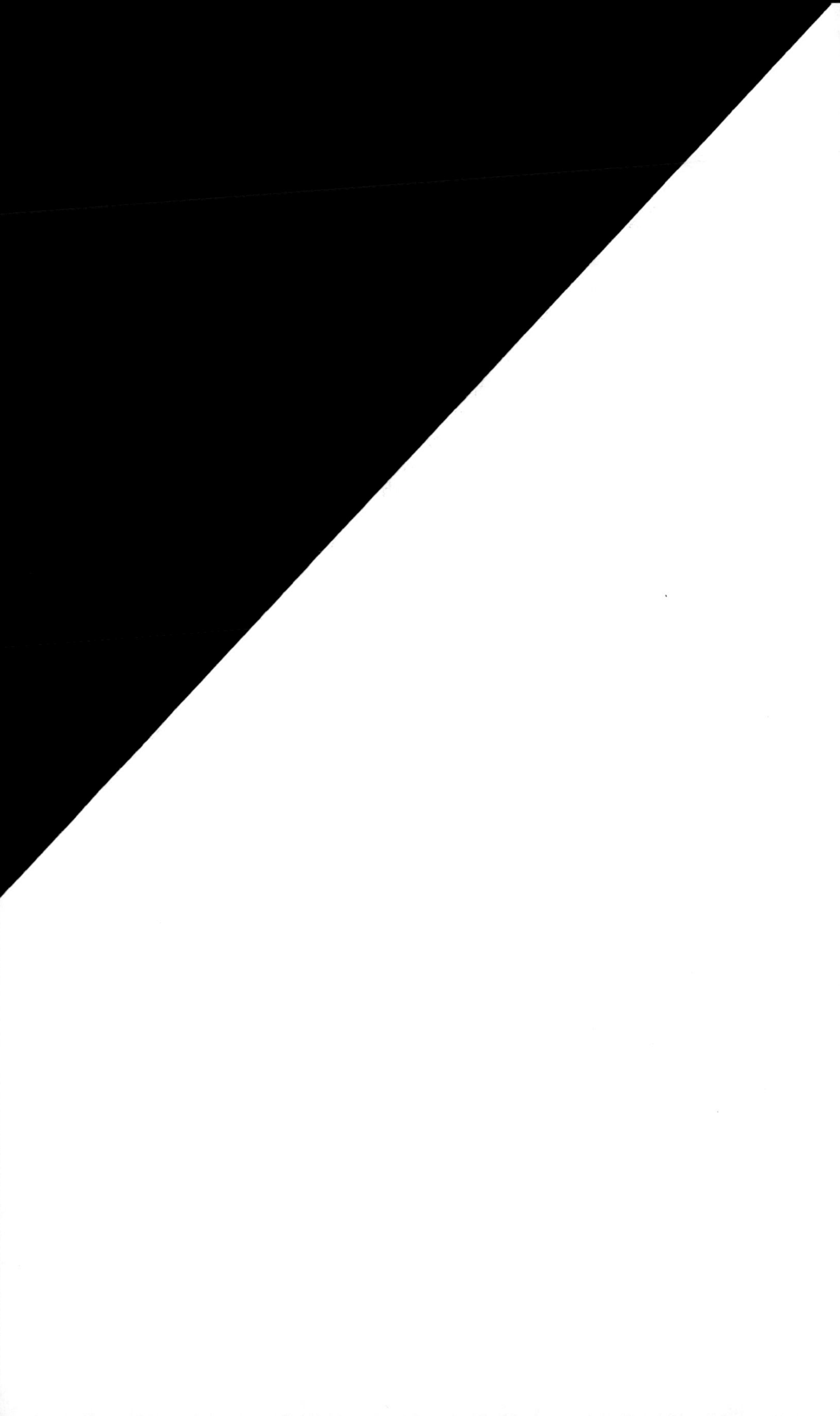

The Wager

Blaise Pascal

If philosophical arguments are inadequate to prove the existence of God and the evidence from miracles and mystical experience is not convincing, might other reasons suffice to justify theism? Blaise Pascal (1623–1662), the French mathematician, physicist, and philosopher, offered an argument that belief in God is useful even if not supported by the available evidence.

According to Pascal's celebrated "wager," if we believe in God, and God exists, then we attain heavenly bliss; if we believe in God, and God doesn't exist, little is lost. On the other hand, if we don't believe in God, and God does exist, then we are doomed to the torments of damnation; if we don't believe in God, and God doesn't exist, little is gained. So belief is the safest strategy.

Do you agree with Pascal's conclusion that by believing in God you have nothing to lose?

If there is a God, he is infinitely beyond our comprehension, since, having neither parts nor limits, he bears no relation to ourselves. We are therefore incapable of knowing either what he is, or if he is. That being so, who will dare to undertake a resolution of this question? It cannot be us, who bear no relationship to him.

Who will then blame the Christians for being unable to provide a rational basis for their belief, they who profess a religion for which they cannot provide a rational basis? They declare that it is a folly (1 Cor. 1: 18) in laying it before the world: and then you complain that they do not prove it! If they did prove it, they would not be keeping their word. It is by the lack of proof that they do not lack sense. "Yes, but although that excuses those who offer their religion as it is, and that takes away the blame from them of producing it without a rational basis, it does not excuse those who accept it."

Let us therefore examine this point, and say: God is, or is not. But towards which side will we lean? Reason cannot decide anything. There is an infinite chaos separating us. At the far end of this infinite distance a game is being played and the coin will come down heads or tails. How will you

From Blaise Pascal, *Pensées,* trans. Honor Levi. Reprinted by permission of Oxford University Press.

wager? Reason cannot make you choose one way or the other, reason cannot make you defend either of the two choices.

So do not accuse those who have made a choice of being wrong, for you know nothing about it! "No, but I will blame them not for having made this choice, but for having made any choice. For, though the one who chooses heads and the other one are equally wrong, they are both wrong. The right thing is not to wager at all."

Yes, but you have to wager. It is not up to you, you are already committed. Which then will you choose? Let us see. Since you have to choose, let us see which interests you the least. You have two things to lose: the truth and the good, and two things to stake: your reason and will, your knowledge and beatitude; and your nature has two things to avoid: error and wretchedness. Your reason is not hurt more by choosing one rather than the other, since you do have to make the choice. That is one point disposed of. But your beatitude? Let us weigh up the gain and the loss by calling heads that God exists. Let us assess the two cases: if you win, you win everything; if you lose, you lose nothing. Wager that he exists then, without hesitating! "This is wonderful. Yes, I must wager. But perhaps I am betting too much." Let us see. Since there is an equal chance of gain and loss, if you won only two lives instead of one, you could still put on a bet. But if there were three lives to win, you would have to play (since you must necessarily play), and you would be unwise, once forced to play, not to chance your life to win three in a game where there is an equal chance of losing and winning. But there is an eternity of life and happiness. And that being so, even though there were an infinite number of chances of which only one were in your favour, you would still be right to wager one in order to win two, and you would be acting wrongly, since you are obliged to play, by refusing to stake one life against three in a game where out of an infinite number of chances there is one in your favour, if there were an infinitely happy infinity of life to be won. But here there is an infinitely happy infinity of life to be won, one chance of winning against a finite number of chances of losing, and what you are staking is finite. That removes all choice: wherever there is infinity and where there is no infinity of chances of losing against one of winning, there is no scope for wavering, you have to chance everything. And thus, as you are forced to gamble, you have to have discarded reason if you cling on to your life, rather than risk it for the infinite prize which is just as likely to happen as the loss of nothingness.

For it is no good saying that it is uncertain if you will win, that it is certain you are taking a risk, and that the infinite distance between the *certainty* of what you are risking and the *uncertainty* of whether you win makes the finite good of what you are certainly risking equal to the uncertainty of the infinite. It does not work like that. Every gambler takes a certain risk for an uncertain gain; nevertheless he certainly risks the finite uncertainty in order to win a finite gain, without sinning against reason. There is no infinite distance between this certainty of what is being risked and the uncertainty of what might be gained: that is untrue. There is, indeed, an infinite distance between the certainty of winning and the certainty of losing. But the uncertainty of winning is proportional to the certainty of the risk, according to the chances of winning or losing. And hence, if there are as many chances on one side as on the other, the odds are even, and then the certainty of what you risk is equal to the uncertainty of winning. It is very far from being infinitely distant from it. So our argument is infinitely strong, when the finite is at stake in a game where there are equal chances of winning and losing, and the infinite is to be won.

That is conclusive, and, if human beings are capable of understanding any truth at all, this is the one.

"I confess it, I admit it, but even so . . . Is there no way of seeing underneath the cards?" "Yes, Scripture and the rest, etc." "Yes, but my hands are tied and I cannot speak a word. I am being forced to wager and I am not free, they will not let me go. And I am made in such a way that I cannot believe. So what do you want me to do?" "That is true. But at least realize that your inability to believe, since reason urges you to do so and yet you cannot, arises from your passions. So concentrate not on convincing yourself by increasing the number of proofs of God but on diminishing your passions. You want to find faith and you do not know the way? You want to cure yourself of unbelief and you ask for the remedies? Learn from those who have been bound like you, and who now wager all they have. They are people who know the road you want to follow and have been cured of the affliction of which you want to be cured. Follow the way by which they began: by behaving just as if they believed, taking holy water, having masses said, etc. That will make you believe quite naturally, and according to your animal reactions." "But that is what I am afraid of." "Why? What do you have to lose?"

Pascal's Wager: A Critique

Simon Blackburn

Simon Blackburn, Professor of Philosophy at the University of Cambridge, does not accept Pascal's reasoning. According to Blackburn, Pascal is assuming that the existence of no God is the only alternative to the existence of a Christian God who cares what people believe but is less concerned with why they believe it. Suppose, however, a God exists who punishes those who hold theistic beliefs without evidence, while rewarding those who in the absence of evidence refrain from believing. In that case, not believing would be the safer bet.

So the key question is: How do we decide on what basis rewards and punishments, if any, will be distributed? Regarding this crucial matter, the wager provides no guidance.

The standard way to present [Pascal's wager] . . . is in terms of a two-by-two box of the options:

	God exists	**God does not**
I believe in him	+infinity!	0
I do not believe in him	–infinity!	0

The zeros on the right correspond to the thought that not much goes better or worse in this life, whether or not we believe. This life is of vanishingly little account compared to what is promised to believers. The plus-infinity figure corresponds to infinite bliss. The minus-infinity figure in the bottom left corresponds to the traditional jealous God, who sends to Hell those who do not believe in him, and of course encourages his followers to give them a hard time here, as well. But the minus-infinity figure can be soft-pedalled. Even if we put 0 in the bottom left-hand box, the wager looks good. It would be good even if God does not punish disbelief, because there is still that terrific payoff of "+infinity" cranking up the choice. In decision-theory terms, the option of belief "dominates," because it can win, and cannot lose. So—go for it!

Unfortunately the lethal problem with this argument is simple, once it is pointed out.

Pascal starts from a position of metaphysical ignorance. We just know nothing about the realm beyond experience. But the set-up of the wager presumes that we *do* know something. We are supposed to know the rewards and penalties attached to belief in a Christian God. This is a God who will be pleasured and reward us for our attendance at mass, and will either be indifferent or, in the minus-infinity option, seriously discombobulated by our nonattendance. But this is a case of false options. For consider that if we are really ignorant metaphysically, then it is at least as likely that the options pan out like this:

> There is indeed a very powerful, very benevolent deity. He (or she or they or it) has determined as follows. The good human beings are those who follow the natural light of reason, which is given to them to control their beliefs. These good humans follow the arguments, and hence avoid religious

convictions. These ones with the strength of mind not to believe in such things go to Heaven. The rest go to Hell.

This is not such a familiar deity as the traditional jealous God, who cares above all that people believe in him. (Why is God so jealous? Alas, might his jealousy be a projection of human sectarian ambitions and emotions? Either you are with us or against us! The French sceptic Voltaire said that God created mankind in his image, and mankind returned the compliment.) But the problem for Pascal is that if we really know nothing, then we do not know whether the scenario just described is any less likely than the Christian one he presented. In fact, for my money, a God that punishes belief is just as likely, and a lot more reasonable, than one that punishes disbelief.

And of course, we could add the Humean point that whilst for Pascal it was a simple two-way question of mass versus disbelief, in the wider world it is also a question of the Koran versus mass, or L. Ron Hubbard versus the Swami Maharishi, or the Aquarian Concepts Community Divine New Order Government versus the First Internet Church of All. The wager has to be silent about those choices.

The Ethics of Belief

W. K. Clifford

Is it ever justified to hold beliefs on the basis of insufficient evidence? W. K. Clifford, an English philosopher and mathematician, thought not. He argued that beliefs influence actions, that our actions may affect others for good or ill, and that believing on weak grounds leads to thoughtless actions that may harm those who rely on us to be conscientious about what we say and do. To stifle doubts and believe more firmly than the available evidence supports is a form of dishonesty that weakens our character by undermining concern for truth.

A shipowner was about to send to sea an emigrant-ship. He knew that she was old, and not over-well built at the first; that she had seen many seas and

---

From W. K. Clifford, *Lectures and Essays*.

climes, and often had needed repairs. Doubts had been suggested to him that possibly she was not seaworthy. These doubts preyed upon his mind, and made him unhappy; he thought that perhaps he ought to have her thoroughly overhauled and refitted, even though this should put him to great expense. Before the ship sailed, however, he succeeded in overcoming these melancholy reflections. He said to himself that she had gone safely through so many voyages and weathered so many storms that it was idle to suppose she would not come safely home from this trip also. He would put his trust in Providence, which could hardly fail to protect all these unhappy families that were leaving their fatherland to seek for better times elsewhere. He would dismiss from his mind all ungenerous suspicions about the honesty of builders and contractors. In such ways he acquired a sincere and comfortable conviction that his vessel was thoroughly safe and seaworthy; he watched her departure with a light heart, and benevolent wishes for the success of the exiles in their strange new home that was to be; and he got his insurance-money when she went down in mid-ocean and told no tales.

What shall we say of him? Surely this, that he was verily guilty of the death of those men. It is admitted that he did sincerely believe in the soundness of his ship; but the sincerity of his conviction can in no wise help him, because *he had no right to believe on such evidence as was before him.* He had acquired his belief not by honestly earning it in patient investigation, but by stifling his doubts. And although in the end he may have felt so sure about it that he could not think otherwise, yet inasmuch as he had knowingly and willingly worked himself into that frame of mind, he must be held responsible for it.

Let us alter the case a little, and suppose that the ship was not unsound after all; that she made her voyage safely, and many others after it. Will that diminish the guilt of her owner? Not one jot. When an action is once done, it is right or wrong for ever; no accidental failure of its good or evil fruits can possibly alter that. The man would not have been innocent, he would only have been not found out. The question of right or wrong has to do with the origin of his belief, not the matter of it; not what it was, but how he got it; not whether it turned out to be true or false, but whether he had a right to believe on such evidence as was before him.

There was once an island in which some of the inhabitants professed a religion teaching neither the doctrine of original sin nor that of eternal punishment. A suspicion got abroad that the professors of this religion had made use of unfair means to get their doctrines taught to children. They were accused of wresting the laws of their country in such a way as to remove children from the care of their natural and legal guardians; and even of stealing them away and keeping them concealed from their friends and relations. A certain number of men formed themselves into a society for the purpose of agitating the public about this matter. They published grave accusations against individual citizens of the highest position and character, and did all in their power to injure these citizens in the exercise of their professions. So great was the noise they made, that a Commission was appointed to investigate the facts; but after the Commission had carefully inquired into all the evidence that could be got, it appeared that the accused were innocent. Not only had they been accused on insufficient evidence, but the evidence of their innocence was such as the agitators might easily have obtained, if they had attempted a fair inquiry. After these disclosures the inhabitants of that country looked upon the members of the agitating society, not only as persons whose judgment was to be distrusted, but also as no longer to be counted honourable men. For although they had sincerely and conscientiously believed in the charges they had made, yet *they had no right to believe on such evidence as was before them.* Their sincere convictions, instead of being honestly earned by patient inquiring, were stolen by listening to the voice of prejudice and passion.

Let us vary this case also, and suppose, other things remaining as before, that a still more accurate investigation proved the accused to have been really guilty. Would this make any difference in the guilt of the accusers? Clearly not; the question is not whether their belief was true or false, but whether they entertained it on wrong grounds. They would no doubt say, "Now you see that we were right after all; next time perhaps you will believe us." And they might be believed, but they would not thereby become honourable men. They would not be innocent, they would only be not found out. Every one of them, if he chose to examine himself *in foro conscientiae,*[1] would know that he had acquired and nourished a belief, when he had no right to believe on such evidence as was before him; and therein he would know that he had done a wrong thing.

It may be said, however, that in both of these supposed cases it is not the belief which is judged to be wrong, but the action following upon it. The ship-owner might say, "I am perfectly certain that my ship is sound, but still I feel it my duty to have her examined, before trusting the lives of so many people to her." And it might be said to the agitator, "However convinced you were of the justice of your cause and the truth of your convictions, you ought not to have made a public attack upon any man's character until you had examined the evidence on both sides with the utmost patience and care."

In the first place, let us admit that, so far as it goes, this view of the case is right and necessary; right, because even when a man's belief is so fixed that he cannot think otherwise, he still has a choice in regard to the action suggested by it, and so cannot escape the duty of investigating on the ground of the strength of his convictions; and necessary, because those who are not yet capable of controlling their feelings and thoughts must have a plain rule dealing with overt acts.

But this being premised as necessary, it becomes clear that it is not sufficient, and that our previous judgment is required to supplement it. For it is not possible so to sever the belief from the action it suggests as to condemn the one without condemning the other. No man holding a strong belief on one side of a question, or even wishing to hold a belief on one side, can investigate it with such fairness and completeness as if he were really in doubt and unbiased; so that the existence of a belief not founded on fair inquiry unfits a man for the performance of this necessary duty.

Nor is that truly a belief at all which has not some influence upon the actions of him who holds it. He who truly believes that which prompts him to an action has looked upon the action to lust after it, he has committed it already in his heart. If a belief is not realized immediately in open deeds, it is stored up for the guidance of the future. It goes to make a part of that aggregate of beliefs which is the link between sensation and action at every moment of all our lives, and which is so organized and compacted together that no part of it can be isolated from the rest, but every new addition modifies the structure of the whole. No real belief, however trifling and fragmentary it may seem, is ever truly insignificant; it prepares us to receive more of its like, confirms those which resembled it before, and weakens others; and so gradually it lays a stealthy train in our inmost thoughts, which may someday explode into overt action, and leave its stamp upon our character for ever.

And no one man's belief is in any case a private matter which concerns himself alone. Our lives are guided by that general conception of the course of things which has been created by society for social purposes. Our words, our phrases, our forms and processes and modes of thought, are common property, fashioned and perfected from age to age; an heirloom which every succeeding generation inherits as a precious deposit and a sacred trust to be handed on to the next one, not unchanged but enlarged and purified, with some clear marks of its proper handiwork. Into this, for good or ill, is woven every belief of every man who has speech of his fellows. An awful privilege, and an awful responsibility, that we should help to create the world in which posterity will live.

In the two supposed cases which have been considered, it has been judged wrong to believe on insufficient evidence, or to nourish belief by suppressing doubts and avoiding investigation. The reason of this judgment is not far to seek; it is that in both these cases the belief held by one man was of great importance to other men. But forasmuch as no belief held by one man, however seemingly trivial the belief, and however obscure the believer, is ever actually insignificant or without its effect on the fate of mankind, we have no choice but to extend our judgment to all cases of belief whatever. Belief, that sacred faculty which prompts the decisions of our will, and knits into harmonious working all the compacted energies of our being, is ours not for ourselves, but for humanity. It is rightly used on truths which have been established by long experience and waiting toil, and which have stood in the fierce light of free and fearless questioning. Then it helps to bind men together, and to strengthen and direct their common action. It is desecrated when given to unproved and unquestioned statements, for the solace and private pleasure of the believer; to add a tinsel splendour to the plain straight road of our life and display a bright mirage beyond it; or even to drown the common sorrows of our kind by a self-deception which allows them not only to cast down, but also to degrade us. Whoso would deserve well of his fellows in this matter will guard the purity of his belief with a very fanaticism of jealous care, lest at any time it should rest on an unworthy object, and catch a stain which can never be wiped away.

It is not only the leader of men, statesman, philosopher, or poet, that owes this bounden duty to mankind. Every rustic who delivers in the village alehouse his slow, infrequent sentences, may help to kill or keep alive the fatal superstitions which clog his race. Every hard-worked wife of an artisan may transmit to her children beliefs which shall knit society together, or rend it in pieces. No simplicity of mind, no obscurity of station, can escape the universal duty of questioning all that we believe.

It is true that this duty is a hard one, and the doubt which comes out of it is often a very bitter thing. It leaves us bare and powerless where we thought that we were safe and strong. To know all about anything is to know how to deal with it under all circumstances. We feel much happier and more secure when we think we know precisely what to do, no matter what happens, than when we have lost our way and do not know where to turn. And if we have supposed ourselves to know all about anything, and to be capable of doing what is fit in regard to it, we naturally do not like to find that we are really ignorant and powerless, that we have to begin again at the beginning, and try to learn what the thing is and how it is to be dealt with—if indeed anything can be learnt about it. It is the sense of power attached to a sense of knowledge that makes men desirous of believing, and afraid of doubting.

This sense of power is the highest and best of pleasures when the belief on which it is founded is a true belief, and has been fairly earned by investigation. For then we may justly feel that it is common property, and hold good for others as well as for ourselves. Then we may be glad, not that I have learned secrets by which I am safer and stronger, but that *we men* have got mastery over more of the world; and we shall be strong, not for ourselves, but in the name of Man and in his strength. But if the belief has been accepted on insufficient evidence, the pleasure is a stolen one. Not only does it deceive ourselves by giving us a sense of power which we do not really possess, but it is sinful, because it is stolen in defiance of our duty to mankind. That duty is to guard ourselves from such beliefs as from a pestilence, which may shortly master our own body and then spread to the rest of the town. What would be thought of one who, for the sake of a sweet fruit, should deliberately run the risk of bringing a plague upon his family and his neighbours?

And, as in other such cases, it is not the risk only which has to be considered; for a bad action is always bad at the time when it is done, no matter what happens afterwards. Every time we let ourselves believe for unworthy reasons, we weaken our powers of self-control, of doubting, of judicially and fairly weighing evidence. We all suffer severely enough from the maintenance and support of false beliefs and the fatally wrong actions which they lead to, and the evil born when one such belief is entertained is great and wide. But a greater and wider evil arises when the credulous character is maintained and supported, when a habit of believing for unworthy reasons is fostered and made permanent. If I steal money from any person, there may be no harm done by the mere transfer of possession; he may not feel the loss, or it may prevent him from using the money badly. But I cannot help doing this great wrong towards Man, that I make myself dishonest. What hurts society is not that it should lose its property, but that it should become a den of thieves, for then it must cease to be society. This is why we ought not to do evil, that good may come; for at any rate this great evil has come, that we have done evil and are made wicked thereby. In like manner, if I let myself believe anything on insufficient evidence, there may be no great harm done by the mere belief; it may be true after all, or I may never have occasion to exhibit it in outward acts. But I cannot help doing this great wrong towards Man, that I make myself credulous. The danger to society is not merely that it should believe wrong things, though that is great enough; but that it should become credulous, and lose the habit of testing things and inquiring into them; for then it must sink back into savagery.

The harm which is done by credulity in a man is not confined to the fostering of a credulous character in others, and consequent support of false beliefs. Habitual want of care about what I believe leads to habitual want of care in others about the truth of what is told to me. Men speak the truth to one another when each reveres the truth in his own mind and in the other's mind; but how shall my friend revere the truth in my mind when I myself am careless about it, when I believe things because I want to believe them, and because they are comforting and pleasant? Will he not learn to cry, "Peace," to me, when there is no peace? By such a course I shall surround myself with a thick atmosphere of falsehood and fraud, and in that I must live. It may matter little to me, in my cloud-castle of sweet illusions and darling lies; but it matters much to Man that I have made my neighbours ready to deceive. The credulous man is father to the liar and the cheat; he lives in the bosom of this his family, and it is no marvel if he should become even as they are. So closely are our duties knit together, that whoso shall keep the whole law, and yet offend in one point, he is guilty of all.

To sum up: it is wrong always, everywhere, and for anyone, to believe anything upon insufficient evidence.

If a man, holding a belief which he was taught in childhood or persuaded of afterwards, keeps down and pushes away any doubts which arise about it in his mind, purposely avoids the reading of books and the company of men that call in question or discuss it, and regards as impious those questions which cannot easily be asked without disturbing it—the life of that man is one long sin against mankind.

If this judgment seems harsh when applied to those simple souls who have never known better, who have been brought up from the cradle with a horror of doubt, and taught that their eternal welfare depends on *what* they believe, then it leads to the very serious question. *Who hath made Israel to sin?*

It may be permitted me to fortify this judgment with the sentence of Milton[2]—

A man may be a heretic in the truth; and if he believe things only because his pastor says so, or the assembly so determine, without knowing other reason, though his belief be true, yet the very truth he holds becomes his heresy.

And with this famous aphorism of Coleridge[3]—

He who begins by loving Christianity better than Truth, will proceed by loving his own sect or Church better than Christianity, and end in loving himself better than all.

Inquiry into the evidence of a doctrine is not to be made once for all, and then taken as finally settled. It is never lawful to stifle a doubt; for either it can be honestly answered by means of the inquiry already made, or else it proves that the inquiry was not complete.

"But," says one, "I am a busy man; I have no time for the long course of study which would be necessary to make me in any degree a competent judge of certain questions, or even able to understand the nature of the arguments."

Then he should have no time to believe.

NOTES

1. [Conscientiously.]
2. *Areopagitica.*
3. *Aids to Reflections.*

The Will to Believe

William James

Williams James, whose work we read previously, disagreed with Clifford. James contended that when you face an important choice between two appealing options and cannot wait for further evidence, you are justified in believing and acting as your passion decides. According to James, we should not allow the fear of holding

---

From William James, "The Will to Believe," *New World,* June 1896.

a false belief to prevent us from losing the benefits of believing what may be true.

James claims that the essence of religion is contained in two fundamental claims: (1) the best things are the more eternal things, and (2) we are better off if we believe (1). Note that in a footnote he says that "if the action required or inspired by the religious hypothesis is in no way different from that dictated by the naturalistic hypothesis, then religious faith is a pure superfluity, better pruned away, and controversy about its legitimacy is a piece of idle trifling, unworthy of serious minds." An intriguing question is whether believing in (1) and (2), which James considers the core of the religious attitude, requires different action than rejecting (1) and (2).

I

Let us give the name of *hypothesis* to anything that may be proposed to our belief; and just as the electricians speak of live and dead wires, let us speak of any hypothesis as either *live* or *dead.* A live hypothesis is one which appeals as a real possibility to him to whom it is proposed. If I ask you to believe in the Mahdi,[1] the notion makes no electric connection with your nature—it refuses to scintillate with any credibility at all. As an hypothesis it is completely dead. To an Arab, however (even if he be not one of the Mahdi's followers), the hypothesis is among the mind's possibilities: it is alive. This shows that deadness and liveness in an hypothesis are not intrinsic properties, but relations to the individual thinker. They are measured by his willingness to act. The maximum of liveness in an hypothesis means willingness to act irrevocably. Practically, that means belief; but there is some believing tendency wherever there is willingness to act at all.

Next, let us call the decision between two hypotheses an *option.* Options may be of several kinds. They may be—1, *living* or *dead;* 2, *forced* or *avoidable;* 3, *momentous* or *trivial;* and for our purposes we may call an option a *genuine* option when it is of the forced, living and momentous kind.

1. A living option is one in which both hypotheses are live ones. If I say to you: "Be a theosophist or be a mahomedan," it is probably a dead option, because for you neither hypothesis is likely to be alive. But if I say "Be an agnostic or be a Christian," it is otherwise: trained as you are, each hypothesis makes some appeal, however small, to your belief.
2. Next, if I say to you: "Choose between going out with your umbrella or without it," I do not offer you a genuine option, for it is not forced. You can easily avoid it by not going out at all. Similarly, if I say "Either

love me or hate me," "Either call my theory true or call it false," your option is avoidable. You may remain indifferent to me, neither loving nor hating, and you may decline to offer any judgment as to my theory. But if I say "Either accept this truth or go without it," I put on you a forced option, for there is no standing place outside of the alternative. Every dilemma based on a complete logical disjunction, with no possibility of not choosing, is an option of this forced kind.

3. Finally, if I were Dr. Nansen and proposed to you to join my North Pole expedition, your option would be momentous; for this would probably be your only similar opportunity, and your choice now would either exclude you from the North Pole sort of immortality altogether or put at least the chance of it into your hands. He who refuses to embrace a unique opportunity loses the prize as surely as if he tried and failed. *Per contra,*[2] the option is trivial when the opportunity is not unique, when the stake is insignificant, or when the decision is reversible if it later proves unwise. Such trivial options abound in the scientific life. A chemist finds an hypothesis live enough to spend a year in its verification: he believes in it to that extent. But if his experiments prove inconclusive either way, he is quit for his loss of time, no vital harm being done.

It will facilitate our discussion if we keep all these distinctions well in mind.

II

The next matter to consider is the actual psychology of human opinion. When we look at certain facts, it seems as if our passional and volitional nature lay at the root of all our convictions. When we look at others, it seems as if they could do nothing when the intellect had once said its say. Let us take the latter facts up first.

Does it not seem preposterous on the very face of it to talk of our opinions being modifiable at will? Can our will either help or hinder our intellect in its perceptions of truth? Can we, by just willing it, believe that Abraham Lincoln's existence is a myth, and that the portraits of him in *McClure's Magazine* are all of someone else? Can we, by any effort of our will, or by any strength of wish that it were true, believe ourselves well and about when we are roaring with rheumatism in bed, or feel certain that the sum of the two one-dollar bills in our pocket must be a hundred dollars? We can *say* any of these things, but we are absolutely impotent to believe them; and of just such things is the whole fabric of the truths that we do believe in made up. . . .

In Pascal's *Thoughts* there is a celebrated passage known in literature as Pascal's wager. In it he tries to force us into Christianity by reasoning as if our concern with truth resembled our concern with the stakes in a game of chance. Translated freely his words are these: You must either believe or not believe that God is—which will you do? Your human reason cannot say. A game is going on between you and the nature of things which at the day of judgment will bring out either heads or tails. Weigh what your gains and your losses would be if you should stake all you have on heads, or God's existence: If you win in such case, you gain eternal beatitude; if you lose, you lose nothing at all. If there were an infinity of chances, and only one for God in this wager, still you ought to stake your all on God; for though you surely risk a finite loss by this procedure, any finite loss is reasonable, even a certain one is reasonable, if there is but the possibility of infinite gain. Go, then, and take holy water, and have masses said; belief will come and stupefy your scruples—*Cela vous fera croire et vous abêtira.*[3] Why should you not? At bottom, what have you to lose?

You probably feel that when religious faith expresses itself thus, in the language of the gaming-table, it is put to its last trumps. Surely Pascal's own personal belief in masses and holy water had far other springs; and this celebrated page of his is but an argument for others, a last desperate snatch at a weapon against the hardness of the unbelieving heart. We feel that a faith in masses and holy water adopted willfully after such a mechanical calculation would lack the inner soul of faith's reality; and if we were ourselves in the place of the Deity, we should probably take particular pleasure in cutting off believers of this pattern from their infinite reward. It is evident that unless there be some pre-existing tendency to believe in masses and holy water, the option offered to the will by Pascal is not a living option. Certainly no Turk ever took to masses and holy water on its account; and even to us Protestants these means of salvation seem such foregone impossibilities that Pascal's logic, invoked for them specifically, leaves us unmoved. As well might the Mahdi write to us, saying "I am the Expected One whom God has created in his effulgence. You shall be infinitely happy if you confess me; otherwise you shall be cut off from the light of the sun. Weigh, then, your infinite gain if I am genuine against your finite sacrifice if I am not!" His logic would be that of Pascal; but he would vainly use it on us, for the hypothesis he offers us is dead. No tendency to act on it exists in us to any degree.

The talk of believing by our volition seems, then, from one point of view, simply silly. From another point of view it is worse than silly, it is vile. When one turns to the magnificent edifice of the physical sciences, and sees how it was reared; what thousands of disinterested moral lives of men lie buried in its mere foundations; what patience and postponement, what choking down of preference, what submission to the icy laws of outer fact are wrought into its very stones and mortar; how absolutely impersonal it stands in its vast augustness—then how besotted and contemptible seems every little sentimentalist who comes blowing his voluntary smoke-wreaths, and pretending to decide things from out of his private dream! Can we wonder if those bred in the rugged and manly school of science should feel like spewing such subjectivism out of their mouths? The whole system of loyalties which grow up in the schools of science go dead against its toleration; so that it is only natural that those who have caught the scientific fever should pass over to the opposite extreme, and write sometimes as if the incorruptibly truthful intellect ought positively to prefer bitterness and unacceptableness to the heart in its cup. . . .

"It fortifies my soul to know
That, though I perish, Truth is so—"

sings Clough, whilst Huxley exclaims: "My only consolation lies in the reflection that, however bad our posterity may become, so long as they hold by the plain rule of not pretending to believe what they have no reason to believe because it may be to their advantage so to pretend [the word 'pretend' is surely here redundant], they will not have reached the lowest depths of immorality." And that delicious *enfant terrible*[4] Clifford writes: "[Belief] is desecrated when given to unproved and unquestioned statements, for the solace and private pleasure of the believer. . . . Whoso would deserve well of his fellows in this matter will guard the purity of his belief with a very fanaticism of jealous care, lest at any time it should rest on an unworthy object, and catch a stain which can never be wiped away. . . . If [a] belief has been accepted on insufficient evidence [even though the belief be true, as Clifford on the same page explains], the pleasure is a stolen one. . . . It is sinful, because it is stolen in defiance of our duty to mankind. That duty is to guard ourselves from such beliefs as from a pestilence, which may shortly master our own body and then spread to the rest of the town. . . . It is wrong always, everywhere, and for anyone, to believe anything upon insufficient evidence."

III

All this strikes one as healthy, even when expressed, as by Clifford, with somewhat too much of robustious pathos in the voice. Free-will and simple wishing do seem, in the matter of our credences, to be only fifth wheels to the coach. Yet if anyone should thereupon assume that intellectual insight is what remains after wish and will and sentimental preference have taken wing, or that pure reason is what then settles our opinions, he would fly quite as directly in the teeth of the facts.

It is only our already dead hypotheses that our willing nature is unable to bring to life again. But what has made them dead for us is for the most part a previous action of our willing nature of an antagonistic kind. When I say "willing nature," I do not mean only such deliberate volitions as may have set up habits of belief that we cannot now escape from—I mean all such factors of belief as fear and hope, prejudice and passion, imitation and partisanship, the circumpressure of our caste and set. As a matter of fact we find ourselves believing, we hardly know how or why. Mr. Balfour gives the name of "authority" to all those influences, born of the intellectual climate, that make hypotheses possible or impossible for us, alive or dead. Here in this room, we all of us believe in molecules and the conservation of energy, in democracy and necessary progress, in Protestant Christianity and the duty of fighting for "the doctrine of the immortal Monroe," all for no reasons worthy of the name. We see into these matters with no more inner clearness, and probably with much less, than any disbeliever in them might possess. His unconventionality would probably have some grounds to show for its conclusions; but for us, not insight, but the *prestige* of the opinions, is what makes the spark shoot from them and light up our sleeping magazines of faith. Our reason is quite satisfied, in nine hundred and ninety-nine cases out of every thousand of us, if it can find a few arguments that will do to recite in case our credulity is criticized by someone else. Our faith is faith in someone else's faith, and in the greatest matters this is most the case. Our belief in truth itself, for instance, that there is a truth, and that our minds and it are made for each other—what is it but a passionate affirmation of desire, in which our social system backs us up? We want to have a truth; we want to believe that our experiments and studies and discussions must put us in a continually better and better position towards it; and on this line we agree to fight out our thinking lives. But if a pyrrhonistic sceptic asks us *how we know* all this, can our logic find a reply? No! Certainly it cannot. It is just one volition against another—we are willing to go in for life upon a trust or assumption which he, for his part, does not care to make.

As a rule we disbelieve all facts and theories for which we have no use. Clifford's cosmic emotions find no use for Christian feelings. Huxley belabors the bishops because there is no use for sacerdotalism in his scheme of life. Newman, on the contrary, goes over to Romanism, and finds all sorts of reasons good for staying there, because a priestly system is for him an organic need and delight. Why do so few "scientists" even look at the evidence for telepathy, so called? Because they think, as a leading biologist, now dead, once said to me, that even if such a thing were true, scientists ought to band together to keep it suppressed and concealed. It would undo the uniformity of Nature and all sorts of other things without which scientists cannot carry on their pursuits. But if this very man had been shown something which as a scientist he might *do* with telepathy, he might not only have examined the evidence, but even have found it good enough. This very law which the logicians would impose upon us—if I may give the name of logicians to those who would rule out our willing nature here—is based on nothing but their own natural wish to exclude all elements for which they, in their professional quality of logicians, can find no use.

Evidently, then, our non-intellectual nature does influence our convictions. There are passional tendencies and volitions which run before and others which come after belief, and it is only the latter that are too late for the fair; and they are not too late when the previous passional work has been already in their own direction. Pascal's argument, instead of being powerless, then seems a regular clincher, and is the last stroke needed to make our faith in masses and holy water complete. The state of things is evidently far from simple; and pure insight and logic, whatever they might do ideally, are not the only things that really do produce our creeds.

IV

Our next duty, having recognized this mixed-up state of affairs, is to ask whether it be simply reprehensible and pathological, or whether, on the contrary, we must treat it as a normal element in making up our minds. The thesis I defend is, briefly stated, this: *Our passional nature not only lawfully may, but must, decide an option between propositions, whenever it is a genuine option that cannot by its nature be decided on intellectual grounds; for to say, under such circumstances, "Do not decide, but leave the question open," is itself a passional decision—just like deciding yes or no—and is attended with the same risk of losing the truth. . . .*

VII

One more point, small but important, and our preliminaries are done. There are two ways of looking at our duty in the matter of opinion—ways entirely different, and yet ways about whose difference the theory of knowledge seems hitherto to have shown very little concern. *We must know the truth;* and *we must avoid error*—these are our first and great commandments as would-be knowers; but they are not two ways of stating an identical commandment, they are two separable laws. Although it may indeed happen that when we believe the truth *A,* we escape as an incidental consequence from believing the falsehood *B,* it hardly ever happens that by merely disbelieving *B* we necessarily believe *A.* We may in escaping *B* fall into believing other falsehoods, *C* or *D,* just as bad as *B;* or we may escape *B* by not believing anything at all, not even *A.*

Believe truth! Shun error!—these, we see, are two materially different laws; and by choosing between them we may end by colouring differently our whole intellectual life. We may regard the chase for truth as paramount, and the avoidance of error as secondary; or we may, on the other hand, treat the avoidance of error as more imperative, and let truth take its chance. Clifford, in the instructive passage which I have quoted, exhorts us to the latter course. Believe nothing, he tells us, keep your mind in suspense forever, rather than by closing it on insufficient evidence incur the awful risk of believing lies. You, on the other hand, may think that the risk of being in error is a very small matter when compared with the blessings of real knowledge, and be ready to be duped many times in your investigation rather than postpone indefinitely the chance of guessing true. I myself find it impossible to go with Clifford. We must remember that these feelings of our duty about either truth or error are in any case only expressions of our passional life. Biologically considered, our minds are as ready to grind out falsehood as veracity, and he who says "Better go without belief forever than believe a lie!" merely shows his own preponderant private horror of becoming a dupe. He may be critical of many of his desires and fears, but this fear he slavishly obeys. He cannot imagine anyone questioning its binding force. For my own part, I have also a horror of being duped; but I can believe that worse things than being duped may happen to a man in this world: so Clifford's exhortation has to my ears a thoroughly fantastic sound. It is like a general informing his soldiers that it is better to keep out of battle forever than to risk a single wound. Not so are victories either over enemies or over nature gained. Our errors are surely not such awfully solemn things. In a world where we are so certain to incur them in spite of all our caution, a certain lightness of heart seems healthier than this excessive nervousness on their behalf. At any rate, it seems the fittest thing for the empiricist philosopher.

VIII

And now, after all this introduction, let us go straight at our question. I have said, and now repeat it, that not only as a matter of fact do we find our passional nature influencing us in our opinions, but that there are some options between opinions in which this influence must be regarded both as an inevitable and as a lawful determinant of our choice.

I fear here that some of you my hearers will begin to scent danger, and lend an inhospitable ear. Two first steps of passion you have indeed had to admit as necessary—we must think so as to avoid dupery, and we must think so as to gain truth; but the surest path to those ideal consummations, you will probably consider, is from now onwards to take no farther passional step.

Well, of course I agree as far as the facts will allow. Wherever the option between losing truth and gaining it is not momentous, we can throw the chance of *gaining truth* away, and at any rate save ourselves from any chance of *believing falsehood,* by not making up our minds at all till objective evidence has come. In scientific questions, this is almost always the case; and even in human affairs in general, the need of acting is seldom so urgent that a false belief to act on is better than no belief at all. Law courts, indeed, have to decide on the best evidence attainable for the moment, because a judge's duty is to make law as well as to ascertain it, and (as a learned judge once said to me) few cases are worth spending much time over: the great thing is to have them decided on *any* acceptable principle, and got out of the way. But in our dealings with objective nature we obviously are recorders, not makers, of the truth; and decisions for the mere sake of deciding promptly and getting on to the next business would be wholly out of place. Throughout the breadth of physical nature facts are what they are quite independently of us, and seldom is there any such hurry about them that the risks of being duped by believing a premature theory need be faced. The questions here are always trivial options, the hypotheses are hardly living (at any rate not living for us spectators), the choice between believing truth or falsehood is seldom forced. The attitude of sceptical balance is therefore the absolutely wise one if we would escape mistakes. What difference, indeed, does it make to most of us whether we have or have not a theory of the Röntgen rays, whether we believe or not in mind-stuff, or have a conviction about the causality of conscious states? It makes no difference. Such options are not forced on us. On every account it is better not to make them, but still keep weighing reasons *pro et contra*[5] with an indifferent hand.

I speak, of course, here of the purely judging mind. For purposes of discovery such indifference is to be less highly recommended, and science would be far less advanced than she is if the passionate desires of individuals to get their own faiths confirmed had been kept out of the game. . . . On the other hand, if you want an absolute duffer in an investigation, you must, after all, take the man who has no interest whatever in its results: he is the warranted incapable, the positive fool. The most useful investigator, because the most sensitive observer, is always he whose eager interest in one side of the question is balanced by an equally keen nervousness lest he become deceived. Science has organized this nervousness into a regular *technique*, her so-called method of verification; and she has fallen so deeply in love with the method that one may even say she has ceased to care for truth by itself at all. It is only truth as technically verified that interests her. The truth of truths might come in merely affirmative form, and she would decline to touch it. Such truth as that, she might repeat with Clifford, would be stolen in defiance of her duty to mankind. Human passions, however, are stronger than technical rules. "Le coeur a ses raisons," as Pascal says, "que la raison ne connaît point";[6] and however indifferent to all but the bare rules of the game the umpire, the abstract intellect, may be, the concrete players who furnish him the materials to judge of are usually, each one of them, in love with some pet "live hypothesis" of his own. Let us agree, however, that wherever there is no forced option, the dispassionately judicial intellect with no pet hypothesis, saving us, as it does, from dupery at any rate, ought to be our ideal.

The question next arises: Are there not somewhere forced options in our speculative questions, and can we (as men who may be interested at least as much in positively gaining truth as in merely escaping dupery) always wait with impunity till the coercive evidence shall have arrived? It seems a priori improbable that the truth should be so nicely adjusted to our needs and powers as that. In the great boarding-house of nature, the cakes and the butter and the syrup seldom come out so even and leave the plates so clean. Indeed, we should view them with scientific suspicion if they did.

IX

Moral questions immediately present themselves as questions whose solution cannot wait for sensible proof. A moral question is a question not of what sensibly exists, but of what is good, or would be good if it did exist. Science can tell us what exists; but to compare the *worths*, both of what exists and of what does not exist, we must consult not science, but what Pascal calls our heart. Science herself consults her heart when she lays it down that the infinite ascertainment of fact and correction of false belief are the supreme goods for man. Challenge the statement and science can only repeat it oracularly, or else prove it by showing that such ascertainment and correction bring man all sorts of other goods which man's heart in turn declares. The question of having moral beliefs at all or not having them is decided by our will. Are our moral preferences true or false, or are they only odd biological phenomena, making things good or bad for *us*, but in themselves indifferent? How can your pure intellect decide? If your heart does not *want* a world of moral reality, your head will assuredly never make you believe in one. Mephistophelian scepticism, indeed, will satisfy the head's play-instincts much better than any rigorous idealism can. Some men (even at the student age) are so naturally cool-hearted that the moralistic hypothesis never has for them any pungent life, and in their supercilious presence the hot young moralist always feels strangely ill at ease. The appearance of knowingness is on their side, of naiveté and gullibility on his. Yet, in the inarticulate heart of him, he clings to it that he is not a dupe, and that there is a realm in which (as Emerson says) all their wit and intellectual superiority is no better than the cunning of a fox. Moral scepticism can no more be refuted or proved by logic than intellectual scepticism can. When we stick to it that there *is* truth (be it of either kind), we do so with our whole nature, and resolve to stand or fall by the results. The sceptic with his whole nature adopts the doubting attitude; but which of us is the wiser, Omniscience only knows.

Turn now from these wide questions of good to a certain class of questions of fact, questions concerning personal relations, states of mind between one man and another. *Do you like me or not?*—for example. Whether you do or not depends, in countless instances, on whether I meet you halfway, am willing to assume that you must like me, and show you trust and expectation. The previous faith on my part in your liking's existence is in such cases what makes your liking come. But if I stand aloof, and refuse to budge an inch until I have objective evidence, until you shall have done something apt, as the absolutists say, *ad extorquendum assensum meum*,[7] ten to one your liking never comes. How many women's hearts are vanquished by the mere sanguine insistence of some man that they *must* love him! he will not consent to the hypothesis that they cannot. The desire for a certain kind of truth here brings about that special truth's existence; and so it is in innumerable cases of other sorts. Who gains promotions, boons, appointments, but the man in whose life they are seen to play the part of live hypotheses, who discounts them, sacrifices other things for their sake before they have come, and takes risks for them in advance? His faith acts on the powers above him as a claim, and creates its own verification.

A social organism of any sort whatever, large or small, is what it is because each member proceeds to his own duty with a trust that the other members will simultaneously do theirs. Wherever a desired result is achieved by the co-operation of many independent persons, its existence as a fact is a pure consequence of the precursive faith in one another of those immediately concerned. A government, an army, a commercial system, a ship, a college, an athletic team, all exist on this condition, without which not only is nothing achieved, but nothing is even attempted. A whole train of passengers (individually brave enough) will be looted by a few highwaymen, simply because the latter can count on one another, while each passenger fears that if he makes a movement of resistance, he will be shot before anyone else backs him up. If we believed that the whole car-full would rise at once with us, we should each severally rise, and train-robbing would never even be attempted. There are, then, cases where a fact cannot come at all unless a preliminary faith exists in it coming. *And where faith in a fact can help create the fact,* that would be an insane logic which should say that faith running ahead of scientific evidence is the "lowest kind of immorality" into which a thinking being can fall. Yet such is the logic by which our scientific absolutists pretend to regulate our lives!

X

In truths dependent on our personal action, then, faith based on desire is certainly a lawful and possibly an indispensable thing.

But now, it will be said, these are all childish human cases, and have nothing to do with great cosmical matter, like the question of religious faith. Let us then pass on to that. Religions differ so much in their accidents that in discussing the religious question we must make it very generic and broad. What then do we now mean by the religious hypothesis? Science says things are; morality says some things are better than other things; and religion says essentially two things.

First, she says that the best things are the more eternal things, the overlapping things, the things in the universe that throw the last stone, so to speak, and say the final word. "Perfection is eternal"—this phrase of Charles Secrétan seems a good way of putting this first affirmation of religion, an affirmation which obviously cannot yet be verified scientifically at all.

The second affirmation of religion is that we are better off even now if we believe her first affirmation to be true.

Now let us consider what the logical elements of this situation are *in case the religious hypothesis in both its branches be really true.* (Of course, we must admit that possibility at the outset. If we are to discuss the question at all, it must involve a living option. If for any of you religion be a hypothesis that cannot, by any living possibility be true, then you need go no farther. I speak to the "saving remnant" alone.) So proceeding, we see, first, that religion offers itself as *a momentous* option. We are supposed to gain, even now, by our belief, and to lose by our non-belief, a certain vital good. Secondly, religion is a *forced* option, so far as that good goes. We cannot escape the issue by remaining sceptical and waiting for more light, because, although we do avoid error in that way *if religion be untrue,* we lose the good, *if it be true,* just as certainly as if we positively chose to disbelieve. It is as if a man should hesitate indefinitely to ask a certain woman to marry him because he was not perfectly sure that she would prove an angel after he brought her home. Would he not cut himself off from that particular angel-possibility as decisively as if he went and married someone else? Scepticism, then, is not avoidance of option; it is option of a certain particular kind of risk. *Better risk loss of truth than chance of error*—that is your faith-vetoer's exact position. He is actively playing his stake as much as the believer is; he is backing the field against the religious hypothesis, just as the believer is backing the religious hypothesis against the field. To preach scepticism to us as a duty until "sufficient evidence" for religion be found, is tantamount therefore to telling us, when in presence of the religious hypothesis, that to yield to our fear of its being error is wiser and better than to yield to our hope that it may be true. It is not intellect against all passions, then; it is only intellect with one passion laying down its law. And by what, forsooth, is the supreme wisdom of this passion warranted? Dupery for dupery, what proof is there that dupery through hope is so much worse than dupery through fear? I, for one, can see no proof; and I simply refuse obedience to the scientist's command to imitate his kind of option, in a case where my own stake is important enough to give me the right to choose my own form of risk. If religion be true and the evidence for it be still insufficient, I do not wish, by putting your extinguisher upon my nature (which feels to me as if it had after all some business in this matter), to forfeit my sole chance in life of getting upon the winning side—that chance depending, of course, on my willingness to run the risk of acting as if my passional need of taking the world religiously might be prophetic and right.

All this is on the supposition that it really may be prophetic and right, and that, even to us who are discussing the matter, religion is a live hypothesis which may be true. Now to most of us religion comes in a still farther way that makes a veto on our active faith even more illogical. The more perfect and more eternal aspect of the universe is represented in our religions as having personal form. The universe is no longer a mere *It* to us, but a *Thou,* if we are religious; and any relation that may be possible from person to person might be possible here. For instance, although in one sense we are passive portions of the universe, in another we show a curious autonomy, as if we were small active centers on our own account. We feel, too, as if the appeal of religion to us were made to our own active goodwill, as if evidence might be forever withheld from us unless we met the hypothesis halfway. To take a trivial illustration: just as a man who in a company of gentlemen made no advances, asked a warrant for every concession, and believed no one's word without proof, would cut himself off by such churlishness from all the social rewards that a more trusting spirit would earn—so here, one who should shut himself up in snarling logicality and try to make the gods extort his recognition willy-nilly, or not get it at all, might cut himself off forever from his only opportunity of making the gods' acquaintance. This feeling, forced on us we know not whence, that by obstinately believing that there are gods (although not to do so would be so easy both for our logic and our life) we are doing the universe the deepest service we can, seems part of the living essence of the religious hypothesis. If the hypothesis *were* true in all its parts, including this one, then pure intellectualism, with its veto on our making willing advances, would be an absurdity; and some participation of our sympathetic nature would be logically required. I, therefore, for one, cannot see my way to accepting the agnostic rules for truth-seeking, or willfully agree to keep my willing nature out of the game. I cannot do so for this plain reason, that *a rule of thinking which would absolutely prevent me from acknowledging certain kinds of truth if those kinds of truth were really there, would be an irrational rule.* That for me is the long and short of the formal logic of the situation, no matter what the kinds of truth might materially be.

I confess I do not see how this logic can be escaped. But sad experience makes me fear that some of you may still shrink from radically saying with me, *in abstracto,*[8] that we have the right to believe at our own risk any hypothesis that is live enough to tempt our will. I suspect, however, that if this is so, it is because you have got away from the abstract logical point of view altogether, and are thinking (perhaps without realizing it) of some particular religious hypothesis which for you is dead. The freedom to "believe what we will" you apply to the case of some patent superstition; and the faith you think of is the faith defined by the schoolboy when he said, "Faith is when you believe something that you know ain't true." I can only repeat that this is misapprehension. *In concreto,*[9] the freedom to believe can only cover living options which the intellect of the individual cannot by itself resolve; and living options never seem absurdities to him who has them to consider. When I look at the religious question as it really puts itself to concrete men, and when I think of all the possibilities which both practically and theoretically it involves, then this command that we shall put a stopper on our heart, instincts and courage, and *wait*—acting of course meanwhile more or less as if religion were *not* true[10]—till doomsday, or till such time as our intellect and senses working together may have raked in evidence enough—this command, I say, seems to me the queerest idol ever manufactured in the philosophic cave. Were we scholastic absolutists, there might be more excuse. If we had an infallible intellect with its objective certitudes, we might feel ourselves disloyal to such a perfect organ of knowledge in not trusting to it exclusively, in not waiting for its releasing word. But if we are empiricists, if we believe that no bell in us tolls to let us know for certain when truth is in our grasp, then it seems a piece of idle fantasticality to preach so solemnly our duty of waiting for the bell. Indeed we *may* wait if we will—I hope you do not think that I am denying that—but if we do so, we do so at our peril as much as if we believed. In either case we *act,* taking our life in our hands. No one of us ought to issue vetoes to the other, nor should we bandy words of abuse. We ought, on the contrary, delicately and profoundly to respect one another's mental freedom—then only shall we bring about the intellectual republic; then only shall we have that spirit of inner tolerance without which all our outer tolerance is soulless, and which is empiricism's glory; then only shall we live and let live, in speculative as well as in practical things.

NOTES

1. [The redeemer, according to Islam, who will come to bring justice on earth and establish universal Islam.]
2. [In contrast.]
3. [Even this will make you believe and deaden your acuity.]
4. [One who is strikingly unorthodox.]
5. [For and against.]
6. [The heart has its reasons, which reason does not know.]
7. [For compelling my assent.]
8. [In abstract.]
9. [In practice.]
10. Since belief is measured by action, he who forbids us to believe religion to be true, necessarily also forbids us to act as we should if we did believe it to be true. The whole defence of religious faith hangs upon action. If the action required or inspired by the religious hypothesis is in no way different from that dictated by the naturalistic hypothesis, then religious faith is a pure superfluity, better pruned away, and controversy about its legitimacy is a piece of idle trifling, unworthy of serious minds. I myself believe, of course, that the religious hypothesis gives to the world an expression which specifically determines our reactions, and makes them in a large part unlike what they might be on a purely naturalistic scheme of belief.

The Will to Believe: A Critique

NICHOLAS EVERITT

How does James's defense of belief differ from Pascal's? Does James's approach avoid the problems that beset Pascal's Wager?

In our next selection, Nicholas Everitt, whose work we read previously, offers answers to these questions. He recognizes important differences between the views of Pascal and James but does not find James's approach any more successful than Pascal's.

James judges as irrational a rule that would forbid us from believing that God exists even if that belief is true. In response, Everitt finds equally irrational a rule that would forbid us from believing that God does not exist even if that belief is true. James allows that the theist may rely on passion to justify belief. Everitt in turn wonders why the atheist may not rely on an opposing passion to justify nonbelief. In short, Everitt finds that James's reasoning can be used to justify nonbelief as well as belief, and thus James's argument favors neither position.

We can note first of all how [James's argument] differs from the Pascalian argument. . . . First, the Wager at least in its extended versions can be applied to the belief in God's existence even if there is some good evidence that God does not exist. So, the Pascalian maintains that even if it is epistemically irrational to believe in God, it can simultaneously be consequentially rational to believe. James, by contrast, invokes the permissibility of accepting a belief which is consequentially rational *only if* the belief is unresolvable, i.e., undecidable in terms of evidence. This means that the potential target audience for the Jamesian argument is to that extent much smaller than for the Wager: the Wager applies equally to those who think that "God exists" is intellectually resolvable, and to those who deny this. But the Jamesian argument applies only to those who think that the belief is intellectually unresolvable, and who further think that the choice whether to accept the belief is living, forced and momentous.

Second, the Wager assumes that you will reap the benefits of believing (and the penalties of disbelieving) only if God exists; for it is only in the afterlife (if there is one) that the pay-offs of the Wager are forthcoming. James, by contrast, locates the benefits and losses in the here-and-now. Even if there is no God and so your belief is false, you will benefit now from holding the belief: it will help make your life go better. The atheist and the agnostic are losing out *now* through not believing. James makes no assumption about any benefits accruing in an afterlife to believers.

Third, the Pascalian . . . has to make some very implausible assumptions about the nature of God and his likely response to belief and disbelief among his creatures. James, on the other hand, makes no explicit assumptions about the nature of God, and all his argument requires are some commonplaces of traditional theism, such as that God cares for us, responds to our needs, helps us in times of difficulty, and so on. And his argument does not require that these commonplaces be true, but only that they be believed, for the benefits come from the belief, whether or not it is true.

There are, then, some important differences between the Pascalian and James. But does James mark an improvement on the Wager? It is difficult to think so, for every step in his argument is open to challenge. First, and perhaps least importantly, we can question whether the existence of God is really intellectually unresolvable. Many people have, of course, thought that it was—but they are generally those who are ignorant of the immensely detailed argumentation that surrounds the claim. It would be a reasonable empirical assumption that the great majority of people who have seriously considered the issue of God's existence have thought that the evidence did favour either belief or disbelief. In other words, they have thought that belief was epistemically rational or irrational, and hence would have denied that a belief in God was the kind of belief to which James's line of thought could apply. To say this is not by itself, of course, to say that they think that the evidence is *overwhelming,* or that it justifies *certainty,* but only that it justifies belief.

Suppose, however, that James is right in his assumption that the existence of God is intellectually unresolvable. A second objection then arises, about James's assumption that a person's passional nature is involved in deciding how to respond to open propositions. James is caught in a strange lack of consistency here. In respect of intellectually resolvable propositions, he accepts that our passional nature has no legitimate role to play: the requirement to believe propositions for which there is overall good evidence, and to disbelieve those for which the evidence is poor, he accepts is a requirement of reason. But if that is so, why is the requirement to suspend judgement in all those cases where the evidence is lacking or evenly balanced not also a requirement of reason? Given that he rightly thinks that reason is the guide in the first two cases, why does it suddenly cease to be so in relation to the third? James provides no explanation or justification for this strange asymmetry.

The third problem focuses on James's negative rule concerning how our passional nature should guide us. He tells us that we should not accept a rule which would prevent us from accepting as true any propositions which in fact are true, i.e., even when we have no evidence that they are true. But on the face of it, the rule he rejects sounds an excellent negative rule to accept! If there are any propositions which are in principle unresolvable, they are propositions for or against which we cannot get good evidence; and in that case, it sounds eminently reasonable to withhold both assent and dissent. . . . [I]t has to be shown that there are beneficial consequences from believing propositions in relation to which one has no evidence. What James really needs is a much more restricted thesis than the one he advances. He rejects a rule which would prevent him from accepting propositions in relation to which he has no evidence. But the most that his argument requires him to reject is a rule which would prevent him from accepting propositions in relation to which he has no evidence, *where the acceptance of the propositions would bring him some benefits.*

More seriously for James's argument, his negative rule does not have the application to theism which he supposes. His actual words were:

(A) "a rule of thinking which would absolutely prevent me from acknowledging certain kinds of truth if those kinds of truth were really there, would be an irrational rule."

Differently expressed, this says:

(B) It would be irrational of me to adopt a rule about belief formation which would forbid me from believing any proposition that is in fact true.

Applied to theism in particular this says:

(C) It would be irrational of me to adopt a rule about belief formation which would forbid me from believing that God exists if in fact he does exist.

But if (C) is true, so presumably is (D):

(D) It would be irrational of me to adopt a rule about belief formation which would forbid me from believing that God does not exist, if in fact he does not exist.

If there were any grounds for accepting (C), they would surely equally be grounds for accepting (D). So if the theist can appeal to his passional nature to justify his acceptance of theism, it seems that the atheist can appeal to *his* passional nature to justify his acceptance of atheism. In other words, what principle (A) licenses is the acceptance of one *or other* in a pair of open propositions: it has no means of picking out which proposition the passionally moved believer should accept.

It might be thought that James does have good grounds for distinguishing between accepting the existence of God, and accepting the non-existence of God. For he tells us that "we are better off even now" if we believe in religion. Although he himself does not elaborate on this claim, a friendly reading of his position could take this to be an omission which can easily be remedied. All that has to be done is to point to the benefits which a belief in God brings to the believer.

However, this reply on James's behalf does mean that his argument is committed to giving further hostages to fortune. For he then needs to supply empirical evidence that belief rather than disbelief does have this beneficial consequence. For some people, no doubt it is belief which makes their life go better; but for other people, it may well be disbelief. And if this is so, the potential audience for James's argument is diminished yet again.

Belief Without Argument

Alvin Plantinga

If the existence of God cannot be proved by reason, might belief in God nevertheless be rational? Alvin Plantinga, who is John A. O'Brien Professor of Philosophy at the University of Notre Dame, answers in the affirmative. He contends that the existence of God is not the conclusion of an argument but a premise, one that should be accepted as a basic belief not in need of support. In other words, belief in the existence of God is an innate tendency, equally as obvious as belief in the existence of one's spouse.

To the objection that this approach to belief in God is akin to a believer in the Great Pumpkin taking as a premise that the Great Pumpkin returns every Halloween, Plantinga replies that belief in the Great Pumpkin is not basic because we have no tendency to accept beliefs about the Great Pumpkin, and furthermore, the Great Pumpkin does not exist. The adequacy of Plantinga's reply is a matter for the reader to ponder.

Suppose we think of natural theology as the attempt to prove or demonstrate the existence of God. This enterprise has a long and impressive history—a history stretching back to the dawn of Christendom and boasting among its adherents many of the truly great thinkers of the Western world. Chief among these is Thomas Aquinas, whose work, I think, is the natural starting point for Christian philosophical reflection, Protestant as well as Catholic. Here we Protestants must be, in Ralph McInerny's immortal phrase, Peeping Thomists. Recently—since the time of Kant, perhaps—the tradition of natural theology has not been as overwhelming as it once was: yet it continues to have able defenders both within and without officially Catholic philosophy.

Many Christians, however, have been less than totally impressed. In particular Reformed or Calvinist theologians have for the most part taken a dim view of this enterprise. A few Reformed thinkers . . . endorse the theistic proofs; but for the most part the Reformed attitude has ranged from indifference, through suspicion and hostility, to outright accusations of blasphemy. And this stance is initially puzzling. It looks a little like the attitude some Christians adopt towards faith healing: it can't be done, but even if it could,

From *Christian Scholar's Review* 11 (1982).

it shouldn't be. What exactly, or even approximately, do these sons and daughters of the Reformation have against proving the existence of God? What *could* they have against it? What could be less objectionable to any but the most obdurate atheist?

Proof and Belief in God

. . . According to John Calvin, who is as good a Calvinist as any, God has implanted in us all an innate tendency, or nisus, or disposition to believe in him:

> "There is within the human mind, and indeed by natural instinct, an awareness of divinity." This we take to be beyond controversy. To prevent anyone from taking refuge in the pretense of ignorance, God himself has implanted in all men a certain understanding of his divine majesty. Ever renewing its memory, he repeatedly sheds fresh drops. Since, therefore, men one and all perceive that there is a God and that he is their Maker, they are condemned by their own testimony because they have failed to honor him and to consecrate their lives to his will. If ignorance of God is to be looked for anywhere, surely one is most likely to find an example of it among the more backward folk and those more remote from civilization. Yet there is, as the eminent pagan says, no nation so barbarous, no people so savage, that they have not a deep-seated conviction that there is a God. So deeply does the common conception occupy the minds of all, so tenaciously does it inhere in the hearts of all! Therefore, since from the beginning of the world there has been no region, no city, in short, no household, that could do without religion, there lies in this a tacit confession of a sense of deity inscribed in the hearts of all.[1]
>
> Indeed, the perversity of the impious, who though they struggle furiously are unable to extricate themselves from the fear of God, is abundant testimony that this conviction, namely, that there is some God, is naturally inborn in all, and is fixed deep within, as it were in the very marrow. . . . From this we conclude that it is not a doctrine that must first be learned in school, but one of which each of us is master from his mother's womb and which nature itself permits no one to forget.[2]

Calvin's claim, then, is that God has created us in such a way that we have a strong propensity or inclination towards belief in him. This tendency has been in part overlaid or suppressed by sin. Were it not for the existence of sin in the world, human beings would believe in God to the same degree and with the same natural spontaneity that we believe in the existence of other persons, an external world, or the past. This is the natural human condition; it is because of our presently unnatural sinful condition that many of us find belief in God difficult or absurd. The fact is, Calvin thinks, one who doesn't believe in God is in an epistemically substandard position—rather like a man who doesn't believe that his wife exists, or thinks she is like a cleverly constructed robot and has no thoughts, feelings, or consciousness.

Although this disposition to believe in God is partially suppressed, it is nonetheless universally present. And it is triggered or actuated by widely realized conditions:

> Lest anyone, then, be excluded from access to happiness, he not only sowed in men's minds that seed of religion of which we have spoken, but revealed himself and daily discloses himself in the whole workmanship of the universe. As a consequence, men cannot open their eyes without being compelled to see him.[3]

Like Kant, Calvin is especially impressed in this connection, by the marvelous compages of the starry heavens above:

> Even the common folk and the most untutored, who have been taught only by the aid of the eyes, cannot be unaware of the excellence of divine art, for it reveals itself in this innumerable and yet distinct and well-ordered variety of the heavenly host.[4]

And Calvin's claim is that one who accedes to this tendency and in these circumstances accepts the belief that God has created the world—perhaps upon beholding the starry heavens, or the splendid majesty of the mountains, or the intricate, articulate beauty of a tiny flower—is entirely within his epistemic rights in so doing. It isn't that such a person is justified or rational in so believing by virtue of having an implicit argument—some version of the teleological argument, say. No; he doesn't need any argument for justification or rationality. His belief need not be based on any other propositions at all; under these conditions he is perfectly rational in accepting belief in God in the utter absence of any argument, deductive or inductive. Indeed, a person in these conditions, says Calvin, *knows* that God exists, has knowledge of God's existence, apart from any argument at all.

Elsewhere Calvin speaks of "arguments from reason" or rational arguments:

> The prophets and apostles do not boast either of their keenness or of anything that obtains credit for them as they speak; nor do they dwell upon rational proofs. Rather, they bring forward God's holy name, that by it the whole world may be brought into obedience to him. Now we ought to see how apparent it is not only by plausible opinion but by dear truth that they do not call upon God's name heedlessly or falsely. If we desire to provide in the best way for our consciences—that they may not be perpetually beset by the instability of doubt or vacillation, and that they may not also boggle at the smallest quibbles—we ought to seek our conviction, in a higher place

than human reasons, judgments, or conjectures, that is, in the secret testimony of the Spirit.[5]

Here the subject for discussion is not belief in the existence of God, but belief that God is the author of the Scriptures; I think it is clear, however, that Calvin would say the same thing about belief in God's existence. The Christian doesn't need natural theology, either as the source of his confidence or to justify his belief. Furthermore, the Christian *ought* not to believe on the basis of argument; if he does, his faith is likely to be unstable and wavering. From Calvin's point of view, believing in the existence of God on the basis of rational argument is like believing in the existence of your spouse on the basis of the analogical argument for other minds—whimsical at best and not at all likely to delight the person concerned.

Foundationalism

We could look further into the precise forms taken by the Reformed objection to Natural Theology; time is short, however; what I shall do instead is tell you what I think underlies these objections, inchoate and unfocused as they are. The reformers mean to say, fundamentally, that belief in God can properly be taken as basic. That is, a person is entirely within his epistemic rights, entirely rational, in believing in God, even if he has no argument for this belief and does not believe it on the basis of any other beliefs he holds. And in taking belief in God as properly basic, the reformers were implicitly rejecting a whole picture or way of looking at knowledge and rational belief; call it *classical foundationalism.* This picture has been enormously popular ever since the days of Plato and Aristotle; it remains the dominant way of thinking about knowledge, justification, belief, faith, and allied topics. Although it has been thus dominant, Reformed theologians and thinkers have, I believe, meant to reject it. What they say here tends to be inchoate and not well-articulated; nevertheless the fact is they meant to reject classical foundationalism. But how shall we characterize the view rejected? The first thing to see is that foundationalism is a *normative* view. It aims to lay down conditions that must be met by anyone whose system of beliefs is *rational;* and here "rational" is to be understood normatively. According to the foundationalist, there is a right way and a wrong way with respect to belief. People have responsibilities, duties and obligations with respect to their believings just as with respect to their (other) actions. Perhaps this sort of obligation is really a special case of a more general moral obligation; or perhaps, on the other hand, it is sui generis. In any event there are such obligations: to conform to them is to be rational and to go against them is to be irrational. To be rational, then, is to exercise one's epistemic powers *properly*—to exercise them in such a way as to go contrary to none of the norms for such exercise.

Foundationalism, therefore, is in part a normative thesis. I think we can understand this thesis more fully if we introduce the idea of a *noetic structure.* A person's noetic structure is the set of propositions he believes together with certain epistemic relations that hold among him and these propositions. Thus some of his beliefs may be *based on* other things he believes; it may be that there are a pair of propositions A and B such that he believes *A on the basis of B.* Although this relation isn't easy to characterize in a revealing and nontrivial fashion, it is nonetheless familiar. I believe that the word "umbrageous" is spelled u-m-b-r-a-g-e-o-u-s: this belief is based on another belief of mine, the belief that that's how the dictionary says it's spelled. I believe that 72 × 71 = 5112. This belief is based upon several other beliefs I hold—such beliefs as that 1 × 72 = 72; 7 × 2 = 14; 7 × 7 = 49; 49 + 1 = 50; and others. Some of my beliefs, however, I accept but don't accept on the basis of any other beliefs. I believe that 2 + 1 = 3, for example, and don't believe it on the basis of other propositions. I also believe that I am seated at my desk, and that there is a mild pain in my right knee. These too are basic for me; I don't believe them on the basis of any other propositions.

An account of a person's noetic structure, then, would include a specification of which of his beliefs are basic and which are non-basic. Of course it is abstractly possible that *none* of his beliefs is basic; perhaps he holds just three beliefs, A, B, and C, and believes each of them on the basis of the other two. We might think this improper or irrational, but that is not to say it couldn't be done. And it is also possible that *all* of his beliefs are basic; perhaps he believes a lot of propositions, but doesn't believe any of them on the basis of any others. In the typical case, however, a noetic structure will include both basic and non-basic beliefs.

Secondly, an account of a noetic structure will include what we might call an index of degree of belief. I hold some of my beliefs much more firmly than others. I believe both that 2 + 1 = 3 and that London, England, is north of Saskatoon, Saskatchewan; but I believe the former more resolutely than the latter. . . .

Thirdly, a somewhat vaguer notion; an account of *S*'s noetic structure would include something like an index of *depth of ingression.* Some of my beliefs are, we might say, on the periphery of my noetic structure. I accept them, and may even accept them quite firmly; but if I were to give them up, not much else in my noetic structure would have to change. I believe there are some large boulders on the top of the Grand Teton. If I come to give up this belief, however (say by climbing it and not finding any), that change wouldn't have extensive reverberations throughout the rest of my noetic structure; it could be accommodated with minimal alteration elsewhere. So its depth of ingression into my noetic structure isn't great. On the other hand, if I were to come to believe that there simply is no such thing as the Grand Teton, or no mountains at all, or no such thing as the state of Wyoming, that would have much greater reverberations. And if, *per impossible,*[6] I were to come to think there hadn't been much of a past (that the world was created just five minutes ago, complete with all its apparent memories and traces of the past), or that there weren't any other persons, that would have even greater reverberations; these beliefs of mine have great depth of ingression into my noetic structure.

Now classical foundationalism is best construed, I think, as a thesis about *rational* noetic structures. A noetic structure is rational if it could be the noetic structure of a person who was completely rational. To be completely rational, as I am here using the term, is not to believe only what is true, or to believe all the logical consequences of what one believes, or to believe all necessary truths with equal firmness, or to be uninfluenced by emotion; it is, instead, to do the right thing with respect to one's believings. As we have seen, the foundationalist holds that there are responsibilities and duties that pertain to believings as well as to actions, or other actions; these responsibilities accrue to us just by virtue of our having the sorts of noetic capabilities we do have. There are norms or standards for beliefs. To criticize a person as irrational, then, is to criticize her for failing to fulfill these duties or responsibilities, or for failing to conform to the relevant norms or standards. From this point of view, a rational person is one whose believings meet the appropriate standards. To draw the ethical analogy, the irrational is the impermissible; the rational is the permissible.

A rational noetic structure, then, is one that could be the noetic structure of a perfectly rational person. And classical foundationalism is, in part, a thesis about such noetic structures. The foundationalist notes, first of all, that some of our beliefs are based upon others. He immediately adds that a belief can't properly be accepted on the basis of just *any* other belief; in a rational noetic structure, *A* will be accepted on the basis of *B* only if *B supports A,* or is a member of a set of beliefs that together support *A*. It isn't clear just what this supports relation is; different foundationalists propose different candidates. One candidate, for example, is *entailment; A* supports *B* only if *B* is entailed by *A,* or perhaps is self-evidently entailed by *A,* or perhaps follows from *A* by an argument where each step is a self-evident entailment. Another and more permissive candidate is probability; perhaps *A* supports *B* if *B* is likely or probable with respect to *A*. And of course there are other candidates.

More important for present purposes, however, is the following claim: in a rational noetic structure, there will be some beliefs that are not based upon others: call these its *foundations.* If every belief in a rational noetic structure were based upon other beliefs, the structure in question would contain infinitely many beliefs. However things may stand for more powerful intellects—angelic intellects, perhaps—human beings aren't capable of believing infinitely many propositions. Among other things, one presumably doesn't believe a proposition one has never heard of, and no one has had time, these busy days, to have heard of infinitely many propositions. So every rational noetic structure has a foundation.

Suppose we say that *weak* foundationalism is the view that (1) every rational noetic structure has a foundation, and (2) in a rational noetic structure, non-basic belief is proportional in strength to support from the foundations.

When I say Reformed thinkers have meant to reject foundationalism, I do not mean to say that they intended to reject weak foundationalism. On the contrary; the thought of many of them tends to support or endorse weak foundationalism. What then do they mean to reject? Here we meet a further and fundamental feature of classic varieties of foundationalism: they all lay down certain conditions of proper or rational basicality. From the foundationalist point of view, not just any kind of belief can be found in the foundations of a rational noetic structure; a belief, to be properly basic (i.e., basic in a rational noetic structure) must meet certain conditions. It is plausible to see Thomas Aquinas, for example, as holding that a proposition is properly basic for a person only if it is self-evident to him (such that his understanding or grasping it is sufficient for his seeing it to be true) or "evident to the senses," as he puts it. By this latter term I think he means to refer to propositions whose truth or falsehood we can determine by looking or listening or employing some other sense—such propositions as

(1) There is a tree before me
(2) I am wearing shoes

and

(3) That tree's leaves are yellow.

Many foundationalists have insisted that propositions basic in a rational noetic structure must be *certain* in some important sense. Thus it is plausible to see Descartes as holding that the foundations of a rational noetic structure don't include such propositions as (1)–(3) but more cautious claims—claims about one's own mental life, for example:

(4) It seems to me that I see a tree
(5) I seem to see something green

or, as Professor Chisholm puts it,

(6) I am appeared greenly to.

Propositions of this latter sort seem to enjoy a kind of immunity from error not enjoyed by those of the former. I could be mistaken in thinking I see a pink rat; perhaps I am hallucinating or the victim of an illusion. But it is at the least very much harder to see that I could be mistaken in believing that I *seem* to see a pink rat, in believing that I am appeared pinkly (or pink ratly) to. Suppose we say that a proposition with respect to which I enjoy this sort of immunity from error is *incorrigible* for me; then perhaps Descartes means to hold that a proposition is properly basic for *S* only if it is either self-evident or incorrigible for *S*.

Aquinas and Descartes, we might say, are *strong* foundationalists; they accept weak foundationalism and add some conditions for proper basicality. Ancient and medieval foundationalists tended to hold that a proposition is properly basic for a person only if it is either self-evident or evident to the senses; modern foundationalists—Descartes, Locke, Leibniz and the like—tended to hold that a proposition is properly basic for *S* only if either self-evident or incorrigible for *S*. Of course this is a historical generalization and is thus subject to contradiction by scholars, such being the penalty for historical generalization; but perhaps it is worth the risk. And now suppose we say that *classical foundationalism* is the disjunction of ancient and medieval with modern foundationalism.

The Reformed Rejection of Classical Foundationalism

These Reformed thinkers, I believe, are best understood as rejecting classical foundationalism. They were inclined to accept weak foundationalism, I think; but they were completely at odds with the idea that the foundations of a rational noetic structure can at most include propositions that are self-evident or evident to the senses or incorrigible. In particular, they were prepared to insist that a rational noetic structure can include belief in God as basic. . . .

In the passages I quoted earlier on, Calvin claims the believer doesn't need argument—doesn't need it, among other things, for epistemic respectability. We may understand him as holding, I think, that a rational noetic structure may perfectly well contain belief in God among its foundations. Indeed, he means to go further, and in two separate directions. In the first place, he thinks a Christian *ought* not believe in God on the basis of other propositions; a proper and well formed Christian noetic structure will *in fact* have belief in God among its foundations. And in the second place Calvin claims that one who takes belief in God as basic can nonetheless know that God exists. Calvin holds that one can *rationally accept* belief in God as basic; he also claims that one can *know* that God exists even if he has no argument, even if he does not believe on the basis of other propositions. A weak foundationalist is likely to hold that some properly basic beliefs are such that anyone who accepts them, *knows* them. More exactly, he is likely to hold that among the beliefs properly basic for a person *S*, some are such that if *S* accepts them *S* knows them. A weak foundationalist could go on to say that *other* properly basic beliefs can't be known, if taken as basic, but only rationally believed; and he might think of the existence of God as a case in point. Calvin will have none of this; as he sees it, one needs no arguments to know that God exists.

Among the central contentions of these Reformed thinkers, therefore, are the claims that belief in God is properly basic, and the view that one who takes belief in God as basic can also *know* that God exists.

The Great Pumpkin Objection

Now I enthusiastically concur in these contentions of Reformed epistemology, and by way of conclusion I want to defend them against a popular objection. It is tempting to raise the following sort of question. If belief in God is properly basic, why can't just any belief be properly basic? Couldn't we say the same for any bizarre aberration we can think of? What about voodoo or astrology? What about the belief that the Great Pumpkin returns every Halloween? Could I properly take *that* as basic? And if I can't, why can I properly take belief in God as basic? Suppose I believe that if I flap my arms with sufficient vigor, I can take off and fly about the room; could I defend myself against the charge of irrationality by claiming this belief is basic? If we say that belief in God is properly basic, won't we be committed to holding that just anything, or nearly anything, can properly be taken as basic, thus throwing wide the gates to irrationalism and superstition?

Certainly not. What might lead one to think the Reformed epistemologist is in this kind of trouble? The fact that he rejects the criteria for proper basicality purveyed by the classical foundationalist? But why should *that* be thought to commit him to such tolerance of irrationality? . . .

[C]riteria for proper basicality must be reached from below rather than above; they should not be presented as obiter dicta, but argued to and tested by a relevant set of examples. But there is no reason to assume, in advance, that everyone will agree on the examples. The Christian will of course suppose that belief in God is entirely proper and rational; if he doesn't accept this belief on the basis of other propositions, he will conclude that it is basic for him and quite properly so. Followers of Bertrand Russell and Madalyn Murray O'Hair may disagree; but how is that relevant? Must my criteria, or those of the Christian community, conform to their examples? Surely not. The Christian community is responsible to its set of examples, not to theirs.

Accordingly, the Reformed epistemologist can properly hold that belief in the Great Pumpkin is not properly basic, even though he holds that belief in God is properly basic and even if he has no full fledged criterion of proper basicality. Of course he is committed to supposing that there is a relevant *difference* between belief in God and belief in the Great Pumpkin, if he holds that the former but not the latter is properly basic. But this should be no great embarrassment; there are plenty of candidates. Thus the Reformed epistemologist may concur with Calvin in holding that God has implanted in us a natural tendency to see his hand in the world around us; the same cannot be said for the Great Pumpkin, there being no Great Pumpkin and no natural tendency to accept beliefs about the Great Pumpkin.

By way of conclusion then, the Reformed objection to natural theology, unformed and inchoate as it is, may best be seen as a rejection of classical foundationalism. As the Reformed thinker sees things, being self-evident, or incorrigible, or evident to the senses is not a necessary condition of proper basicality. He goes on to add that belief in God is properly basic. He is not thereby committed, even in the absence of a general criterion of proper basicality, to suppose that just any or nearly any belief—belief in the Great Pumpkin, for example—is properly basic. Like everyone should, he begins with examples; and he may take belief in the Great Pumpkin as a paradigm of irrational basic belief.

NOTES

1. *Institutes of the Christian Religion,* ed. J. T. McNeill and trans. Ford Lewis Battles (Philadelphia: Westminster Press, 1960), Book I, Chap. iii, sec. 1.
2. *Institutes,* I, iii, 3.
3. *Institutes,* V, v, 1.
4. *Institutes,* V, v, 2.
5. *Institutes,* I, vii, 4.
6. [although impossible.]

Belief Without Argument: A Critique

Michael Martin

Michael Martin, who is Professor Emeritus of Philosophy at Boston University, does not find Plantinga's position persuasive. Martin points out that if theists can take belief in God as basic, atheists can take disbelief in God as basic. Furthermore, believers in the Great Pumpkin can take belief in the Great Pumpkin as basic. If Plantinga were correct, no reliable method would be available to evaluate any of these claims.

Belief in the existence of a spouse might be basic because no plausible alternatives are workable. Belief in the existence of God, however, is only one possibility among others, many of which can be adopted without difficulty. Thus the justifications for the two sorts of belief are not parallel.

What can one say about Plantinga's ingenious attempt to save theism from the charge of irrationality by making beliefs about God basic?

(1) Plantinga's claim that his proposal would not allow just any belief to become a basic belief is misleading. It is true that it would not allow just any belief to become a basic belief *from the point of view of Reformed epistemologists.* However it would seem to allow any belief at all to become basic from the point of view of *some* community. Although reformed epistemologists would not have to accept voodoo beliefs as rational, voodoo followers would be able to claim that insofar as they are basic in the voodoo community they are rational and, moreover, that reformed thought was irrational in this community. Indeed, Plantinga's proposal would generate many different communities that could *legitimately* claim that their basic beliefs are rational and that these beliefs conflict with basic beliefs of other communities. Among the communities generated might be devil worshipers, flat earthers, and believers in fairies just so long as belief in the devil, the flatness of the earth, and fairies was basic in the respective communities.

(2) On this view the rationality of any belief is absurdly easy to obtain. The cherished belief that is held without reason by *any* group could be considered properly basic by the group's members. There would be no way to make a critical evaluation of any beliefs so considered. The community's most cherished beliefs and the conditions that, according to the community, correctly trigger such beliefs would be accepted uncritically by the members of the community as just so many more examples of basic beliefs and justifying conditions. The more philosophical members of the community could go on to propose hypotheses as to the necessary and sufficient conditions for inclusion in this set. Perhaps, using this inductive procedure, a criterion could be formulated. However, what examples the hypotheses must account for would be decided by the community. As Plantinga says, each community would be responsible only to its own set of examples in formulating a criterion, and each would decide what is to be included in this set.

(3) Plantinga seems to suppose that there is a consensus in the Christian community about what beliefs are basic and what conditions justify these beliefs. But this is not so. Some Christians believe in God on the basis of the traditional arguments or on the basis of religious experiences; their belief in God is not basic. There would, then, certainly be no agreement in the Christian community over whether belief in God is basic or nonbasic. More important, there would be no agreement on whether doctrinal beliefs concerning the authority of the pope, the makeup of the Trinity, the nature of Christ, the means of salvation, and so on were true, let alone basic. Some Christian sects would hold certain doctrinal beliefs to be basic and rational; others would hold the same beliefs to be irrational and, indeed, the gravest of heresies. Moreover, there would be no agreement over the conditions for basic belief. Some Christians might believe that a belief is properly basic when it is triggered by listening to the pope. Others would violently disagree. Even where there was agreement over the right conditions, these would seem to justify

conflicting basic beliefs and, consequently, conflicting religious sects founded on them. For example, a woman named Jones, the founder of sect S_1, might read the Bible and be impressed that God is speaking to her and telling her that p. A man named Smith, the founder of sect S_2, might read the Bible and be impressed that God is speaking to him and telling him that ~p. So Jones's belief that p and Smith's belief that ~p would both be properly basic. One might wonder how this differs from the doctrinal disputes that have gone on for centuries among Christian sects and persist to this day. The difference is that on Plantinga's proposal each sect could *justifiably* claim that its belief, for which there might be no evidence or argument, was completely rational.

(4) So long as belief that there is no God was basic for them, atheists could also justify the claim that belief in God is irrational relative to their basic beliefs and the conditions that trigger them without critically evaluating any of the usual reasons for believing in God. Just as theistic belief might be triggered by viewing the starry heavens above and reading the Bible, so atheistic beliefs might be triggered by viewing the massacre of innocent children below and reading the writings of Robert Ingersoll. Theists may disagree, but is that relevant? To paraphrase Plantinga: Must atheists' criteria conform to the Christian communities' criteria? Surely not. The atheistic community is responsible to *its* set of examples, not to theirs.

(5) There may not at present be any clear criterion for what can be a basic belief, but belief in God seems peculiarly inappropriate for inclusion in the class since there are clear disanalogies between it and the basic beliefs allowable by classical foundationalism. For example, in his critique of classical foundationalism, Plantinga has suggested that belief in other minds and the external world should be considered basic. There are many plausible alternatives to belief in an all-good, all-powerful, all-knowing God, but there are few, if any, plausible alternatives to belief in other minds and the external world. Moreover, even if one disagrees with these arguments that seem to provide evidence against the existence of God, surely one must attempt to meet them. Although there are many skeptical arguments against belief in other minds and the external world, there are in contrast no seriously accepted arguments purporting to show that there are no other minds or no external world. In this world, atheism and agnosticism are live options for many intelligent people; solipsism is an option only for the mentally ill.

(6) As we have seen, Plantinga, following Calvin, says that some conditions that trigger belief in God or particular beliefs about God also justify these beliefs and that, although these beliefs concerning God are basic; they are not groundless. Although Plantinga gave no general account of what these justifying conditions are, he presented some examples of what he meant and likened these justifying conditions to those of properly basic perceptual and memory statements. The problem here is the weakness of the analogy. As Plantinga points out, before we take a perceptual or memory belief as properly basic we must have evidence that our perception or memory is not faulty. Part of the justification for believing that our perception or memory is

not faulty is that in general it agrees with the perception or memory of our epistemological peers—that is, our equals in intelligence, perspicacity, honesty, thoroughness, and other relevant epistemic virtues, as well as with our other experiences. For example, unless my perceptions generally agreed with other perceivers with normal eyesight in normal circumstances and with my nonvisual experience—for example, that I feel something solid when I reach out—there would be no justification for supposing that my belief that I see a rose-colored wall in front of me is properly basic. Plantinga admits that if I know my memory is unreliable, my belief that I had breakfast should not be taken as properly basic. However, one knows that one's memory is reliable by determining whether it coheres with the memory reports of other people whose memory is normal and with one's other experiences.

As we have already seen, lack of agreement is commonplace in religious contexts. Different beliefs are triggered in different people when they behold the starry heavens or when they read the Bible. Beholding the starry heavens can trigger a pantheistic belief or a purely aesthetic response without any religious component. Sometimes no particular response or belief at all is triggered. From what we know about the variations of religious belief, it is likely that people would not have theistic beliefs when they beheld the starry heavens if they had been raised in nontheistic environments. Similarly, a variety of beliefs and responses are triggered when the Bible is read. Some people are puzzled and confused by the contradictions, others become skeptical of the biblical stories, others believe that God is speaking to them and has appointed them as his spokesperson, others believe God is speaking to them but has appointed no one as His spokesperson. In short, there is no consensus in the Christian community, let alone among Bible readers generally. So unlike perception and memory, there are no grounds for claiming that a belief in God is properly basic since the conditions that trigger it yield widespread disagreement among epistemological peers.

Faith

Richard Taylor

Suppose you arrive at the conclusion that your religious belief is unreasonable. Should you abandon that belief? In our next reading,

---

From Sidney Hook, ed., *Religious Experience and Truth.* Reprinted by permission of Ernest B. Hook.

Richard Taylor, whose work we read previously, accepts as obvious the claim that Christianity is not reasonable. But rather than concluding that Christian belief should be abandoned, he urges that reason should give way to faith. Such an approach has strong appeal to many religious adherents, and Taylor's defense of the appropriateness of their devotion is uncompromising and unapologetic.

"Our most holy religion," David Hume said, "is founded on *faith,* not on reason." (All quotations are from the last two paragraphs of Hume's essay "Of Miracles.") He did not then conclude that it ought, therefore, to be rejected by reasonable men. On the contrary, he suggests that rational evaluation has no proper place in this realm to begin with, that a religious man need not feel in the least compelled to put his religion "to such a trial as it is, by no means, fitted to endure," and he brands as "dangerous friends or disguised enemies" of religion those "who have undertaken to defend it by the principles of human reason."

I want to defend Hume's suggestion, and go a bit farther by eliciting some things that seem uniquely characteristic of *Christian* faith, in order to show what it has, and what it has not, in common with other things to which it is often compared. I limited myself to Christian faith, because I know rather little of any other, and faith is, with love and hope, supposed to be a uniquely Christian virtue.

Faith and Reason

Faith is not reason, else religion would be, along with logic and metaphysics, a part of philosophy, which it assuredly is not. Nor is faith belief resting on scientific or historical inquiry, else religion would be part of the corpus of human knowledge, which it clearly is not. More than that, it seems evident that by the normal, common-sense criteria of what is reasonable, the content of Christian faith is *un*reasonable. This, I believe, should be the starting point, the *datum,* of any discussion of faith and reason. It is, for instance, an essential content of the Christian faith that, at a certain quite recent time, God became man, dwelt among us in the person of a humble servant, and then, for a sacred purpose, died, to live again. Now, apologetics usually addresses itself to the *details* of this story, to show that they are not inherently incredible, but this is to miss the point. It is indeed *possible* to believe it, and in the strict sense the story is credible. Millions of people do most deeply and firmly believe it. But even the barest statement of the content of that belief makes it manifest that it does not and, I think, could not, ever result from rational inquiry. "Mere reason," Hume said, "is insufficient to convince us of its veracity." The Christian begins the recital of his faith with the words, "I believe," and it would be an utter distortion to construe this as anything like "I have inquired, and found it reasonable to conclude." If there were a man who could say that in honesty, as I think there is not, then he would, in a clear and ordinary sense, believe, but he would have no religious faith whatsoever, and his beliefs themselves would be robbed of what would make them religious.

Now if this essential and (it seems to me) obvious unreasonableness of Christian belief could be recognized at the outset of any discussion of religion, involving rationalists on the one hand and believers on the other, we would be spared the tiresome attack and apologetics upon which nothing ultimately turns, the believer would be spared what is, in fact, an uncalled-for task of reducing his faith to reason or science, which can, as Hume noted, result only in "exposing" it as neither, and the rationalist would be granted his main point, not as a conclusion triumphantly extracted, but as a datum too obvious to labor.

Faith and Certainty

Why, then, does a devout Christian embrace these beliefs? Now this very question, on the lips of a philosopher, is wrongly expressed, for he invariably intends it as a request for reasons, as a means of putting the beliefs to that unfair "trial" of which Hume spoke. Yet there is a clear and definite answer to this question, which has the merit of being true and evident to anyone who has known intimately those who dwell in the atmosphere of faith. The reason the Christian believes that story around which his whole life turns is, simply, that he cannot help it. If he is trapped into eliciting grounds for it, they are grounds given after the fact of conviction. . . . One neither seeks nor needs grounds for the acceptance of what he cannot help believing. "Whoever is moved by *faith* to assent," Hume wrote, "is conscious of a continued miracle in his own person, which subverts all the principles of his understanding, and gives him a determination to believe. . . ." It is this fact of faith which drives philosophers to such exasperation, in the face of which the believer is nonetheless so utterly unmoved.

The believer sees his life as a gift of God, the world as the creation of God, his own purposes, insofar as they are noble, as the purposes of God, and history as exhibiting a divine plan, made known to him through the Christian story. He sees things this way, just because they do seem so, and he cannot help it. This is why, for him, faith is so "easy," and secular arguments to the contrary so beside the point. No one seeks evidence for that of which he is entirely convinced, or regards as relevant what seems to others to cast doubt. The believer is like a child who recoils from danger, as exhibited, for instance, in what he for the first time sees as a fierce animal; the child has no difficulty *believing* he is in peril, just because he cannot help believing it, yet his belief results not at all from induction based on past experience with fierce animals, and no reassurances, garnered from *our* past experience, relieve his terror at all.

Some Confusions

If this is what religious faith essentially is—if, as a believer might poetically but, I think, correctly describe it, faith is an involuntary conviction, often regarded as a "gift," on the part of one who has voluntarily opened his mind and heart to receive it—then certain common misunderstandings can be removed.

In the first place, faith should never be likened to an *assumption,* such as the scientist's assumption of the uniformity of nature, or what not. An assumption is an intellectual device for furthering inquiry. It need not be a conviction nor, indeed, even a belief. But a half-hearted faith is no religious faith. Faith thus has that much, at least, in common with knowledge, that it is a *conviction,* and its subjective state is *certainty.* One thus wholly distorts faith if he represents the believer as just "taking" certain things "on faith," and then reasons, like a philosopher, from these beginnings, as though what were thus "taken" could, like an assumption, be rejected at will.

Again, it is a misunderstanding to represent faith as "mere tenacity." Tenacity consists in stubbornly clinging to what one hopes, but of which one is not fully convinced. The child who is instantly convinced of danger in the presence of an animal is not being tenacious or stubborn, even in the face of verbal reassurances, and no more is the Christian whose acts are moved by faith. The believer does not so much *shun* evidence as something that might *shake* his faith, but rather regards it as not to the point. In this he may appear to philosophers to be mistaken, but only if one supposes, as he need not, that one should hold only such beliefs as are rational.

Again, it is misleading to refer to any set of propositions, such as those embodied in a creed, as being this or that person's "faith." Concerning that content of belief in which one is convinced by faith, it is logically (though I think not otherwise) possible that one might be convinced by evidence, in which case it would have no more to do with faith or religion than do the statements in a newspaper. This observation has this practical importance, that it is quite possible—in fact, common—for the faith of different believers to be one and the same, despite creedal differences.

And finally, both "faith" (or "fideism") and "reason" (or "rationalism") can be, and often are, used as pejorative terms, and as terms of commendation. Which side one takes here is arbitrary, for there is no non-question-begging way of deciding. A rationalist can perhaps find reasons for being a rationalist, though this is doubtful; but in any case it would betray a basic misunderstanding to expect a fideist to do likewise. This is brought out quite clearly by the direction that discussions of religion usually take. A philosophical teacher will often, for instance, labor long to persuade his audience that the content of Christian faith is unreasonable, which is a shamefully easy task for him, unworthy of his learning. Then suddenly, the underlying assumption comes to light that Christian beliefs ought, therefore, to be abandoned by rational people! A religious hearer of this discourse might well reply that, religion being unreasonable but nonetheless manifestly worthy of belief, we should conclude with Hume that reason, in this realm at least, ought to be rejected. Now, one can decide *that* issue by any light that is granted him, but it is worth stressing that the believer's position on it is just exactly as good, and just as bad, as the rational sceptic's.

Faith and Reason

MICHAEL SCRIVEN

In the previous selection, Richard Taylor maintained that in deciding matters of religious belief, the appeal to faith is as appropriate as the use of reason. According to him, the choice between the two approaches is arbitrary.

Michael Scriven, who is Professor of Philosophy at Western Michigan University, disagrees. He argues that reason and faith are not on a par because reason has passed tests of effectiveness that faith has not. Furthermore, while every religious believer relies on reason to assess the claims of ordinary experience, those who are not religious believers have no need to rely on religious faith in any aspect of their lives. If the criteria for religious truth are not connected with the criteria for everyday truth, faith, unlike reason, does not provide a reliable guide for our lives in this world.

We must now contend with the suggestion that reason is irrelevant to the commitment to theism because this territory is the domain of another faculty: the faculty of faith. It is sometimes even hinted that it is morally wrong and certainly foolish to suggest we should be reasoning about God. For this is the domain of faith or of the "venture of faith," of the "knowledge that passeth understanding," of religious experience and mystic insight.

Now the normal meaning of *faith* is simply "confidence"; we say that we have great faith in someone or in some claim or product, meaning that we believe and act as if they were very reliable. Of such faith we can properly

---

From Michael Scriven, *Primary Philosophy*. Reprinted by permission of The McGraw-Hill Companies.

say that it is well founded or not, depending on the evidence for whatever it is in which we have faith. So there is no incompatibility between this kind of faith and reason; the two are from different families and can make a very good marriage. Indeed if they do not join forces, then the resulting ill-based or inadequate confidence will probably lead to disaster. So faith, in this sense, means only a high degree of belief and may be reasonable or unreasonable.

But the term is sometimes used to mean an *alternative to reason* instead of something that should be founded on reason. Unfortunately, the mere use of the term in this way does not demonstrate that faith is a possible route to truth. It is like using the term "winning" as a synonym for "playing" instead of one possible outcome of playing. This is quaint, but it could hardly be called a satisfactory way of proving that we are winning; any time we "win" by changing the meaning of winning, the victory is merely illusory. And so it proves in this case. To use "faith" *as if* it were an alternative way to the truth cannot by-pass the crucial question whether such results really have any likelihood of being true. A rose by any other name will smell the same, and the inescapable facts about "faith" in the new sense are that it is still *applied to* a belief and is still supposed to imply *confidence in* that belief: the belief in the existence and goodness of God. So we can still ask the same old question about that belief: Is the confidence justified or misplaced? To say we "take it on faith" does not get it off parole.

Suppose someone replies that theism is a kind of belief that does not need justification by evidence. This means either that no one cares whether it is correct or not or that there is some other way of checking that it is correct besides looking at the evidence for it, i.e., giving reasons for believing it. But the first alternative is false since very many people care whether there is a God or not; and the second alternative is false because any method of showing that belief is likely to be true is, by definition, a justification of that belief, i.e., an appeal to reason. You certainly cannot show that a belief in God is likely to be true just by having confidence in it and by saying this is a case of knowledge "based on" faith, any more than you can win a game just by playing it and by calling that winning.

It is psychologically possible to have faith in something without any basis in fact, and once in a while you will turn out to be lucky and to have backed the right belief. This does not show you "really knew all along"; it only shows you cannot be unlucky all the time. . . . But, in general, beliefs without foundations lead to an early grave or to an accumulation of superstitions, which are usually troublesome and always false beliefs. It is hardly possible to defend this approach just by *saying* that you have decided that in this area confidence is its own justification.

Of course, you might try to *prove* that a feeling of great confidence about certain types of propositions is a reliable indication of their truth. If you succeeded, you would indeed have shown that the belief was justified; you would have done *this* by justifying it. To do this you would have to show what the real facts were and show that when someone had the kind of faith we are now talking about, it usually turned out that the facts were as he believed, just as we might justify the claims of a telepath. The catch in all this is simply that you have got to show what the real facts are in some way *other* than by appealing to faith, since that would simply be assuming what you are trying to prove. And if you can show what the facts are in this other way, you do not need faith in any new sense at all; you are already perfectly entitled to confidence in any belief that you have shown to be well supported.

How are you going to show what the real facts are? You show this by any method of investigation that has itself been tested, the testing being done by still another tested method, etc., through a series of tested connections that eventually terminates in our ordinary everyday reasoning and testing procedures of logic and observation.

Is it not prejudiced to require that the validation of beliefs always involve ultimate reference to our ordinary logic and everyday-plus-scientific knowledge? May not faith (religious experience, mystic insight) give us access to some new domain of truth? It is certainly possible that it does this. But, of course, it is also possible that it lies. One can hardly accept the reports of those with faith or, indeed, the apparent revelations of one's own religious experiences on the ground that they *might* be right. So *might* be a fervent materialist who saw his interpretation as a revelation. Possibility is not veracity. Is it not of the very greatest importance that we should try to find out whether we really can justify the use of the term "truth or knowledge" in describing the content of faith? If it is, then we must find something in that content that is known to be true in some other way, because to get off the ground we must first push off against the ground—we cannot lift ourselves by our shoelaces. If the new realm of knowledge is to be a realm of knowledge and not mythology, then it must tell us something which relates it to the kind of case that gives meaning to the term "truth." If you want to use the old word for the new events, you must show that it is applicable.

Could not the validating experience, which religious experience must have if it is to be called true, be the experience of others who also have or have had religious experiences? The religious community could, surely, provide a basis of agreement analogous to that which ultimately underlies scientific truth. Unfortunately, agreement is not the only requirement for avoiding error, for all may be in error. The difficulty for the religious community is to show that its agreement is not simply agreement about a shared mistake. If agreement were the only criterion of truth, there could never be a shared mistake; but clearly either the atheist group or the theist group shares a mistake. To decide which is wrong must involve appeal to something other than mere agreement. And, of course, it is clear that particular religious beliefs are mistaken, since religious groups do not all agree and they cannot all be right.

Might not some or all scientific beliefs be wrong, too? This is conceivable, but there are crucial differences between the two kinds of belief. In the first place, any commonly agreed religious beliefs concern only one or a few entities and their properties and histories. What for convenience we are here calling "scientific belief" is actually the sum total of all conventionally founded human knowledge, much of it not part of any science, and it embraces billions upon billions of facts, each of them perpetually or frequently subject to checking by independent means, each connected with a million others. The success of *this* system of knowledge shows up every day in everything that we do: we eat, and the food is not poison; we read, and the pages do not turn to dust; we slip, and gravity does not fail to pull us down. We are not just relying on the existence of agreement about the interpretation of a certain experience among a small part of the population. We are relying directly on our extremely reliable, nearly universal, and independently tested senses, and each of us is constantly obtaining independent confirmation for claims based on these, many of these confirmations being obtained for many claims, independently of each other. It is the wildest flight of fancy to suppose that there is a body of common religious beliefs which can be set out to exhibit this degree of repeated checking by religious experiences. In fact, there is not only gross disagreement on even the most fundamental claims in the creeds of different churches, each of which is supported by appeal to religious experience or faith, but where there is agreement by many people, it is all too easily open to the criticism that it arises from the common cultural exposure of the child or the adult convert and hence is not independent in the required way.

This claim that the agreement between judges is spurious in a particular case because it only reflects previous common indoctrination of those in agreement is a serious one. It must always be met by direct disproof whenever agreement is appealed to in science, and it is. The claim that the food is not poison cannot be explained away as a myth of some subculture, for anyone, even if told nothing about the eaters in advance, will judge that the people who ate it are still well. The whole methodology of testing is committed to the doctrine that any judges who could have learned what they are expected to say about the matter they are judging are completely valueless. Now anyone exposed to religious teaching, whether a believer or not, has long known the standard for such experiences, the usual symbols, the appropriate circumstances, and so on. These suggestions are usually very deeply implanted, so that they cannot be avoided by good intentions, and consequently members of our culture are rendered entirely incapable *of* being independent observers. Whenever observers are not free from previous contamination in this manner, the only way to support their claims is to examine independently testable *consequences* of the novel claims, such as predictions about the future. In the absence of these, the religious-experience gambit, whether involving literal or analogical claims, is wholly abortive.

A still more fundamental point counts against the idea that agreement among the religious can help support the idea of faith as an alternative path to truth. It is that every sane theist also believes in the claims of ordinary experience, while the reverse is not the case. Hence, the burden of proof is on the theist to show that the *further step* he wishes to take will not take him beyond the realm of truth. The two positions, of science and religion, are not symmetrical; the adherent of one of them suggests that we extend the range of allowable beliefs and yet is unable to produce the same degree of acceptance or "proving out" in the ordinary field of human activities that he insists on before believing in a new instrument or source of information. The atheist obviously cannot be shown his error in the way someone who thinks that there are no electrons can be shown his, *unless some of the arguments for the existence of God are sound. . . .* If some of them work, the position of religious knowledge is secure; if they do not, nothing else will make it secure.

In sum, the idea of separating religious from scientific knowledge and making each an independent realm with its own basis in experience of quite different kinds is a counsel of despair and not a product of true sophistication, for one cannot break the connection between everyday experience and religious claims, for purposes of defending the latter, without eliminating the consequences of religion for everyday life. There is no way out of this inexorable contract: if you want to support your beliefs, you must produce some experience which can be shown to be a reliable indicator of truth, and that can be done only by showing a connection between the experience and what we know to be true in a previously established way.

So, if the criteria of religious truth are not connected with the criteria of everyday truth, then they are not criteria of truth at all and the beliefs they "establish" have no essential bearing on our lives, constitute no explanation of what we see around us, and provide no guidance for our course through time.

Theology and Falsification

Antony Flew, R. M. Hare, and Basil Mitchell

The exchange that follows has probably given rise to more commentary than any other single work in twentieth-century philosophy of religion. The central issue is not whether God exists but whether the claim that God exists has meaning.

From Antony Flew and Alasdair MacIntyre, eds., *New Essays in Philosophical Theology.* SCM Press, 1995. Reprinted by permission of Scribner, an imprint of Simon & Schuster Adult Publishing Group, and SCM Press. I am grateful to Dr. Victor Goldenberg for suggesting to me that Hare's term *blik* may have been derived from the German word *Blick.*

Antony Flew, Professor Emeritus of Philosophy at York University, argues that in order for a belief to be meaningful, it must be open to the possibility of disproof. For instance, my belief that my computer works well would be disproved by its going on and off uncontrollably. What evidence, however, would theists accept as a disproof of either God's existence or God's love for us? If a person maintains that God is good, no matter what evils may occur, then against what evils does God's goodness offer protection? In other words, if God's goodness is compatible with all possible events, how does a world filled with God's goodness differ from one without it?

R. M. Hare (1919–2002), who was White's Professor of Moral Philosophy at the University of Oxford, responds to Flew's challenge by introducing the notion of a *blik*, an undefined term that appears akin to an unprovable assumption. (Perhaps Hare derived the word from the German word *Blick* meaning "view.") In any case Hare claims that we all have *bliks* about the world and that Christian belief is one example. He grants that some *bliks* are sane and others insane but does not explain his basis for drawing this distinction.

Basil Mitchell, who was Nolloth Professor of the Christian Religion at the University of Oxford, claims that evidence does count against Christian doctrines but that for a person of faith such evidence can never be allowed to be decisive. Does this reply, however, lead theism to suffer what Flew calls "death by a thousand qualifications"? This question is but one of many provocative issues raised in the much-discussed selection that follows.

A

Antony Flew

Let us begin with a parable. It is a parable developed from a tale told by John Wisdom in his haunting and revelatory article "Gods."[1] Once upon a time two explorers came upon a clearing in the jungle. In the clearing were growing many flowers and many weeds. One explorer says, "Some gardener must tend this plot." The other disagrees, "There is no gardener." So they pitch their tents and set a watch. No gardener is ever seen. "But perhaps he is an invisible gardener." So they set up a barbed-wire fence. They electrify it. They patrol with bloodhounds. (For they remember how H. G. Wells's *The Invisible Man* could be both smelt and touched though he could not be seen.) But no shrieks ever suggest that some intruder has received a shock. No movements of the wire ever betray an invisible climber. The bloodhounds never give cry. Yet still the Believer is not convinced. "But there is a gardener, invisible, intangible, insensible to electric shocks, a gardener who has no scent and makes no sound, a gardener who comes secretly to look after the garden which he loves." At last the Sceptic despairs, "But what remains of your original assertion? Just how does what you call an invisible, intangible, eternally elusive gardener differ from an imaginary gardener or even from no gardener at all?"

In this parable we can see how what starts as an assertion, that something exists or that there is some analogy between certain complexes of phenomena, may be reduced step by step to an altogether different status, to an expression perhaps of a "picture preference."[2] The Sceptic says there is no gardener. The Believer says there is a gardener (but invisible, etc.). One man talks about sexual behaviour. Another man prefers to talk of Aphrodite (but knows that there is not really a superhuman person additional to, and somehow responsible for, all sexual phenomena). The process of qualification may be checked at any point before the original assertion is completely withdrawn and something of that first assertion will remain (Tautology). Mr. Wells's invisible man could not, admittedly, be seen, but in all other respects he was a man like the rest of us. But though the process of qualification may be, and of course usually is, checked in time, it is not always judiciously so halted. Someone may dissipate his assertion completely without noticing that he has done so. A fine brash hypothesis may thus be killed by inches, the death by a thousand qualifications.

And in this, it seems to me, lies the peculiar danger, the endemic evil, of theological utterance. Take such utterances as "God has a plan," "God created the world," "God loves us as a father loves his children." They look at first sight very much like assertions, vast cosmological assertions. Of course, this is no sure sign that they either are, or are intended to be, assertions. But let us confine ourselves to the cases where those who utter such sentences intend them to express assertions. (Merely remarking parenthetically that those who intend or interpret such utterances as crypto-commands, expressions of wishes, disguised ejaculations, concealed ethics, or as anything else but assertions, are unlikely to succeed in making them either properly orthodox or practically effective).

Now to assert that such and such is the case is necessarily equivalent to denying that such and such is not the case. Suppose then that we are in doubt as to what someone who gives vent to an utterance is asserting, or suppose that, more radically, we are sceptical as to whether he is really asserting anything at all, one way of trying to understand (or perhaps it will be to expose) his utterance is to attempt to find what he would regard as counting against, or as being incompatible with, its truth. For if the utterance is indeed an assertion, it will necessarily be equivalent to a denial of the negation of that assertion. And anything which would count against the assertion, or which would induce the speaker to withdraw it and to admit that it had been mistaken, must be part of (or the whole of) the meaning of the negation of that assertion. And to know the meaning of the negation of an assertion, is as near as makes no matter, to know the meaning of that assertion. And if there is nothing which a putative assertion denies then there is nothing which it asserts either: and so it is not really an assertion. When the Sceptic in the parable asked the Believer, "Just how does what you call an invisible, intangible, eternally elusive gardener differ from an imaginary gardener or even from no gardener at all?" he was suggesting that the Believer's earlier statement had been so eroded by qualification that it was no longer an assertion at all.

Now it often seems to people who are not religious as if there was no conceivable event or series of events the occurrence of which would be admitted by sophisticated religious people to be a sufficient reason for conceding "There wasn't a God after all" or "God does not really love us then." Someone tells us that God loves us as a father loves his children. We are reassured. But then we see a child dying of inoperable cancer of the throat. His earthly father is driven frantic in his efforts to help, but his Heavenly Father reveals no obvious sign of concern. Some qualification is made—God's love is "not a merely human love" or it is "an inscrutable love," perhaps—and we realize that such sufferings are quite compatible with the truth of the assertion that "God loves us as a father (but, of course, . . .)." We are reassured again. But then perhaps we ask: what is this assurance of God's (appropriately qualified) love worth, what is this apparent guarantee really a guarantee against? Just what would have to happen not merely (morally and wrongly) to tempt but also (logically and rightly) to entitle us to say "God does not love us" or even "God does not exist"? I therefore put to the succeeding symposiasts the simple central questions, "What would have to occur or to have occurred to constitute for you a disproof of the love of, or of the existence of, God?"

B

R. M. Hare

I wish to make it clear that I shall not try to defend Christianity in particular, but religion in general—not because I do not believe in Christianity, but because you cannot understand what Christianity is, until you have understood what religion is.

I must begin by confessing that, on the ground marked out by Flew, he seems to me to be completely victorious. I therefore shift my ground by relating anothe parable. A certain lunatic is convinced that all dons want to murder him. His friends introduce him to all the mildest and most respectable dons that they can find, and after each of them has retired, they say, "You see, he doesn't really want to murder you; he spoke to you in a most cordial manner; surely you are convinced now?" But the lunatic replies "Yes, but that was only his diabolical cunning; he's really plotting against me the whole time, like the rest of them; I know it I tell you." However many kindly dons are produced, the reaction is still the same.

Now we say that such a person is deluded. But what is he deluded about? About the truth or falsity of an assertion? Let us apply Flew's test to him. There is no behaviour of dons that can be enacted which he will accept as counting against his theory; and therefore his theory, on this test, asserts nothing. But it does not follow that there is no difference between what he thinks about dons and what most of us think about them—otherwise we should not call him a lunatic and ourselves sane, and dons would have no reason to feel uneasy about his presence in Oxford.

Let us call that in which we differ from this lunatic, our respective *bliks.* He has an insane *blik* about dons; we have a sane one. It is important to realize that we have a sane one, not no *blik* at all; for there must be two sides to any argument—if he has a wrong *blik,* then those who are right about dons must have a right one. Flew has shown that a *blik* does not consist in an assertion or system of them; but nevertheless it is very important to have the right *blik.*

Let us try to imagine what it would be like to have different *bliks* about other things than dons. When I am driving my car, it sometimes occurs to me to wonder whether my movements of the steering-wheel will always continue to be followed by corresponding alterations in the direction of the car. I have never had a steering failure, though I have had skids, which must be similar. Moreover, I know enough about how the steering of my car is made, to know the sort of thing that would have to go wrong for the steering to fail—steel joints would have to part, or steel rods break, or something—but how do I know that this won't happen? The truth is, I don't know; I just have a *blik* about steel and its properties, so that normally I trust the steering of my car; but I find it not at all difficult to imagine what it would be like to lose this *blik* and acquire the opposite one. People would say I was silly about steel; but there would be no mistaking the reality of the difference between our respective *bliks*—for example, I should never go in a motor-car. Yet I should hesitate to say that the difference between us was the difference between contradictory assertions. No amount of safe arrivals or bench-tests will remove my *blik* and restore the normal one; for my *blik* is compatible with any finite number of such tests.

It was Hume who taught us that our whole commerce with the world depends upon our *blik* about the world; and that differences between *bliks* about the world cannot be settled by observation of what happens in the world. That was why, having performed the interesting experiment of doubting the ordinary man's *blik* about the world, and showing that no proof could be given to make us adopt one *blik* rather than another, he turned to backgammon to take his mind off the problem. It seems, indeed, to be impossible even to formulate as an assertion the normal *blik* about the world which makes me put my confidence in the future reliability of steel joints, in the continued ability of the road to support my car, and not gape beneath it revealing nothing below; in the general non-homicidal tendencies of dons; in my own continued well-being (in some sense of that word that I may not now fully understand) if I continue to do what is right according to my lights; in the general likelihood of people like Hitler coming to a bad end. But perhaps a formulation less inadequate than most is to be found in the Psalms: "The earth is weak and all the inhabiters thereof: I bear up the pillars of it."

The mistake of the position which Flew selects for attack is to regard this kind of talk as some sort of *explanation,* as scientists are accustomed to use the word. As such, it would obviously be ludicrous. We no longer believe in God as an Atlas—*nous n'avons pas besoin de cette hypothèse.*[3] But it is nevertheless true to say that, as Hume saw, without a *blik* there can be no explanation; for it is by our *bliks* that we decide what is and what is not an explanation. Suppose we believed that everything that happened, happened by pure chance. This would not of course be an assertion; for it is compatible with anything happening or not happening, and so, incidentally, is its contradictory. But if we had this belief, we should not be able to explain or predict or plan anything. Thus, although we should not be *asserting* anything different from those of a more normal belief, there would be a great difference between us; and this is the sort of difference that there is between those who really believe in God and those who really disbelieve in him.

The word "really" is important, and may excite suspicion. I put it in, because when people have had a good Christian upbringing, as have most of those who now profess not to believe in any sort of religion, it is very hard to discover what they really believe. The reason why they find it so easy to think that they are not religious, is that they have never got into the frame of mind of one who suffers from the doubts to which religion is the answer. Not for them the terrors of the primitive jungle. Having abandoned some of the more picturesque fringes of religion, they think that they have abandoned the whole thing—whereas in fact they still have got, and could not live without, a religion of a comfortably substantial, albeit highly sophisticated, kind, which differs from that of many "religious people" in little more than this, that "religious people" like to sing Psalms about theirs—a very natural and proper thing to do. But nevertheless there may be a big difference lying behind—the difference between two people who, though side by side, are walking in different directions. I do not know in what direction Flew is walking; perhaps he does not know either. But we have had some examples recently of various ways in which one can walk away from Christianity, and there are any number of possibilities. After all, man has not changed biologically since primitive times; it is his religion that has changed, and it can easily change again. And if you do not think that such changes make a difference, get acquainted with some Sikhs and some Mussulmans of the same Punjabi stock; you will find them quite different sorts of people.

There is an important difference between Flew's parable and my own which we have not yet noticed. The explorers do not *mind* about their garden; they discuss it with interest, but not with concern. But my lunatic, poor fellow, minds about dons; and I mind about the steering of my car; it often has people in it that I care for. It is because I mind very much about what goes on in the garden in which I find myself, that I am unable to share the explorers' detachment.

C

Basil Mitchell

Flew's article is searching and perceptive, but there is, I think, something odd about his conduct of the theologian's case. The theologian surely would not deny that the fact of pain counts against the assertion that God loves men. This very incompatibility generates the most intractable of theological problems—the problem of evil. So the theologian *does* recognize the fact of pain as counting against Christian doctrine. But it is true that he will not allow it—or anything—to count decisively against it; for he is committed by his faith to trust in God. His attitude is not that of the detached observer, but of the believer.

Perhaps this can be brought out by yet another parable. In time of war in an occupied country, a member of the resistance meets one night a stranger who deeply impresses him. They spend that night together in conversation. The Stranger tells the partisan that he himself is on the side of the resistance—indeed that he is in command of it, and urges the partisan to have faith in him no matter what happens. The partisan is utterly convinced at that meeting of the Stranger's sincerity and constancy and undertakes to trust him.

They never meet in conditions of intimacy again. But sometimes the Stranger is seen helping members of the resistance, and the partisan is grateful and says to his friends, "He is on our side."

Sometimes he is seen in the uniform of the police handing over patriots to the occupying power. On these occasions his friends murmur against him: but the partisan still says, "He is on our side." He still believes that, in spite of appearances, the Stranger did not deceive him. Sometimes he asks the Stranger for help and receives it. He is then thankful. Sometimes he asks and does not receive it. Then he says, "The Stranger knows best." Sometimes his friends, in exasperation, say "Well, what *would* he have to do for you to admit that you were wrong and that he is not on our side?" But the partisan refuses to answer. He will not consent to put the Stranger to the test. And sometimes his friends complain, "Well, if *that's* what you mean by his being on our side, the sooner he goes over to the other side the better."

The partisan of the parable does not allow anything to count decisively against the proposition "The Stranger is on our side." This is because he has committed himself to trust the Stranger. But he of course recognizes that the Stranger's ambiguous behaviour *does* count against what he believes about him. It is precisely this situation which constitutes the trial of his faith.

When the partisan asks for help and doesn't get it, what can he do? He can (*a*) conclude that the stranger is not on our side or; (*b*) maintain that he is on our side, but that he has reasons for withholding help.

The first he will refuse to do. How long can he uphold the second position without its becoming just silly?

I don't think one can say in advance. It will depend on the nature of the impression created by the Stranger in the first place. It will depend, too, on the manner in which he takes the Stranger's behaviour. If he blandly dismisses it as of no consequence, as having no bearing upon his belief, it will be assumed that he is thoughtless or insane. And it quite obviously won't do for him to say easily, "Oh, when used of the Stranger the phrase 'is on our side' *means* ambiguous behaviour of this sort." In that case he would be like the religious man who says blandly of a terrible disaster "It is God's will." No, he will only be regarded as sane and reasonable in his belief, if he experiences in himself the full force of the conflict.

It is here that my parable differs from Hare's. The partisan admits that many things may and do count against his belief: whereas Hare's lunatic who has a *blik* about dons doesn't admit that anything counts against his *blik*. Nothing *can* count against *bliks*. Also the partisan has a reason for having in the first instance committed himself, viz. the character of the Stranger; whereas the lunatic has no reason for his *blik* about dons—because, of course, you can't have reasons for *bliks*.

This means that I agree with Flew that theological utterances must be assertions. The partisan is making an assertion when he says, "The Stranger is on our side."

Do I want to say that the partisan's belief about the Stranger is, in any sense, an explanation? I think I do. It explains and makes sense of the Stranger's behaviour: it helps to explain also the resistance movement in the context of which he appears. In each case it differs from the interpretation which the others put upon the same facts.

"God loves men" resembles "the Stranger is on our side" (and many other significant statements, e.g., historical ones) in not being conclusively falsifiable. They can both be treated in at least three different ways: (1) As provisional hypotheses to be discarded if experience tells against them; (2) As significant articles of faith; (3) As vacuous formulae (expressing, perhaps, a desire for reassurance) to which experience makes no difference and which make no difference to life.

The Christian, once he has committed himself, is precluded by his faith from taking up the first attitude: "Thou shalt not tempt the Lord thy God." He is in constant danger, as Flew has observed, of slipping into the third. But he need not; and, if he does, it is a failure in faith as well as in logic.

D

Antony Flew

It has been a good discussion: and I am glad to have helped to provoke it. But now—at least in *University*—it must come to an end: and the Editors of *University* have asked me to make some concluding remarks. Since it is impossible to deal with all the issues raised or to comment separately upon each contribution, I will concentrate on Mitchell and Hare, as representative of two very different kinds of response to the challenge made in "Theology and Falsification."

The challenge, it will be remembered, ran like this. Some theological utterances seem to, and are intended to, provide explanations or express assertions. Now an assertion, to be an assertion at all, must claim that things stand thus and thus; *and not otherwise.* Similarly an explanation, to be an explanation at all, must explain why this particular thing occurs; *and not something else.* Those last clauses are crucial. And yet sophisticated religious people—or so it seemed to me—are apt to overlook this, and tend to refuse to allow, not merely that anything actually does occur, but that anything conceivably could occur, which would count against their theological assertions and explanations. But in so far as they do this their supposed explanations are actually bogus, and their seeming assertions are really vacuous.

Mitchell's response to this challenge is admirably direct, straightforward, and understanding. He agrees "that theological utterances must be assertions." He agrees that if they are to be assertions, there must be something that would count against their truth. He agrees, too, that believers are in constant danger of transforming their would-be assertions into "vacuous formulae." But he takes me to task for an oddity in my "conduct of the theologian's case. The theologian surely would not deny that the fact of pain counts against the assertion that God loves men. This very incompatibility generates the most intractable of theological problems, the problem of evil." I think he is right. I should have made a distinction between two very different ways of dealing with what looks like evidence against the love of God: the way I stressed was the expedient of qualifying the original assertion; the way the theologian usually takes, at first, is to admit that it looks bad but to insist that there is—there must be—some explanation which will show that, in spite of appearances, there really is a God who loves us. His difficulty, it seems to me, is that he has given God attributes which rule out all possible saving explanations. In Mitchell's parable of the Stranger it is easy for the believer to find plausible excuses for ambiguous behaviour: for the Stranger is a man. But suppose the Stranger is God. We cannot say that he would like to help but cannot: God is omnipotent. We cannot say that he would help if he only knew: God is omniscient. We cannot say that he is not responsible for the wickedness of others: God creates those others. Indeed an omnipotent, omniscient God must be an accessory before (and during) the fact to every human misdeed; as well as being responsible for every non-moral defect in the unverse. So, though I entirely concede that Mitchell was absolutely right to insist against me that the theologian's first move is to look for an *explanation,* I still think that in the end, if relentlessly pursued, he will have to resort to the avoiding action of *qualification.* And there lies the danger of that death by a thousand qualifications, which would, I agree, constitute "a failure in faith as well as in logic."

Hare's approach is fresh and bold. He confesses that "on the ground marked out by Flew, he seems to me to be completely victorious." He therefore introduces the concept of *blik.* But while I think that there is room for some such concept in philosophy, and that philosophers should be grateful to Hare for his invention, I nevertheless want to insist that any attempt to analyse Christian religious utterances as expressions or affirmations of a *blik* rather than as (at least would-be) assertions about the cosmos is fundamentally misguided. *First,* because thus interpreted they would be entirely unorthodox. If Hare's religion really is a *blik,* involving no cosmological assertions about the nature and activities of a supposed personal creator, then surely he is not a Christian at all? *Second,* because thus interpreted, they could scarcely do the job they do. If they were not even intended as assertions then many religious activities would become fradulent, or merely silly. If "You ought *because* it is God's will" asserts no more than "You ought," then the person who prefers the former phraseology is not really giving a reason, but a fraudulent substitute for one, a dialectical dud cheque. If "My soul must be immortal *because* God loves his children, etc." asserts no more than "My soul must be immortal," then the man who reassures himself with theological arguments for immortality is being as silly as the man who tries to clear his overdraft by writing his bank a cheque on the same account. (Of course neither of these utterances would be distinctively Christian: but this discussion never pretended to be so confined.) Religious utterances may indeed express false or even bogus assertions: but I simply do not believe that they are not both intended and interpreted to be or at any rate to presuppose assertions, at least in the context of religious practice; whatever shifts may be demanded, in another context, by the exigencies of theological apologetic.

One final suggestion. The philosophers of religion might well draw upon George Orwell's last appalling nightmare *1984* for the concept of *doublethink.* "*Doublethink* means the power of holding two contradictory beliefs simultaneously, and accepting both of them. The party intellectual knows that he is playing tricks with reality, but by the exercise of *doublethink* he also satisfies himself that reality is not violated" (*1984,* p. 220). Perhaps religious intellectuals too are sometimes driven to doublethink in order to retain their faith in a loving God in face of the reality of a heartless and indifferent world. But of this more another time, perhaps.

NOTES

1. P. A. S., 1944–5, reprinted as Chap. X of *Logic and Language,* Vol. I (Blackwell, 1951), and in his *Philosophy and Psychoanalysis* (Blackwell, 1953).

2. Cf. J. Wisdom, "Other Minds," *Mind*, 1940; reprinted in his *Other Minds* (Blackwell, 1952).
3. [We have no need for that hypothesis.]

The Hiddenness of God

Robert McKim

Is it important whether we believe in God? If so, why does God remain hidden to us? Why does God not take steps to be revealed in a manner accessible to all?

According to Robert McKim, Associate Professor of Philosophy at the University of Illinois at Urbana-Champaign, the evidence suggests that whether we believe in God doesn't much matter because if believing made an important difference, the evidence of God's existence would be more apparent.

The Hidden Emperor

Once upon a time, in a faraway and geographically isolated land, there was a small community that had lived without contact with other communities for so long that the very memory that there were other peoples had been lost almost entirely. Only a few of the elders could recall from their childhood the stories that used to be told of visitors from afar, of distant peoples and communities, of powerful princes and lords, and of their vast empires. Some of the very oldest people with the best memories could recall that back in the old days there were some who said (or was it that they remembered hearing reports about its having been said?—it was so long ago and so hard to tell) that their territory was actually itself part of one of those great empires, and one that was ruled over by a great and good emperor. But these stories had not been told for so long that even the old people had difficulty remembering them, and the young were downright skeptical.

From Robert McKim, *Religious Ambiguity and Religious Diversity*. Reprinted by permission of Oxford University Press.

And then one day there arrived an outsider who claimed to be an emissary and who bore astonishing news. He declared that some of the old stories were true. He said that the small, isolated community was indeed part of a great empire, an empire that stretched farther than anyone could have imagined. And—more astonishing still—the ruler of all this, the emissary said, pointing to the familiar hillsides and fields, to the rude dwellings and away to the horizon in all directions, is a great and wise emperor who deserves loyalty and obedience from all his subjects. And that includes you, said the visitor. And—could it be yet more astonishing?—the emperor is generally known to his subjects throughout the rest of the empire as the "Hidden Emperor," for he never lets himself be seen clearly by any of his subjects. Not even his closest, most loyal, and most devoted servants are sure exactly what he looks like. But it is widely believed that he travels incognito throughout the empire, for he has various remarkable powers that make this possible, including the power to make himself invisible, the power to travel from place to place with great speed, and even the power to understand what people are thinking. Indeed, so great are his powers in these respects, said the visitor, that it is hardly an exaggeration to say that he is always present throughout the entire empire.

Never had anything quite like this been heard. Mouths were agape, eyes were wide in astonishment. What are we to do, what does the emperor want from us and what are we to expect from him? people asked. "He wants your loyalty, trust, and obedience, and he offers protection and help in time of trouble," replied the emissary.

At this point a man in the crowd, a tallish bearded man with a puzzled expression, and of the sort that is inclined to twiddle with his beard in an irritating way, replied as follows. "But why," he asked—and the emissary knew what was coming, for he had been through this many times and knew that in every community there is a trouble–maker or two and that beard twiddling and a puzzled expression are among the best indicators that trouble is brewing—"why does the emperor have to be hidden? Why can't we see the emperor for ourselves? I know that it is not my place to ask"—a familiar line to the seasoned emissary, who has heard it all before and can recognize false modesty at a glance—"but why couldn't the emperor's existence and presence be as clear as *your* presence and existence? And"—now for the coup de grâce, thought the emissary, the sign that we are contending here with a *serious* thinker—"if it is important for the emperor to be hidden, why are you here informing us about him?"

After the tall bearded man had spoken, there was silence for a few minutes. The fact was that no one quite knew what would happen next, or what it was proper to say to the emissary. Had the bearded man gone too far? Had he spoken improperly? Would he be reprimanded or punished? Would they all be reprimanded or punished? Should he be silenced?

Then an old woman, known for her wisdom and insight, and of that generation among whom belief in the great empêror had not entirely been lost, spoke up. "I, for one, think that things are much better this way. As long as the emperor, and may he and his blessed relatives live for ever," she added, with a glance at the emissary," as long as the emperor is hidden, we have a type of freedom that would otherwise be unavailable to us. We are free to decide whether or not to believe that there is an emperor. If the facts of the matter were clear to us, and it were just plain obvious that the emperor exists, belief would be forced on us. As long as the facts are unclear, we are in a position to exercise control over what we think. And even though our esteemed visitor has come to explain the situation to us, we are still in a position to decide whether or not to believe what he says."

At this the bearded man became downright exasperated, saying, "Listen here. What is so great about being able to make up your mind in conditions in which the facts are unclear? Surely if the facts are unclear, we ought simply to believe that the facts are unclear. It's absurd to suggest that there is something especially admirable or good about deciding that the emperor exists under circumstances in which it is unclear whether the emperor exists. Do you think that it would also be good for us to be able to choose whether or not to believe, say, that two plus two equals four in circumstances in which *that* is not clear, or for us to be able to choose what to believe about who our parents are in circumstances in which *that* is not clear?"

"This may seem absurd to you," interjected the woman, "since you are the sort of man who likes to strut around as if you had all the answers to life's questions even though nobody else has quite noticed, but what you have to understand is that this arrangement has the great advantage of permitting our willingness to acknowledge our status as subservient underlings in the emperor's realm to play a role in determining whether or not we believe that the emperor exists."

"And I will tell you," said the woman, warming to her theme and enjoying the attention of the crowd, and what she took to be the approving look of the visiting emissary, "I will tell you about another benefit of our current situation. The fact that we do not know what the emperor looks like permits him to come among us, looking like one of us. Long ago, when I was a little girl, it used to be said that when you entertain a stranger, you should remember that you might be entertaining the emperor. In fact people used to say, 'Every poor stranger is the emperor.' I don't suppose that they really meant it, but you can see what they had in mind. And there was another saying, too, now that I remember it. We used to say, when we wished to show respect for someone, that 'You are He.' Of course, if you knew that a visitor in your house really was the emperor, you would be quite dazed and overwhelmed, and even ashamed by how little you had to offer such a guest."

"Damn it all," said the man with the puzzled look, "this is all nonsense. If the emperor wanted us to believe in him, he would make his existence apparent to us. Don't listen to that old bag. It's as simple as this. If the emperor existed, he would want us to know him and to know about him. If so, he would make his presence apparent to us. He does not do so even though he could do so. The only sensible conclusion is that *there is no emperor. There is no emperor! There is no emperor!*"

After this intemperate outburst yet another voice was heard from the crowd, the voice of one who prides himself on taking a sober, comprehensive, and balanced view of things, and in the process takes himself much too seriously. "Maybe we *are* part of the empire," said this new interlocutor. "Certainly we have some evidence that this is so, not least of which is the fact that our honored visitor, who appears to me to have an open and trustworthy countenance, has come to tell us that this is so. The recollections of some of our senior members are also relevant here. Surely they give us some reason to believe there to be an emperor. But if there is an emperor—and I certainly do not rule out this possibility—it is hard to believe that it matters to him whether we believe that he exists. If it mattered very much to the emperor that we believe that he exists, then surely it would be clearer than it now is that there is an emperor. After all, where has the emperor been all this time? Furthermore, the beliefs that we hold about the emperor under current conditions, if we hold any, ought to reflect the fact that they are held under conditions of uncertainty. Any beliefs we hold in this area ought in fact to be held with tentativeness, and with an awareness that we may be wrong."

In the fullness of time, and after the emissary had gone his way, it came to pass that three schools of thought developed, each of which embraced one of the views that were expressed on that day. There were those who agreed with the old woman, and who were known by their opponents as the "Imperialists." Then there were the Skeptics. All of their bearded members had a strong inclination toward beard-twiddling. And there were the Tentative Believers. They were known to their detractors as "the half-baked believers." So who was right? . . .

The Disadvantages of God's Hiddenness

If God exists but is hidden, this is a perplexing state of affairs. One reason that it is perplexing is internal to theism and arises from the fact that the theistic traditions place such importance on belief. Typically each theistic tradition asserts that to fail to hold theistic beliefs, and especially to fail to hold its theistic beliefs, or at least what it considers to be the most important among them, is to go wrong in a very serious way whereas to adopt theistic beliefs, and especially the set of theistic beliefs associated with it, is a worthwhile and important thing to do. These traditions say, too, that one ought to regret or even feel guilty about a failure to believe. Yet if God is hidden, belief is more difficult than it would be if God were not hidden. If God exists, and if the facts about God's existence and nature were clear, belief would be ever so much easier for us. The theistic traditions are inclined to hold human beings responsible and even to blame them if they are nonbelievers or if their belief is weak. But does this make any sense?

God's hiddenness creates uncertainty and contributes to profound disagreement about the existence and nature of God. Indeed, I would suggest that it contributes *more* to the occurrence of nonbelief than does the presence of evil in the world (or of *other* evil in the world, if the hiddenness of God is understood as a type of evil). This is not to deny that there are people who are nontheists because of evils that they either encounter or are familiar with; but it seems that the explanation in most cases of how it has come about that people do not believe that God exists (whether they are atheists or agnostics or members of nontheistic religions) is not that they consider God's existence to be incompatible with various evils. Rather, it is that they have nothing that they understand as an awareness of God. They do not understand themselves to be familiar with God. Consequently, they do not even reach a point where evil is perceived as a problem. . . .

Another reason that the hiddenness of God is perplexing has to do with the sort of personal relationship with God that some theists advocate. This is also a reason that is internal to theism, or at least to theism of a certain sort, especially evangelical and fundamentalist Christianity. The personal relationship in question is understood to involve trust, respect, and, above all, ongoing intimate communication. Is it not reasonable to suppose that if God were less hidden, this sort of relationship would be more widespread?

The hiddenness of God, therefore, seems to be a particularly acute problem for strands of theism that emphasize the importance of fellowship and communication with God. But it is also a problem for the other major strands of theism because they all emphasize the importance and value of belief. And they declare that God cares about us; if God exists and if God cares about us, why does God leave human beings to such an extent in the dark about various religiously important facts? If God does not care about us, there is less to explain. Theism typically requires, too, that we put our trust and confidence in God: But why, then, are the facts about God not more clear? If God exists and the facts about God's existence and nature were more clear, people would be more likely to see that they ought to put their trust and confidence in God and would be more willing and more able to do so.

Another important, and related, disadvantage associated with divine hiddenness is this. If God exists, God is worthy of adoration and worship: given the good, wise, just (etc.) nature of God, and the relation between God and God's creatures, a worshipful response from human beings would be appropriate. For if God exists, God is our Creator and we owe all we have to God. But if many of us are in the dark about the existence and nature of God, then this appropriate human response is made more difficult than it otherwise would be. So part of the cost of divine hiddenness is its contribution to the large-scale failure of human beings to respond to God in ways that seem appropriate in the case of a good, just, and wise creator.

And there are further costs. The profound disagreements about God, and more broadly the profound disagreements that there are about numerous matters of religious importance, often play a role in promoting and exacerbating social conflict. If God exists and if the facts about God were as clear as they could be, there might not be as much room for disagreement, and hence such disagreements would not contribute to social conflict. The mystery surrounding God also provides opportunities for charlatans and frauds to pose as experts on the nature and activities of God, and for religious authorities in numerous traditions to acquire and exercise, and sometimes abuse, power and control over others.

To each of these apparent disadvantages, or costs, of God's hiddenness there corresponds an advantage or benefit that, it appears, would accrue if God were not hidden. Thus if God were not hidden, and the facts about God were clear for all to see, it appears that belief would be easier for us, a personal relationship with God would be facilitated, more people would worship God, religious disagreement would be less likely to exacerbate social tensions, and there would be fewer opportunities for people to pose as experts and to acquire power and influence over others. . . .

There is, then, some reason to think that, if God exists, it must not matter greatly to God whether we believe. This applies to belief that God exists, to various standard theistic beliefs about God, such as beliefs about the activities and character of God, and to belief in God. At least that we should hold such beliefs . . . here and now and under our current circumstances probably does not matter greatly. There is also considerable reason to believe that it is not important that everyone should accept any particular form of theism, such as Judaism or Islam. If it were very important that we should accept theism or any particular form of theism, our circumstances probably would be more conducive to it.

PART 6

RESURRECTION AND IMMORTALITY

Resurrection

John H. Hick

The doctrine of the resurrection of the dead plays a central role in Christianity. But how is the concept of resurrection to be understood? Can it be explained so as to make it intelligible? In our next selection, answers to these questions are offered by John H. Hick, whose work we read previously.

Hick finds that resurrection is implicit in God's love for creatures made in God's image. How could God allow loved ones to pass out of existence? Furthermore, recall that in a previous selection Hick argues that life after death is required to justify all the world's pains and sorrows. In accord with that view, he asserts that God's purposes for us can only be realized in an existence beyond this life. Thus Hick concludes that God's plan for humanity would not be complete without resurrection.

What does "the resurrection of the dead" mean? Saint Paul's discussion provides the basic Christian answer to this question.[1] His conception of the general resurrection (distinguished from the unique resurrection of Jesus) has nothing to do with the resuscitation of corpses in a cemetery. It concerns God's re-creation or reconstitution of the human psychophysical individual, not as the organism that has died but as a *soma pneumatikon,* a "spiritual body," inhabiting a spiritual world as the physical body inhabits our present physical world.

A major problem confronting any such doctrine is that of providing criteria of personal identity to link the earthly life and the resurrection life. Paul does not specifically consider this question, but one may, perhaps, develop his thought along lines such as the following.

Suppose, first, that someone—John Smith—living in the USA were suddenly and inexplicably to disappear from before the eyes of his friends, and that at the same moment an exact replica of him were inexplicably to appear in India. The person who appears in India is exactly similar in both physical and mental characteristics to the person who disappeared in America. There is continuity of memory, complete similarity of bodily features including fingerprints, hair and eye coloration, and stomach contents, and also of beliefs,

---

habits, emotions, and mental dispositions. Further, the "John Smith" replica thinks of himself as being the John Smith who disappeared in the USA. After all possible tests have been made and have proved positive, the factors leading his friends to accept "John Smith" as John Smith would surely prevail and would cause them to overlook even his mysterious transference from one continent to another, rather than treat "John Smith," with all John Smith's memories and other characteristics, as someone other than John Smith.

Suppose, second, that our John Smith, instead of inexplicably disappearing, dies, but that at the moment of his death a "John Smith" replica, again complete with memories and all other characteristics, appears in India. Even with the corpse on our hands we would, I think, still have to accept this "John Smith" as the John Smith who died. We would have to say that he had been miraculously re-created in another place.

Now suppose, third, that on John Smith's death the "John Smith" replica appears, not in India, but as a resurrection replica in a different world altogether, a resurrection world inhabited only by resurrected persons. This world occupies its own space distinct from that with which we are now familiar. That is to say, an object in the resurrection world is not situated at any distance or in any direction from the objects in our present world, although each object in either world is spatially related to every other object in the same world.

This supposition provides a model by which one may conceive of the divine re-creation of the embodied human personality. In this model, the element of the strange and the mysterious has been reduced to a minimum by following the view of some of the early Church Fathers that the resurrection body has the same shape as the physical body,[2] and ignoring Paul's own hint that it may be as unlike the physical body as a full grain of wheat differs from the wheat seed.[3]

What is the basis for this Judaic-Christian belief in the divine re-creation or reconstitution of the human personality after death? There is, of course, an argument from authority, in that life after death is taught throughout the New Testament (although very rarely in the Old Testament). But, more basically, belief in the resurrection arises as a corollary of faith in the sovereign purpose of God, which is not restricted by death and which holds man in being beyond his natural mortality. In the words of Martin Luther, "Anyone with whom God speaks, whether in wrath or in mercy, the same is certainly immortal. The Person of God who speaks, and the Word, show that we are creatures with whom God wills to speak, right into eternity, and in an immortal manner." In a similar vein it is argued that if it be God's plan to create finite persons to exist in fellowship with himself, then it contradicts both his own intention and his love for the creatures made in his image if he allows men to pass out of existence when his purpose for them remains largely unfulfilled.

It is this promised fulfillment of God's purpose for man, in which the full possibilities of human nature will be realized, that constitutes the "heaven" symbolized in the New Testament as a joyous banquet in which all and sundry rejoice together.

NOTES

1. I Corinthians 15.
2. For example, Irenaeus, *Against Heresies,* Book II, Chap. 34, para. 1.
3. I Corinthians, 15:37.

Life After Death

TERENCE PENELHUM

The doctrine of life after death most often takes the form of either the resurrection of the body or the immortality of the soul. Both versions of postmortem survival, however, present two fundamental problems: (1) envisioning the kind of life survivors after death could lead and (2) finding some means of determining whether the person who might survive death would be the same person who had lived.

In the next selection, Terence Penelhum, Professor Emeritus of Religious Studies at the University of Calgary, explores the ways these difficulties apply to each version of life after death. He concludes that the notion of postmortem disembodied existence, that is, the immortality of the soul, is unintelligible, and that the doctrine of bodily resurrection, while not absurd, cannot be shown to be true.

Two Concepts of Survival

. . . There can be no doubt that the doctrine of the immortality of the soul, even though Greek in origin, has been held by many members of the Christian tradition, whether it belonged originally to that tradition or not. The

From Terence Penelhum, *Religion and Rationality.* Reprinted by permission of the author.

doctrine of the resurrection of the body, certainly authentically a part of the Christian tradition (since some form of it is clearly held by St. Paul),[1] is part of the most widely used creed of the Christian Church. Let us leave aside their historical relationship and look at the logical possibilities they present. I shall begin with the doctrine of the immortality of the soul, or, as I prefer to word it, the doctrine of disembodied survival. Before doing so, however, I shall attempt to clear the ground a little by indicating the major sources of difficulty that philosophers have discovered in these doctrines.

These difficulties divide themselves naturally into two groups. There are, first of all, difficulties about envisaging the kind of life that survivors of death in either sense could be said to lead. It is not enough to say that the nature of this life is totally unknown, for if this is taken seriously to the extent of our being unable to say that these beings will possess personal characteristics as we now understand these, it seems to leave the belief that they will survive without any content. If one wishes to avoid this pitfall, one has to ascribe to the survivors some characteristics that persons as we know them possess. This does not seem impossible in the case of the doctrine of the resurrection of the body; though it can be made impossible if unlimited stress is placed on the claim that the body of the survivor is transformed. Radical transformation is to be expected as part of such a doctrine, but total transformation would rob the notion of survival of all clear meaning, for it is part of that notion that the *person* survives, and this seems to entail that the resulting being is a person also. But if the doctrine of the resurrection of the body is expressed in ways that avoid this danger, it is clearly possible for us to form a rough notion (which is all one can reasonably demand) of what such a future state would be like.

The difficulty seems much greater, however, when we consider the doctrine of disembodied survival. For it is not obviously intelligible to ascribe personal characteristics to a being that is denied to have any physical ones. The notion of human intelligence, for example, seems closely bound up with the things men can be seen to do and heard to say; the notion of human emotion seems closely bound up with the way men talk and behave; and the notion of human action seems closely bound up with that of physical movement. There is plenty of room for disagreement over the nature of these connections, but they cannot even exist in the case of an allegedly disembodied being. So can we understand what is meant by talk of disembodied intelligences, or disembodied sufferers of emotion, or disembodied agents? A natural answer to our present problem is: Disembodied survivors might have mental lives. They might, that is, think, imagine, dream, or have feelings. This looks coherent enough. On the other hand, for them to have anything to think *about* or have feelings *toward*, it might be necessary for them also to have that which supplies us with our objects of reflection or emotion, namely, perception. Some might also want to add the notion of agency (especially if they wish to use the doctrine of disembodied survival to offer explanations of the phenomena of psychical research). We must bear in mind, further, that disembodied persons could, of course, never perceive or meet each other, in any normal sense of these words. What we need to do, even at the risk of spinning fantasies, is to see how severely the belief in their disembodiment restricts the range of concepts that we can apply to them.

The second group of difficulties affects both doctrines, though in different ways. These are difficulties about the self-identity of the survivors. The belief that people survive is not merely the belief that after people's deaths there will be personal beings in existence. It is the belief that those beings will be the same ones that existed before death. One of the reasons for concern about the nature of the life a disembodied person might lead is that if this mode of life were *too* radically different from the sort of life we lead, those beings leading it could not be identified with us. This difficulty is critical, for even if we can readily understand what the future life that is spoken of would be like, its coming to pass would only be an interesting cosmic hypothesis, lacking any personal relevance, if the beings living that life were not ourselves. This requirement connects with another. We have to be able to form some concept of what it is for the future, post-mortem being to remain the same through time in the future life, quite apart from his also being identifiable with some previous person who existed in *this* life. If, for instance, our being able to identify a person whom we meet now as some person we knew previously depends on our being able to discern some feature that he still possesses; and if that feature is something that a being in the future life could not possess, then it needs to be shown that there could be post-mortem persons who persist through time at all. There would have to be some substitute, in the case of post-mortem persons, for the feature that establishes identity for pre-mortem persons. If we are not able to indicate what this would be, we have no adequately clear concept of what talk of post-mortem persons means.

These problems about identity arise in quite different ways for the two doctrines of disembodied survival and bodily resurrection. A proponent of the doctrine of disembodied survival has to face the problem of the continuing identity of the disembodied person through time, by showing that what makes that person identical through time could be some wholly *mental* feature and that the absence of a body does not render the notion of a body inapplicable. (He may or may not do this by claiming that we use mental rather than physical features to identify pre-mortem beings through time.) This task may not be hopeless, though it looks as though we depend on the physical continuity of people for our ability to reidentify them. He must also succeed in showing that some purely mental feature will serve to identify the post-mortem person with his pre-mortem predecessor.

In the case of the doctrine of the resurrection of the body, the problem of how the post-mortem, resurrected person can remain identical through time in the future state does not look very difficult, since the sort of life envisaged for this being is an embodied one, similar in enough respects (one may suppose) to our own. So even if we decided that the continuity of the body is a necessary condition of the continuance of a person through time, this condition could easily be said to be satisfied in the case of a resurrected person. Yet we still have a difficulty: Could a post-mortem person, even in this embodied state, be identified with any pre-mortem person? For if the doctrine of resurrection is presented in a form that entails the annihilation of a person at death, it could reasonably be argued that what is predicted as happening at the resurrection is not, after all, the reappearance of the original person but the (first) appearance of a *duplicate* person—no doubt resembling the former one but not numerically identical with him. If this can be argued and cannot be refuted, we are in the odd position of being unsure whether or not to say that the future persons are the former ones. Philosophers have often noted the extent to which problems of identity seem to involve not discoveries but decisions—decisions on what to *call* a particular situation. The literature of personal identity is full of actual and imagined stories introduced to help us discover, by deciding how to talk of them, what the conditions of application of our concepts are. The doctrine of the resurrection of the body seems to present us with just such a matter of decision—namely, would this admittedly conceivable future state properly be described as the reappearance of a former person or as the first appearance of a duplicate of him?

Disembodied Personality

Let us now look at the first group of difficulties, those connected with the possibility of applying our normal concepts of personal life to post-mortem beings. These seem to arise, as we have seen already, only in connection with the belief that men survive without their bodies, and I shall therefore only discuss them in this connection. . . .

Disembodied persons can conduct no physical performances. They cannot walk or talk (or, therefore, converse), open and close their eyes or peer (or, therefore, look), turn their heads and incline their ears (or, therefore, listen), raise their hands in anger or weep (or, therefore, give bodily expression to their emotions), or touch or feel physical objects. Hence they cannot perceive each other or be perceived by us. Can they, still, be said without absurdity to perceive physical things? Perhaps we could say so if we were prepared to allow that a being having a set of visual images corresponding to the actual disposition of some physical things was thereby *seeing* those things. We could say so if we were prepared to allow that a being having a sequence of auditory experiences that made him think correctly that a certain object was giving off a particular sound was thereby *hearing* that object. The notions of seeing and hearing would be attenuated, since they would not, if applied in such cases, entail that the person who saw was physically in front of the object he saw with his face turned toward it or that the person who heard was receiving sound waves from the object that was giving them off. On the other hand, many philosophers hold that such implications are at most informal ones that are not essential to the concepts in question. Perhaps we could also say even that disembodied percipients could *do* things to the objects (or persons) they see and hear. We might be able to say this if we imagined that sometimes these percipients had wishes that were immediately actualized in the world, without any natural explanation for the strange things that occurred; though obviously such fantasies would involve the ascription of occult powers to the spirits. We might prefer to avoid all talk of interaction between the world of the spirits and ours, however, by denying that a disembodied being can see or hear or act in our world at all. Perhaps their lives consist exclusively of internal processes—acts of imagination and reflection. Such a life would be life in a dream world; and each person would have his own private dream. It might include dream images "of" others, though the accuracy of any reflections they occasioned would be purely coincidental.

These informal suggestions indicate that it might be possible, given a good deal of conceptual elasticity, to accord to disembodied persons at least some of the forms of mental life with which we are familiar. It therefore seems overdoctrinaire to refuse to admit that such beings could be called persons. We must bear in mind, however, that they could hardly be said to have an *inter*personal existence. Not only would we be unable to perceive a disembodied person; but a disembodied person, being unable to perceive another disembodied person, could have no more reason than we have to believe that others besides himself existed. Only if he can perceive embodied persons would he be in a position to know from anything other than memory that they exist or that they act in particular ways. The logic of the concept of disembodied persons clearly rules out the possibility of there being a community of such persons, even though by exercising conceptual care and tolerance we do seem able to ascribe some sort of life to disembodied individuals. In response to this, a verificationist might demand that before we can understand the ascriptions we have considered we should be able to say how we would *know* that a disembodied individual was having some experience or performing some act. But since we are dealing with a possible use of predicates that we have already learned, this verificationist demand seems too stringent.

We have also had to put aside another question whose bearing cannot be disputed, since it casts doubt on our ability to think of disembodied individuals. In asking whether some of the notions of a personal mental life can be applied, we have had to assume that there is a continuing, nonphysical subject to whom they can be applied, who has the experience or who does the action. This notion is essential to our understanding of the suggestion that there is a plurality of distinct individuals (whether they form a community or not), that on some occasion an experience is had by one of them rather than another, and that on another occasion a second experience is had by the same individual (or, indeed, a different individual) as had the first. In daily life the distinction between individuals and the continuing identity of individuals through time seems to depend upon the fact that each individual person has a distinguishable and persisting body. In the absence of a body are we able to form any notion of what has the experience or does the actions, has certain other experiences or actions in its past, and will have others in its future? In what follows, in order to retain some degree of clarity and simplicity in a philosophical area where obscurity is especially easy, I shall concentrate on trying to provide some account of what it might be for a disembodied person to retain identity through time. The philosophical theories we shall look at are usually also intended to offer some answer to the problem of distinguishing between two or more contemporaries—the problem, that is, of individuation. It is in any case hard to see how that question could have an answer if the problem of identity through time does not. I shall now turn, then, to the second, and more fundamental, of our two problems in the logic of the concept of survival.

The Problem of Identity

The logical problems one has to contend with when examining the concept of survival are to a large extent extensions of those that have puzzled philosophers when they have tried to analyze the notion of personal identity. We all recognize one another; we are all familiar enough with the experience of wondering who someone is; and most of us know the embarrassment that follows when one makes a mistake about who someone is. Our day-to-day thinking about these matters suggests that we take it for granted that there are clearly understood factors that determine whether the man before us is Smith or not, or is who he says he is or not, even though we may be unable to decide sometimes, through lack of information, whether these factors obtain. Philosophers have been puzzled, however, when they have tried to say what these factors are. Skeptical philosophers have even wondered whether any such factors can be isolated; and if they cannot be, they have suggested, our assumption that people do retain their identities from one period of time to the next may be an illusion. . . .

Mental and Bodily Criteria of Identity

One way of trying to avoid this confusion is to resort to . . . the doctrine of spiritual substance. This is the doctrine that in spite of the changingness of our mental lives, there is some hidden core to it that persists unchanged throughout, thus providing a backdrop against which the changes occur. This backdrop need not be *un*changing: It could be subject only to gradual change. The tacit assumption that it cannot change at all is only the result of assuming that identity and change are always inconsistent. But even if we allow that the spiritual substance to which the occurrences in our mental lives belong might itself be subject to gradual change, the doctrine is without value. For if the doctrine implies that we can find this relatively permanent core within by looking into ourselves, then it is false; for we cannot. . . . If on the other hand, it is admitted that the doctrine postulates something that is not accessible to observation, there is another difficulty: It can at best be a matter of happy accident that when we judge someone before us to be the same person as someone we knew before, we are right. For the only thing that would make this judgment reliable is the knowledge that the features possessed by the present and the past person belonged to the same substance. Yet when the substance is inaccessible even to the person himself, how could we ever know that an identity judgment was true? It is obvious that our basis for such judgments must be something other than what the doctrine requires it to be, for how, otherwise, could we learn to make such judgments in the first place?

We base our identity judgments, at least of others, upon the observation of their physical appearance. This fact, plus the mysteriousness of the doctrine of spiritual substance, has made it very tempting for philosophers to say that what makes a person the same from one period to the next is the continuance of his body throughout the two periods. The human body has the relative stability that we associate with a great many observable material objects and is not usually subject to the rapid changes that go on in the human mind. The plausibility of the claim that bodily continuity is a necessary and sufficient condition of personal identity derives also from the fact that our judgments about the identity of persons are in the vast majority of cases based on our having looked at them, talked to them, and recognized them. This may be why even philosophers who have tacitly identified the person with his mind have assumed that a person cannot consist only of thoughts, feelings, images, and other fleeting and changing phenomena, but must consist, beneath this, of something more stable. For they have, perhaps, been looking within the mind itself for something that has the relative stability of the body, even though they have officially abandoned any belief that the body provides persons with their continuing identity.

Suppose, however, that they were to abandon body surrogates like spiritual substance. Suppose they were not to assume that the identity of a person consists in the persistence of some relatively stable element such as his body, but were to concentrate their attention solely upon what they consider to be the contents of his mental life. If they were to do this, it would seem that their only hope of giving an account of the self-identity of persons would be to suggest the existence of some relationship among the fleeting elements of which human mental life is composed. An appropriate relationship does seem available. Some of the later experiences in a man's life history are, the story might go, memories of the earlier ones. And only the same person who had the earlier experiences could have a memory of one of them among his later experiences. So we have here the possibility of a purely mental standard of identity: that person *A* at time T_2 is the same as person *B* at some earlier time T_1 if and only if, among the experiences that person A has at T_2 there are memories of experiences that person B had at T_1. In the literature of the subject these two criteria of identity (bodily continuity and memory) have contended for priority.

The claim that personal identity can be understood solely in terms of memory can be accepted by someone who does not believe that a person can be identified with his mind or that anyone ever survives physical death. A philosopher who does not believe these things might still believe that the embodied person before him can be identified with Smith, whom he used to know, only if the person before him has the appropriate memories. But it is clear that someone who does believe those things must reject the thesis that only bodily continuity can be a criterion of personal identity. For if it is a necessary condition of a person's continuing that his body should continue, no one could survive in a disembodied form. Someone who accepts the doctrine of disembodied survival, therefore, will naturally incline toward the view that memory is the one necessary and sufficient condition of personal identity, since he must reject the traditional alternative position.

There is an artificiality about speaking, as I have, about two competing positions here. For in daily life it looks as though we use both standards of identity, resorting to one or the other depending on circumstances. Sometimes we decide who someone is by ascertaining facts about their physical appearance, height, weight, and the rest. Sometimes we decide who someone is by trying to determine whether or not they can remember certain past events that the person they claim to be could not fail, we think, to recall. Indeed, the barrier between these two methods becomes less clear than it first seems, when we reflect that we might try to reach our decision by seeing what skills a person has retained or what performances he can carry out. But although both standards are used, one might still have priority over the other. This would be the case if the other would not be available to us if the one were not or if the description of the one required some reference to the other.

It might look as though the use of the bodily criterion of identity presupposes that of memory in some way. For we cannot know, without resorting to our own or someone else's memory of the person in question, whether the body before us is the same one that the person we think he is had in the past. This is true, but it does not show that the man's own memories determine who he is. It only shows that other people could not determine the necessary physical facts about him unless they could rely on their own memories to do it, and this is not the same thing.

There are two arguments that tend to show, I think, that the bodily criterion has priority over the memory criterion. The first one, which is the less fundamental, rests on the fact that people forget things. We cannot say that the man before us is the man who performed some past action if and only if he remembers doing that action, for people forget actions they have done. But one might object on two counts that this need not refute the claim that his having the memory of that action is what makes that action his rather than someone else's. For, first, all we mean by this is that he *could* remember doing it, not that he *does* remember doing it; and, second, all we need is that he be able to remember doing some action or having some experience that the person who did the original action also did, or had.

Let us take these objections in order. The first will not do, for what do we mean when we say that he could remember doing the action in question? If we mean that it is in practice possible to get him to recall doing it, for instance, by psychoanalysis, then the retort is that all practicable methods might fail without thereby showing that the action was not done by him. If, on the other hand, we merely mean that it is in theory possible, then this requires further elucidation: Something that is possible in theory but not in practice is possible in virtue of some condition that in practice cannot bring it about. And this condition can only be the very fact that we are trying to elucidate, namely, the fact that the action was done by him and not by someone else. The other objection does not hold either, for a similar sort of reason. If we say that although the man before us cannot remember doing the action in question, he did do it because he can remember having some experience that the past person who did that action had, this presupposes that we understand what makes the past person who had that experience the same past person who did the original action. There must therefore be some standard of identity, actually satisfied, that we are appealing to in order to presuppose this. To say that this standard is itself that of memory is to raise our original question all over again.

The second and more fundamental argument rests on the fact that the notion of remembering is ambiguous. To say that someone remembers some action or event may mean merely that he believes he did it or witnessed it (without, at least consciously, basing this belief upon being told about it). It is possible, of course, for someone to remember something in this sense without what he remembers having happened at all and without its having happened to *him* even if it did occur. The more common use of the notion of remembering, however, concedes the truth of the man's belief, so that to say that the man remembers some action or event is to say that his claim to know about it is correct. Let us call these sense (i) and sense (ii) of "remember." Then we can say that to remember in sense (i) is to believe that one remembers in sense (ii).

It is apparent that memory in sense (i) cannot provide a criterion of personal identity. It is certainly not a sufficient condition of a man before us being the person that he claims to be that he remembers, in sense (i), doing or experiencing something done or experienced by the man he claims to be. For he could believe that he remembered doing something in this sense, even if nobody had done it. So we have to lean on sense (ii) of "remember." But this leads into a deeper problem. Let us simplify our discussion by concentrating solely upon a person's remembering doing an action or having an experience or witnessing an event and leave aside the complexities involved in someone's remembering some fact, such as that Cáesar was murdered. To say that someone, in sense (ii), remembers, is not merely to report that he believes something, but to accept his belief to be true. But an integral part of his belief is not only that some action was done, some experience had, or some event witnessed, but that it was done or had or witnessed *by him*. In other words, to say that he remembers in sense (ii) is not just to say that he now has some mental image or some conviction, even though it is likely to include this; it is to say that the past action, experience, or event that he refers to is part of his own past. But it now becomes clear that we cannot even state the memory criterion of identity without having some prior (and therefore independent) notion of the identity of the person. So the identity of the person must in the end rest upon some other condition, and the claim that it could rest solely upon memory must be false. The bodily criterion of identity is the natural one to refer to here. If, because of some commitment to dualism, one refuses to resort to it, it becomes wholly mysterious what the criterion of personal identity can be.

Identity and Survival

We can now return to the problem of survival. We were considering how far it is possible to make sense of the notion of the persistence of a disembodied person through time and of the claim that some particular future disembodied person will be identical with one of us in this world here and now. We can also ask how far the doctrine of the resurrection of the body frees us from the difficulties that the doctrine of disembodied survival encounters.

If bodily continuity is a necessary condition of the persistence of a person through time, then we cannot form any clear conception of the persistence of a person through time without a body nor of the identity of such a person with some previous embodied person. The previous reflections about the notion of personal identity leave us with two results: first, that to attempt to understand the self-identity of a person solely in terms of memory is impossible and, second, that when we are considering the case of flesh-and-blood persons there seems no alternative but to conclude that bodily continuity is a necessary condition of personal identity. These conclusions by themselves do not show that no substitute for bodily continuity could be invented when discussing the case of disembodied personality. But some substitute for it would have to be supplied by invention, and until it is, the notion of disembodied personal identity makes no sense.

The main line of argument is now plain, but for greater completeness it may be desirable to apply it to the doctrine of disembodied survival in a little more detail. An adherent of this doctrine, anxious to avoid admitting the necessity of the bodily criterion of personal identity, might perhaps claim that a survivor of death would intelligibly be said to be identical with someone who had died, because he remembered the actions and experiences of that person. And he might be said intelligibly to persist through time in his disembodied state because later and earlier experiences in the afterlife could be similarly connected by memories.

Let us take the latter suggestion first. It is that the disembodied person who has some experience at some future time FT_2 will be identical with the disembodied person who will have had some experience at an earlier future time FT_1 if, along with the experience at FT_2, there is a memory of the one he had at FT_1. The difficulty is to make sense not only of a phrase like "along with the experience there is a memory," but also, of what it means to speak of a memory here at all. For it will have to be a memory in sense (ii). And to say that the disembodied person has a memory at FT_2 in sense (ii) of some experience had at FT_1 is to assume that the two experiences will have been had by the same person; and this time, since we have no bodily criterion of identity to fall back on, we have no way of interpreting this claim.

If we turn now to the problem of identifying the disembodied person with some person who has died, we find the same difficulty. To say that he can be so identified because he remembers the deeds or experiences of that person is once again to use the notion of remembering in sense (ii). But to do this is to presuppose that we understand what it is for the remembering to be identical with the person who did those deeds or had those experiences. And we do not actually understand this. For although the person who did those deeds had a body, the rememberer, by hypothesis, does not have one and therefore cannot have the same body. It does not seem possible, therefore, to find any answer to the problem of self-identity for disembodied persons.

What about the doctrine of the resurrection of the body? Given that we are talking of the future existence of persons with bodies, the notion of their lasting through time in their future state does not seem to present any logical difficulties. But what of their identity with ourselves? If we assume some one-to-one correspondence between the inhabitants of the next world and of this (that is, assume at least that the inhabitants of the next world each resemble, claim to be, and claim to remember the doings of inhabitants of this one), it might seem foolish to deny that they will be identical with ourselves. But foolishness is not logical absurdity. It is conceivable that there might be a future existence in which there were large numbers of persons each resembling one of us and having uncanny knowledge of our pasts. And if that world does come to be in the future, we shall not be in it. What would make it a world with us in it, rather than a world with duplicates of us in it and not ourselves? Unless we can give a clear answer to this, it seems, very paradoxically, to be a matter of arbitrary choice whether to say these future people are us or not.

Surely, the answer might run, they will have the same bodies that we now have. But this is precisely what is not obvious. Apart from questions about whether the future bodies are like ours in youth, maturity, or old age, the dissolution of the earthly body means that the future body will be in some sense new. To say that it is the old one re-created is merely to say it is the same one without giving any reason for saying it is identical with the original body rather than one very much like it. To answer this way, then, seems merely to face the same puzzle again. To say that the future beings will remember in sense (ii) our doings and feelings is to raise the same questions here as before. The only possible solution seems to be to insist that in spite of the time gap between the death of the old body and the appearance of the new one, something persists in between. But what? The person disembodied? If so, then the doctrine of the resurrection of the body does not avoid the difficulties that beset the doctrine of disembodied survival, for the simple reason that it falls back upon that very doctrine when its own implications are understood.

This argument does not show that the doctrine of the resurrection of the body is absurd in the way in which the doctrine of disembodied survival is. It shows rather that the doctrine of resurrection is merely one way, and a question-begging way, of describing a set of circumstances that can be described equally well in another fashion. Yet the difference between the two alternative descriptions is a vital one. For it comes to no less than the original question, namely, do we survive? It is a question that the doctrine provides an answer to but one that seems to have no conclusive grounds, even if the circumstances envisaged in the doctrine were admitted to be forthcoming.

The belief in survival, then, at least in this version, does not run into insuperable difficulties of logic. But it does not seem possible to describe a set of future circumstances that will unambiguously show it to be true.

NOTE

1. See I Corinthians, Chapter 15.

Do We Need Immortality?

GRACE M. JANTZEN

Without life after death, would religion be pointless? In the next selection, Grace M. Jantzen (1948–2006), who was Professor of Religion, Culture, and Gender at the University of Manchester, argues that a belief in immortality is not central to religion, not even to Christianity.

From Grace M. Jantzen, "Do We Need Immortality?" Modern Theology 1 (1984). Reprinted by permission of Blackwell Publishing Ltd.

In a previous selection, John H. Hick observed that if God loved human beings, God would not allow them to pass out of existence. Jantzen replies that most species of animals who have lived on earth are now extinct. Did God not value them?

Jantzen interprets eternal life not as endless survival but as a quality of present existence that can be found here and now. She concludes that if we have only one life, then we cannot postpone seeking enjoyment and fulfillment both for ourselves and for those about whom we care.

The doctrine of life after death is often taken to be an essential ingredient in Christian theology. Baron Friedrich Von Hügel, when he said that "Religion, in its fullest development, essentially requires, not only this our little span of earthly years, but a life beyond,"[1] was only echoing the words of St Paul: "If in this life only we have hope in Christ, we are of all men most miserable."[2] And more recently, others, among them John Hick, have devoted much energy to a consideration of life after death. Hick writes that "Any religious understanding of human existence—not merely one's own existence but the life of humanity as a whole—positively requires some kind of immortality belief and would be radically incoherent without it."[3]

In this article I propose to look behind the arguments for and against the possibility of life after death, to investigate the various motives for wanting it, ranging from the frivolously irreligious to the profound. I shall argue that the belief in immortality is not so central to Christian thought and practice as is often believed, and indeed that a rich Christian faith does not require a doctrine of life after death in order to be profound and meaningful.

Self-Regarding Motives

To begin with the obvious, our desire for immortality is not a desire for just any sort of continued existence: the less musical among us might prefer extinction to an eternity of playing harps and singing hymns, and given a choice, we would all prefer extinction to hell. H. H. Price has offered a picture of a life after death which is entirely the product of our desires—but which might turn out to be a highly undesirable state. In his description, the postmortem world is a world in which our wishes would immediately fulfil themselves, a world whose laws "would be more like the laws of Freudian psychology than the laws of physics."[4] As Price points out, this might be much less pleasant than we might have thought; because our desires, when we include all those we have repressed, are not in mutual harmony. They incorporate, for instance, desires for punishment and suffering for the wrongs we have done. He offers the following grim comments: "Each man's purgatory, would be just the automatic consequence of his own desires; if you like, he would punish himself by having just those images which his own good feelings demand. But, if there is any consolation in it, he would have those unpleasant experiences because he wanted to have them; exceedingly unpleasant as they might be, there would still be something in him which was satisfied by them."[5] Price's point is that if all our repressed desires suddenly came true, this would be horrifying, and we would have to set about the difficult process of altering our characters so that when we get what we want, we want what we get.

The popular desire for immortality is very little like this. Life after death is often pictured, rather, as the fulfilment of longings for pleasure: it will be a paradise where there will be no more suffering and pain, where we will be happily reunited with those we love in perpetual feasting and gladness. It must be admitted that some religious pictures of heaven reinforce this frankly hedonistic conception. In the Koran we find that heaven is a beautiful garden filled with fruits and flowers. "There the Muslims drink the wine they have been denied on earth, wine that has no after-effects. It is brought to them by handsome youths, and dark-eyed houris wait on their every pleasure."[6] Similar descriptions of a hedonistic paradise of feasting and delight can be found in Christian writings, except that the dark-eyed houris are conspicuously absent, probably because of Christianity's long-standing suspicion of the sorts of delights the presence of these creatures would signal.

One of the appeals of such a description of paradise is that in this eternal delight there is no more separation from those we love; we are all eternally reunited. This, however, might prove a mixed blessing. Apart from the fact that with some of those we love, the relationship improves if there are periods of space between our togetherness, there is also the consideration that heaven would not be a private party—everyone is invited. Now, what might it be like to find oneself at the heavenly feast seated next to a Neanderthal man? Surely conversation would lag, and it is doubtful whether the silences could be filled by enjoyment of the same food. Christianity has sometimes avoided this social embarrassment by consigning the vast majority of mankind to hell, but that is not a possibility with which many of us could acquiesce and still enjoy the feast.

The point behind these frivolous comments is that it is not quite so easy to give a picture of unending delight as might be thought; it is against scenarios of this sort that Bernard Williams' comments on the tedium of immortality have some point.[7] A paradise of sensuous delights would become boring; it would in the long run be pointless and utterly unfulfilling. We can perhaps imagine ways of making a very long feast meaningful; we do, after all, cope with lengthy terrestrial social occasions by choosing interesting conversational partners, and making the dinner occasions not merely for food and drink but also for stimulating discussion and for giving and receiving friendship the value of which extends beyond the termination of the dinner. But if the feasting literally never came to an end, if there were no progress possible from the sensuous enjoyment of paradise to anything more meaningful, then we might well wish, like Elina Macropolis, to terminate the whole business and destroy the elixir of youth. It is important to notice, however, that on this view survival is tedious simply because there is no progress, no point to the continued existence except the satisfaction of hedonistic desires. But this picture is much too simple-minded. Christians (and Muslims too, of course) have long recognized this, and have taken the hedonistic descriptions of the Scriptures as symbolic of something more meaningful than eternal self-indulgence, as we shall see.

Death is sometimes seen as evil because it means the curtailment of projects; immortality would be required to give significance to life because it would allow those projects to be meaningfully continued. Of course, most of our projects would not require all eternity to complete. But even in this life, one enterprise leads to another, and provided endless progress were possible, we might pursue an endless series of challenging and absorbing tasks, each one developing into another, without any risk of boredom. This might also give more point to some of our earthly projects: the painstaking acquisition of languages and techniques would be worthwhile beyond the few years we have to employ them here. This way of thinking about survival is probably more attractive to an intellectual whose current projects could easily be extended into the future, than, say, to a labourer who considers the prospect of endless projects as enough to make him feel tired already. Still, given the opportunity, perhaps he too would develop interests which he would genuinely like to pursue.

The notion that life after death would provide an opportunity for the fulfilment of projects is not, of course, presented as an argument for the likelihood of survival but as an argument for its desirability. But does it succeed? There is considerable pull toward saying that it does, especially for those who have far more interests than they can possibly develop even assuming an average life-span. An after-life in which we could all pursue what we are really interested in without worrying about earning daily bread or having the notion that the project itself is fulfilling—so that a fulfilled person is one who completes fulfilling projects—but then we have gone round in a circle. Personal fulfilment involves something like actualizing our potential, completing projects which "do ourselves justice." But this then is problematical again: what is meant by "our potential"? If it means the whole variety of things that many of us would enjoy doing and could do well with suitable training, then this life is much too short for fulfilment, and immortality appears attractive.

But while this shows that immortality may be desirable (for some people, in some forms) it is possible to give an alternative account of fulfilment which does not require survival. If death is seen as the limit of life, then "death gains what significance it has, not by serving as a state characterizing things, but as a function which orders members of the limited series."[8] Thus if we take seriously the fact that our existence will terminate, this will affect our choice about life: if we will not live forever, then we must do while we can those things which are really important to do. On this view, a fulfilled person would be a person who picked such projects for his life that were genuinely worthwhile and suitable for his abilities and aptitudes, and was able to bring them to completion: Einstein, who lived to an old age and had accomplished significant projects, would be described as fulfilled, but a person who never had any projects at all, and lived in continuous aimless frustration, "In the evening saying 'Would it were morning' and in the morning saying 'Would it were evening'" would not be so describable. Neither would be the person who had projects but died before he could accomplish them. We do distinguish fulfilled and unfulfilled people in these ways, without reference to immortality. This does not of course mean that immortality is not desirable, especially for those who through no fault of their own are not able to complete their projects in their life-times. But it does mean that we do not have to postulate an after-life to make sense of the very concept of fulfilled and meaningful human life.

Also, if death is a limit, this gives a significance and urgency to our choices which they would not otherwise have. If we could go on pursuing an endless series of projects, it might not matter very much which ones we chose first: we could always do others later. Nor would it matter how vigorously we pursued them—for there would always be more time—nor how challenging they were or how well they developed us and brought out the best in us—for there would always be other opportunities. But if fulfilment is something which must be reached in this life if it is to be reached at all, we will be far less cavalier about the choices we make affecting our own fulfilment, and also, very importantly, in our relationships with others for whose fulfilment we are partly responsible. A great many of our projects, and arguably the most significant of them, have to do not merely with ourselves but with others: our fulfilment is not simply a matter of, say, satisfying our individual intellectual curiosities, but is bound up with the fulfilment of family, friends, students. If we really have only this life, then enjoyment and fulfilment cannot be postponed to another, either for ourselves or for those we care about.

Moral Motives

It is sometimes argued that immortality is required on moral grounds. Such an argument can take the Kantian form: immortality is necessary as a postulate of practical reason. Since the Summum Bonum involves happiness as well as virtue, and since in this life we often find a disparity between the two, it is necessary to postulate a life after death where the imbalance will be redressed. Otherwise the universe is ultimately unjust, out of joint.

I do not wish to linger long over this, but simply make three points, none of them original. First, maybe we should just admit that the universe is out of joint; it hardly seems obvious, even (or especially) from the point of view of Christian theology, that it is not. Second, even if it is, that does not rob morality—even on a Kantian system—of its point. An act of intrinsic worth is still worthwhile even if it will never receive any happiness in reward; furthermore, morality retains its meaning even if we are all going to perish. (It is not pointless for the dying to show kindness to one another.) Those who say that if there is no life after death then nothing—including morality—in this life is meaningful are implicitly admitting that there is nothing in this life which is worthwhile for its own sake, independent of eternal consequences; that everything, even love, is only a means to an end, and an end which this life cannot give. Kant himself could not have accepted such a view. Third, the Kantian view of reward has a peculiarity. What sort of happiness is it which is to be the reward of virtue? Suppose we think of it as some variant of the hedonistic paradise described earlier: then for reasons already given, the more moral one was—the more one valued that which was intrinsically good—the less happiness one would find in such ultimately pointless eternal self-indulgence. On the other hand, if Kant was speaking of the satisfactions of fulfilment rather than of a hedonistic utopia, then for the one who truly pursues virtue, becoming virtuous will itself be the fulfilment; virtue will be its own reward.

A more interesting argument for the requirement of immortality arises, not from the idea that virtue needs to be rewarded, but from the fact that none of us is sufficiently virtuous. If part of the point of life is moral development, and none of us develops fully in this life, would it not be desirable for this process to continue beyond the grave? There is considerable connection between this argument and the previous ones; except that here there is no request for happiness as a compensation for virtue, but rather for fulfilment of the very virtue that one has sought, albeit with only moderate success. There are at least two aspects of this, which I shall consider separately.

The first is encapsulated by Dostoyevsky in *The Brothers Karamazov.* "Surely I haven't suffered simply that I, my crimes and my sufferings, may manure the soil of the future harmony for somebody else. I want to see with my own eyes the hind lie down with the lion and the victim rise up and embrace his murderer. I want to be there when everyone suddenly understands what it has all been for."[9] This is not a desire for happiness in any hedonistic sense, but a desire to see the point, the fruition of all one's efforts. It is a natural enough human desire, of course; yet I do not think that it can be used as an argument that morality requires immortality, for the assumption here surely is that all the toil and suffering does have a point, whether we are "there" to understand it in the end or not. Even if we are not present at the final denouement, this does not make working toward it less worthwhile, for once again, the value of doing that cannot depend on what we individually get out of it. Although Dostoyevsky here touches, as he so often does, a very deep nerve of desire, he surely cannot be interpreted to mean that if that desire remains forever unfulfilled, there was no meaning to the suffering in the first place.

The second aspect of the longing for immortality is the longing for perfection in virtue. This is part of what prompted the more positive conceptions of purgatory, where that was seen not as a place of retributive punishment until one had suffered proportionately to the sins one had committed on earth, but rather as a place of moral purification and advance, "Where human spirits purge themselves, and train/To leap up into joy celestial."[10] This, clearly, is not an unworthy motive for desiring life after death (though in more cynical moments one might wonder how universally it is shared—how many people desire immortality because they truly want to become better). Yet it too has some problems.

In the first place, it is not obvious that simple extension of life would result in moral improvement: more time can be opportunity for deterioration as well as for advance; the person who says, "I would be better, if only I had a little longer" is justifiably suspect. Still, although time does not automatically produce growth, it may be true that it is necessary for growth. But once again it is worth thinking about the concept of death as a limit. If immortality is denied, and if moral growth is valued, there is an urgency to moral improvement, both for oneself and for others, which might easily be ignored if it were thought that there was endless time available. And as we have already seen, it will not do to say that such moral improvement, with its struggle and frequent failure, would be worthless if all ends at death, for this would hold true only if moral improvement were a means to an end, rather than intrinsically valuable.

Religious Motives

Those who say that immortality will be the scene of moral progress do not, of course, usually have in mind nothing but temporal extension to bring this about: as Fichte once said, "By the mere getting oneself buried, one cannot arrive at blessedness."[11] Rather, they believe that in the life after death there will be some strong inducements to improvement. In Price's non-theistic purgatory the unpleasantness of getting what we want may lead us to revise our desires and characters, while according to some theistic conceptions of purgatory, the punishments for our sins will purge us—sometimes in Clockwork Orange fashion—of our innate sinfulness. The most interesting theory of inducement to moral perfection, and one that forms a bridge to specifically religious arguments for the need for immortality, is the idea that the lure of divine love, more obvious in the next life than in this one, will progressively wean us from our self-centeredness and purify us so that at last our response will be perfect love reciprocated. John Hick, in his discussion of universal salvation, argues that given the assumption that man has been created by God and is "basically oriented towards him, there is no final opposition between God's saving will and our human nature acting in freedom."[12] Thus God, extending his love ever again towards us, will not take "no" for an answer but will ultimately woo successfully, not by overriding our freedom, but by winning us over so that eventually we freely choose him and his perfection. Hick says, "if there is continued life after death, and if God is ceaselessly at work for the salvation of his children, it follows that he will continue to be at work until the work is done; and I have been arguing that it is logically possible for him eventually to fulfil his saving purpose without at any point overriding our human freedom."[13]

But even granting Hick's basic assumptions of humanity's created bias toward God, God in loving pursuit of men and women, and endless time for "the unhurried chase," there are still problems with his conclusion. It is not clear that genuine freedom could be preserved while still guaranteeing the ultimate result: surely if there is freedom there is always the possibility of refusal. Hick's response, presumably, would be to agree that refusal is possible but that, given his assumptions, it becomes less and less likely as time goes on. Yet significantly to the extent that theists, Hick among them, wish to use the fact of human freedom as a (partial) resolution of the problem of evil, one aspect of their defence is that, though persons were created with a bias toward God, their freedom made it possible for them to choose rebellion, thus bringing moral evil in its train: evil is the price of freedom gone wrong. I do not see how one can have it both ways: if evil choices were made in the past even when there seemed no particular reason for them, how can Hick be confident that they will not be repeated endlessly in the future, especially since in the latter case they are made by characters already considerably warped by previous evil choices? The only way that I can see out of this for Hick is by increasing the emphasis on the divine pressure, but that runs the risk of undermining the very freedom which must here be preserved.

It is important to see the implications of human freedom for a Christian doctrine of redemption. One aspect of choice not sufficiently considered is its finality. Of course decisions can sometimes be reversed; we can often change our minds. And when we do so, when there is genuine repentance and conversion, Christianity teaches that God "makes all things new," brings creativity out of chaos, Easter out of Calvary. But the fact that we can sometimes freely change our minds is not the same as saying that in the end it makes no difference what our intermediate choices are because ultimately we will all (freely) be brought to the same goal. If it is true that whether I choose p or not-p, in the end I will get p, the idea of choice has been robbed of all significance—and that is so even if I can be persuaded that in the end it will really be p that I do want. So if I perpetually choose selfishness and distrust and dishonesty, and my character is formed by these choices, it seems perverse to say that eventually these choices will be reversed and I will attain the same moral perfection as I would have if I had all along chosen integrity and compassion. Part of what it means to be free is that our choices have consequences; it is playing much too lightly with the responsibility of freedom to suggest that these consequences, at least in their effects upon ourselves, are always reversible, even if only in the endless life to come. For that matter, if everyone is perfected, then even the consequences of our choices upon others will finally be overridden: all, in the end, will be as though no one had ever chosen evil at all. Morally revolting as is the thought of God committing people to eternal flames, one of the reasons why traditional theology has so long retained a doctrine of hell is surely to guard this aspect of freedom: there is no such thing as automatic salvation.

In spite of the strong reinforcement which the belief in immortality receives from Scripture and Christian tradition, a surprising amount can also be found which calls into question the idea that immortality is a religious requirement. In the first place, it is sometimes held that, of all the evils and sufferings in this world, death is the worst. On a traditional theistic view, evil must eventually be overcome, and all the wrongs made good; and this requires that death, "the last enemy," may not be proud. Death, too, shall die, when all who have ever lived will live again. This assumes, of course, that death is an evil; and if what I have said about death as a limit is correct, then that cannot be retained without some qualifications. Still, although death is not the worst evil, and not an unqualified evil, this does not amount to saying that it is not an evil at all; consequently in a world where evil was eradicated, death, too, would have no place.

But can this be used as an argument for a religious requirement of life after death? I am not sure that it can. If the perfect world dawns, death will perhaps not be found in it; but does this mean that death in this very imperfect world is followed by immortality? One might argue that only if it is, is God just: the sufferings of this present world can only be justified by the compensation of eternal life. But this, in the first place, is shocking theodicy: it is like saying that I may beat my dog at will provided that I later give him a dish of his favourite liver chowder. What happens after death—no matter how welcome—does not make present evil good.[14] But if life after death cannot be thought of as a compensation for otherwise unjustified present evils, surely death itself—permanent extinction–must be an evil from which a Christian may hope to escape? Well, on what grounds? We do not escape other evils and sufferings which a perfect world would not contain; why should we expect to escape this one? A Christian surely must recognize that there are many aspects of the problem of evil which he cannot explain; maybe he should just accept that death is another one. But would not death make the problem of evil not just more mysterious than it already is, but actually in principle unsolvable? Wouldn't we have to conclude that God is unjust? I don't know. If we can retain a belief in divine justice amid present evil and suffering, horrific as it is, I am not sure that relinquishing the prospect of life after death would necessarily alter the case. Of course it might tip the balance psychologically, making us "of all men, most miserable," but that is another matter. If the present evils can be relegated to the mysterious purposes of God, it seems presumptuous to assume that these purposes could not include our extinction.

A very persuasive argument for the requirement for immortality for Christian theology gathers up strands from several of these lines of thought, but places special emphasis on the personal love of God. If, as Christians maintain, God loves and values each of us individually, then we can trust him not to allow us to perish forever. We are worth more to him than that. Thus Helen Oppenheimer, in her discussion of problems of life after death, recognizes the great philosophical complexities regarding personal identity, resurrection, and the rest, but finally says that if we believe in God at all, we must also believe that if we keep on looking we will find the solution to these problems, because it is as unthinkable that a loving God would permit a relationship with one he loves to be severed by extinction of that loved one as it is to think that we would willingly allow our dearest friends to perish if it were in our power to provide them with a full and rich life.[15]

This approach has the merit, first of not pretending that the puzzles of identity and/or resurrection are easily solvable, second, of treating death seriously, and third, of placing the doctrine of immortality within the context of a doctrine of personal relationship with God. Death is not seen as a mild nuisance which can be quickly left behind never to be repeated; immortality is not automatic, and could not be expected at all were it not for the intervention of an omnipotent God. It is only because Christianity stakes itself on the unfailing love of God, following the man who dared to call God "Father" rather than "Judge," that life after death can even be considered.

But even though this seems to me a sounder starting place, given basic assumptions of Christian theology, than the belief that human beings are endowed with naturally immortal souls, I still have problems with it. It is comforting to be told that the love of God will not allow the termination of a relationship with him; it is also much more religiously satisfying to see this relationship as of central importance, and all the descriptions of the delights of paradise as mere symbolic gropings after the enjoyment of this divine fellowship. Nevertheless, Christian theology does hold that there are other things which are precious to God and which, in spite of that, perish forever. Christian theologians increasingly recognize that it is not the case that the whole earth, every primrose, every songbird, all the galaxies of all the heavens, exist for the benefit of humanity alone. Yet if it is true that God brought about the existence of all these things and takes delight in them, then it is also true that some of the things he delights in perish forever: a popular book of natural history estimates that 99 percent of all species of animals which have lived on earth are now extinct.[16]

We cannot have it both ways. "Are not three sparrows sold for a farthing?" Jesus asked. "Yet not one of them falls to the ground without your heavenly Father's knowledge."[17] These words of Jesus have often (and rightly) been taken as his teaching of the tender concern of the Father for all his creatures; what has not been noticed so often is that Jesus never denies that sparrows do fall. If the analogy which Jesus is drawing to God's care for persons (who, he says, "are of more value than many sparrows") is taken to its logical conclusion, the implication, surely, is not that we will not die but that our death will not go unnoticed. If a Christian admits that God allows some things which he values to perish, it will need further argument to show why this should not also be true of human beings: the primroses, presumably, are not loved less simply because they are temporary.

But perhaps they are temporary because they are loved less? Because they are not of such enduring worth to God (as human beings are) they are allowed to perish? This still leaves me uneasy. It is one thing to believe that we are individually valued by God, and valued perhaps in a way that other things are not; it is quite another to say that this value must result in our immortality. How can we be so sure? The analogy with persons we love whom we would not willingly allow to perish assumes that our relationship with God is in this respect just like our relationship with them. But even if we accept this analogy as the best we have for our relationship with God, we must still admit that there must be considerable disanalogies as well: how do we know that the case of endless preservation is not one of them? We may believe that God looks upon us with love and compassion, but that does not seem to me to be any guarantee that he wills our everlasting existence—that is a further (very large) step. We are taught, to be sure, that God wishes to bring us to eternal life; but it is a glaring confusion to equate eternal life with endless survival. As the notion of eternal life is used in the Johannine writings, for instance, it is spoken of as a present possession, a quality of life, not a limitless quantity; nor is it something that happens after death but in this present lifetime.

Furthermore, if there were no life after death, this in itself would not mean that religion would be pointless. Just as that which is morally valuable is valuable for its own sake and not for the reward it can bring, so also trust in God, if it is worthwhile at all, is worthwhile even if it cannot go on forever. A relationship with another human being does not become pointless just because at some time it will end with the death of one of the partners; why should it be thought that a relationship with God would be pointless if one day it too should end? Shneur Zalman, the Jewish founder of the Chabad, once exclaimed, "Master of the Universe! I desire neither Paradise nor Thy bliss in the world to come. I desire Thee and Thee alone."[18] And the hymn of Fenelon has become the common property of Christendom:

> My God I love Thee: not because I hope for
> heaven thereby,
> Nor yet because who love Thee not are lost
> eternally . . .
> Not for the sake of winning heaven, nor of
> escaping hell;
> Not from the hope of gaining aught, not
> seeking a reward;
> But as thyself hast loved me, O ever loving
> Lord . . .
> Solely because thou art my God and my most
> loving King.[19]

It is true, of course, that these words (and many more examples could be given) were written by men who did believe in immortality; the point, however, is that according to them, the value of the relationship with God, the vision of God, cannot be measured by measuring its temporal duration.

But perhaps it will still be objected that if God will one day allow me to perish, this shows that all the teaching about his love for me is a vast fraud—if he really loved me, he would preserve my life. I can only reply that for reasons already given, this does not seem obvious to me. I cannot forget the primroses. They perish. Must we conclude that they are not precious to God?

I am not arguing that there is no life beyond the grave or that it is irrational to hope for it or for Christians to commit their future to God in trust. But if what I have said is correct, then it would be presumptuous to be confident that life after death is a matter of course, guaranteed, whatever the problems, by the requirements of morality and religion. We should not neglect the significant change of verb in the Nicene Creed: from affirmations "I believe in God," "I believe in Jesus Christ," and so on, we come to the rather more tentative "And I look for the resurrection of the dead and the life of the world to come." Christian faith and Christian commitment bases itself not first and foremost on a hope of survival of death, but on the intrinsic value of a relationship with God, without any reservations about what the future holds—here or hereafter.

NOTES

1. Baron F. Von Hügel, *Eternal Life*, 2nd edition (Edinburgh: T. & T. Clark, 1913), p. 396.
2. I Cor. 15: 19.
3. John Hick, *Death and Eternal Life* (London: Fontana, 1976), p. 11.
4. H. H. Price, "Survival and the Idea of 'Another World'," in J. Donnelly (ed.), *Language, Metaphysics and Death* (New York: Fordham University Press, 1978), p. 193.
5. Ibid., p. 192.
6. Alfred Guillaume, *Islam*, 2nd edition (Harmondsworth, Middlesex: Penguin, 1954), p. 198.
7. Bernard Williams, "The Macropolis Case: Reflections of the Tedium of Immortality," in his *Problems of the Self* (Cambridge: Cambridge University Press, 1973).
8. James Van Evra, "On Death as a Limit," in Donnelly, *Language, Metaphysics and Death*, p. 25.
9. F. Dostoyevsky, *The Brothers Karamazov*, II. V. 4.
10. Dante, *The Divine Comedy: Purgatory*, I. 5 & 6.
11. Fichte, *Sämmtliche Werke Vol. 5* (1845–6), p. 403, quoted in Von Hügel, *Eternal Life*, p. 176.
12. Hick, *Death and Eternal Life*, p. 254.
13. Ibid., p. 258. "Salvation" as Hick uses the term involves moral perfection.
14. And of course it may put a different complexion on things that were perceived as evil in our imperfect state of knowledge, so that we see that it was a necessary condition for good; but that is not at issue here.

15. Helen Oppenheimer in a University Sermon preached in St Mary's, Oxford, in 1979.
16. Richard E. Leakey, *The Making of Mankind* (London: Book Club Associates, 1981), p. 20.
17. Matt. 10: 29.
18. Quoted in Isidore Epstein, *Judaism* (Harmondsworth, Middlesex: Penguin, 1959), p. 279.
19. Quoted from *Hymns Ancient and Modern*, 106.

PART 7

RELIGIOUS PLURALISM

The Dimensions of Religion

Ninian Smart

In discussing religion most of us generalize from the one religion we happen to know best. The principal religions of the world, however, differ in important ways.

For an account of the main aspects of religion, we turn to the writing of Ninian Smart (1927–2001), who taught religious studies at the University of Lancaster and the University of California, Santa Barbara. In the selection that follows, he concludes that every religion contains doctrines, myths, ethical teachings, rituals, and social institutions, all of which are animated by various kinds of religious experiences.

He emphasizes that although religions resemble one another, each is unique and needs to be understood in its own terms. In other words, he stresses that we need to keep in mind the multiplicity of religious traditions while still recognizing their points of unity.

[E]ach religion has its own style, its own inner dynamic, its own special meanings, its uniqueness. Each religion is an organism, and has to be understood in terms of the interrelation of its different parts. Thus though there are resemblances between religions or between parts of religions, these must not be seen too crudely.

For example, it is correct to say that some religions are monotheistic. They each worship a single God. But the conception of God can vary subtly. For instance, though Islam and Christianity both draw upon the Old Testament heritage, and though Allah has many characteristics of the Christian God, such as being Creator, judge, merciful, providential, nevertheless even the points of resemblance are affected by the rest of the milieu. Thus the Christian idea of the Creator is affected by the fact that creation is not just seen in relation to Genesis but also in relation to the opening verses of John. Belief in Christ seen as the Logos affects belief in God and affects one's view of creation.

It is like a picture. A particular element, such as a patch of yellow, may occur in two different pictures. One can point to the resemblance. Yet the meaning of one patch of yellow can still be very different from the meaning of the other. What it means, how it looks—these depend on what other

---

patches of color surround it. Likewise, elements in a religious organism are affected by the other elements present.

So although we are inevitably drawn to compare religions in order to make sense of the patterns of religious experience found in the history of men's faiths, we also have to recognize that each religion must also be seen essentially in its own terms, from within, as it were. This means that we have to have a sense of the multiplicity of man's religious life, as well as for its points of unity and contact. We are not only concerned with religion: we are concerned also with religions. And we have to see them in the perspective of the world's history.

[T]here are different aspects or, as I shall call them, *dimensions* of religion. . . .

The Ritual Dimension

If we were asked the use or purpose of such buildings as temples and churches, we would not be far wrong in saying that they are used for ritual or ceremonial purposes. Religion tends in part to express itself through such rituals: through worship, prayers, offerings, and the like. We may call this the *ritual* dimension of religion. About this, some important comments need to be made.

First, when we think of ritual we often think of something very formal and elaborate, like a High Mass or the Liturgy of the Eastern Orthodox Church. But it is worth remarking that even the simplest form of religious service involves ritual, in the sense of some form of outer behavior (such as closing one's eyes in prayer) coordinated to an inner intention to make contact with, or to participate in, the invisible world. I am not concerned here with those who deny the existence of such an "invisible world," however interpreted, whether as God's presence, as nirvana, as a sacred energy pervading nature. Whether or not such an invisible world exists, it forms an aspect of the world seen from the point of view of those who participate in religion. It is believed in. . . .

Second, since ritual involves both an inner and an outer aspect it is always possible that the latter will come to dominate the former. Ritual then degenerates into a mechanical or conventional process. If people go through the motions of religious observance without accompanying it with the intentions and sentiments which give it human meaning, ritual is merely an empty shell. This is the reason why some religious activities are condemned as "ritualistic." But it would be wrong to conclude that because ritualism in this bad sense exists, therefore ritual is an unimportant or degenerate aspect of religion.

It should not be forgotten that there are secular rituals which we all use, and these can form an integral part of personal and social relationships. Greeting someone with a "Good morning," saying goodbye, saluting the flag—all these in differing ways are secular rituals. Very often in society they are integrated with religious rituals, as when men say "God be with you," which is more than taking leave of someone: it is invoking a blessing upon the other person.

Third, it will prove convenient to extend the meaning of "ritual" beyond its reference to the forms of worship, sacrifice, etc., directed toward God or the gods.

It happens that a crucial part is played in India and elsewhere by yoga and analogous techniques of self-training. The ultimate aim of such methods is the attainment of higher states of consciousness, through which the adept has experience of release from worldly existence, of nirvana, of ultimate reality (the interpretation partly depends on the system of doctrines against which the adept tests his experience). Thus the essence of such religion is contemplative or mystical. Sometimes, it is pursued without reference to God or the gods—for example, in Buddhism, where the rituals of a religion of worship and sacrifice are regarded as largely irrelevant to the pursuit of nirvana. Nevertheless, the techniques of self-training have an analogy to ritual: the adept performs various physical and mental exercises through which he hopes to concentrate the mind on the transcendent, invisible world, or to withdraw his senses from their usual immersion in the flow of empirical experiences. This aspect of religion, then, we shall include in our definition of the ritual dimension. It can be classified as pragmatic (aimed at the attainment of certain experiences) in distinction from sacred ritual (directed toward a holy being, such as God). Sometimes the two forms of ritual are combined, as in Christian mysticism.

The meaning of ritual cannot be understood without reference to the environment of belief in which it is performed. Thus prayer in most ritual is directed toward a divine being. Very often, legends about the gods are used to explain the features of a ceremony or festival; and often the important events of human life, such as birth, marriage, death, are invested with a sacred significance by relating them to the divine world.

All this can happen before a religion has any theology or formal system of doctrines. Theology is an attempt to introduce organization and intellectual power into what is found in less explicit form in the deposit of revelation or traditional mythology of a religion. The collection of myths, images, and stories through which the invisible world is symbolized can suitably be called the *mythological* dimension of religion.

The Mythological Dimension

Some important comments need to be made about this mythological dimension. First, in accordance with modern usage in theology and in the comparative study of religion, the terms "myth," "mythological," etc., are *not* used to mean that the content is false. Perhaps in ordinary English to say

"It's a myth" is just a way of saying "It's false." But the use of the term *myth* in relation to religious phenomena is quite neutral as to the truth or falsity of the story enshrined in the myth. In origin, the term "myth" means "story," and in calling something a story we are not thereby saying that it is true or false. We are just reporting on what has been said. Similarly, here we are concerned with reporting on what is believed.

Second, it is convenient to use the term to include not merely stories about God (for instance the story of the creation in Genesis), about the gods (for instance in Homer's *Iliad*), etc., but also the historical events of religious significance in a tradition. For example, the Passover ritual in Judaism reenacts a highly important event that once occurred to the children of Israel; their delivery from bondage in Egypt. The historical event functions as a myth. Thus we shall include stories relating to significant historical events under the head of the mythological dimension—again without prejudice to whether the stories accurately describe what actually occurred in history.

The Doctrinal Dimension

Third, it is not always easy to differentiate the mythological and the symbolic from what is stated in theology. Doctrines are an attempt to give system, clarity, and intellectual power to what is revealed through the mythological and symbolic language of religious faith and ritual. Naturally, theology must make use of the symbols and myths. For example, when the Christian theologian has to describe the meaning of the Incarnation, he must necessarily make use of Biblical language and history. Thus the dividing line between the mythological and what I shall call the *doctrinal* dimension is not easy to draw. Yet there is clearly a distinction between Aquinas's treatment of creation at the philosophical level and the colorful story of creation in Genesis. The distinction is important, because the world religions owe some of their living power to their success in presenting a total picture of reality, through a coherent system of doctrines.

The Ethical Dimension

Throughout history we find that religions usually incorporate a code of ethics. Ethics concern the behavior of the individual and, to some extent, the code of ethics of the dominant religion controls the community. Quite obviously, men do not always live up to the standards they profess. And sometimes the standards which are inculcated by the dominant faith in a particular society may not be believed by all sections of that society.

Even so, there is no doubt that religions have been influential in molding the ethical attitudes of the societies they are part of. It is important, however, to distinguish between the moral teaching incorporated in the doctrines and mythology of a religion, and the social facts concerning those who adhere to the faith in question. For instance, Christianity teaches "Love thy neighbor as thyself." As a matter of sociological fact, quite a lot of people in so-called Christian countries, where Christianity is the official, or dominant religion, fail to come anywhere near this ideal. The man who goes to church is not necessarily loving; nor is the man who goes to a Buddhist temple necessarily compassionate. Consequently, we must distinguish between the ethical teachings of a faith, which we shall discuss as the *ethical* dimension of religion, and the actual sociological effects and circumstances of a religion.

Pertinent to this point is the consideration that most religions are institutionalized. This is most obvious in technologically primitive societies, where the priest, soothsayer, or magician is closely integrated into the social structure. Religion is not just a personal matter here: it is part of the life of the community. It is built into the institutions of daily life. But even in sophisticated communities where a line is drawn between religious and secular concerns, as in contemporary America, churches exist as institutions to be reckoned with. They are part of the "establishment." In areas where there is active or latent persecution of religious faith, as in the Soviet Union, there are still organizations for continuing religious activities.

The Social Dimension

Religions are not just systems of *belief*: they are also organizations, or parts of organizations. They have a communal and social significance. This social shape of a religion is, of course, to some extent determined by the religious and ethical ideals and practices that it harbors. Conversely, it often happens that the religious and ethical ideals are adapted to existing social conditions and attitudes. For example, Japanese fishermen reconcile the Buddhist injunction against taking life (even animal or fish life) to their activity as fishermen. The Christian's dedication to brotherly love or his attitude to war may be determined more by patriotism and a national crisis than by the Gospel. Thus, it is important to distinguish between the ethical dimension of religion and the *social* dimension. The latter is the mode in which the religion in question is institutionalized, whereby, through its institutions and teachings, it affects the community in which it finds itself. The doctrinal, mythological, and ethical dimensions express a religion's claims about the nature of the invisible world and its aims about how men's lives ought to be shaped: the social dimension indicates the way in which men's lives are in fact shaped by these claims and the way in which religious institutions operate.

It is, incidentally, clear that the ongoing patterns of ritual are an important element in the institutionalization of religion. For example, if it is believed that certain ceremonies and sacraments can only be properly performed by a priest, then the religious institution will be partly determined by the need to maintain and protect a professional priesthood.

The Experiential Dimension

The dimensions we have so far discussed would indeed be hard to account for were it not for the dimension . . . of experience, the *experiential* dimension. Although men may hope to have contact with, and participate in, the invisible world through ritual, personal religion normally involves the hope of, or realization of, experience of that world. The Buddhist monk hopes for nirvana, and this includes the contemplative experience of peace and of insight into the transcendent. The Christian who prays to God believes normally that God answers prayer—and this not just "externally" in bringing about certain states of affairs, such as a cure for illness, but more importantly "internally" in the personal relationship that flowers between the man who prays and his Maker. The prayerful Christian believes that God does speak to men in an intimate way and that the individual can and does have an inner experience of God. Hence, personal religion necessarily involves what we have called the experiential dimension.

The factor of religious experience is even more crucial when we consider the events and the human lives from which the great religions have stemmed. The Buddha achieved Enlightenment as he sat in meditation beneath the Bo-Tree. As a consequence of his shattering mystical experience, he believed that he had the secret of the cure for the suffering and dissatisfactions of life in this world. We have records of the inaugural visions of some of the Old Testament prophets, of the experiences that told them something profoundly important about God and that spurred them on to teach men in his name. It was through such experiences that Mohammad began to preach the unity of Allah—a preaching that had an explosive impact upon the world from Central Asia to Spain. One cannot read the Upanishads, the source of so much of Hindu doctrine, without feeling the experience on which their teachings are founded. The most striking passage in the *Bhagavadgita*, perhaps the greatest religious document of Hinduism, is that in which the Lord reveals himself in terrifying splendor to Arjuna. Arjuna is overwhelmed by awe and filled with utter devotion. . . .

The words of Jesus Christ reveal his sense of intimate closeness to the Father; there is little doubt that this rested upon highly significant personal experiences. These and other examples can be given of the crucial part played by religious experience in the genesis of the great faiths. . . .

There is a special difficulty, however, in undertaking a description of a religious experience. We have to rely upon the testimony of those who have the experience, and their reports must be conveyed to us either by telling or writing. Sometimes accounts of prophetic or mystical experience of important religious leaders have been preserved by oral tradition through many generations before being written down. But for the most part, the individual religious experiences that have influenced large segments of mankind occurred in cultures that knew the art of writing.

This means that the experience occurred in the context of the existing religions which already had a doctrinal dimension. This raises a problem for us in our attempt to understand the unique religious experience of the prophets or founders of religions, for their experiences are likely to be interpreted in the light of existing doctrines, as well as clothed in the mythological and symbolic forms of the age. There is less difficulty when we consider the "lesser" figures of the religions—not the founders, but those saints and visionaries who come after. They interpret their experiences in terms of received doctrines and mythologies.

For these reasons, it is not easy to know about a given report which of the elements in it are based, so to say, purely on the experience itself, and which are due to doctrinal and mythological interpretation. To some extent the problem can be overcome by comparing the reports of men of different cultures—such as India and the West—which had virtually no contact during the periods crucial for the formation and elaboration of the dominant religious beliefs.

Moreover, it is worth noting that there is a *dialectic* between experience and doctrine. Thus, though the Buddha, for example, took over elements from the thought-forms of his own age, he was genuinely a creative teacher, who introduced new elements and transmuted the old. The Old Testament prophets fashioned a genuinely original ethical monotheism from an existant belief in Yahweh. The changes they made in the simple tribal religious teaching they inherited can be understood, to some degree, in terms of the impact of the personal religious experiences that were revelatory for these men. Thus experience and doctrinal interpretation have a dialectical relationship. The latter colors the former, but the former also shapes the latter. . . .

This dialectical interplay also helps us to understand some of the features of personal religion at a humbler level. The Christian, for example, is taught certain doctrines and mythological symbols by his parents. He learns to call God "Our Father"; he is instructed to believe that the world is created by God and sustained by God. These ideas will at first simply be "theoretical" as far as the young Christian is concerned, on a par with other non-observable theories he learns about the world, such as that the earth goes round the sun. But suppose he progresses to a deeper understanding of the Christian faith through a particular personal experience, or through his response to the ritual and ethical demands of the religion. Then he will come to see that in some mysterious way God is a person with whom he can have contact; God is not just like the sun, to be thought of speculatively, or to be looked at. Personally, then, he discovers that he can worship and pray to God. In short, "I believe in God the Father Almighty, Maker of Heaven and Earth" will come to have a new meaning for him. In a sense, he will now believe something other than what he first believed. In this way, the interplay between doctrine and experiences is fundamental to personal religion. . . .

Religion as an Organism

To sum up our account . . . of what religion is: it is a six-dimensional organism, typically containing doctrines, myths, ethical teachings, rituals, and social institutions, and animated by religious experiences of various kinds. To understand the key ideas of religion, such as God and nirvana, one has to understand the pattern of religious life directed toward these goals. God is the focus of worship and praise; nirvana is found by treading the Noble Eightfold Path, culminating in contemplation. . . .

Religious Pluralism and Salvation

JOHN H. HICK

John H. Hick, whose work we read previously, believes that despite the differences among religions, in at least one crucial respect all are fundamentally similar. Each can be viewed as offering a path to salvation, a way of shifting believers from self-centeredness to concentration on a divine reality. In light of this consideration, Hick urges all religious adherents to reject the view that their own religions are superior to all others.

In particular, Hick maintains that Christians should recognize the "arbitrary and contrived notion" that the salvation of all persons depends on their believing in the Trinity and resurrection. Whether such a doctrinal transformation would undermine or enhance Christianity is a crucial question for readers to consider.

I

The fact that there is a plurality of religious traditions, each with its own distinctive beliefs, spiritual practices, ethical outlook, art forms, and cultural ethos, creates an obvious problem for those of us who see them, not simply as human phenomena, but as responses to the Divine. For each presents itself,

From *Faith and Philosophy* 5 (1988). Reprinted by permission of the journal.

implicitly or explicitly, as in some important sense absolute and unsurpassable and as rightly claiming a total allegiance. The problem of the relationship between these different streams of religious life has often been posed in terms of their divergent belief-systems. For whilst there are various overlaps between their teachings there are also radical differences: is the divine reality (let us refer to it as the Real) personal or non-personal; if personal, is it unitary or triune; is the universe created, or emanated, or itself eternal; do we live only once on this earth or are we repeatedly reborn? and so on and so on. When the problem of understanding religious plurality is approached through these rival truth-claims it appears particularly intractable.

I want to suggest, however, that it may more profitably be approached from a different direction, in terms of the claims of the various traditions to provide, or to be effective contexts of, salvation. "Salvation" is primarily a Christian term, though I shall use it here to include its functional analogues in the other major world traditions. In this broader sense we can say that both Christianity and these other faiths are paths of salvation. For whereas preaxial religion was (and is) centrally concerned to keep life going on an even keel, the post-axial traditions, originating or rooted in the "axial age" of the first millennium B.C.E.—principally Hinduism, Judaism, Buddhism, Christianity, Islam—are centrally concerned with a radical transformation of the human situation.

It is of course possible, in an alternative approach, to define salvation in such a way that it becomes a necessary truth that only one particular tradition can provide it. If, for example, from within Christianity we define salvation as being forgiven by God because of Jesus' atoning death, and so becoming part of God's redeemed community, the church, then salvation is by definition Christian salvation. If on the other hand, from within Mahayana Buddhism, we define it as the attainment of *satori* or awakening, and so becoming an ego-free manifestation of the eternal Dharmakaya, then salvation is by definition Buddhist liberation. And so on. But if we stand back from these different conceptions to compare them, we can, I think, very naturally and properly see them as different forms of the more fundamental conception of a radical change from a profoundly unsatisfactory state to one that is limitlessly better because rightly related to the Real. Each tradition conceptualizes in its own way the wrongness of ordinary human existence—as a state of fallenness from paradisal virtue and happiness, or as a condition of moral weakness and alienation from God, or as the fragmentation of the infinite One into false individualities, or as a self-centeredness which pervasively poisons our involvement in the world process, making it to us an experience of anxious, unhappy unfulfillment. But each at the same time proclaims a limitlessly better possibility, again conceptualized in different ways—as the joy of conforming one's life to God's law; as giving oneself to God in Christ, so that "it is no longer I who live, but Christ who lives in me" (Galatians 2:20), leading to eternal life in God's presence; as a complete surrender (*islam*) to God, and hence peace with God, leading to the bliss of paradise; as transcending the ego and realizing oneness with the limitless being-consciousness-bliss (*satchitananda*) of Brahman; as overcoming the ego point of view and entering into the serene selflessness of nirvana. I suggest that these different conceptions of salvation are specifications of what, in a generic formula, is the transformation of human existence from self-centeredness to a new orientation, centered in the divine Reality. And in each case the good news that is proclaimed is that this limitlessly better possibility is actually available and can be entered upon, or begin to be entered upon, here and now. Each tradition sets forth the way to attain this great good: faithfulness to the Torah, discipleship to Jesus, obedient living out of the Qur'anic way of life, the Eightfold Path of the Buddhist dharma, or the three great Hindu *margas* of mystical insight, activity in the world, and self-giving devotion to God.

II

The great world religions, then, are ways of salvation. Each claims to constitute an effective context within which the transformation of human existence can and does take place from self-centeredness to Reality-centeredness. How are we to judge such claims? We cannot directly observe the inner spiritual quality of a human relationship to the Real; but we can observe how that relationship, as one's deepest and most pervasive orientation, affects the moral and spiritual quality of a human personality and of a man's or woman's relationship to others. It would seem, then, that we can only assess these salvation-projects insofar as we are able to observe their fruits in human life. The inquiry has to be, in a broad sense, empirical. For the issue is one of fact, even though hard to define and difficult to measure fact, rather than being settleable by a priori stipulation.

The word "spiritual" which occurs above is notoriously vague; but I am using it to refer to a quality or, better, an orientation which we can discern in those individuals whom we call saints—a Christian term which I use here to cover such analogues as arahat, bodhisattva, jivanmukti, mahatma. In these cases the human self is variously described as becoming part of the life of God, being "to the Eternal Goodness what his own hand is to a man"; or being permeated from within by the infinite reality of Brahman; or becoming one with the eternal Buddha nature. There is a change in their deepest orientation from centeredness in the ego to a new centering in the Real as manifested in their own tradition. One is conscious in the presence of such a person that he or she is, to a startling extent, open to the transcendent, so as to be largely free from self-centered concerns and anxieties and empowered to live as an instrument of God/Truth/Reality.

It is to be noted that there are two main patterns of such a transformation. There are saints who withdraw from the world into prayer or meditation and saints who seek to change the world—in the medieval period a contemplative Julian of Norwich and a political Joan of Arc, or in our own century a mystical Sri Aurobindo and a political Mahatma Gandhi. In our present age of sociological consciousness, when we are aware that our inherited political and economic structures can be analyzed and purposefully changed, saintliness is more likely than in earlier times to take social and political forms. But, of whichever type, the saints are not a different species from the rest of us; they are simply much more advanced in the salvific transformation.

The ethical aspect of this salvific transformation consists in observable modes of behavior. But how do we identify the kind of behavior which, to the degree that it characterizes a life, reflects a corresponding degree of reorientation to the divine Reality? Should we use Christian ethical criteria, or Buddhist, or Muslim . . . ? The answer, I suggest, is that at the level of their most basic moral insights the great traditions use a common criterion. For they agree in giving a central and normative role to the unselfish regard for others that we call love or compassion. This is commonly expressed in the principle of valuing others as we value ourselves, and treating them accordingly. Thus in the ancient Hindu *Mahabharata* we read that "One should never do to another that which one would regard as injurious to oneself. This, in brief, is the rule of Righteousness" (*Anushana parva*, 113:7). Again, "He who . . . benefits persons of all orders, who is always devoted to the good of all beings, who does not feel aversion to anybody . . . succeeds in ascending to Heaven" (*Anushana parva*, 145:24). In the Buddhist *Sutta Nipata* we read, "As a mother cares for her son, all her days, so towards all living things a man's mind should be all-embracing" (149). In the Jain scriptures we are told that one should go about "treating all creatures in the world as he himself would be treated" (*Kitanga Sutra*, I.ii.33). Confucius, expounding humaneness (*jen*), said, "Do not do to others what you would not like yourself" (*Analects*, xxi, 2). In a Taoist scripture we read that the good man will "regard [others'] gains as if they were his own, and their losses in the same way" (*Thai Shang*, 3). The Zoroastrian scriptures declare, "That nature only is good when it shall not do unto another whatever is not good for its own self" (*Dadistan-i-dinik*, 94:5). We are all familiar with Jesus' teaching, "As ye would that men should do to you, do ye also to them likewise" (Luke 6:31). In the Jewish Talmud we read "What is hateful to yourself do not do to your fellow man. That is the whole of the Torah" (*Babylonian Talmud*, Shabbath 31a). And in the Hadith of Islam we read Muhammad's words, "No man is a true believer unless he desires for his brother that which he desires for himself" (*Ibn Madja*, Intro. 9). Clearly, if everyone acted on this basic principle, taught by all the major faiths, there would be no injustice, no avoidable suffering, and the human family would everywhere live in peace.

When we turn from this general principle of love/compassion to the actual behavior of people within the different traditions, wondering to what extent they live in this way, we realize how little research has been done on so important a question. We do not have, much more to go on than general impressions, supplemented by travellers' tales and anecdotal reports. We observe among our neighbors within our own community a great deal of practical loving-kindness; and we are told, for example, that a remarkable degree of self-giving love is to be found among the Hindu fishing families in the mud huts along the Madras shore; and we hear various other similar accounts from other lands. We read biographies, social histories, and novels of Muslim village life in Africa, Buddhist life in Thailand, Hindu life in India, Jewish life in New York, as well as Christian life around the world, both in the past and today, and we get the impression that the personal virtues (as well as vices) are basically much the same within these very different religion-cultural settings and that in all of them unselfish concern for others occurs and is highly valued. And, needless to say, as well as love and compassion we also see all-too-abundantly, and apparently spread more or less equally in every society, cruelty, greed, hatred, selfishness, and malice.

All this constitutes a haphazard and impressionistic body of data. Indeed I want to stress, not how easy it is, but on the contrary how difficult it is, to make responsible judgments in this area. For not only do we lack full information, but the fragmentary information that we have has to be interpreted in the light of the varying natural conditions of human life in different periods of history and in different economic and political circumstances. And I suggest that all that we can presently arrive at is the cautious and negative conclusion that we have no good reason to believe that any one of the great religious traditions has proved itself to be more productive of love/compassion than another.

The same is true when we turn to the large-scale social outworkings of the different salvation-projects. Here the units are not individual human lives, spanning a period of decades, but religious cultures spanning many centuries. For we can no more judge a civilization than a human life by confining our attention to a single temporal cross-section. Each of the great streams of religious life has had its times of flourishing and its times of deterioration. Each has produced its own distinctive kinds of good and its own distinctive kinds of evil. But to assess either the goods or the evils cross-culturally is difficult to say the least. How do we weigh, for example, the lack of economic progress, and consequent widespread poverty, in traditional Hindu and Buddhist cultures against the endemic violence and racism of Christian civilization, culminating in the twentieth century Holocaust? How do we weigh what the west regards as the hollowness of arranged marriages against what the east regards as the hollowness of a marriage system that leads to such a high proportion of divorces and broken families? From within each culture one can see clearly enough the defects of the others. But an objective ethical comparison of such vast and complex totalities is at present an unattainable ideal. And the result is that we are not in a position to claim an over-all moral superiority for any one of the great living religious traditions.

Let us now see where we have arrived. I have suggested that if we identify the central claim of each of the great religious traditions as the claim to provide, or to be an effective context of, salvation; and if we see salvation as an actual change in human beings from self-centeredness to a new orientation centered in the ultimate divine Reality; and if this new orientation has both a more elusive "spiritual" character and a more readily observable moral aspect—then we arrive at the modest and largely negative conclusion that, so far as we can tell, no one of the great world religions is salvifically superior to the rest.

III

If this is so, what are we to make of the often contradictory doctrines of the different traditions? In order to make progress at this point, we must distinguish various kinds and levels of doctrinal conflict.

There are, first, conceptions of the ultimate as Jahweh, or the Holy Trinity, or Allah, or Shiva, or Vishnu, or as Brahman, or the Dharmakaya, the Tao, and so on.

If salvation is taking place, and taking place to about the same extent, within the religious systems presided over by these various deities and absolutes, this suggests that they are different manifestations to humanity of a yet more ultimate ground of all salvific transformation. Let us then consider the possibility that an infinite transcendent divine reality is being differently conceived, and therefore differently experienced, and therefore differently responded to from within our different religio-cultural ways of being human. This hypothesis makes sense of the fact that the salvific transformation seems to have been occurring in all the great traditions. Such a conception is, further, readily open to philosophical support. For we are familiar today with the ways in which human experience is partly formed by the conceptual and linguistic frameworks within which it occurs. The basically Kantian insight that the mind is active in perception, and that we are always aware of our environment as it appears to a consciousness operating with our particular conceptual resources and habits, has been amply confirmed by work in cognitive psychology and the sociology of knowledge and can now be extended with some confidence to the analysis of religious awareness. If, then, we proceed inductively from the phenomenon of religious experience around the world, adopting a religious as distinguished from a naturalistic interpretation of it, we are likely to find ourselves making two moves. The first is to postulate an ultimate transcendent divine reality (which I have been referring to as the Real) which, being beyond the scope of our human concepts, cannot be directly experienced by us as it is in itself but only as it appears through our various human thought-forms. And the second is to identify the thought-and-experienced deities and absolutes as different manifestations of the Real within different historical forms of human consciousness. In Kantian terms, the divine noumenon, the Real *an sich*, is experienced through different human receptivities as a range of divine phenomena, in the formation of which religious concepts have played an essential part.

These different "receptivities" consist of conceptual schemas within which various personal, communal, and historical factors have produced yet further variations. The most basic concepts in terms of which the Real is humanly thought-and-experienced are those of (personal) deity and of the (non-personal) absolute. But the Real is not actually experienced either as deity in general or as the absolute in general. Each basic concept becomes (in Kantian terminology) schematized in more concrete form. It is at this point that individual and cultural factors enter the process. The religious tradition of which we are a part, with its history and ethos and its great exemplars, its scriptures feeding our thoughts and emotions, and perhaps above all its devotional or meditative practices, constitutes an uniquely shaped and coloured "lens" through which we are concretely aware of the Real specifically as the personal Adonai, or as the Heavenly Father, or as Allah, or Vishnu, or Shiva . . . or again as the non-personal Brahman, or Dharmakaya, or the Void or the Ground. . . . Thus, one who uses the forms of Christian prayer and sacrament is thereby led to experience the Real as the divine Thou, whereas one who practices advaitic yoga or Buddhist zazen is thereby brought to experience the Real as the infinite being-consciousness-bliss of Brahman, or as the limitless emptiness of *sunyata* which is at the same time the infinite fullness of immediate reality as "wondrous being."

Three explanatory comments at this point before turning to the next level of doctrinal disagreement. First, to suppose that the experienced deities and absolutes which are the intentional objects of worship or content of religious meditation, are appearances or manifestations of the Real, rather than each being itself the Real *an sich*, is not to suppose that they are illusions—any more than the varying ways in which a mountain may appear to a plurality of differently placed observers are illusory. That the same reality may be variously experienced and described is true even of physical objects. But in the case of the infinite, transcendent divine reality there may well be much greater scope for the use of varying human conceptual schemas producing varying modes of phenomenal experience. Whereas the concepts in terms of which we are aware of mountains and rivers and houses are largely (though by no means entirely) standard throughout the human race, the religious concepts in terms of which we become aware of the Real have developed in widely different ways within the different cultures of the earth.

As a second comment, to say that the Real is beyond the range of our human concepts is not intended to mean that it is beyond the scope of purely formal, logically generated concepts—such as the concept of being beyond the range of (other than purely formal) concepts. We would not be able to refer at all to that which cannot be conceptualized in any way, not even by the concept of being unconceptualizable! But the other than purely formal concepts by which our experience is structured must be presumed not to apply to its noumenal ground. The characteristics mapped in thought and language are those that are constitutive of human experience. We have no warrant to apply them to the noumenal ground of the phenomenal, i.e., experienced, realm. We should therefore not think of the Real *an sich* as singular or plural, substance or process, personal or non-personal, good or bad, purposive or non-purposive. This has long been a basic theme of religious thought. For example, within Christianity, Gregory of Nyssa declared that:

> The simplicity of the True Faith assumes God to be that which He is, namely, incapable of being grasped by any term, or any idea, or any other device of our apprehension, remaining beyond the reach not only of the human but of the angelic and all supramundane intelligence, unthinkable, unutterable, above all expression in words, having but one name that can represent His proper nature, the single name being "Above Every Name" (*Against Eunomius*, I, 42).

Augustine, continuing this tradition, said that "God transcends even the mind" (*True Religion*, 36:67), and Aquinas that "by its immensity, the divine substance surpasses every form that our intellect reaches" (*Contra Gentiles*, I, 14, 3). In Islam the Qur'an affirms that God is "beyond what they describe" (6:101). The Upanishads declare of Brahman, "There the eye goes not, speech goes not, nor the mind" (*Kena Up.*, 1, 3), and Shankara wrote that Brahman is that "before which words recoil, and to which no understanding has ever attained" (Otto, *Mysticism East and West*, E. T. 1932, p. 28).

But, third, we might well ask, why postulate an ineffable and unobservable divine-reality-in-itself? If we can say virtually nothing about it, why affirm its existence? The answer is that the reality or non-reality of the postulated noumenal ground of the experienced religious phenomena constitutes the difference between a religious and a naturalistic interpretation of religion. If there is no such transcendent ground, the various forms of religious experience have to be categorized as purely human projections. If on the other hand there is such a transcendent ground, then these phenomena may be joint products of the universal presence of the Real and of the varying sets of concepts and images that have crystallized within the religious traditions of the earth. To affirm the transcendent is thus to affirm that religious experience is not solely a construction of the human imagination but is a response—though always culturally conditioned—to the Real.

Those doctrinal conflicts, then, that embody different conceptions of the ultimate arise, according to the hypothesis I am presenting, from the variations between different sets of human conceptual schema and spiritual practice. And it seems that each of these varying ways of thinking-and-experiencing the Real has been able to mediate its transforming presence to human life. For the different major concepts of the ultimate do not seem—so far as we can tell—to result in one religious totality being soteriologically more effective than another.

IV

The second level of doctrinal difference consists of metaphysical beliefs which cohere with although they are not exclusively linked to a particular conception of the ultimate. These are beliefs about the relation of the material universe to the Real: creation ex nihilo, emanation, an eternal universe, an unknown form of dependency . . . ? And about human destiny: reincarnation or a single life, eternal identity or transcendence of the self . . . ? Again, there are questions about the existence of heavens and hells and purgatories and angels and devils and many other subsidiary states and entities. Out of this mass of disputed religious issues let me pick two major examples: is the universe created ex nihilo, and do human beings reincarnate?

I suggest that we would do well to apply to such questions a principle that was taught by the Buddha two and a half millennia ago. He listed a series of "undetermined questions" (*avyakata*)—whether the universe is eternal, whether it is spatially infinite, whether (putting it in modern terms) mind and brain are identical, and what the state is of a completed project of human existence (a Tathagata) after bodily death. He refused to answer these questions, saying that we do not need to have knowledge of these things in order to attain liberation or awakening (nirvana); and indeed that to regard such information as soteriologically essential would only divert us from the single-minded quest for liberation. I think that we can at this point profitably learn from the Buddha, even extending his conception of the undetermined questions further than he did—for together with almost everyone else in his own culture he regarded one of our examples, reincarnation, as a matter of assured knowledge. Let us, then, accept that we do not *know* whether, e.g., the universe was created ex nihilo, nor whether human beings are reincarnated; and, further, that it is not necessary for salvation to hold a correct opinion on either matter.

I am not suggesting that such issues are unimportant. On their own level they are extremely important, being both of great interest to us and also having widely ramifying implications within our belief systems and hence for our lives. The thought of being created out of nothing can nourish a salutary sense of absolute dependence. (But other conceptions can also nurture that sense.) The idea of reincarnation can offer the hope of future spiritual progress; though, combined with the principle of karma, it can also serve to validate the present inequalities of human circumstances. (But other eschatologies also have their problems, both theoretical and practical). Thus these—and other—disputed issues do have a genuine importance. Further, it is possible that some of them may one day be settled by empirical evidence. It might become established, for example, that the "big bang" of some fifteen billion years ago was an absolute beginning, thus ruling out the possibility that the universe is eternal. And again, it might become established, by an accumulation of evidence, that reincarnation does indeed occur in either some or all cases. On the other hand it is possible that we shall never achieve agreed knowledge in these areas. Certainly, at the present time, whilst we have theories, preferences, hunches, inherited convictions, we cannot honestly claim to have secure knowledge. And the same is true, I suggest, of the entire range of metaphysical issues about which the religions dispute. They are of intense interest, properly the subject of continuing research and discussion, but are not matters concerning which absolute dogmas are appropriate. Still less is it appropriate to maintain that salvation depends upon accepting some one particular opinion or dogma. We have seen that the transformation of human existence from self-centeredness to Reality-centeredness seems to be taking place within each of the great traditions despite their very different answers to these debated questions. It follows that a correct opinion concerning them is not required for salvation.

V

The third level of doctrinal disagreement concerns historical questions. Each of the great traditions includes a larger or smaller body of historical beliefs. In the case of Judaism these include at least the main features of the history described in the Hebrew scriptures; in the case of Christianity, these plus the main features of the life, death, and resurrection of Jesus as described in the New Testament; in the case of Islam, the main features of the history described in the Qur'an; in the case of Vaishnavite Hinduism, the historicity of Krishna; in the case of Buddhism, the historicity of Guatama and his enlightenment at Bodh Gaya; and so on. But although each tradition thus has its own records of the past, there are rather few instances of direct disagreement between these. For the strands of history that are cherished in these different historical memories do not generally overlap; and where they do overlap they do not generally involve significant differences. The overlaps are mainly within the thread of ancient Near Eastern history that is common to the Jewish, Christian, and Muslim scriptures; and within this I can only locate two points of direct disagreement—the Torah's statement that Abraham nearly sacrificed his son Isaac at Mount Moriah (Genesis 22) versus the Muslim interpretation of the Qur'anic version (in Sura 37) that it was his other son Ishmael; and the New Testament witness that Jesus died on the cross versus the Qur'anic teaching that "they did not slay him, neither crucified him, only a likeness of that was shown them" (Sura 4:156). (This latter however would seem to be a conflict between an historical report, in the New Testament, and a theological inference—that God would not allow so great a prophet to be killed—in the Qur'an.)

All that one can say in general about such disagreements, whether between two traditions or between any one of them and the secular historians, is that they could only properly be settled by the weight of historical evidence. However, the events in question are usually so remote in time, and the evidence so slight or so uncertain, that the question cannot be definitively settled. We have to be content with different communal memories, enriched as they are by the mythic halo that surrounds all long-lived human memories of events of transcendent significance. Once again, then, I suggest that differences of historical judgment, although having their own proper importance, do not prevent the different traditions from being effective, and so far as we can tell equally effective, contexts of salvation. It is evidently not necessary for salvation to have correct historical information. (It is likewise not necessary for salvation, we may add, to have correct scientific information.)

VI

Putting all this together, the picture that I am suggesting can be outlined as follows: our human religious experience, variously shaped as it is by our sets of religious concepts, is a cognitive response to the universal presence of the ultimate divine Reality that, in itself, exceeds human conceptuality. This Reality is however manifested to us in ways formed by a variety of human concepts, as the range of divine personae and metaphysical impersonae witnessed to in the history of religions. Each major tradition, built around its own distinctive way of thinking-and-experiencing the Real, has developed its own answers to the perennial questions of our origin and destiny, constituting more or less comprehensive and coherent cosmologies and eschatologies. These are human creations which have, by their association with living streams of religious experience, become invested with a sacred authority. However they cannot all be wholly true; quite possibly none is wholly true; perhaps all are partly true. But since the salvific process has been going on through the centuries despite this unknown distribution of truth and falsity in our cosmologies and eschatologies, it follows that it is not necessary for salvation to adopt any one of them. We would therefore do well to learn to tolerate unresolved, and at present unresolvable, differences concerning these ultimate mysteries.

One element, however, to be found in the belief-systems of most of the traditions raises a special problem, namely that which asserts the sole salvific efficacy of that tradition. I shall discuss this problem in terms of Christianity because it is particularly acute for those of us who are Christians. We are all familiar with such New Testament texts as "There is salvation in no one else [than Jesus Christ], for there is no other name under heaven given among men by which we must be saved" (Acts 4:12), and with the Catholic dogma *Extra ecclesiam nulla salus* (No salvation outside the church) and its Protestant equivalent—never formulated as an official dogma but nevertheless implicit within the eighteenth and nineteenth century Protestant missionary expansion—no salvation outside Christianity. Such a dogma differs from other elements of Christian belief in that it is not only a statement about the potential relationship of Christians to God but at the same time about the actual relationship of non-Christians to God. It says that the latter, in virtue of being non-Christians, lack salvation. Clearly such a dogma is incompatible with the insight that the salvific transformation of human existence is going on, and so far as we can tell going on to a more or less equal extent, within all the great traditions. Insofar, then, as we accept that salvation is not confined to Christianity we must reject the old exclusivist dogma.

This has in fact now been done by most thinking Christians, though exceptions remain, mostly within the extreme Protestant fundamentalist constituencies. The *Extra ecclesiam* dogma, although not explicitly repealed, has been outflanked by the work of such influential Catholic theologians as Karl Rahner, whose new approach was in effect endorsed by Vatican II. Rahner expressed his more inclusivist outlook by suggesting that devout people of other faiths are "anonymous Christians," within the invisible church even without knowing it, and thus within the sphere of salvation. The Pope [John Paul II] in his Encyclical *Redemptor Hominis* (1979), expressed this thought even more comprehensively by saying that "every man without exception has been redeemed by Christ" and "with every man without any exception whatever Christ is in a way united, even when man is unaware of it" (para. 14). And a number of Protestant theologians have advocated a comparable position.

The feature that particularly commends this kind of inclusivism to many Christians today is that it recognizes the spiritual values of other religions, and the occurrence of salvation within them, and yet at the same time preserves their conviction of the ultimate superiority of their own religion over all others. For it maintains that salvation, wherever it occurs, is Christian salvation; and Christians are accordingly those who alone know and preach the source of salvation, namely in the atoning death of Christ.

This again, like the old exclusivism, is a statement not only about the ground of salvation for Christians but also for Jews, Muslims, Hindus, Buddhists, and everyone else. But we have seen that it has to be acknowledged that the immediate ground of their transformation is the particular spiritual path along which they move. It is by living in accordance with the Torah or with the Qur'anic revelation that Jews and Muslims find a transforming peace with God; it is by one or other of their great *margas* that Hindus attain to *moksha*; it is by the Eightfold Path that Theravada Buddhists come to *nirvana*; it is by *zazen* that Zen Buddhists attain to *satori*; and so on. The Christian inclusivist is, then, by implication, declaring that these various spiritual paths are efficacious, and constitute authentic contexts of salvation, because Jesus died on the cross; and, by further implication, that if he had not died on the cross they would not be efficacious.

This is a novel and somewhat astonishing doctrine. How are we to make sense of the idea that the salvific power of the dharma taught five hundred years earlier by the Buddha is a consequence of the death of Jesus in approximately 30 C.E.? Such an apparently bizarre conception should only be affirmed for some very good reason. It was certainly not taught by Jesus or his apostles. It has emerged only in the thought of twentieth century Christians who have come to recognize that Jews are being salvifically transformed through the spirituality of Judaism, Muslims through that of Islam, Hindus and Buddhists through the paths mapped out by their respective traditions, and so on, but who nevertheless wish to retain their inherited sense of the unique superiority of Christianity. The only outlet left for this sense, when one has acknowledged the salvific efficacy of the various great spiritual ways, is the arbitrary and contrived notion of their metaphysical dependency upon the death of Christ. But the theologian who undertakes to spell out this invisible causality is not to be envied. The problem is not one of logical possibility—it only requires logical agility to cope with that—but one of religious or spiritual plausibility. It would be a better use of theological time and energy, in my opinion, to develop forms of trinitarian, christological, and soteriological doctrine which are compatible with our awareness of the independent salvific authenticity of the other great world faiths. Such forms are already available in principle in conceptions of the Trinity, not as ontologically three but as three ways in which the one God is humanly thought and experienced; conceptions of Christ as a man so fully open to and inspired by God as to be, in the ancient Hebrew metaphor, a "son of God"; and conceptions of salvation as an actual human transformation which has been powerfully elicited and shaped, among his disciples, by the influence of Jesus.

There may indeed well be a variety of ways in which Christian thought can develop in response to our acute late twentieth century awareness of the other world religions, as there were of responding to the nineteenth century awareness of the evolution of the forms of life and the historical character of the holy scriptures. And likewise there will no doubt be a variety of ways in which each of the other great traditions can rethink its inherited assumption of its own unique superiority. But it is not for us to tell people of other traditions how to do their own business. Rather, we should attend to our own.

A Defense of Religious Exclusivism

Alvin Plantinga

In response to those like John Hick who urge religious adherents to reject the superiority of their own religion, Alvin Plantinga, whose work we read previously, maintains that his belief in Christianity is true, whereas beliefs incompatible with Christianity are false. Is he, therefore, intellectually mistaken or morally arrogant? He denies these charges. Assessing his defense is the responsibility of each reader.

From *Philosophy of Religion: An Anthology*, Fifth Edition, ed. Louis P. Pojman. Reprinted by permission of the author.

I find myself with religious beliefs . . . that I realize aren't shared by nearly everyone else. For example, I believe both

(1) The world was created by God, an almighty, all-knowing, and perfectly good personal being (one that holds beliefs; has aims, plans, and intentions; and can act to accomplish these aims).
(2) Human beings require salvation, and God has provided a unique way of salvation through the incarnation, life, sacrificial death, and resurrection of his divine son.

Now there are many who do not believe these things. First, there are those who agree with me on (1) but not (2): They are non-Christian theistic religions. Second, there are those who don't accept either (1) or (2) but nonetheless do believe that there is something beyond the natural world, a something such that human well-being and salvation depend upon standing in a right relation to it. Third, in the West and since the Enlightenment, anyway, there are people—*naturalists*, we may call them—who don't believe any of these three things. And my problem is this: When I become really aware of these other ways of looking at the world, these other ways of responding religiously to the world, what must or should I do? What is the right sort of attitude to take? What sort of impact should this awareness have on the beliefs I hold and the strength with which I hold them? My question is this: How should I think about the great religious diversity the world in fact displays? Can I sensibly remain an adherent of just one of these religions, rejecting the others? And here I am thinking specifically of *beliefs*. Of course, there is a great deal more to any religion or religious practice than just belief, and I don't for a moment mean to deny it. But belief is a crucially important part of most religions; it is a crucially important part of *my* religion; and the question I mean to ask here is, What does the awareness of religious diversity mean or should mean for my religious beliefs? . . .

Now there are several possible reactions to awareness of religious diversity. One is to continue to believe—what you have all along believed; you learn about this diversity but continue to believe that is, take to be true—such propositions as (1) and (2) above, consequently taking to be false any beliefs, religious or otherwise, that are incompatible with (1) and (2). Following current practice, I will call this *exclusivism*; the exclusivist holds that the tenets or some of the tenets of *one* religion—Christianity, let's say—are in fact true; he adds, naturally enough, that any propositions, including other religious beliefs, that are incompatible with those tenets are false. And there is a fairly widespread apprehension that . . . exclusivism as such is or involves a vice of some sort: It is wrong or deplorable. It is this claim I want to examine. I propose to argue that exclusivism need not involve either epistemic or moral failure and that, furthermore, something like it is wholly unavoidable, given our human condition.

These objections, of course, are not to the *truth* of (1) or (2) or any other proposition someone might accept in this exclusivist way (although objections of that sort are also put forward); they are instead directed to the *propriety or rightness* of exclusivism. There are initially two different kinds of indictments of exclusivism: broadly moral, or ethical, indictments and other broadly intellectual, or epistemic, indictments. These overlap in interesting ways as we will see below. But initially, anyway, we can take some of the complaints about exclusivism as *intellectual* criticisms: It is *irrational* or *unjustified* to think in an exclusivistic way. The other large body of complaint is moral: There is something *morally* suspect about exclusivism—it is arbitrary, or intellectually arrogant, or imperialistic. . . . I want to consider both kinds of claims or criticisms; I propose to argue that the exclusivist as such is not necessarily guilty of any of these charges.

I turn to the moral complaints: that the exclusivist is intellectually arrogant, or egotistical or self-servingly arbitrary, or dishonest, or imperialistic, or oppressive. But first, I provide three qualifications. An exclusivist, like anyone else, will probably be guilty of some or of all of these things to at least some degree, perhaps particularly the first two. The question, however, is whether she is guilty of these things just by virtue of being an exclusivist. Second, I will use the term *exclusivism* in such a way that you don't count as an exclusivist unless you are rather fully aware of other faiths, have had their existence and their claims called to your attention with some force and perhaps fairly frequently, and have to some degree reflected on the problem of pluralism, asking yourself such questions as whether it is or could be really true that the Lord has revealed Himself and His programs to us Christians, say, in a way in which He hasn't revealed Himself to those of other faiths. Thus, my grandmother, for example, would not have counted as an exclusivist. She had, of course, *heard* of the heathen, as she called them, but the idea that perhaps Christians could learn from them, and learn from them with respect to religious matters, had not so much as entered her head; and the fact that it *hadn't* entered her head, I take it, was not a matter of moral dereliction on her part. This same would go for a Buddhist or Hindu peasant. These people are not, I think, properly charged with arrogance or other moral flaws in believing as they do.

Third, . . . an exclusivist, as I use the term, not only believes something like (1) or (2) and thinks false any proposition incompatible with it; she also meets a further condition C that . . . includes (a) being rather fully aware of other religions, (b) knowing that there is much that at the least looks like genuine piety and devoutness in them, and (c) believing that you know of no arguments that would necessarily convince all or most honest and intelligent dissenters.

Given these qualifications then, why should we think that an exclusivist is properly charged with these moral faults? I will deal first and most briefly with charges of oppression and imperialism: I think we must say that they are on the face of it wholly implausible. I daresay there are some among you who reject some of the things I believe; I do not believe that you are thereby oppressing me, even if you do not believe you have an argument that would convince me. It is conceivable that exclusivism might in some way *contribute* to oppression, but it isn't in itself oppressive.

The more important moral charge is that there is a sort of self-serving arbitrariness, an arrogance or egotism, in accepting such propositions as (1) or (2) under condition *C*; exclusivism is guilty of some serious moral fault or flaw. According to Wilfred Cantwell Smith, ". . . except at the cost of insensitivity or delinquency, it is morally not possible actually to go out into the world and say to devout, intelligent, fellow human beings: '. . . we believe that we know God and we are right; you believe that you know God, and you are totally wrong.'"[1]

So what can the exclusivist have to say for himself: Well, it must be conceded immediately that if he believes (1) or (2), then he must also believe that those who believe something incompatible with them are mistaken and believe what is false. That's no more than simple logic. Furthermore, he must also believe that those who do not believe as he does—those who believe neither (1) nor (2), whether or not they believe their negations—*fail* to believe something that is deep and important and that he *does* believe. He must therefore see himself as *privileged* with respect to those others—those others of both kinds. There is something of great value, he must think, that *he* has and *they* lack. They are ignorant of something—something of great importance—of which he has knowledge. But does this make him properly subject to the above censure?

I think the answer must be no. Or if the answer is yes, then I think we have here a genuine moral dilemma; for in our earthly life here below, as my Sunday School teacher used to say, there is no real alternative; there is no reflective attitude that is not open to the same strictures. These charges of arrogance are a philosophical tar baby: Get close enough to them to use them against the exclusivist and you are likely to find them stuck fast to yourself. How so? Well, as an exclusivist, I realize that I can't convince others that they should believe as I do, but I nonetheless continue to believe as I do. The charge is that I am, as a result, arrogant or egotistical, arbitrarily preferring my way of doing things to other ways.[2] But what are my alternatives with respect to a proposition like (1)? There seem to be three choices. I can continue to hold it; I can withhold it, . . . believing neither it nor its denial, and I can accept its denial. Consider the third way, a way taken by those pluralists who, like John Hick, hold that such propositions as (1) and (2) and their colleagues from other faiths are literally false, although in some way still valid responses to the Real. This seems to me to be no advance at all with respect to the arrogance or egotism problem; this is not a way out. For if I do this, I will then be in the very same condition as I am now: I will believe many propositions others don't believe and will be in condition *C* with respect to those propositions. For I will then believe the denials of (1) and (2) (as well as the denials of many other propositions explicitly accepted by those of other faiths). Many others, of course, do not believe the denials of (1) and (2) and in fact believe (1) and (2). Further, I will not know of any arguments that can be counted on to persuade those who do believe (1) or (2) (or propositions accepted by the adherents of other religions). I am therefore in the condition of believing propositions that many others do not believe and furthermore am in condition C. If, in the case of those who believe (1) and (2), that is sufficient for intellectual arrogance or egotism, the same goes for those who believe their denials.

So consider the second option: I can instead *withhold* the proposition in question. I can say to myself: "The right course here, given that I can't or couldn't convince these others of what I believe, is to believe neither these propositions nor their denials." The pluralist objector to exclusivism can say that the right course, under condition *C*, is to abstain from believing the offending proposition and also abstain from believing its denial; call him, therefore, "the abstemious pluralist." But does he thus really avoid the condition that, on the part of the exclusivist, leads to the charges of egotism and arrogance in this way? Think, for a moment, about disagreement. Disagreement, fundamentally, is a matter of adopting conflicting propositional attitudes with respect to a given proposition. In the simplest and most familiar case, I disagree with you if there is some proposition *p* such that I believe *p* and you believe $-p$. But that's just the simplest case; there are also others. The one that is presently of interest is this: I believe *p* and you withhold it, fail to believe it. Call the first kind of disagreement "contradicting"; call the second "dissenting."

My claim is that if contradicting others (under the condition C spelled out above) is arrogant and egotistical, so is dissenting (under that same condition). Suppose you believe some proposition *p* but I don't; perhaps you believe that it is wrong to discriminate against people simply on the grounds of race, but I, recognizing that there are many people who disagree with you, do not believe this proposition. I don't disbelieve it either, of course, but in the circumstances I think the right thing to do is to abstain from belief. Then am I not implicitly condemning your attitude, your *believing* the proposition, as somehow improper—naive, perhaps, or unjustified, or in some other way less than optimal? I am implicitly saying that my attitude is the superior one; I think my course of action here is the right one and yours somehow wrong, inadequate, improper, in the circumstances at best second-rate. Of course, I realize that there is no question, here, of *showing* you that your attitude is wrong or improper or naive; so am I not guilty of intellectual arrogance? Of a sort of egotism, thinking I know better than you, arrogating to myself a privileged status with respect to you? The problem for the exclusivist was that she was obliged to think she possessed a truth missed by many others; the problem for the abstemious pluralist is that he is obliged to think that he possesses a virtue others don't or acts rightly where others don't. If, in condition *C*, one is arrogant by way of believing a proposition others don't, isn't one equally, under those reflective conditions, arrogant by way of withholding a proposition others don't? . . .

So the abstemious pluralist is hoist with his own petard; but even apart from this dialectical argument (which in any event some will think unduly cute), aren't the charges unconvincing and implausible? I must concede that there are a variety of ways in which I can be and have been intellectually arrogant and egotistic; I have certainly fallen into this vice in the past and no doubt am not free of it now. But am I really arrogant and egotistic just by virtue of believing what I know others don't believe, where I can't show them that I am right? Suppose I think the matter over, consider the objections as carefully as I can, realize that I am finite and furthermore a sinner, certainly no better than those with whom I disagree; but suppose it still seems clear to me that the proposition in question is true. Can I really be behaving immorally in continuing to believe it? I am dead sure that it is wrong to try to advance my career by telling lies about my colleagues; I realize there are those who disagree; I also realize that in all likelihood there is no way I can find to show them that they are wrong; nonetheless I think they are wrong. If I think this after careful reflection, if I consider the claims of those who disagree as sympathetically as I can, if I try my level best to ascertain the truth here, and it *still* seems to me sleazy, wrong, and despicable to lie about my colleagues to advance my career, could I really be doing what is immoral by continuing to believe as before? I can't see how. If, after careful reflection and thought, you find yourself convinced that the right propositional attitude to take to (1) and (2) in the face of the facts of religious pluralism is abstention from belief, how could you properly be taxed with egotism, either for so believing or for so abstaining? Even if you knew others did not agree with you? . . .

Return to the case of moral belief. King David took Bathsheba, made her pregnant, and then, after the failure of various stratagems to get her husband Uriah to think the baby was his, arranged for him to be killed. The prophet Nathan came to David and told him a story about a rich man and a poor man. The rich man had many flocks and herds; the poor man had only a single ewe lamb, which grew up with his children, "ate at his table, drank from his cup, lay in his bosom, and was like a daughter to him." The rich man had unexpected guests. Rather than slaughter one of his own sheep, he took the poor man's single ewe lamb, slaughtered it, and served it to his guests. David exploded in anger: "The man who did this deserves to die!" Then, in one of the most riveting passages in all the Bible, Nathan turns to David and declares, "You are that man!" And then David sees what he has done.

My interest here is in David's reaction to the story. I agree with David: Such injustice is utterly and despicably wrong; there are really no words for it. I believe that such an action is wrong, and I believe that the proposition that it *isn't* wrong—either because really *nothing* is wrong, or because even if some things are wrong, *this* isn't—is false. As a matter of fact, there isn't a lot I believe more strongly. I recognize, however, that there are those who disagree with me; and once more, I doubt that I could find an argument to show them that I am right and they wrong. Further, for all I know, their conflicting beliefs have for them the same internally available epistemic markers, the same phenomenology, as mine have for me. Am I then being arbitrary, treating similar cases differently in continuing to hold, as I do, that in fact that kind of behavior *is* dreadfully wrong? I don't think so. Am I wrong in thinking racial bigotry despicable, even though I know that there are others who disagree, and even if I think they have the same internal markers for their beliefs as I have for mine? I don't think so. I believe in serious actualism, the view that no objects have properties in worlds in which they do not exist, not even nonexistence. Others do not believe this, and perhaps the internal markers of their dissenting views have for them the same quality as my views have for me. Am I being arbitrary in continuing to think as I do? I can't see how.

And the reason here is this: in each of these cases, the believer in question doesn't really think the beliefs in question *are* on a relevant epistemic par. She may agree that she and those who dissent are equally convinced of the truth of their belief and even that they are internally on a par, that the internally available markers are similar, or relevantly similar. But she must still think that there is an important epistemic difference, she thinks that somehow the other person has *made a mistake*, or *has a blind spot*, or hasn't been wholly attentive, or hasn't received some grace she has, or is in some way epistemically less fortunate. And, of course, the pluralist critic is in no better case. He thinks the thing to do when there is internal epistemic parity is to withhold judgment; he knows that there are others who don't think so, and for all he knows that belief has internal parity with his; if he continues in that belief, therefore, he will be in the same condition as the exclusivist; and if he doesn't continue in this belief, he no longer has an objection to the exclusivist.

But couldn't I be wrong? Of course I could! But I don't avoid that risk by withholding all religious (or philosophical or moral) beliefs; I can go wrong that way as well as any other, treating all religions, or all philosophical thoughts, or all moral views as on a par. Again, there is no safe haven here, no way to avoid risk. In particular, you won't reach a safe haven by trying to take the same attitude toward all the historically available patterns of belief and withholding; for in so doing, you adopt a particular pattern of belief and withholding, one incompatible with some adopted by others. "You pays your money and you takes your choice," realizing that you, like anyone else, can be desperately wrong. But what else can you do? You don't really have an alternative. And how can you do better than believe and withhold according to what, after serious and responsible consideration, seems to you to be the right pattern of belief and withholding?

NOTES

1. Wilfred Cantwell Smith, *Religious Diversity* (New York: Harper & Row, 1976), p. 14.
2. John Hick, *An Interpretation of Religion* (New Haven, Conn.: Yale Univ. Press, 1989), p. 2.

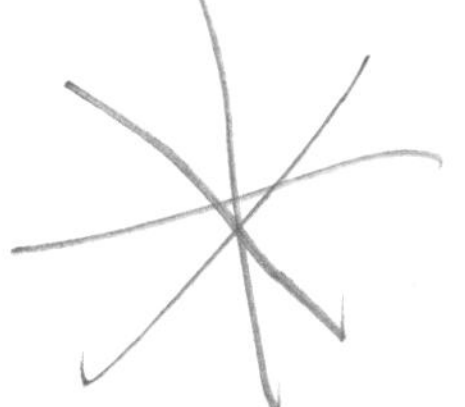

Religion Versus the Religious

JOHN DEWEY

John Dewey (1859–1952), the leading American philosopher of the first half of the twentieth century, urged that we abandon the supernaturalism associated with traditional religion and embrace instead an attitude that he termed "religious." He found this quality in those experiences he describes as the pursuit of ideals that lead individuals to be at peace with the conditions of their lives.

For Dewey, faith in the continued discovery of truth through cooperative human inquiry was more religious in quality than any faith in a supposedly supernatural revelation. Thus he sought to dissolve the links between religious values and the creeds of any particular religion.

Never before in history has mankind been so much of two minds, so divided into two camps, as it is today. Religions have traditionally been allied with ideas of the supernatural, and often have been based upon explicit beliefs about it. Today there are many who hold that nothing worthy of being called religious is possible apart from the supernatural. Those who hold this belief differ in many respects. They range from those who accept the dogmas and sacraments of the Greek and Roman Catholic church as the only sure means of access to the supernatural to the theist or mild deist. Between them are the many Protestant denominations who think the Scriptures, aided by a pure conscience, are adequate avenues to supernatural truth and power. But they agree in one point: the necessity for a Supernatural Being and for an immortality that is beyond the power of nature.

The opposed group consists of those who think the advance of culture and science has completely discredited the supernatural and with it all religions that were allied with belief in it. But they go beyond this point. The extremists in this group believe that with elimination of the supernatural not only must historic religions be dismissed but with them everything of a religious nature. When historical knowledge has discredited the claims made for the supernatural character of the persons said to have founded historic religions; when the supernatural inspiration attributed to literatures held sacred has been riddled, and when anthropological and psychological knowledge has disclosed the all-too-human source from which religious beliefs and practices have sprung, everything religious must, they say, also go.

There is one idea held in common by these two opposite groups: identification of the religious with the supernatural. The question I shall raise . . . concerns the ground for and the consequences of this identification: its reasons and its value. In the discussion I shall develop another conception of the nature of the religious phase of experience, one that separates it from the supernatural and the things that have grown up about it. I shall try to show that these derivations are encumbrances and that what is genuinely religious will undergo an emancipation when it is relieved from them; that then, for the first time, the religious aspect of experience will be free to develop freely on its own account.

This view is exposed to attack from both the other camps. It goes contrary to traditional religions, including those that have the greatest hold upon the religiously minded today. The view announced will seem to them to cut the vital nerve of the religious element itself in taking away the basis upon which traditional religions and institutions have been founded. From the other side, the position I am taking seems like a timid halfway position, a concession and compromise unworthy of thought that is thoroughgoing. It is regarded as a view entertained from mere tendermindedness, as an emotional hangover from childhood indoctrination, or even as a manifestation of a desire to avoid disapproval and curry favor.

The heart of my point . . . is that there is a difference between religion, *a* religion, and the religious; between anything that may be denoted by a noun substantive and the quality of experience that is designated by an adjective. It is not easy to find a definition of religion in the substantive sense that wins general acceptance. However, in the *Oxford Dictionary* I find the following: "Recognition on the part of man of some unseen higher power as having control of his destiny and as being entitled to obedience, reverence and worship."

This particular definition is less explicit in assertion of the supernatural character of the higher unseen power than are others that might be cited. It is, however, surcharged with implications having their source in ideas connected with the belief in the supernatural, characteristic of historic religions. Let us suppose that one familiar with the history of religions, including those called primitive, compares the definition with the variety of known facts and by means of the comparison sets out to determine just what the definition means. I think he will be struck by three facts that reduce the terms of the definition to such a low common denominator that little meaning is left.

He will note that the "unseen powers" referred to have been conceived in a multitude of incompatible ways. Eliminating the differences, nothing is left beyond the bare reference to something unseen and powerful. This has been conceived as the vague and undefined Mana of the Melanesians; the Kami of primitive Shintoism; the fetish of the Africans; spirits, having some human properties, that pervade natural places and animate natural forces; the ultimate and impersonal principle of Buddhism; the unmoved mover of

Greek thought; the gods and semi-divine heroes of the Greek and Roman Pantheons; the personal and loving Providence of Christianity, omnipotent, and limited by a corresponding evil power; the arbitrary Will of Moslemism; the supreme legislator and judge of deism. And these are but a few of the outstanding varieties of ways in which the invisible power has been conceived.

There is no greater similarity in the ways in which obedience and reverence have been expressed. There has been worship of animals, of ghosts, of ancestors, phallic worship, as well as of a Being of dread power and of love and wisdom. Reverence has been expressed in the human sacrifices of the Peruvians and Aztecs; the sexual orgies of some Oriental religions; exorcisms and ablutions; the offering of the humble and contrite mind of the Hebrew prophet, the elaborate rituals of the Greek and Roman Churches. Not even sacrifice has been uniform; it is highly sublimated in Protestant denominations and in Moslemism. Where it has existed it has taken all kinds of forms and been directed to a great variety of powers and spirits. It has been used for expiation, for propitiation and for buying special favors. There is no conceivable purpose for which rites have not been employed.

Finally, there is no discernible unity in the moral motivations appealed to and utilized. They have been as far apart as fear of lasting torture, hope of enduring bliss in which sexual enjoyment has sometimes been a conspicuous element; mortification of the flesh and extreme asceticism; prostitution and chastity; wars to extirpate the unbeliever; persecution to convert or punish the unbeliever, and philanthropic zeal; servile acceptance of imposed dogma, along with brotherly love and aspiration for a reign of justice among men.

I have, of course, mentioned only a sparse number of the facts which fill volumes in any well-stocked library. It may be asked by those who do not like to look upon the darker side of the history of religions why the darker facts should be brought up. We all know that civilized man has a background of bestiality and superstition and that these elements are still with us. Indeed, have not some religions, including the most influential forms of Christianity, taught that the heart of man is totally corrupt? How could the course of religion in its entire sweep not be marked by practices that are shameful in their cruelty and lustfulness, and by beliefs that are degraded and intellectually incredible? What else than what we find could be expected, in the case of people having little knowledge and no secure method of knowing; with primitive institutions, and with so little control of natural forces that they lived in a constant state of fear?

I gladly admit that historic religions have been relative to the conditions of social culture in which peoples lived. Indeed, what I am concerned with is to press home the logic of this method of disposal of outgrown traits of past religions. Beliefs and practices in a religion that now prevails are by this logic relative to the present state of culture. If so much flexibility has obtained in the past regarding an unseen power, the way it affects human destiny, and the attitudes we are to take toward it, why should it be assumed that change in conception and action has now come to an end? The logic involved in getting rid of inconvenient aspects of past religions compels us to inquire how much in religions now accepted are survivals from outgrown cultures. It compels us to ask what conception of unseen powers and our relations to them would be consonant with the best achievements and aspirations of the present. It demands that in imagination we wipe the slate clean and start afresh by asking what would be the idea of the unseen, of the manner of its control over us and the ways in which reverence and obedience would be manifested, if whatever is basically religious in experience had the opportunity to express itself free from all historic encumbrances.

So we return to the elements of the definition that has been given. What boots it to accept, in defense of the universality of religion, a definition that applies equally to the most savage and degraded beliefs and practices that have related to unseen powers and to noble ideals of a religion having the greatest share of moral content? There are two points involved. One of them is that there is nothing left worth preserving in the notions of unseen powers, controlling human destiny to which obedience, reverence and worship are due, if we glide silently over the nature that has been attributed to the powers, the radically diverse ways in which they have been supposed to control human destiny, and in which submission and awe have been manifested. The other point is that when we begin to select, to choose, and say that some present ways of thinking about the unseen powers are better than others; that the reverence shown by a free and self-respecting human being is better than the servile obedience rendered to an arbitrary power by frightened men; that we should believe that control of human destiny is exercised by a wise and loving spirit rather than by madcap ghosts or sheer force—when I say, we begin to choose, we have entered upon a road that has not yet come to an end. We have reached a point that invites us to proceed farther.

For we are forced to acknowledge that concretely there is no such thing as religion in the singular. There is only a multitude of religions. "Religion" is a strictly collective term and the collection it stands for is not even of the kind illustrated in textbooks of logic. It has not the unity of a regiment or assembly but that of any miscellaneous aggregate. Attempts to prove the universality prove too much or too little. It is probable that religions have been universal in the sense that all the peoples we know anything about have had *a* religion. But the differences among them are so great and so shocking that any common element that can be extracted is meaningless. The idea that religion is universal proves too little in that the older apologists for Christianity seem to have been better advised than some modern ones in condemning every religion but one as an impostor, as at bottom some kind of demon worship or at any rate a superstitious figment. Choice among religions is imperative, and the necessity for choice leaves nothing of any force in the argument from universality. Moreover, when once we enter upon the road of choice, there is at once presented a possibility not yet generally realized.

For the historic increase of the ethical and ideal content of religions suggests that the process of purification may be carried further. It indicates that further choice is imminent in which certain values and functions in experience may be selected. This possibility is what I had in mind in speaking of the difference between the religious and a religion. I am not proposing a religion, but rather the emancipation of elements and outlooks that may be called religious. For the moment we have a religion, whether that of the Sioux Indian or of Judaism or of Christianity, that moment the ideal factors in experience that may be called religious take on a load that is not inherent in them, a load of current beliefs and of institutional practices that are irrelevant to them.

I can illustrate what I mean by a common phenomenon in contemporary life. It is widely supposed that a person who does not accept any religion is thereby shown to be a non-religious person. Yet it is conceivable that the present depression in religion is closely connected with the fact that religions now prevent, because of their weight of historic encumbrances, the religious quality of experience from coming to consciousness and finding the expression that is appropriate to present conditions, intellectual and moral. I believe that such is the case. I believe that many persons are so repelled from what exists as a religion by its intellectual and moral implications, that they are not even aware of attitudes in themselves that if they came to fruition would be genuinely religious. I hope that this remark may help make clear what I mean by the distinction between "religion" as a noun substantive and "religious" as adjectival.

To be somewhat more explicit, a religion (and as I have just said there is no such thing as religion in general) always signifies a special body of beliefs and practices having some kind of institutional organization, loose or tight. In contrast, the adjective "religious" denotes nothing in the way of a specifiable entity, either institutional or as a system of beliefs. It does not denote anything to which one can specifically point as one can point to this and that historic religion or existing church. For it does not denote anything that can exist by itself or that can be organized into a particular and distinctive form of existence. It denotes attitudes that may be taken toward every object and every proposed end or ideal.

Before, however, I develop my suggestion that realization of the distinction just made would operate to emancipate the religious quality from encumbrances that now smother or limit it, I must refer to a position that in some respects is similar in words to the position I have taken, but that in fact is a whole world removed from it. I have several times used the phrase "religious elements of experience." Now at present there is much talk, especially in liberal circles, of religious experience as vouching for the authenticity of certain beliefs and the desirability of certain practices, such as particular forms of prayer and worship. It is even asserted that religious experience is the ultimate basis of religion itself. The gulf between this position and that which I have taken is what I am now concerned to point out.

Those who hold to the notion that there is a definite kind of experience which is itself religious, by that very fact make out of it something specific, as a kind of experience that is marked off from experience as aesthetic, scientific, moral, political; from experience as companionship and friendship. But "religious" as a quality of experience signifies something that may belong to all these experiences. It is the polar opposite of some type of experience that can exist by itself. The distinction comes out clearly when it is noted that the concept of this distinct kind of experience is used to validate a belief in some special kind of object and also to justify some special kind of practice.

For there are many religionists who are now dissatisfied with the older "proofs" of the existence of God, those that go by the name of ontological, cosmological and teleological. The cause of the dissatisfaction is perhaps not so much the arguments that Kant used to show the insufficiency of these alleged proofs, as it is the growing feeling that they are too formal to offer any support to religion in action. Anyway, the dissatisfaction exists. Moreover, these religionists are moved by the rise of the experimental method in other fields. What is more natural and proper, accordingly, than that they should affirm they are just as good empiricists as anybody else—indeed, as good as the scientists themselves? As the latter rely upon certain kinds of experience to prove the existence of certain kinds of objects, so the religionists rely upon a certain kind of experience to prove the existence of the object of religion, especially the supreme object, God.

The discussion may be made more definite by introducing, at this point, a particular illustration of this type of reasoning. A writer says: "I broke down from overwork and soon came to the verge of nervous prostration. One morning after a long and sleepless night . . . I resolved to stop drawing upon myself so continuously and begin drawing upon God. I determined to set apart a quiet time every day in which I could relate my life to its Ultimate Source, regain the consciousness that in God I live, move and have my being. That was thirty years ago. Since then I have had literally not one hour of darkness or despair."

This is an impressive record. I do not doubt its authenticity nor that of the experience related. It illustrates a religious aspect of experience. But it illustrates also the use of that quality to carry a superimposed load of a particular religion. For having been brought up in the Christian religion, its subject interprets it in the terms of the personal God characteristic of that religion. Taoists, Buddhists, Moslems, persons of no religion including those who reject all supernatural influence and power, have had experiences similar in their effect. Yet another author commenting upon the passage says: "The religious expert can be more sure that this God exists than he can of either the cosmological God of speculative surmise or the Christlike God involved in the validity of moral optimism," and goes on to add that such experiences "mean that God the Savior, the Power that gives victory over sin on certain conditions that man can fulfill, is an existent, accessible and scientifically knowable reality." It should be clear that this inference is sound only if the conditions, of whatever sort, that produce the effect are called "God." But most readers will take the inference to mean that the existence of a particular Being, of the type called "God" in the Christian religion, is proved by a method akin to that of experimental science.

In reality, the only thing that can be said to be "proved" is the existence of some complex of conditions that have operated to effect an adjustment in life, an orientation, that brings with it a sense of security and peace. The particular interpretation given to this complex of conditions is not inherent in the experience itself. It is derived from the culture with which a particular person has been imbued. A fatalist will give one name to it; a Christian Scientist another, and the one who rejects all supernatural being still another. The determining factor in the interpretation of the experience is the particular doctrinal apparatus into which a person has been inducted. The emotional deposit connected with prior teaching floods the whole situation. It may readily confer upon the experience such a peculiarly sacred preciousness that all inquiry into its causation is barred. The stable outcome is so invaluable that the cause to which it is referred is usually nothing but a reduplication of the thing that has occurred, plus some name that has acquired a deeply emotional quality.

The intent of this discussion is not to deny the genuineness of the result nor its importance in life. It is not, save incidentally, to point out the possibility of a purely naturalistic explanation of the event. My purpose is to indicate what happens when religious experience is already set aside as something sui generis. The actual religious quality in the experience described is the *effect* produced, the better adjustment in life and its conditions, not the manner and cause of its production. The way in which the experience operated, its function, determines its religious value. If the reorientation actually occurs, it, and the sense of security and stability accompanying it, are forces on their own account. It takes place in different persons in a multitude of ways. It is sometimes brought about by devotion to a cause; sometimes by a passage of poetry that opens a new perspective; sometimes as was the case with Spinoza—deemed an atheist in his day—through philosophical reflection.

The difference between an experience having a religious force because of what it does in and to the processes of living and religious experience as a separate kind of thing gives me occasion to refer to a previous remark. If this function were rescued through emancipation from dependence upon specific types of beliefs and practices, from those elements that constitute a religion, many individuals would find that experiences having the force of bringing about a better, deeper and enduring adjustment in life are not so rare and infrequent as they are commonly supposed to be. They occur frequently in connection with many significant moments of living. The idea of invisible powers would take on the meaning of all the conditions of nature and human association that support and deepen the sense of values which carry one through periods of darkness and despair to such an extent that they lose their usual depressive character.

I do not suppose for many minds the dislocation of the religious from a religion is easy to effect. Tradition and custom, especially when emotionally charged, are a part of the habits that have become one with our very being. But the possibility of the transfer is demonstrated by its actuality. Let us then for the moment drop the term "religious," and ask what are the attitudes that lend deep and enduring support to the processes of living. I have, for example, used the words "adjustment" and "orientation." What do they signify?

While the words "accommodation," "adaptation," and "adjustment" are frequently employed as synonyms, attitudes exist that are so different that for the sake of clear thought they should be discriminated. There are conditions we meet that cannot be changed. If they are particular and limited, we modify our own particular attitudes in accordance with them. Thus we accommodate ourselves to changes in weather, to alterations in income when we have no other recourse. When the external conditions are lasting we become inured, habituated, or, as the process is now often called, conditioned. The two main traits of this attitude, which I should like to call accommodation, are that it affects *particular* modes of conduct, not the entire self, and that the process is mainly *passive*. It may, however, become general and then it becomes fatalistic resignation or submission. There are other attitudes toward the environment that are also particular but that are more active. We react against conditions and endeavor to change them to meet our wants and demands. Plays in a foreign language are "adapted" to meet the needs of an American audience. A house is rebuilt to suit changed conditions of the household; the telephone is invented to serve the demand for speedy communication at a distance; dry soils are irrigated so that they may bear abundant crops. Instead of accommodating ourselves to conditions, we modify conditions so that they will be accommodated to our wants and purposes. This process may be called adaptation.

Now both of these processes are often called by the more general name of adjustment. But there are also changes in ourselves in relation to the world in which we live that are much more inclusive and deep seated. They relate not to this and that want in relation to this and that condition of our surroundings, but pertain to our being in its entirety. Because of their scope, this modification of ourselves is enduring. It lasts through any amount of vicissitude of circumstances, internal and external. There is a composing and harmonizing of the various elements of our being such that, in spite of changes in the special conditions that surround us, these conditions are also arranged, settled, in relation to us. This attitude includes a note of submission. But it is voluntary, not externally imposed; and as voluntary it is something more than a mere Stoical resolution to endure unperturbed throughout the buffetings of fortune. It is more outgoing, more ready and glad, than the latter attitude, and it is more active than the former. And in calling it voluntary, it is not meant that it depends upon a particular resolve or volition. It is a change *of* will conceived as the organic plenitude of our being, rather than any special change *in* will.

It is the claim of religions that they effect this generic and enduring change in attitude. I should like to turn the statement around and say that whenever this change takes place there is a definitely religious attitude. It is not *a* religion that brings it about, but when it occurs, from whatever cause and by whatever means, there is a religious outlook and function. As I have said before, the doctrinal or intellectual apparatus and the institutional accretions that grow up are, in a strict sense, adventitious to the intrinsic quality of such experiences. For they are affairs of the traditions of the culture with which individuals are inoculated. Mr. Santayana has connected the religious quality of experience with the imaginative, as that is expressed in poetry. "Religion and poetry," he says, "are identical in essence, and differ merely in the way in which they are attached to practical affairs. Poetry is called religion when it intervenes in life, and religion, when it merely supervenes upon life, is seen to be nothing but poetry." The difference between intervening *in* and supervening *upon* is as important as is the identity set forth. Imagination may play upon life or it may enter profoundly into it. As Mr. Santayana puts it, "poetry has a universal and a moral function," for "its highest power lies in its relevance to the ideals and purposes of life." Except as it intervenes, "all observation is observation of brute fact, all discipline is mere repression, until these facts digested and this discipline embodied in humane impulses become the starting-point for a creative movement of the imagination, the firm basis for ideal constructions in society, religion, and art."

If I may make a comment upon this penetrating insight of Mr. Santayana, I would say that the difference between imagination that only supervenes and imagination that intervenes is the difference between one that completely interpenetrates all the elements of our being and one that is interwoven with only special and partial factors. There actually occurs extremely little observation of brute facts merely for the sake of the facts, just as there is little discipline that is repression and nothing but repression. Facts are usually observed with reference to some practical end and purpose, and that end is presented only imaginatively. The most repressive discipline has some end in view to which there is at least imputed an ideal quality; otherwise it is purely sadistic. But in such cases of observation and discipline imagination is limited and partial. It does not extend far; it does not permeate deeply and widely.

The connection between imagination and the harmonizing of the self is closer than is usually thought. The idea of a whole, whether of the whole personal being or of the world, is an imaginative, not a literal, idea. The limited world of our observation and reflection becomes the Universe only through imaginative extension. It cannot be apprehended in knowledge nor realized in reflection. Neither observation, thought, nor practical activity can attain that complete unification of the self which is called a whole. The *whole* self is an ideal, an imaginative projection. Hence the idea of a thoroughgoing and deep-seated harmonizing of the self with the Universe (as a name for the totality of conditions with which the self is connected) operates only through imagination—which is one reason why this composing of the self is not voluntary in the sense of an act of special volition or resolution. An "adjustment" possesses the will rather than is its express product. Religionists have been right in thinking of it as an influx from sources beyond conscious deliberation and purpose—a fact that helps explain, psychologically, why it has so generally been attributed to a supernatural source and that, perhaps, throws some light upon the reference of it by William James to unconscious factors. And it is pertinent to note that the unification of the self throughout the ceaseless flux of what it does, suffers, and achieves, cannot be attained in terms of itself. The self is always directed toward something beyond itself and so its own unification depends upon the idea of the integration of the shifting scenes of the world into that imaginative totality we call the Universe.

The intimate connection of imagination with ideal elements in experience is generally recognized. Such is not the case with respect to its connection with faith. The latter has been regarded as a substitute for knowledge, for sight. It is defined, in the Christian religion, as *evidence* of things not seen. The implication is that faith is a kind of anticipatory vision of things that are now invisible because of the limitations of our finite and erring nature. Because it is a substitute for knowledge, its material and object are intellectual in quality. As John Locke summed up the matter, faith is "assent to a proposition . . . on the credit of its proposer." Religious faith is then given to a body of propositions as true on the credit of their supernatural author, reason coming in to demonstrate the reasonableness of giving such credit. Of necessity there results the development of theologies, or bodies of systematic propositions, to make explicit in organized form the content of the propositions to which belief is attached and assent given. Given the point of view, those who hold that religion necessarily implies a theology are correct.

But belief or faith has also a moral and practical import. Even devils, according to the older theologians, believe—and tremble. A distinction was made, therefore, between "speculative" or intellectual belief and an act called "justifying" faith. Apart from any theological context, there is a difference between belief that is a conviction that some end should be supreme over conduct, and belief that some object or being exists as a truth for the intellect. Conviction in the moral sense signifies being conquered, vanquished, in our active nature by an ideal end; it signifies acknowledgment of its rightful claim over our desires and purposes. Such acknowledgment is practical, not primarily intellectual. It goes beyond evidence that can be presented to *any* possible observer. Reflection, often long and arduous, may be involved in arriving at the conviction, but the import of thought is not exhausted in discovery of evidence that can justify intellectual assent. The authority of an ideal over choice and conduct is the authority of an ideal, not of a fact, of a truth guaranteed to intellect, not of the status of the one who propounds the truth.

Such moral faith is not easy. It was questioned of old whether the Son of Man should find faith on the earth in his coming. Moral faith has been bolstered by all sorts of arguments intended to prove that its object is not ideal and that its claim upon us is not primarily moral or practical, since the ideal in question is already embedded in the existent frame of things. It is argued that the ideal is already the final reality at the heart of things that exist, and that only our senses or the corruption of our natures prevents us from apprehending its prior existential being. Starting, say, from such an idea as that justice is more than a moral ideal because it is embedded in the very makeup of the actually existent world, men have gone on to build up vast intellectual schemes, philosophies, and theologies, to prove that ideals are real not as ideals but as antecedently existing actualities. They have failed to see that in converting moral realities into matters of intellectual assent they have evinced lack of *moral* faith. Faith that something should be in existence as far as lies in our power is changed into the intellectual belief that it is already in existence. When physical existence does not bear out the assertion, the physical is subtly changed into the metaphysical. In this way, moral faith has been inextricably tied up with intellectual beliefs about the supernatural.

The tendency to convert ends of moral faith and action into articles of an intellectual creed has been furthered by a tendency of which psychologists are well aware. What we ardently desire to have thus and so, we tend to believe is already so. Desire has a powerful influence upon intellectual beliefs. Moreover, when conditions are adverse to realization of the objects of our desire—and in the case of significant ideals they are extremely adverse—it is an easy way out to assume that after all they are already embodied in the ultimate structure of what is, and that appearances to the contrary are *merely* appearances. Imagination then merely supervenes and is freed from the responsibility for intervening. Weak natures take to reverie as a refuge as strong ones do to fanaticism. Those who dissent are mourned over by the first class and converted through the use of force by the second.

What has been said does not imply that all moral faith in ideal ends is by virtue of that fact religious in quality. The religious is "morality touched by emotion" only when the ends of moral conviction arouse emotions that are not only intense but are actuated and supported by ends so inclusive that they unify the self. The inclusiveness of the end in relation to both self and the "universe" to which an inclusive self is related is indispensable. According to the best authorities, "religion" comes from a root that means being bound or tied. Originally, it meant being bound by vows to a particular way of life—as *les religieux* were monks and nuns who had assumed certain vows. The religious attitude signifies something that is bound through imagination to a *general* attitude. This comprehensive attitude, moreover, is much broader than anything indicated by "moral" in its usual sense. The quality of attitude is displayed in art, science and good citizenship.

If we apply the conception set forth to the terms of the definition earlier quoted, these terms take on a new significance. An unseen power controlling our destiny becomes the power of an ideal. All possibilities, as possibilities, are ideal in character. The artist, scientist, citizen, parent, as far as they are actuated by the spirit of their callings, are controlled by the unseen. For all endeavor for the better is moved by faith in what is possible, not by adherence to the actual. Nor does this faith depend for its moving power upon intellectual assurance or belief that the things worked for must surely prevail and come into embodied existence. For the authority of the object to determine our attitude and conduct, the right that is given it to claim our allegiance and devotion is based on the intrinsic nature of the ideal. The outcome, given our best endeavor, is not with us. The inherent vice of all intellectual schemes of idealism is that they convert the idealism of action into a system of beliefs about antecedent reality. The character assigned this reality is so different from that which observation and reflection lead to and support that these schemes inevitably glide into alliance with the supernatural.

All religions, marked by elevated ideal quality, have dwelt upon the power of religion to introduce perspective into the piecemeal and shifting episodes of existence. Here too we need to reverse the ordinary statement and say that whatever introduces genuine perspective is religious, not that religion is something that introduces it. There can be no doubt (referring to the second element of the definition) of our dependence upon forces beyond our control. Primitive man was so impotent in the face of these forces that, especially in an unfavorable natural environment, fear became a dominant attitude, and, as the old saying goes, fear created the gods.

With increase of mechanisms of control, the element of fear has, relatively speaking, subsided. Some optimistic souls have even concluded that the forces about us are on the whole essentially benign. But every crisis, whether of the individual or of the community, reminds man of the precarious and partial nature of the control he exercises. When man, individually and collectively, has done his uttermost, conditions that at different times and places have given rise to the ideas of Fate and Fortune, of Chance and Providence, remain. It is the part of manliness to insist upon the capacity of mankind to strive to direct natural and social forces to humane ends. But unqualified absolutistic statements about the omnipotence of such endeavors reflect egoism rather than intelligent courage.

The fact that human destiny is so interwoven with forces beyond human control renders it unnecessary to suppose that dependence and the humility that accompanies it have to find the particular channel that is prescribed by traditional doctrines. What is especially significant is rather the form which the sense of dependence takes. Fear never gave stable perspective in the life of anyone. It is dispersive and withdrawing. Most religions have in fact added rites of communion to those of expiation and propitiation. For our dependence is manifested in those relations to the environment that support our undertakings and aspirations as much as it is in the defeats inflicted upon us. The essentially unreligious attitude is that which attributes human achievement and purpose to man in isolation from the world of physical nature and his fellows. Our successes are dependent upon the cooperation of nature. The sense of the dignity of human nature is as religious as is the sense of awe and reverence when it rests upon a sense of human nature as a cooperating part of a larger whole. Natural piety is not of necessity either a fatalistic acquiescence in natural happenings or a romantic idealization of the world. It may rest upon a just sense of nature as the whole of which we are parts, while it also recognizes that we are parts that are marked by intelligence and purpose, having the capacity to strive by their aid to bring conditions into greater consonance with what is humanly desirable. Such piety is an inherent constituent of a just perspective in life.

Understanding and knowledge also enter into a perspective that is religious in quality. Faith in the continued disclosing of truth through directed cooperative human endeavor is more religious in quality than is any faith in a completed revelation. It is of course now usual to hold that revelation is not completed in the sense of being ended. But religions hold that the essential framework is settled in its significant moral features at least, and that new elements that are offered must be judged by conformity to this framework. Some fixed doctrinal apparatus is necessary for *a* religion. But faith in the possibilities of continued and rigorous inquiry does not limit access to truth to any channel or scheme of things. It does not first say that truth is universal and then add there is but one road to it. It does not depend for assurance upon subjection to any dogma or item of doctrine. It trusts that the natural interactions between man and his environment will breed more intelligence and generate more knowledge provided the scientific methods that define intelligence in operation are pushed further into the mysteries of the world, being themselves promoted and improved in the operation. There is such a thing as faith in intelligence becoming religious in quality—a fact that perhaps explains the efforts of some religionists to disparage the possibilities of intelligence as a force. They properly feel such faith to be a dangerous rival.

Lives that are consciously inspired by loyalty to such ideals as have been mentioned are still comparatively infrequent to the extent of that comprehensiveness and intensity which arouse an ardor religious in function. But before we infer the incompetency of such ideals and of the actions they inspire, we should at least ask ourselves how much of the existing situation is due to the fact that the religious factors of experience have been drafted into supernatural channels and thereby loaded with irrelevant encumbrances. A body of beliefs and practices that are apart from the common and natural relations of mankind must, in the degree in which it is influential, weaken and sap the force of the possibilities inherent in such relations. Here lies one aspect of the emancipation of the religious from religion.

Any activity pursued in behalf of an ideal end against obstacles and in spite of threats of personal loss because of conviction of its general and enduring value is religious in quality. Many a person, inquirer, artist, philanthropist, citizen, men and women in the humblest walks of life, have achieved, without presumption and without display, such unification of themselves and of their relations to the conditions of existence. It remains to extend their spirit and inspiration to ever wider numbers. If I have said anything about religions and religion that seems harsh, I have said those things because of a firm belief that the claim on the part of religions to possess a monopoly of ideals and of the supernatural means by which alone, it is alleged, they can be furthered, stands in the way of the realization of distinctively religious values inherent in natural experience. For that reason, if for no other, I should be sorry if any were misled by the frequency with which I have employed the adjective "religious" to conceive of what I have said as a disguised apology for what have passed as religions. The opposition between religious values as I conceive them and religions is not to be bridged. Just because the release of these values is so important, their identification with the creeds and cults of religions must be dissolved.

Conclusion

We have come to the end of our selections exploring the major issues in the philosophy of religion. At this point you may wonder whether the whole subject coheres or is merely a collection of unconnected problems.

What follows is a monograph of mine intended to offer a distinctive overview of the field. Using a variety of unusual examples as well as references drawn from perhaps unexpected sources, I attempt to provide an accessible and provocative treatment of the subject taken in its totality.

You may agree with much of what I have to say; you may, however, disagree. In any case, I place my own views before you not as in any way definitive but as encouragement for you to think comprehensively as you develop your own position.

Remember that philosophers do not show respect for a work by uncritically accepting it; instead, they subject it to the most careful scrutiny. I ask you to proceed ahead in that spirit and consider my presentation in the light of all the reading you have already done.

If you are prepared to weigh some words from Woody Allen, think along with Sherlock Holmes, ponder The Book of Job, pay a visit to *The Twilight Zone*, and read in its entirety a revelatory story by the Yiddish writer I. L. Peretz, then please turn the page and accompany me as I take an uncommon path through the field of philosophy of religion.

"Oh, I know He works in mysterious ways, but if I worked that mysteriously I'd get fired."

Appendix

God, Reason, and Religion

STEVEN M. CAHN

Introduction

In *Stardust Memories*, one of Woody Allen's lesser known movies, Allen plays the role of a troubled film director who imagines various encounters, including one with a group of otherworldly, superintelligent creatures who are prepared to respond to any of his queries. He asks, "Why is there so much human suffering?" The reply comes back, "This is unanswerable." So he tries again: "Is there a God?" This time he is told, "These are the wrong questions."[1]

The exchange is not only humorous but revelatory, for if these questions are intended to shed light on the human condition, then I believe they are, indeed, the wrong ones. But why? If we could be assured that God exists, shouldn't that knowledge change our lives? Wouldn't it provide a foundation for morality and a justification for religion? Wouldn't we gain a deepened understanding of life's triumphs and tragedies?

I think not. In my view, belief in God does not imply religious commitment, nor does religious commitment imply belief in God. Furthermore, in appealing to God's will, we explain neither the world's goods nor its evils. Indeed, to echo David Hume, the existence of God, even if provable, "affords no inference that affects human life."[2]

These claims, however, are mere assertions. In the pages that follow, I shall try to justify them.

My conclusions may be surprising, for although I am not a traditional theist, I find much to admire in a religious life, so long as its beliefs and practices do not violate the methods and results of scientific inquiry. Those who suppose that no religion can meet such a standard are among the readers I am addressing.

From Steven M. Cahn, *God, Reason, and Religion*. Reprinted by permission of Wadsworth, a division of Thomson Learning.

1. Proving God's Existence?

A theist believes God exists. An atheist believes God does not exist. An agnostic believes the available evidence is insufficient to decide the matter. Which of these positions is the most reasonable?

The first step is to determine what is meant by the term *God*. The word has been used in various ways, ranging from the Greek concept of the Olympian gods to the proposal by John Dewey that the divine is the "active relation between ideal and actual."[3] Let us adopt the more usual view, common to many religious believers, that *God* refers to an all-good, all-powerful, all-knowing, eternal creator of the world. The question is whether a being of that description exists.

Throughout the centuries, various arguments have been put forth to prove the existence of God. One of the best known is the *cosmological argument*, which rests on the assumption that everything that exists is caused to exist by something else. For example, a house is caused to exist by its builder, and rain is caused to exist by certain meteorological conditions. But if everything that exists is caused to exist by something else, then the world itself must be caused to exist by something else. This "something else" is God.

Although the cosmological argument may seem initially plausible, it has a major difficulty: if everything that exists is caused to exist by something else, then the cause of the world's existence is itself caused to exist by something else. In that case, the cause of the world's existence is not God, for God is an all-powerful being and thus does not depend on anything else for His[4] existence.

A defender of the cosmological argument might try to surmount this difficulty by claiming that the cause of the world's existence is not caused to exist by something else but is self-caused: that is, the reason for its existence lies within itself. However, if we admit the possibility that something is self-caused, the cosmological argument crumbles, for if the cause of the world's existence can be self-caused, why cannot the world be self-caused? In that case, no need would arise to postulate an external cause of the world's existence, for its existence would be self-explanatory.

In an attempt to salvage the cosmological argument, a defender might argue simply that something must have started everything, and this "something" is God. Yet even if we grant the claim that something must have started everything (and this supposition could be contested by appealing to the mathematical notion of an infinite series), the "something" may not be all-good, all-powerful, all-knowing, or eternal. Perhaps the first cause is evil or ceased to exist after a brief life. No such possibilities are excluded by the cosmological argument; thus it is not successful.

A second classic proof for the existence of God is the *ontological argument*. It makes no appeal to empirical evidence but purports to demonstrate that the essence of God implies His existence.

This argument has various versions, the best known of which share a basic structure. God is defined as the greatest of all conceivable beings, one who possesses every perfection. Assuming that a being who exists is greater than one who doesn't, God must exist.

Although this argument has been defended in subtle ways, it is open to the crucial criticism, stated succinctly by Immanuel Kant that existence is not an attribute. In other words, the definition of anything remains the same regardless of whether that thing exists. For example, the definition of a unicorn would not be altered if we discovered a living unicorn, just as our definition of a whooping crane would not be altered if whooping cranes became extinct. In short, whether unicorns or whooping cranes exist does not affect the meaning of the terms *unicorn* and *whooping crane*.

To clarify the point, imagine a ferocious tiger. Now imagine a ferocious tiger that exists. What more is there to imagine in the second case than in the first? Our concept of a ferocious tiger remains the same whether or not any ferocious tigers exist.

Applying this insight to the ontological argument, we can see why it is unsound. Because the definition of a thing remains the same whether or not it exists, the definition of *God* remains the same whether or not He exists. Thus existence cannot be part of the definition of God. God may be defined as the greatest conceivable being, one who possesses every perfection, but existence does not render something greater, since existence is no attribute at all. To assert that something exists is not to ascribe greatness or perfection to the thing but to state a fact about the world. What we mean by the term *God* is one matter; whether God exists is another. The ontological argument, however, conflates the two and thereby goes awry.

The third argument we shall consider, the *teleological argument*, is much less abstruse. Its defenders point out that the world possesses a highly ordered structure, just like an extraordinarily complex machine. Each part is adjusted to the other parts with wondrous precision. For instance, the human eye, which so many of us take for granted, is a mechanism of such intricacy that its design is breathtaking. But doesn't a design require a designer? The magnificent order of our world cannot be a result of pure chance but must be the work of a supreme mind that is responsible for the order. That supreme mind is God.

Although this argument has persuasive power, it suffers from several critical flaws. To begin with, any world would exhibit some kind of order. Were you to drop at random ten coins on the floor, they would exhibit an order. An order, therefore, does not imply an orderer. If we use the term *design* to mean "a consciously established order," then a design implies a designer. But the crucial question is whether our world exhibits mere order or design.

If the world were just like a machine, as the teleological argument claims, then because a machine has a design and a designer, so would the world. But is it obvious that the world is just like a machine? David Hume, in his *Dialogues Concerning Natural Religion*, argues that our experience is too limited for us to accept such an analogy. He notes that although the world bears some slight resemblance to a machine, the world is also similar to an animal in that "A continual circulation of matter in it produces no disorder; a continual waste in every part is incessantly repaired; the closest sympathy is perceived throughout the entire system; and each part or member, in performing its proper offices, operates both to its own preservation and to that of the whole."[5] Hume further points out that the world is somewhat like a vegetable because neither has sense organs or brains, although both exhibit life and movement. But whereas any machine requires a designer of the machine, animals and vegetables come into being very differently from machines.

Hume is not suggesting that the world came into being as does an animal or vegetable, but he wishes to demonstrate that the world is not sufficiently like an animal, a vegetable, or a machine to permit us to draw reasonable conclusions from such weak analogies. Lacking them, the teleological argument collapses, for we are left with no reason to believe that the world exhibits a design rather than an order.

As Hume points out, however, even if we were to accept the analogy to a machine, the argument still fails. Let us grant, he says, that like effects prove like causes. If the world is like a machine, the cause of the world is like the cause of a machine. Machines are usually built after many trials; so the world was probably built after many attempts. Machines are usually built by many workers; so the world was probably built by many deities. Those who build machines are often inexperienced, careless, or foolish; so the gods, too, may be inexperienced, careless, or foolish. As Hume suggests, perhaps this world "was only the first rude essay of some infant deity who afterwards abandoned it, ashamed of his lame performance." Or perhaps "it is the work only of some dependent, inferior deity, and is the object of derision to his superiors." It might even be "the production of old age and dotage in some superannuated deity; and ever since his death has run on at adventures, from the first impulse and active force which it received from him."[6] By suggesting such possibilities, Hume demonstrates that even if we grant an analogy between the world and a machine, and agree that both were designed, we are not committed to believing that the world's design is the work of one all-good, all-powerful, all-knowing eternal designer.

What, then, is the source of order? The world may have gone through innumerable structural changes until a stable pattern was reached, and the existence of such complex phenomena as the human eye may be a result of the process of natural selection whereby surviving forms of life are those that can adjust. Such an explanation of the world's order not only requires no recourse to the hypothesis of a supreme designer but has also been confirmed by biological research since the time of Charles Darwin.

This reply to the teleological argument may appear conclusive. Yet some of the argument's proponents have responded that the existence of God is not implied merely by the order in the world but, as the ingenious Anglo-Irish philosopher and clergyman George Berkeley (1685–1753) put it, by the "surprising magnificence, beauty, and perfection" of that order.[7] In other words, such a perfect world as ours could not be either the work of an inferior deity or the outcome of impersonal natural processes. Only an all-good, all-powerful, all-knowing creator could have produced such a flawless masterpiece.

This defense of the teleological argument, however, rests on the highly dubious premise that the world is perfect. In fact, the evidence against this view is overwhelming. Consider droughts, floods, famines, hurricanes, tornadoes, earthquakes, tsunamis, and the innumerable varieties of disease that plague us. Is it a perfect world in which babies are born deformed, infants are bitten by rats, and young people die from leukemia? And what of the evils people cause each other? The savageries of war, the indignities of slavery, and the torments of injustice and treachery extend far beyond the limits of our imagination. In short, the human condition is of such a nature that, as Hume observed, "The man of a delicate, refined temper, by being so much more alive than the rest of the world, is only so much more unhappy. . . ."[8]

We need not go on enumerating the ills of our world before the teleological argument loses its plausibility. Thus I conclude that none of the three best-known arguments for the existence of God is successful.

2. The Problem of Evil

The lack of proof that God exists is not by itself a proof that God does not exist. To reach that conclusion requires a separate argument, and a much-discussed one is the problem of evil. The Greek philosopher Epicurus (341–270 B.C.E.) put it most succinctly: Is God willing to prevent evil, but not able? Then He is impotent. Is He able, but not willing? Then He is malevolent. Is He both able and willing? From where, then, comes evil?

In other words, an all-good being would do everything possible to abolish evil. An all-powerful being would be able to abolish evil. So if an all-good, all-powerful being existed, evil would not. But evil does exist. Therefore, an all-good, all-powerful being does not.

Numerous attempts have been made to provide a *theodicy*, a defense of God's goodness in the face of evil. A promising approach, offered by John Hick,[9] begins by distinguishing two types of evil: moral and physical. *Moral evils* are those for which human beings are responsible, such as murder, theft, and oppression. *Physical evils* are those for which human beings are not responsible, such as typhoons, locusts, and viruses.

Moral evils are justified by the hypothesis that God has given us free will, the power to do good and the power to do evil. Which we do is up to us. God could have ensured that we always act rightly, but had He done so, He would have had to take away our free will, because a person who is forced to act rightly is not free. God is all-powerful but cannot perform an act whose description is contradictory, because such a supposed act is no act at all. For example, God cannot draw a square circle, but His inability to do so is no limitation on His power, for by definition a circle cannot be square. Similarly, it is no limitation on God's ability that He cannot create free persons who must always do what is right, because by definition a free person is one who does not always have to do what is right. God, therefore, had to choose between creating beings who always did what was right and creating beings who were free to do both right and wrong. In his wisdom He chose the latter, because it constituted the greater good. Thus all moral evils are justified as necessary concomitants of the best possible world God could have created, namely, a world in which persons can do good freely.

Physical evils are justified by their providing the opportunity for human beings to develop moral attributes. If the world were a paradise without hardships and dangers, people would be unable to acquire the strength of character that results from standing firm in the face of difficulties. The world was not intended as a pleasure palace but as an arena of "soul making" in which human beings grapple with their weaknesses and in so doing acquire the strength that will serve them well in some future life.

Hick defends his position further by employing what he terms the "method of negative theodicy." Suppose, contrary to fact, the world were arranged so that nothing could ever go badly. No one could harm anyone else, no one could perform a cowardly act, no one could fail to complete any worthwhile project. Presumably, such a world could be created through innumerable acts of God, who would alter the laws of nature as necessary.

Our present ethical concepts would thereby become useless. What would fortitude mean in an environment without difficulties? What would kindness be if no one needed help? Such a world, however efficiently it promoted pleasure, would be ill-adapted for the development of the best qualities of the human personality.

Hick emphasizes that this theodicy points forward in two ways to life after death. First, although we can find many striking instances of good resulting from evil, such as dangers that produce courage or calamities that develop patience, still in many cases evils lead to selfishness or disintegration of character. So any divine purpose of soul making in earthly history must continue beyond this life to achieve more than a fragmentary success.

Second, if we ask whether the business of soul making is so good as to nullify all the evils we find, the theist's answer must be in terms of a future good that is great enough to justify all that has happened.

Does this two-pronged reply to the problem of evil succeed in blunting its force? To some extent. Those who pose the problem may claim that it is logically impossible that an all-good, all-powerful being would permit the existence of evil. As we have seen, under certain circumstances an all-good, all-powerful being might have to allow evil to exist, for if the evil were a necessary component of the best possible world, then a being who wished to bring about that world would have to utilize whatever evil was necessary for the achievement of that goal. Thus no contradiction is involved in asserting that a world containing evil was created by an all-good, all-powerful being.

Yet how likely is it that we live in the best possible world and that all the evils are logically necessary? Do the greatest of horrors and tragedies enhance our lives? Are we better off because of them? How plausible, after all, is Hick's theodicy? Let us test it by considering the effectiveness of a similar approach to an analogous issue I call "the problem of goodness."

3. The Problem of Goodness

Suppose someone claims that the world was created by an all-powerful, all-knowing, all-evil Demon. Even if no proof of the Demon's existence is offered, the absence of such proof does not by itself demonstrate the Demon's nonexistence. To reach that conclusion requires a separate argument, and a plausible one is "the problem of goodness": An all-evil being would do everything possible to abolish goodness. An all-powerful being would be able to abolish goodness. So if an all-evil, all-powerful being existed, goodness would not. But goodness does exist. Therefore an all-evil, all-powerful being does not.

To paraphrase Epicurus: Is the Demon willing to prevent good, but not able? Then He[10] is impotent. Is He able, but not willing? Then He is benevolent. Is He both able and willing? From where, then, comes goodness?

Surprisingly, we can develop a reply to the problem of goodness along the same lines suggested by John Hick's reply to the problem of evil. We begin by distinguishing two types of goodness: moral and physical. *Moral goods* are those for which human beings are responsible, such as acts of altruism, generosity, and kindheartedness. *Physical goods* are those for which human beings are not responsible, such as sunshine, breathable air, and drinkable water.

The justification of moral goods proceeds by tying their existence to our free will. Surely, performing a bad act freely is more evil than performing it involuntarily. The Demon could have ensured that human beings would always perform bad actions, but then those actions would not have been free, because the Demon would have ensured their occurrence. Simply performing them, therefore, would not have produced the greatest possible evil, because greater evil can be produced by free persons than by unfree ones. The Demon had to provide human beings with freedom so that they might perform their bad actions voluntarily, thus maximizing evil.

As for the justification of physical goods, we should not suppose that the Demon's purpose in creating the world was to construct a chamber of tortures in which the inhabitants would be forced to endure a succession of unrelieved pains. The world can be viewed, instead, as a place of "soul breaking," in which free human beings, by grappling with the exhausting tasks and challenges in their environment, can have their spirits broken and their wills to live destroyed.

This conception of the world can be supported by what, following Hick, we might call the "method of negative justification." Suppose, contrary to fact, the world were arranged so that nothing could ever go well. No one could help anyone else, no one could perform a courageous act, no one could complete any worthwhile project. Presumably, such a world could be created through innumerable acts of the Demon, who would alter the laws of nature as necessary.

Our present ethical concepts would thereby become useless. What would frustration mean in an environment without hope? What would selfishness be if no one could make use of help? Such a world, however efficiently it promoted pain, would be ill adapted for the development of the worst qualities of the human personality.

This justification, just as Hick's, points forward in two ways to life after death. First, although we can find many striking instances of evil's being produced from good, such as the pollution of beautiful lakes or the slashing of great paintings, still in many cases goods lead to altruism or strengthening of character. So any demonic purpose of soul breaking at work in earthly history must continue beyond this life to achieve more than a fragmentary success.

Second, if we ask whether the business of soul breaking is so evil that it nullifies all the goodness we find, the demonist's answer must be in terms of a future evil great enough to justify all that has happened.

Does this two-pronged reply to the problem of goodness succeed? To some extent. Those who pose the problem may claim that it is logically impossible that an all-evil, all-powerful being would permit the existence of goodness. As we have seen, under certain circumstances an all-evil, all-powerful being might have to allow goodness to exist, for if the goodness were a necessary component of the worst possible world, then a being who wished to bring about that world would have to utilize whatever goodness was necessary for the achievement of that goal. Thus no contradiction is involved in asserting that a world containing goodness was created by an all-evil, all-powerful being.

Yet how likely is it that we live in the worst possible world and that all the goods are logically necessary? The answer is that it is highly unlikely, just as it is highly unlikely that we live in the best possible world and that all the evils are logically necessary. What is the evidence that, as Hick proposes, the horrors of bubonic plague somehow contribute to a better world? What is the evidence, as the believer in the Demon suggests, that the beauty of a sunset somehow contributes to a worse world? What is the evidence that, as Hick proposes, the free will of a Hitler achieved greater good than would have been achieved by his performing right actions involuntarily? What is the evidence that, as the believer in the Demon suggests, the free will of a Socrates achieved greater evil than would have been achieved by his performing wrong actions involuntarily?

If this world is neither the worst possible nor the best possible, then it could not have been created by either an all-powerful, all-evil Demon or an all-powerful, all-good God. Thus although the problem of goodness and the problem of evil do not show either demonism or theism to be impossible, the problems show both doctrines to be highly improbable. If demonists or theists can produce any other evidence in favor of their positions, then they can increase the plausibility of their views, but otherwise the reasonable conclusion is that neither the Demon nor God exists.

4. The Moriarty Hypothesis

The supposition that the world was created by an omnipotent, omnimalevolent Demon may appear strange. Yet stranger is the realization that its defenders may have the same expectations about the events of this world as do theists. In other words, both demonists and theists may choose to interpret their contrary views as supported equally by any future occurrences, no matter how good or evil they may be.

To illustrate this admittedly counterintuitive claim, consider the fictional example of Sherlock Holmes and his archenemy Professor Moriarty. Holmes believed that Moriarty was the "great malignant brain" behind crime in London, the "deep organizing power" that unified "every deviltry" into "one connected whole," the "foul spider which lurks in the center," "never caught—never so much as suspected."[11] Now suppose Moriarty's power extended throughout the universe, so that all events (perhaps excluding acts of human freedom) were the work of one omnipotent, omniscient, omnimalevolent Demon. Let us call this theory the *Moriarty hypothesis*.

Does the presence of various goods refute the Moriarty hypothesis? No, for just as theism has been shown to be logically consistent with the world's most horrendous evils, the Moriarty hypothesis can be shown to be logically consistent with the world's most wonderful goods. While any evil can be viewed as logically necessary for a greater good, any good can be viewed as logically necessary for a greater evil. Thus, the Moriarty hypothesis is not obviously false.

Now consider the following two assessments of the human condition:

1. "Is not all life pathetic and futile? . . . We reach. We grasp. And what is left in our hands at the end? A shadow. Or worse than a shadow—misery."
2. "The first entrance into life gives anguish to the new-born infant and to its wretched parent; weakness, impotence, distress attend each stage of that life, and it is, at last, finished in agony and horror."

Which is the viewpoint of a theist and which that of a believer in the Moriarty hypothesis? As it happens, (1) is uttered by Sherlock Holmes,[12] and (2) by the orthodox believer Demea in Hume's *Dialogues Concerning Natural Religion*.[13] The positions appear interchangeable.

Both the theist and the believer in the Moriarty hypothesis recognize that life contains happiness as well as misery. No matter how terrible the misery, the theist may regard it as unsurprising; after all, aren't all evils, in principle, explicable? To believers in the Moriarty hypothesis, happiness may be regarded as unsurprising; after all, aren't all goods, in principle, explicable? Supporters of both positions are apt to view events that appear to conflict with their fundamental principles merely as tests of fortitude, opportunities to display strength of commitment.

If defenders of either view modified their beliefs in the light of changing circumstances, then their expectations would differ. But believers are loath to admit doubt. They admire those who stand fast in their faith, regardless of appearances.

Any seemingly contrary evidence can be considered ambiguous. St. Paul says, "we see in a mirror, dimly,"[14] and Sherlock Holmes speaks of seeking the truth "through the veil which shrouded it."[15] If events are so difficult to interpret, they provide little reason for believers to abandon deep-seated tenets. Those who vacillate are typically viewed by other members of their communities as weakhearted and faithless.

One other attempt to differentiate the expectations of the theist and the believer in the Moriarty hypothesis is to suppose that theists have reason to be more optimistic than their counterparts. But this presumption is unwarranted. Recall the words from the Book of Ecclesiastes: "Then I accounted those who died long since more fortunate than those who are still living; and happier than either are those who have not yet come into being and have never witnessed the miseries that go on under the sun."[16] A more pessimistic view is hard to imagine.

We may be living, as the theist supposes, in the best of all possible worlds, but if so, the best of all possible worlds contains immense torments. On the other hand, we may be living, as the believer in the Moriarty hypothesis supposes, in the worst of all possible worlds, but if so, the worst of all possible worlds contains enormous delights. Both scenarios offer us reason to be cheerful and reason to be gloomy. Our outlook depends on our personalities, not our theology or demonology.

Thus, as we seek to understand life's vicissitudes, does it make any difference whether we believe in God or in the Moriarty hypothesis? Not if we hold either of these beliefs unshakably. For the more tenaciously we cling to one of them, the less it matters which one.

5. Dummy Hypotheses

To hold to an explanation of events in the face of conflicting facts is not to protect one's view but to render it pointless. As an illustration of this principle, consider the following anecdote, found in Anita Shreve's novel *All He Ever Wanted*:

> A man is propelled one minute sooner to his automobile because he decides not to stop to kiss his wife goodbye. As a consequence of this omission, he

> then crosses a bridge one minute before it collapses, taking all its traffic and doomed souls into the swirling and angry depths below. Oblivious, and safely out of harm's way, our man continues on his journey.[17]

Let us first suppose this man is a theist and, when he becomes aware of his good fortune, attributes it to the benevolence of God. What are we to make of his claim?

To begin with, whatever goodness God displayed in this man's case did not extend to the many others who fell to their death. How is God's benevolence compatible with such a tragedy? Our man does not know, but when he ponders the matter, he is likely to suppose that the chain of events serves a divine purpose that lies beyond human understanding.

Next, suppose this man believes in the Moriarty hypothesis and, when he becomes aware of the circumstances, attributes them to the malevolence of the Demon. What are we to make of this claim?

To begin with, whatever evil the Demon displayed in these horrific events did not extend to the man himself, for he was saved. How is the Demon's malevolence compatible with this man's good fortune? He does not know, but when he ponders the matter, he is likely to suppose that the chain of events serves a demonic purpose that lies beyond human understanding.

A third hypothesis the man might accept is that the world is the scene of a struggle between God and the Demon. Both are powerful, but neither is omnipotent. When events go well, God's benevolence is in the ascendancy; when events go badly, the Demon's malevolence is in the ascendancy. In the tragic case under consideration the Demon caused the collapse of the bridge, while God arranged for the one man to be saved.

Is this third explanation unnecessarily complex and therefore to be rejected? No, for even though in one sense it is more complex than the other two, because it involves two supernatural beings rather than only one, in another sense the third explanation is simpler than the other two, because it leaves no aspect of the situation beyond human understanding.

The crucial point is that all three hypotheses (as well as innumerable others of this sort that one might imagine) can be maintained regardless of the facts. For instance, suppose the bridge had collapsed at a time when all vehicles but one had already crossed. The theist would thank God for having saved the lives of so many, while considering it a mystery why the one vehicle was lost; the believer in the Moriarty hypothesis would attribute the loss of the one vehicle to the work of the Demon, while considering it a mystery why the lives of so many were saved; the believer in God and the Demon would thank God for having saved the lives of so many, while attributing the loss of the one vehicle to the work of the Demon.

Any of these incompatible hypotheses can be interpreted to account for whatever events occur. Using them in this way turns them into dummy hypotheses, compatible with all possible facts. Like a dummy bell rope that makes no sound, a dummy hypothesis makes no sense.[18] Its compatibility with all possible situations robs it of any explanatory power.

Contrast a dummy hypothesis with a scientific one, which is typically tested by the following four-step procedure: (1) Formulate the hypothesis clearly; (2) work out the implications of the hypothesis; (3) perform controlled experiments to verify whether these implications hold; (4) observe the consequences of these experiments and, as a result, accept or reject the hypothesis. In practice, complications may abound at each stage. Moreover, the method yields only high probabilities, not certainties, for a hypothesis may pass numerous tests, yet fail additional ones. But the crucial point is that scientific hypotheses are tested, then rejected if inconsistent with the outcome of the tests.

As an example of how scientific method works, consider the case of the American army surgeon Dr. Walter Reed (1851–1902), who sought to control yellow fever. He hypothesized that the disease was caused by a specific type of mosquito. To test this hypothesis, he quarantined some individuals so that they would not come into contact with any of the insects, but did not quarantine the other test subjects. When those exposed developed the disease and those quarantined did not, Reed had strong evidence that the mosquitoes were the cause of the disease.

Had the results of the experiment been different, Reed's hypothesis might have turned out to be false. If those quarantined had developed the disease at the same rate as those exposed, then Reed would have rejected his hypothesis and been led to develop and test others.

That a hypothesis can be disproved by testing is not a weakness of the hypothesis but a strength. Any genuine hypothesis is open to possible refutation. Dummy hypotheses are not open to refutation and therefore do not provide understanding. They may be psychologically comforting but do not enable us to gain any control over our environment.

Some may choose to attribute an outbreak of yellow fever to God or the Demon or a struggle between them. Such hypotheses are untestable, however, and therefore do not help us eradicate or control the disease.

Finally, a few thoughts about the story of the fallen bridge, with which we began. Why did it collapse? The answer is most likely to be found by calling in engineers who can determine the cause, learn from the case, and build a new bridge that will be safer. At no point will they use theories involving any divine or demonic beings.

Yet some may persist in asking why the one man was saved. The answer is that he arrived one minute sooner because of not stopping to kiss his wife goodbye. Why didn't he kiss his wife goodbye? Perhaps he was distracted by thoughts of an upcoming business meeting. Why was that meeting so critical? We can continue such speculation endlessly, but the crucial point is that no question we may ask will be answered satisfactorily by appealing to any dummy hypothesis.

6. The Appeal to Faith

Few theists view their belief in God as resting on a scientific assessment of empirical data. Rather, they see themselves as persons of faith, firm in their convictions regardless of any apparent evidence to the contrary. I have already suggested the pitfalls in disregarding facts that conflict with one's beliefs, but here I want to focus directly on the nature of faith and offer another example to clarify further its inherent dangers.

To have faith is to put aside any doubts, and doing so is sometimes beneficial, because doubt may be counterproductive. Golfers who doubt they will hole their putts almost surely will miss them. Teachers who doubt their students' ability to learn are less effective instructors. A crucial component of achievement is perseverance, and those who doubt themselves are less likely to persist in the face of difficulty or opposition. In short, certitude often correlates with success, whereas doubt is apt to lead to failure.

To describe someone as a person of faith suggests that the individual is strong-willed, fearless, and unwavering. To describe someone as a person without faith suggests that the individual is weak-willed, fearful, and faltering.

Faith, however, can be misplaced. If you are not an experienced mountain climber, but set out to scale Mount Everest because you have faith in your ability to do so, then you are reckless. If your supposed friend routinely betrays your confidence but you continue to have faith in this individual, then you are gullible. If you have faith in your ability to master the violin in ten easy lessons, then you are ignorant.

So faith in the sense of assurance can be wise or foolish. The circumstances of the case make all the difference. But faith in the sense of an unwillingness to acknowledge evidence contrary to one's beliefs is never wise and may be disastrous.

Consider a fictional clairvoyant named, Sibyl, who is asked to help in the search for a missing friend of yours. After undergoing a trance, Sibyl emerges to announce that your friend can be found in a place where darkness dwells. Subsequently, your friend is found tending bar in a Manhattan nightclub. Sibyl's followers acclaim her insight because, as they point out, a nightclub dwells in darkness.

You are impressed with Sibyl and recommend her to someone else searching for a lost cousin. Sibyl is consulted, and after undergoing another trance, emerges to announce that the cousin is to be found in a place where darkness dwells. Subsequently, the cousin is found on Cape Cod. Sibyl's followers again acclaim her insight because, as they point out, recently the weather on the Cape has been rainy and the skies dark.

As it turns out, whenever Sibyl is consulted regarding a person's whereabouts, she announces that the individual is in a place where darkness dwells. Regardless of the outcome of subsequent searches, her followers acclaim her insight and interpret her prediction so that it conforms with the outcome of the search. If the person being sought is no longer living, that individual surely dwells in darkness, while if the person cannot be located at all, that individual has vanished into darkness.

Are Sibyl's predictions true? Are they false? They are neither, for they are consistent with all possible situations and are thus useless, wholly without any significance. Because the place darkness dwells can turn out to be any place, Sibyl's words do not identify any particular site or eliminate any possibilities. To use previous terminology, she has offered a dummy hypothesis. Her followers may find that she provides them with psychological comfort. In a crisis, however, paying close attention to her pronouncement and attempting to act on it could be fatal.

Suppose a man is kidnapped and the police need to find out his whereabouts as soon as possible. Every minute counts. Hearing from Sibyl's admirers of her reputation for helping to find missing persons, the police consult her and, not surprisingly, she tells them that the victim is to be found where darkness dwells. If the police spend any time trying to decipher what she says and search where she is suggesting, all may be lost, for *we* know, even if the police do not, that her words provide no clue to any particular location.

A similar problem undermines the claim that a certain occurrence is in accord with God's plan, for whatever happens can be understood as in accord with the plan. Such a plan is no plan at all, and having faith in it is akin to having faith in Sibyl's predictions.

Believing in God's providence may provide theists with a sense of calm during trying times. In a medical emergency, for example, those who have faith in God may find that prayer helps them deal with the stress of the situation. But before taking time to pray, theists are well advised to seek the services of a reliable physician. For even though having faith in God may offer the best chance for comfort to those who are worried, relying on science offers the best chance for health to those who are ill.

Faith also opens the door to intolerance. If the majority hold a particular faith and are unwilling to be proven wrong, what may be the consequences for a minority? Will the majority permit the minority to believe differently, even if certain that what the minority believes is mistaken?

The historical record is not encouraging. If my belief can be wrong, then your opposing belief can be right, and I am inclined to listen to your arguments. But if my belief cannot be wrong, then your opposing belief cannot be right, and I have no need to listen to your arguments. Indeed, I may set out to save you from your errors. Thus arises persecution, carried out in the name of the good but inevitably leading to a reign of evil. For even though a faith may lack meaning, its adherents may not lack malice.

7. Skepticism About Faith

A devout person of blameless character may suffer a series of terrible misfortunes. Why would an all-good, all-powerful God allow such injustice? To many theists, the most appropriate response in such a situation is not to doubt God's power or goodness but to assume that the evils would be explicable if only we could understand God's plan.

Surprisingly, a powerful challenge to such faith in God is found in the Bible, in particular, in the Book of Job. Although commonly misinterpreted as a defense of faith in God, the book instead suggests that the more we know of God's intentions, the less they justify His actions. This scriptural story merits careful attention.

Consider the plot. After a short introduction in which Job's exemplary piety and extraordinary good fortune are described, the scene shifts to heaven, where a dialogue takes place between God and Satan. God proudly comments to Satan about Job's great spiritual qualities. Satan scoffs at Job's devoutness, claiming that Job is obedient only because God has given Job good health, a fine family, and untold wealth. Although God Himself testifies to Job's genuine piety, He permits Satan to test Job by inflicting on him the severest personal losses. Suddenly, all ten of Job's children die and his wealth is destroyed. When Job does not relinquish his faith in God, Satan, claiming that Job has maintained his faith only because his own body has been spared, obtains further permission from God to inflict on Job a most painful disease.

The scene now shifts to the land of Uz, the place of Job's residence. Having heard of his misfortunes, Job's three friends Eliphaz, Bildad, and Zophar come to comfort him. Job gives vent to his feelings of despair, cursing the day he was born and avowing that under his circumstances death is better than life. Eliphaz advises Job to calm himself and not despise the chastening of the Almighty. Eliphaz believes that because Job is suffering, he must have sinned, for God does not punish the innocent. Eliphaz also counsels Job to repent of his sins and so be restored to God's favor.

In response, Job points out that Eliphaz has not understood Job's outburst. Job has not lost faith in God. Rather, he longs for death because his life has become intolerable. In a harsh rejoinder, Bildad tells Job that God does not pervert justice, and that if Job were upright he would be prosperous. Job once again pleads with his friends that they do not understand the point of his complaint. He recognizes, as they do, the majesty of God, but he claims to be innocent. He wishes only to know in what way he has erred, so that he might wholeheartedly repent. Finally Job cries to God that he would willingly present his case before Him, if the Almighty would only permit the opportunity.

The three friends and a newcomer, Elihu, repeat Eliphaz's basic argument: Job is suffering and therefore is a sinner; if he would repent his sins, God would pardon him. Job's response continues to be that although he claims innocence, he is prepared to be judged, and if found guilty, stands ready to accept just punishment.

The climax of the story comes when God answers Job from out of a whirlwind. God speaks of His own wisdom and power in the creation and control of the mighty forces of nature. He points out the utter insignificance of humanity in the presence of God. He then questions Job's right even to inquire of God, for how could humanity ever hope to understand the workings of the Almighty?

Finally, he urges Job to renew his faith in the wisdom, goodness, and justice of God, even though Job cannot hope to understand their workings.

In the divine presence Job is overawed. He humbles himself before God, promising never to inquire of God again but forever to believe fervently in the greatness and power of the Lord. The story concludes as God rebukes Eliphaz, Bildad, and Zophar for the advice they gave Job, pardoning them only out of regard for him. He heals Job, restores to him twice as much wealth as he had possessed before his misfortunes, and blesses him with ten children and a long and happy life.

Now let us examine the traditional interpretation of the Book of Job, which views it as a defense of God's power, knowledge, and goodness as well as an admission of human ignorance regarding the divine. Here is one such account:

> The Book of Job teaches us that God's ways are beyond the complete understanding of our little minds. Like Job, we must believe that God, who placed us in this world, knows what is best for us. Such faith in the goodness of God, even though we cannot altogether understand it, brings us strength and confidence to face our calamities and sorrows and sufferings.[19]

Again:

> The total mystery of God can be gleaned from the Book of Job. There we are presented with a deity whose workings in nature can in no way be inferred from a knowledge of nature's order. For how did that order come into existence? That is God's secret. Nor can man's moral intuitions be trusted. Job *knows* he is innocent, yet in the end he is satisfied to accept the dictate that the conventional-minded friends with whom he has carried on a courageous, honest debate are in a sense correct. Who is he, a mere mortal, to challenge God's justice? There is infinitely more to it than even his clear conscience can hope to fathom. Indeed he cannot any longer allow himself to think of God as just or unjust, at least as these terms are understood by man. These categories have no meaning when applied to God.[20]

And again:

> The positive contribution of the *Book of Job* comes in the "Speeches of the Lord" which give Job something better than that which is provided by the feeble remarks of his friends. The essential point of these final speeches is that the problem is too great for the finite mind, that Job sees only a small segment of reality, and that his criticisms are accordingly inappropriate. How can Job *know* that either God's power or goodness is limited? His knowledge of temporal things is admittedly slight; his knowledge of eternal things is still more slight. The conclusion of the book is Job's recognition of his own humble status with the consequent mood of childlike trust.[21]

All these variations on the basic interpretation overlook a key passage: the opening dialogue in heaven. If this scene were eliminated, the traditional understanding of the book would be persuasive. Readers would be in the place of Job. They would not know why he was suffering and would, like Job, be overawed by God's appearance from out of the whirlwind.

But readers are not in this position. We were told explicitly at the outset of the story why Job would suffer. Satan had, in effect, made a wager with God about the strength of Job's faith, and the wager required Job's suffering. God's words from out of the whirlwind at the climax of the plot appear childish when we are, in effect, behind the scenes. For God to have answered Job's question truthfully would have shown Him to be anything but a great moral force. Does a righteous being make a wager involving human lives? Thus, much in the manner of the bully who, when engaged in a philosophical dispute, challenges opponents to a fistfight to settle the issue, God attacks Job's position ad hominem, trying to disallow Job's right to ask an embarrassing question by emphasizing his inability to control nature.

Job does not possess God's power, but Job's question remains unanswered. Job may be overawed, but readers should not be, for we are aware of the circumstances surrounding God's actions. God's ways may be beyond Job's understanding, but they are not beyond the readers'. We can hardly be expected to have "childlike trust" in the goodness of a God who not only punishes Job unfairly but kills his ten children without any possible justification. Had these individuals done anything unjust? Their lives were sacrificed as part of the wager. The ten children who are given to Job at the end of the story may to some extent compensate Job for his previous losses, but are the dead children compensated? Are they restored to life?

What, then, is the significance of the Book of Job? It stands opposed to the prevailing theology of almost all the rest of the Bible. The doctrine of retributive justice, as presented in Deuteronomy, Psalms, Proverbs, and elsewhere, states that a pious person will be rewarded with wealth and happiness; a sinner will suffer both economic and physical adversity. Traditional believers supposed that the righteous were favored by God with material rewards, whereas sinners were punished with calamities. The Book of Job is a criticism of this theology. Later thinkers, however, could not accept this protest. They tried to torture the text into a pattern of orthodoxy. In effect, they turned a challenge to the righteousness of God's justice into a defense of unquestioning faith.

The Book of Job does not justify God's ways; rather, it doubts God's goodness. The book does not provide support for faith in the divine; to the contrary, it offers powerful support for skepticism about such faith.

8. The Problem of Meaning

In attempting to explain why a world created by an all-good, all-powerful God contains so much evil, theists are tempted to respond that the reasons are known to God but not to us, for we lack the intellectual powers to grasp His plan. In the words of one of the commentators on the Book of Job whom I quoted previously, "God's ways are beyond the complete understanding of our little minds."

To deny *complete* understanding of God, however, is a dodge, because we may not completely understand anyone, even ourselves. What we seek is at least partial understanding of God. Do we possess it?

To assert that we do reopens the problem of evil, for even a partial understanding of God should include a partial understanding of evil, a burden theists don't wish to shoulder. After all, who is prepared to offer even a partial explanation of how the best possible world contains the Holocaust? The sure way to avoid the question is to deny any understanding of God. To adopt this position, however, is fatal to theism. For how can we make sense of the view that something exists if it is a total mystery?

Suppose, for instance, we are asked whether we believe in the existence of a snark.[22] We inquire what a snark is, what specific characteristics it possesses. If we are told its nature is unknowable, what would be the sense of our affirming or denying its existence? What would we be talking about? Belief in the existence of a wholly incomprehensible snark is empty. So is belief in the existence of a wholly incomprehensible God.

To avoid this pitfall, theists may claim that we do have some knowledge of God's nature, because, for example, we know He is wise and just, although the words *wise* and *just* have a different meaning when applied to God than when applied to human beings. What is this meaning? One possible answer is that no one knows. But this reply leads to a dead end, for we cannot speak intelligently using words we don't understand. If the meaning of the words we apply to God is unknown, then God is unknown.

One traditional response to this difficulty is to maintain that God's attributes cannot be conceived in positive terms but only negatively. For example, to say that "God knows" is to deny that He does not know. This approach is supposed to make it possible to avoid applying human concepts to the divine essence.

But to deny that someone does not possess knowledge is to affirm that the individual does possess knowledge. If that implication fails to hold, then we do not understand the meaning of our own words, and we cannot use them to make meaningful claims.

If God's knowledge has nothing in common with human knowledge, then, as Gersonides argued, we might as well say that God *lacks* knowledge, adding the proviso that the term *knowledge* applied to God does not have the same meaning as it does ordinarily.[23] In other words, once we allow ourselves to use words without being able to offer any explanation of them, we might as well say anything at all, for none of what we say makes any sense.

What if the words we apply to God are to be taken not literally but metaphorically? Does that approach help deal with the problem? Only if the metaphors can be explained in nonmetaphorical language. Otherwise, we are attempting to elucidate a mystery by means of an enigma.

To see how a normal metaphor can be unpacked, consider an example offered by Janet Martin Soskice, who has developed a sophisticated defense of the use of metaphor in speaking of God. Commenting on e. e. cummings's line "nobody, not even the rain, has such small hands," she proposes that "the power of the metaphor rests in its casting up in the reader's mind thoughts of what kinds of hands rain might have, suggestions of fragility, delicacy, transience, ability to reach the smallest places."[24] Thus does Soskice intend to show that a metaphor may offer "a new vision, the birth of a new understanding, a new referential access."[25]

She stresses that science as well as literature uses metaphor. In both cases, the figure of speech arises from a model, which she defines as "an object or state of affairs viewed in terms of its resemblance, real or hypothetical, to some other object or state of affairs."[26] The brain may thus be modeled on a computer, leading to talk of "programming," "inputs," and "feedback."

If, however, theological models are analogous to scientific ones, shouldn't the former, like the latter, be causually explanatory, falsifiable, revisable? Soskice agrees, arguing that "the Christian realist must concede that there is a point, theoretically at least, at which he would be committed to surrendering his theism."[27] But where is this point? The question is invariably left unanswered.

In offering her account of cummings's line, Soskice explains its metaphor in nonmetaphorical language. After she does so, the metaphor yields the nonmetaphorical assertion that the rain is delicate and transient. If that rain is part of a major hurricane, then the claim is false.

Can theological metaphors also be explained so as to yield nonmetaphorical claims? If so, we can speak of God literally, a position theists seek to deny.

But if the metaphors cannot be explained, why is one more appropriate than another? We talk of God the Father or, possibly, God the Mother. But why not God the Aunt or Uncle, God the Cousin, or God the Neighbor? Some may protest that these phrases are inexplicable. Perhaps so. But one inexplicable metaphor is as good as another.

Thus we are left with the problem of meaning: How can we describe an indescribable God?

9. Miracles

If we cannot speak of God, can we at least experience the workings of His will? Do some events bear the stamp of divine intervention?

Return to the case of the man who crosses a bridge one minute before it collapses. Let us alter the circumstances and suppose the man is driving on the bridge when the tragedy occurs. No one on the bridge survives, except for him. He is thrown from his car, lands in soft soil, and is unharmed. Has a miracle occurred?

In one sense of the word it has, for a miracle may be understood as an unexpected, wonderful event, and the man's escape from death is in that sense miraculous. But is it miraculous in a stronger sense of the word—is it an act of God that suspends the laws of nature?

Some theists may be tempted to believe so, especially when several members of a local church come forward to say that as they were watching the events unfold, they saw a fiery chariot appear from the heavens, pick up the man as he was falling, and bring him safely to earth.[28] Do their reports increase the likelihood that a miracle occurred?

Testimony offered in court is subject to cross-examination and may turn out to be mistaken. Assume two witnesses say that they observed the defendant Smith commit a robbery. Yet forty reliable others are prepared to testify that at the time in question Smith was playing in a volleyball game many miles away. So the two witnesses who thought they saw Smith commit the crime were apparently mistaken. When challenged, though, the two insist they couldn't be wrong because they certainly seemed to see Smith.

To assess their claim we need to draw a distinction between statements such as "I see a star" and statements such as "I seem to see a star." If I see a star, then a star is present for me to see. I may be wrong that I am seeing a star, for perhaps I am seeing an airplane instead, but if I am right that I am seeing a star, the truth of my statement implies the existence of a star. If it turns out that I only thought I was seeing a star, but in fact I was seeing an airplane, I can still claim that I *seemed* to see a star. In making that claim sincerely, I am safe from error, but my saying that I seemed to see something doesn't imply the existence of what I seemed to see. In other words, statements such as "I see a star" may be false, but if they are true, they imply the existence of the thing perceived. Statements such as "I seem to see a star," if sincere, cannot be false but do not imply the existence of the thing seemingly perceived.

Confusion sets in if some persons claim that a thing exists because they seem to see it. What is necessary is that *if* they see something, it is present. What is also necessary is that if they *seem* to see something, they can't be wrong that they *seem* to see it; they can, however, be wrong that it is present.

In the case of the witnesses who seemed to see Smith commit the robbery, did they actually see what they thought they saw? To determine the reliability of a person's testimony, we assess it in light of answers to questions such as:

(1) How many witnesses saw the event?
(2) Do the witnesses agree in all important respects?
(3) Are they widely regarded as persons of reliable judgment?
(4) Do they have any reason to want to see what they claim to have seen?
(5) Is anyone trying to mislead them?

(6) Is their testimony incompatible with other evidence?
(7) How likely is their testimony compared to the likelihood of any widely accepted views with which it is incompatible?
(8) How plausible is an alternative explanation of why they seemed to see what they thought they saw?

In Smith's case, forty witnesses testify that they saw him playing volleyball, whereas only two say they saw him commit the robbery. Let us presume that the testimony of the forty is in all important respects identical, that they are reliable persons with no reason to lie, that no one is trying to mislead them, that their testimony fits all the facts except for the accounts of the two dissenting witnesses, that the testimony of the forty is not incompatible with any laws of nature or other widely believed claims, and that Smith has an identical twin brother who doesn't play volleyball but has previously been convicted of crimes and was known to be in the vicinity of the crime scene when the robbery occurred. Given all these factors, any reasonable jury would find Smith "not guilty."

Let us now use these same criteria to judge the plausibility of those who reported seeing a fiery chariot save the man falling from the bridge. The number of witnesses was small, probably they each described the chariot somewhat differently, their reliability may be suspect in view of their previous accounts of equally strange sightings, their commitment to a particular type of theism may give them reason to wish to witness miracles, they may be subject to the will of a leader who praises them for reporting supposed miracles, and no traces of any chariot tracks are found in the ground where the man came to rest.

Most important, however, their reports imply the suspension of the law of gravity, a law as highly confirmed as any could be. So the weight of the evidence suggests not that the law ceased to operate but that these observers made a mistake.

As to how they were misled, we might suppose that remains of a burning car are found near where the man landed, and these burning parts might have been mistaken for a chariot. Granted, this hypothesis is not highly plausible, but it is far more so than the possibility that the law of gravity was suspended while a fiery chariot appeared and disappeared.

Admittedly, I have stacked the deck against those reporting the miracle by assuming weaknesses in their testimony that may not fit the facts in every case. Suppose the witnesses were more numerous, independent, and reliable. Would such conditions increase the probability that a miracle occurred?

Not to a significant degree, for as Hume noted in his much-discussed account of miracles, "There must . . . be a uniform experience against every miraculous event, otherwise the event would not merit that appellation. And as a uniform experience amounts to a proof, there is here a direct and full *proof*, from the nature of the fact, against the existence of any miracle. . . ."[29] In other words, because a miracle suspends a natural law, and because the evidence for the operation of such laws is overwhelming, the probability that a miracle occurred is always far less than the probability that the law suddenly stopped functioning. Thus invariably any report of a miracle is highly unlikely.

Theists are most tempted to believe in a miracle when it involves the triumph of good over evil. If the man saved in the collapse of the bridge was of saintly character whereas those killed in the accident were seeking to harm him, then considering the event miraculous is nearly irresistible. But to assume that God acts so that the good prosper while evildoers are punished is to agree with Job's friends, whom God rebuked for their mistaken views. After all, if we attribute wondrous events to God, who is supposed to be responsible for horrendous ones?

10. God Without Religion

So far I have focused on belief in God without making any reference to religious commitment. Yet often theism and religiosity are treated as equivalent. For example, a public opinion survey may ask Americans whether they believe in God and, when a high percentage say they do, the results are said to show that a high percentage of Americans are religious. This conclusion, however, is not implied by the data.

To see why, suppose that contrary to what most philosophers believe, the cosmological, ontological, and teleological arguments for the existence of God are all sound. Let us grant the existence of the most perfect conceivable being, the all-good, all-powerful creator of the universe. What implications follow from this premise that would suggest participation in any religion?

Some people would feel more secure in the knowledge that the world had been planned by an all-good being. Others would feel insecure, realizing the extent to which their existence depended on a decision of this being. In any case, most people, either out of fear or respect, would wish to act in accord with God's will.

None of the arguments for believing in God, however, provides any hint as to which actions God wishes us to perform or what we ought to do to please or obey Him. We may affirm that God is all-good yet have no way of knowing the highest moral standards. All we may presume is that, whatever these standards, God always acts in accordance with them. We might expect God to have implanted the correct moral intuitions in our minds, but this supposition is doubtful in view of the conflicts among people's intuitions. Furthermore, even if a consensus prevailed, it might be only a means by which God tests us to see whether we have the courage to dissent from popular opinion.

Some would argue that if God exists, then at least it follows that murder is immoral, because it would be immoral to destroy what God in His infinite wisdom created. This argument, however, fails on several grounds. First, God also created germs, viruses, and disease-carrying rats. Does it follow that because God created these things they ought not be eliminated? Second, if God arranged for us to live, He also arranged for us to die. Does it follow that by killing we are assisting the work of God? Third, God provided us with the mental and physical potential to commit murder. Does it follow that God wishes us to fulfill this potential?

To attempt to deduce moral precepts from God's existence is to try to deduce normative conclusions from purely factual premises, a move Hume showed to be logically impossible.[30] No such deduction is valid, and thus any moral principle is consistent with the existence of God.

Because the arguments for believing in God afford no means of distinguishing good from evil, no person can be sure how to obey God and do what is best in His eyes. We may hope our actions are in accord with God's standards, but no test is available to check. Some seemingly good persons suffer great ills, while some seemingly evil persons achieve great happiness. Perhaps in a future life these outcomes are reversed, but we have no way of ascertaining who, if anyone, is ultimately punished and who ultimately rewarded.

Over the course of history, those who believed in God's existence typically were eager to learn His will and tended to rely on those individuals who claimed to possess such insight. Diviners, seers, and priests were given positions of great influence. Competition among them was severe, for no one could be sure which oracle to believe.

In any case, prophets died, and their supposedly revelatory powers disappeared with them. For practical purposes, what was needed was a permanent record of God's will. This requirement was met by the writing of holy books in which God's will was revealed for all to know.

But even though many such books were supposed to embody the will of God, they conflicted with one another. Which was to be believed? Theism by itself yields no answer. The only direct avenue to the divine will is a personal, self-validating experience in which one senses the presence of God and apprehends which of the putative holy books is genuine.

Drawing on a distinction made in the discussion of miracles, however, we need to distinguish between seeming to see God and seeing God. Anyone may claim to have seemed to see God, and we ordinarily have no reason to doubt that the person did *seem* to see the divine. But such testimony is fallible; it does not prove that the person saw God. As Sidney Hook wrote, "Whether an actual angel speaks to me in my beatific vision or whether I only dreamed he spoke, the truth of what he says can only be tested in the same way as I test what my neighbor says to me. For even my neighbor may claim to be a messenger of the Lord."[31] Testimony of revelations, like testimony of miracles, has to meet standards of reliability. Yet claims to have seen and heard God are invariably dubious, especially because they imply the suspension of accepted laws of nature related to optics and acoustics, and for that reason alone are highly implausible.

Suppose you are convinced that God exists but are not persuaded that anyone knows His will. In that case you might choose not to practice any religion. Your position would be coherent and best described as that of a non-religious theist or, to use a term popular in the seventeenth and eighteenth centuries, a deist. Among those who held this view were Benjamin Franklin, George Washington, and Thomas Jefferson, an estimable group indeed.

11. Playing the Odds

Assuming we agree with those who deny insight into God's will, might prudence nevertheless dictate that we participate in an established religion, because each offers a well-trodden path to understanding the divine? Isn't it likely that millions of believers are on the right track to truth? Even if they are not, what has been lost by joining them and trying their ways?

This line of argument is similar to *Pascal's wager*, the reasoning offered by Blaise Pascal, for why one should believe in God even without any proof of His existence. Pascal argues that if you believe, and God exists, then you attain heavenly bliss; if you believe, and God doesn't exist, little is lost. On the other hand, if you don't believe, and God does exist, then you are doomed to the torments of damnation; if you don't believe, and God doesn't exist, little is gained. Thus belief is the safest strategy.[32]

Pascal, however, failed to consider the possibility that a different kind of God might exist, for example, one who wishes us to hold only those beliefs supported by the available evidence. If such a God exists, then in the absence of evidence, *not* believing is the safest strategy.

A similar difficulty undermines the supposition that in the absence of knowledge about God, the safest strategy is to join a religion, worship God, pray to Him, and hope for the best. After all, suppose God doesn't approve of any religion and doesn't wish to be worshipped or prayed to. What if He rewards those who shun such activities? In that case, avoiding them is the safest strategy.

Admittedly, this account of the divine nature is contrary to what many people suppose. They take as obvious that God wishes to receive our veneration and supplications. But leaving aside for a moment the incomprehensibility of God, which would make it impossible for anyone to know His nature, let me offer an analogy to suggest that what God wills may be contrary to widespread expectations.

Most children, although sadly not all, enter this world beloved by their parents who, having created them, make every effort to nurture and support them, sometimes even at great cost to the parents' own ambitions. In response, the children may dearly love one or both of their parents, not merely honoring them in accord with the biblical injunction, but adoring them.

Yet sensible parents would not wish to be the object of their children's worship. To the contrary, they would find the situation distressing and believe that in some way they had failed as parents, for even though they welcomed the love of an independent child who had learned to make decisions and take responsibilities, they did not seek nor would they want the single-minded devotion of a dependent child who relied on them for all decisions and was unwilling to shoulder any responsibilities.

If we are children of God, might not God, like a wise parent, wish those He created to be independent, not dependent? Might He disapprove of being worshipped at public services and prayed to at times of hardship? Might He instead favor those who meditated privately, if at all, performed good deeds rather than godly rituals, and displayed the fortitude to persevere in the face of difficulties without appealing for His help? Perhaps, as Benjamin Franklin wrote, "God helps them who help themselves."[33] Indeed, God's will may have been best understood by the prophet Amos, when he attributed to Him the following words:

> I loathe, I spurn your festivals,
> I am not appeased by your solemn assemblies.
> If you offer Me burnt offerings—or your meal offerings—
> I will not accept them;
> I will pay no heed
> To your gifts of fatlings.
> Spare Me the sound of your hymns,
> And let Me not hear the music of your lutes.
> But let justice well up like water,
> Righteousness like an unfailing stream.[34]

Thus, rather than venerating God and offering Him supplications, we should focus our efforts on being considerate to others.

Granted, I have been speculating about matters that may lie beyond human understanding. If they do not, I believe my account of God's will is as plausible as another's. But if grasping the nature of the divine is impossible, then joining an established religion in an effort to find the truth is no more reasonable than not joining. In the absence of any relevant information, all bets are off.

12. Religions

In the last section, I considered the decision to accept a religion as if the choice among religions did not matter. But the divergences among them are vast, including different rituals, different prayers, different theistic systems, and different moral beliefs.[35]

Judaism believes in a unitary god, Zoroastrianism in two gods, Christianity in a triune god, Shinto in gods too numerous to count; Theravada Buddhism and Samkhya and Mimamsa Hinduism believe in no god at all. The Confucian Mencius teaches that human nature is essentially good; Christians view human nature as tainted by original sin. Hindus consider the soul immortal; Buddhists view it as impermanent. Christians place a heavy emphasis on an afterlife; the central concern of Judaism is life in this world. Moslems practice *purdah*, the seclusion of women; in Shinto female priests conduct religious ceremonies. The Sikh religion is unique in requiring its members to have long hair, a bracelet, a dagger, a comb, and short pants.

Indeed, every belief and practice of any particular religion is rejected by some other religions. Furthermore, although each religion has its own holy writings that are thought to embody the divine will as revealed to inspired prophets, within each religion interpretations of scripture differ and have frequently given rise to fierce internal doctrinal disputes. Recall that despite the many matters about which Protestants and Catholics agree, their disagreements have led to centuries of bloodshed.

Such differences cannot be overcome by embracing all religions as variations on a single theme, because religions are exclusive: accepting one implies not accepting others. We may respect a religion or admire aspects of it, but to accept it fully requires conversion, for each religion claims to be correct in belief and practice, and these claims are in conflict. But what arguments can establish the truth of one religion and the falsity of all others?

As a test case consider Jainism, an ancient faith from India. It denies a creator God and is thus atheistic. Through self-mortification, its adherents seek to transcend the world and achieve a peace beyond all concerns. The central virtue is nonviolence against any living being. To this end all adherents must be vegetarians and cannot serve as butchers or soldiers. Its monks wear a gauze mask over the mouth to prevent the unintentional inhalation of an innocent insect. They are also required to sweep the ground in front of them as they walk, so as not to crush anything alive. They renounce all worldly attachments as well as any sexual pleasures, and they vow not to eat after sunset. If psychologically strong enough to achieve the goal of neglecting every personal interest, the monks commit suicide by self-starvation, thereby ridding the soul of all passions and bringing an appropriate close to an ethical life. The two main sects of the religion are divided over the question of whether the monks, to symbolize their complete renunciation of the material world, should practice nudity.

Can any argument demonstrate why Christianity, for example, is superior to Jainism? Granted, any one of their differing metaphysical and ethical principles could be isolated and subjected to critical scrutiny. But in view of their disagreements about so many fundamental matters, how could advocates for the two religions profitably debate their opposing outlooks and practices?

Note that an appeal to numbers would not settle the issue. Worldwide, Christianity has nearly 500 times as many adherents as Jainism, but Buddhism, Hinduism, and Islam together have hundreds of millions more adherents than Christianity. Whatever may be the relevance of such statistics to a sociologist of religion, they bear no philosophical significance. After all, at one time most people thought the sun went around the earth; nevertheless, this belief was false.

Some Christians might argue that the beliefs and practices of Jainism are too strange to be taken seriously. But how would the beliefs and practices of Christianity appear to Jains? What would they think of the immaculate conception, virgin birth, transubstantiation, and resurrection? What would they think of using a Roman device of torture as a central religious symbol? What would they think of the claim that the moral lapses of a person living today are forgiven because approximately two thousand years ago the son of God in the person of a Jewish teacher was put to death?

Each religion reflects the culture in which it develops, and cultures are not true or false, provable or disprovable, although one may be richer in some respects than another. Yet a culture is not tested by arguments, nor are religions. They are less like scientific theories and more like works of art, not adding to our factual knowledge but enabling many to enrich their response to the challenges of the human condition.

Some have said that religions, regardless of the chasms between them, have been a force for good in human history. Hume, on the other hand, a leading historian as well as philosopher, forcefully expressed the opposite view, saying of religion: "Factions, civil wars, persecutions, subversions of government, oppression, slavery—these are the dismal consequences which always attend its prevalence over the minds of men. If the religious spirit be ever mentioned in any historical narration, we are sure to meet afterwards with a detail of the miseries which attend it."[36]

Surely the record of religion is mixed: sublime ideals and saintly acts are balanced by ignoble sentiments and horrendous practices. Religion as such is neither good nor evil. Religions have been both.

13. Religion Without God

In the previous section, I referred to religions that do not affirm the existence of God. Yet how is it possible for religious adherents to deny any concept of a deity separate from the natural world? Isn't it a contradiction to speak of religion without a supernatural God?

I propose to show that nothing in the theory or practice of religion—not ritual, not prayer, not metaphysical belief, not moral commitment—necessitates a commitment to theism. In other words, just as one may be a nonreligious theist, so one can be a religious agnostic or atheist.

Consider the concept of a ritual. It is a prescribed symbolic action. In the case of religion, the ritual is prescribed by the religious organization and the act symbolizes some aspect of religious belief. If the religion is supernaturalistic (that is, if it believes in a supernatural God), then those who reject such theology may, as a result, consider any ritual irrational. Yet although particular rituals may be based on irrational beliefs, nothing about the practice of ritual is inherently irrational.

Think of two people shaking hands when meeting. This act is a ritual, prescribed by our society and symbolic of the individuals' mutual respect. The act is in no way irrational. If people shook hands in order to ward off evil demons, then shaking hands would indeed be irrational. But that reason is not why people shake hands. The ritual has no connection with God or demons but indicates the attitude one person has toward another.

It might be assumed that the ritual of handshaking escapes irrationality only because the ritual is not prescribed by any specific organization and is not part of an elaborate ceremony. To see that this assumption is false, consider the graduation ceremony at a college. The graduates and faculty members all wear peculiar hats and robes, and the participants stand and sit at appropriate times. The ceremony, however, is not at all irrational. Indeed, the rites of graduation day, far from being irrational, are symbolic of commitment to the process of education and the life of reason.

At first glance, rituals may seem a comparatively insignificant feature of life; yet they are a pervasive and treasured aspect of human experience. Who would want to eliminate the festivities associated with holidays such as Independence Day or Thanksgiving? What would college football be without songs, cheers, flags, and the innumerable other symbolic features surrounding the game? Those who disdain popular rituals typically proceed to establish their own distinctive ones, ranging from characteristic habits of dress to the use of drugs, symbolizing a rejection of traditional mores.

Religious persons, like all others, search for an appropriate means of emphasizing their commitment to a group or its values. Rituals provide such a means. Granted, supernaturalistic religion has often infused its rituals with superstition, but nonreligious rituals can be equally superstitious. For instance, most Americans view the Fourth of July as an occasion on which they can express pride in their country's heritage. With this purpose in mind, the holiday is one of great significance. However, if the singing of the fourth verse of "The Star-Spangled Banner" four times on the Fourth of July were thought to protect our country against future disasters, then the original meaning of the holiday would soon be lost in a maze of superstition.

A naturalistic (that is, nonsupernaturalistic) religion need not utilize ritual in a superstitious manner, because such a religion does not employ rituals to please a benevolent deity or appease an angry one. Rather, naturalistic religion views rituals, as one of its exponents has put it, as "the enhancement of life through the dramatization of great ideals."[37] If a group places great stress on justice or freedom, why should it not utilize ritual in order to emphasize these goals? Such a use of ritual serves to solidify the group and strengthen its devotion to its expressed purposes. These are buttressed if the ritual in question has the force of tradition, having been performed by many generations who have belonged to the same group and struggled to achieve the same goals. Ritual so conceived is not a form of superstition; rather, it is a reasonable means of strengthening religious commitment, as useful to naturalistic as to supernaturalistic religion.

Let us next turn to the concept of prayer. Some might suppose that naturalistic religion could have no use for prayer, because prayer is supposedly addressed to a supernatural being, and proponents of naturalistic religion do not believe in the existence of such a being. But this objection oversimplifies the concept of prayer, focusing attention on one type while neglecting an equally important but different sort.

Supernaturalistic religion makes extensive use of petitionary prayer, prayer that petitions a supernatural being for various favors. These may range from the personal happiness of the petitioner to the general welfare of all society. Because petitionary prayer rests on the assumption that a supernatural being exists, such prayer clearly has no place in a naturalistic religion.

Not all prayers, however, are prayers of petition. Some prayers are prayers of meditation. These are not directed to any supernatural being and are not requests for granting favors. Rather, these prayers provide the opportunity for persons to rethink their ultimate commitments and rededicate themselves to their ideals. Such prayers may take the form of silent devotion or involve oral repetition of certain central texts. Just as Americans repeat the Pledge of Allegiance and reread the Gettysburg Address, so adherents of naturalistic religion repeat the statements of their ideals and reread the documents that embody their traditional beliefs.

Granted, supernaturalistic religions, to the extent that they utilize prayers of meditation, tend to treat these prayers irrationally by supposing that if the prayers are not uttered a precise number of times under certain specific conditions, then the prayers lose all value. Yet prayer need not be viewed in this way. Rather, as the English biologist Sir Julian Huxley wrote, prayer "permits the bringing before the mind of a world of thought which in most people must inevitably be absent during the occupation of ordinary life. . . . [I]t is the means by which the mind may fix itself upon this or that noble or beautiful or awe-inspiring idea, and so grow to it and come to realize it more fully."[38]

Such a use of prayer may be enhanced by song, instrumental music, and various types of symbolism. These elements, fused together, provide the means for adherents of naturalistic religion to engage in religious services akin to those engaged in by adherents of supernaturalistic religion. The difference between the two services is that those who participate in the latter come to relate themselves to God, whereas those who participate in the former come to relate themselves to their fellow human beings and the world in which we live.

Thus far we have examined how ritual and prayer can be utilized in naturalistic religion, but to adopt a religious perspective also involves metaphysical beliefs and moral commitments. Can these be maintained without recourse to supernaturalism?

If we use the term *metaphysics* in its usual sense, referring to the systematic study of the most basic features of existence, then a metaphysical system may be either supernaturalistic or naturalistic. Representative of a supernaturalistic theory are the views of Descartes and the illustrious German philosopher and mathematician Gottfried Leibniz (1646–1716). Representative of a naturalistic theory are the views of the eminent Dutch philosopher Baruch Spinoza (1632–1677) and John Dewey.

Spinoza's *Ethics*, for example, one of the greatest of all metaphysical works, explicitly rejects the view that any being exists apart from Nature itself. Spinoza identifies God with Nature as a whole and urges that the good life consists in coming to understand Nature. In his words, "our salvation, or blessedness, or freedom consists in a constant and eternal love toward God."[39] Spinoza's concept of God, however, is explicitly not the supernaturalistic concept of God, and Spinoza's metaphysical system thus exemplifies not only a naturalistic metaphysics but also the possibility of reinterpreting the concept of God within a naturalistic framework.

Can those who do not believe in a supernaturalistic God commit themselves to moral principles, or is the acceptance of moral principles dependent on the acceptance of supernaturalism? Some have assumed that those who reject a supernaturalistic God are necessarily immoral, for their denial of the existence of such a God leaves them free to act without fear of divine punishment. This assumption, however, is seriously mistaken.

The refutation of the view that morality must rest on belief in a supernatural God was provided more than two thousand years ago in Plato's remarkable dialogue, the *Euthyphro*. Plato's teacher, Socrates, who in most of Plato's works is given the leading role, asks the overconfident Euthyphro the following question: Are actions right because God says they are right, or does God say actions are right because they are right? This question is not a verbal trick; on the contrary, it poses a serious dilemma for those who believe in a supernatural deity.

Socrates was inquiring whether actions are right because of God's fiat or whether God is Himself subject to moral standards. If actions are right because of God's command, then anything God commands is right, including torture or murder. Some may accept this discomforting view, but then their assertion that God is good becomes pointless, for if the good is whatever God commands, to say that God commands rightly is simply to say that He commands as He commands, which is a tautology. This approach makes a mockery of morality, for might does not make right, even if the might is the infinite might of God. To act morally is not to act out of fear of punishment; it is not to act as one is commanded to act. Rather, it is to act as one ought to act, and how one ought to act is not dependent on anyone's power, even if the power be divine.

Thus actions are not right because God commands them; on the contrary, God commands them because they are right. What is right is independent of what God commands, for what He commands must conform with an independent standard in order to be right. Because one could act intentionally in accord with this independent standard without believing in the existence of a supernatural God, it follows that morality does not rest on supernaturalism. Consequently, naturalists can be highly moral (as well as immoral) persons, and supernaturalists can be highly immoral (as well as moral) persons. This conclusion should come as no surprise to anyone who has contrasted the benevolent life of the inspiring teacher Buddha (563–483 B.C.E.), an atheist, with the malevolent life of the churchman Tomás de Torquemada (1420–1498), who devised and enforced the unimaginable cruelties of the Spanish Inquisition.

We have now seen that naturalistic religion is a genuine possibility, because reasonable individuals may perform rituals, utter prayers, accept metaphysical beliefs, and commit themselves to moral principles without believing in supernaturalism. Indeed, even a supernaturalistic religion such as Christianity or Judaism may be reinterpreted to eliminate any commitment to supernaturalism. Consider, for example, those Christians who accept the "Death of God"[40] or those Jews who belong to the influential Reconstructionist movement in Judaism.[41]

Such options are philosophically respectable. Whether to choose any of them is for each person to decide.

14. Heaven and Hell

One feature of some supernaturalist religions, including traditional Christianity and Islam, is the belief that life on earth is followed by an afterlife in which some persons abide forever in a place of joy while others endure everlasting suffering in a place of doom. Many people find these visions compelling and therefore embrace a religion that emphasizes them. But are the concepts of heaven and hell viable?

They raise more questions than they resolve. Why should finite wickedness deserve infinite punishment? Why should finite goodness deserve infinite reward? Is heaven reserved for adherents of only one religion? Are all other believers assigned to hell? What is the fate of those who lived before the development of any particular religion? Are they condemned to hell for not believing in a doctrine that had not yet been formulated when they lived? What about infants who die? How are they to be judged? What about beloved dogs, cats, and other creatures who have enriched the lives of so many persons? Might some of these animals merit a place in heaven? If not, how joyful can heaven be for those deprived of their faithful companions?

This last question is explored in "The Hunt," a provocative episode of the award-winning television series *The Twilight Zone*. An old hillbilly named Simpson and his hound dog Rip appear to drown in a backwoods pond but awake the next morning near the water, walk toward the local graveyard, come to an unfamiliar fence, follow it, and arrive at a gate. The gatekeeper explains to Simpson that he is at the entrance to heaven. He is welcome, but Rip is not; no dogs are allowed. Simpson becomes infuriated, declaring that he would rather stay with Rip than go to heaven, and man and dog walk away together. Soon they meet an angel sent to accompany them to heaven. Simpson protests that he won't go without Rip, and the angel tells Simpson that Rip is welcome in heaven. The angel explains that if

Simpson had left Rip and gone through the gate, he would have made a terrible mistake, for the gatekeeper had lied: the gate was the entrance to hell. Why had Rip been excluded? He would have smelled the brimstone and warned Simpson away. As the angel says, "You see, Mr. Simpson, a man, well he'll walk right into Hell with both eyes open—but even the Devil can't fool a dog!"[42]

The effectiveness of this story depends in part on our being able to envision hell but not heaven. For when we realize that Simpson nearly made the mistake of going to hell, we can easily imagine the horrors that awaited him. We all are familiar with the nature of misery. Who among us has not known sorrow or suffering? Most have experienced anguish and agony. Too many have suffered tortures of mind and body. Could the horrors of hell be worse than those suffered by many in their dreadful lives on earth? I doubt it. As the visionary English poet William Blake (1757–1827) wrote,

> Every Night & every Morn
> Some to Misery are Born.
> Every Morn & every Night
> Some are Born to sweet delight.
> Some are Born to sweet delight,
> Some are Born to Endless Night.[43]

Those born on earth to endless night might welcome whatever hell offers.

Heaven, however, defies description. What events take place there? How do individuals relate to each other? What activities occupy them? A familiar supposition is that harps are played, but how long can harp music suffice for felicity? We understand the happiness that Rip brings Simpson. But how does it compare to the joys Simpson would experience in heaven? Not knowing, we are comfortable with Simpson rejecting heaven and staying with Rip.

To see additional difficulties involved in grasping the concept of heaven, consider the case of Willie Mays, the spectacular baseball player whose greatest joy was to play the game he loved. What does heaven offer him? Presumably bats, balls, and gloves are not found there. So what does Willie Mays do? Assuming he is the same person who made that spectacular catch in the 1954 World Series, how can the delights that supposedly await him in heaven match those he knew on earth?

Furthermore, some of Mays's fans found their greatest delight in watching him play baseball. Won't they be denied this joy in heaven? Whatever heaven may offer them, they will miss watching Willie in action.

The problems mount. Consider two individuals, Peters and Peterson, and suppose that Peters looks forward to the joy of spending eternity with Peterson, whereas Peterson looks forward to the joy of being forever free of Peters. Assuming they retain their distinctive personalities, including their fundamental likes and dislikes, how can they both attain heavenly bliss?

More questions arise in attempting to understand the supposition that our bodies will be resurrected. Will they appear as they did when we were ten, forty, or eighty years old? If a person suffered from diabetes, will the resurrected body suffer from the disease? In what sense would a resurrected person be identical to the person who died? If a ship is destroyed and an identical one is built, the second is a different ship from the first. Similarly, if a person is destroyed and an identical one is created, the second is a different person from the first.

One way to avoid these difficulties is to suppose that after death what survives are not bodies but souls. Thus although Simpson appeared to have a body, in reality he was only a soul. Was Rip also a soul, or do dogs not have souls? Can two souls inhabit a single body, or is it one soul to a customer?

What, after all, is a soul? Supposedly, when added to a body, a soul converts that body into a person. Does the soul itself think and feel? In that case, it is already a person and needs no body. If it doesn't think and feel, how does it start to do so when it enters a body?

This problem can be avoided by recognizing that some bodies can think and feel. They do so as a result of possessing brains, which are physical objects and not immaterial souls. Yet brains cease functioning. People die.

Despite all the conceptual difficulties, some may continue to believe in heaven and hell. But given the bewildering questions that make it difficult to provide a persuasive, or even coherent, account of survival in a next world, trying to imagine such a possible state of affairs provides no help in enabling us to understand our lives in the world we actually inhabit.

15. Life Without God

An assumption common to many theists is that if we do not believe in the existence of God, our life is somehow diminished. Why accept this view? After all, even if God does not exist, we are still alive, as are others we cherish, we still experience times of health and sickness, we still strive to achieve goals, we still relish successes and regret failures, we still witness inspiring acts of goodness and disheartening deeds of evil, and we still face moral problems and have to make difficult decisions.

Granted, we cannot expect help from God. But even if He exists, our choices are our own, not His. We cannot look to God for guidance, because what He wills is unknown. We cannot rest secure in the belief that God is taking care of us, because in any case bad things happen to good people, and good things happen to bad people.

Would life without God lack meaning? The answer depends on what sort of meaning a life can have. If a meaningful life is one in which each individual plays a role in a divine drama, entering and exiting the stage at an appointed time in order to serve God's purposes, then in the absence of God, life has no meaning.

Why assume that people cannot have their own purposes, independent of any divine playwright? Suppose I wish to devote my life to teaching philosophy, you wish to devote your life to providing medical care to the sick, and others wish to devote their lives to composing music, cultivating a garden, or raising a family. Why aren't these activities meaningful? None of them depends on the existence of God. They nevertheless provide life with significance. They are freely chosen, not preordained, but so much the better. They are expressions of our own personalities and values.

Or is the problem supposed to be that in the absence of God, we are unable to decide which values or moral principles to accept? This problem can be solved by using reason to assess specific value judgments in the light of shared human concerns and our common experience.

To illustrate the process, let us examine in turn various ethical principles that have been thought by many to embody the will of God but that, regardless of whether God exists, fall short of providing an entirely satisfactory foundation for morality. These rules, whatever their origin, are not immune from difficulties that can be recognized by theists and nontheists alike. Both groups can assess such moral guidelines.

Consider the Golden Rule, a moral principle endorsed by various religious traditions, both theistic and nontheistic. Its positive formulation, attributed to Jesus, is: "In everything do to others as you would have them do to you."[44] The negative formulation, which appeared five centuries earlier, is attributed to the Chinese sage Confucius (c. 551–479 B.C.E.) and was later proposed by the Jewish scholar Hillel (c. 30 B.C.E.–10 C.E.) The latter put it as follows: "What is hateful to you, do not to your neighbor."[45] Is either of these versions entirely acceptable?

Consider first the positive formulation. Granted, we should usually treat others as we would wish them to treat us. For instance, we should go to the aid of an injured person, just as we would wish that person to come to our aid if we were injured. If we always followed this rule, however, the results would be unfortunate. Consider masochists, who derive pleasure from being hurt. Were they to act according to the principle in question, their duty would be to inflict pain, thereby doing to others as they wish done to themselves. Similarly, consider a person who enjoys receiving telephone calls, regardless of who is calling. The principle would require that person to telephone everyone, thereby reciprocating preferred treatment. Indeed, strictly speaking, to fulfill the positive formulation of the Golden Rule would be impossible because we wish so many others to do so much for us that we would not have time to do all that is necessary to treat them likewise. As Walter Kaufman commented, "anyone who tried to live up to Jesus's rule would become an insufferable nuisance."[46]

In this respect the negative formulation of the Golden Rule is preferable because it does not imply that we have innumerable duties toward everyone else. Neither does it imply that masochists ought to inflict pain on others, nor that those who enjoy receiving telephone calls ought themselves to make calls. However, while the negative formulation does not require these actions, neither does it forbid them. It enjoins us not to do to others what is hateful to ourselves, but pain is not hateful to the masochist and calls are not hateful to the telephone enthusiast. Thus the negative formulation of the Golden Rule, though superior in one way to the positive formulation, is not without weakness, because it does not prohibit actions that ought to be prohibited.

Whether the Golden Rule in either formulation is supposed to be of divine origin makes no difference in its assessment. Whatever its source, all can agree that it does not by itself serve as the ultimate moral touchstone.

The Ten Commandments, accepted by adherents of a variety of religions, also have their limitations. Consider the Second Commandment, which, after prohibiting the making or serving of sculptured images, goes on to say, "For I the LORD your God am an impassioned God, visiting the guilt of the parents upon the children, upon the third and upon the fourth generations of those who reject Me, but showing kindness to the thousandth generation of those who love Me and keep My commandments."[47] But to punish one person for the moral lapses of another is unethical, as is rewarding a person for the good deeds done by another. This point was made emphatically by the prophet Ezekiel, who declared: "A child shall not share the burden of a parent's guilt, nor shall a parent share the burden of a child's guilt; the righteousness of the righteous shall be accounted to him alone, and the wickedness of the wicked shall be accounted to him alone."[48] Incidentally, Ezekiel's principles rule out the possibility that anyone, including God, could act in such a way as to absolve us of responsibility for our failings. Only we as individuals can atone for our own errors.

The Fifth Commandment instructs individuals to honor their father and mother. Suppose, however, parents break the Second Commandment by making and worshipping sculptured images. Or perhaps they break some of the remaining commandments by coveting a neighbor's property, bearing false witness, stealing, engaging in adultery, or even committing murder. Although they might still merit their child's concern, parents who acted in such ways would not deserve to be honored.

Two of the commandments take slavery for granted. The Fourth, which requires individuals to remember the Sabbath day and keep it holy, prohibits work at that time by "you, your son or daughter, your male or female slave."[49] The Tenth prohibits coveting anything that belongs to a neighbor, including his "wife, or his male or female slave."[50] Slavery we all now agree is immoral, yet the Ten Commandments treat it as an acceptable practice.

A further problem is that the commandments are stated as if they allowed no exceptions. Yet under certain circumstances, not to break a commandment would be widely regarded as unethical. For example, if a young girl's life depended on her mother's stealing a small amount of money from a wealthy, immoral person, most of us would view the theft favorably.

Not only do certain circumstances call for making exceptions to the commandments, but situations can develop in which fulfilling one commandment would amount to breaking another. If, for instance, a man had to work on the Sabbath in order to take his critically ill father to the hospital, the commandment to honor one's father and mother would take precedence over the commandment not to work on the Sabbath. The commandments have exceptions, but do not themselves provide any guidance for when or how to make such exceptions. Thus regardless of claims of their divine origin and despite their moral worth, the Ten Commandments fall short as an ultimate guide to morality.

The same is true of that sacred Christian text, the Sermon on the Mount. Amid its beauties of language and thought, we find such an unacceptable principle as "[I]f your right hand causes you to sin, cut it off and throw it away . . ."[51] Any statement, of course, can be interpreted to render it sensible, but taken literally, thieves cutting off their hands would be acts of lunacy. If the statement is not to be taken literally, however, it does not provide an unambiguous guide to moral action.

A similar problem is implicit in Jesus's instruction that "whoever marries a divorced woman commits adultery."[52] Few would find such a principle morally acceptable. What of Jesus's saying, "[D]o not worry about your life, what you will eat or what you will drink. . . ."[53] Wouldn't such a lack of concern for oneself be a sign of a psychological problem as well as an unfair drain on family and friends?

If these sayings appear peripheral to Jesus's principal message, consider this central passage: "Do not resist an evildoer. But if anyone strikes you on the right cheek, turn the other also; and if anyone wants to sue you and take your coat, give your cloak as well. . . ."[54] The difficulty with such pacifism is that those who adhere to it depend on others' not adhering to it in order to avoid the triumph of evil. Turning the other cheek to a Hitler is death. Not to fight for the right is wrong. Throughout history, when those who consider themselves devout Christians have come under attack, they have temporarily put aside the Sermon on the Mount and picked up their weapons. To have done otherwise would have led to the destruction of Christianity. Recall that when Jesus entered Jerusalem, he "drove out all who were selling and buying in the temple, and he overturned the tables of the money changers and the seats of those who sold doves."[55] So much for turning the other cheek.

Over the course of centuries many persons have found the Golden Rule, the Ten Commandments, or the Sermon on the Mount inspirational and worthy of devotion. Yet these statements of principle, like all others, require interpretation by the use of reason and testing by appeal to the lessons of experience. If God exists, our principles, even if attributed to the divine, still need to be evaluated. Theism doesn't solve our moral problems. And even if

God does not exist, we may still commit ourselves to care for others. A world without God need not be a world without love.

16. A Religious Life

Many suppose that a religious life necessarily involves believing in God, doing what is right in order to serve God's will, and hoping thereby to attain the bliss supposedly found in heaven. I propose instead that someone may lead a religious life without believing in God, but by doing what is right in response to the needs of others, thereby potentially achieving the joys that can be found on earth.

For illustration, I turn to a Yiddish tale authored by I. L. Peretz, described by one notable critic as "arguably the most important figure in the development of modern Jewish culture."[56] To summarize the story would fail to do it justice, and so I present it in its entirety.[57]

If Not Higher

Early every Friday morning, at the time of the Penitential Prayers,[58] the rabbi of Nemirov[59] would vanish.

He was nowhere to be seen—neither in the synagogue nor in the two study houses nor at a minyan.[60] And he was certainly not at home. His door stood open: whoever wished could go in and out; no one would steal from the rabbi. But not a living creature was within.

Where could the rabbi be? Where should he be? In heaven, no doubt. A rabbi has plenty of business to take care of just before the Days of Awe.[61] Jews, God bless them, need livelihood, peace, health, and good matches. They want to be pious and good, but our sins are so great, and Satan of the thousand eyes watches the whole earth from one end to the other. What he sees, he reports; he denounces, informs. Who can help us if not the rabbi!

That's what the people thought.

But once a Litvak[62] came, and he laughed. You know the Litvaks. They think little of the holy books but stuff themselves with Talmud[63] and law. So this Litvak points to a passage in the Gemara—it sticks in your eyes—where it is written that even Moses our Teacher did not ascend to heaven during his lifetime but remained suspended two and a half feet below. Go argue with a Litvak!

So where can the rabbi be?

"That's not my business," said the Litvak, shrugging. Yet all the while—what a Litvak can do!—he is scheming to find out.

That same night, right after the evening prayers, the Litvak steals into the rabbi's room, slides under the rabbi's bed, and waits. He'll watch all night and discover where the rabbi vanishes and what he does during the Penitential Prayers.

Someone else might have gotten drowsy and fallen asleep, but a Litvak is never at a loss; he recites a whole tractate of the Talmud by heart.

At dawn he hears the call to prayers.

The rabbi has already been awake for a long time. The Litvak has heard him groaning for a whole hour.

Whoever has heard the rabbi of Nemirov groan knows how much sorrow for all Israel, how much suffering, lies in each groan. A man's heart might break, hearing it. But a Litvak is made of iron; he listens and remains where he is. The rabbi—long life to him!—lies on the bed, and the Litvak under the bed.

Then the Litvak hears the beds in the house begin to creak; he hears people jumping out of their beds, mumbling a few Jewish words, pouring water on their fingernails, banging doors. Everyone has left. It is again quiet and dark; a bit of light from the moon shines through the shutters.

(Afterward, the Litvak admitted that when he found himself alone with the rabbi a great fear took hold of him. Goose pimples spread across his skin, and the roots of his sidelocks pricked him like needles. A trifle: to be alone with the rabbi at the time of the Penitential Prayers! But a Litvak is stubborn. So he quivered like a fish in water and remained where he was.)

Finally the rabbi—long life to him!—arises. First, he does what befits a Jew.[64] Then he goes to the clothes closet and takes out a bundle of peasant clothes: linen trousers, high boots, a coat, a big felt hat, and a long, wide leather belt studded with brass nails. The rabbi gets dressed. From his coat pocket dangles the end of a heavy peasant rope.

The rabbi goes out, and the Litvak follows him.

On the way the rabbi stops in the kitchen, bends down, takes an ax from under the bed, puts it into his belt, and leaves the house. The Litvak trembles but continues to follow.

The hushed dread of the Days of Awe hangs over the dark streets. Every once in a while a cry rises from some minyan reciting the Penitential Prayers, or from a sickbed. The rabbi hugs the sides of the streets, keeping to the shade of the houses. He glides from house to house, and the Litvak after him. The Litvak hears the sound of his heartbeats mingling with the sound of the rabbi's heavy steps. But he keeps on going and follows the rabbi to the outskirts of the town.

A small wood stands just outside the town.

The rabbi—long life to him!—enters the wood. He takes thirty or forty steps and stops by a small tree. The Litvak, overcome with amazement, watches the rabbi take the ax out of his belt and strike the tree. He hears the tree creak and fall. The rabbi chops the tree into logs and the logs into sticks. Then he makes a bundle of the wood and ties it with the rope in his pocket. He puts the bundle of wood on his back, shoves the ax back into his belt, and returns to the town.

He stops at a back street beside a small, broken-down shack and knocks at the window.

"Who is there?" asks a frightened voice. The Litvak recognizes it as the voice of a sick Jewish woman.

"I," answers the rabbi in the accent of a peasant.

"Who is I?"

Again the rabbi answers in Russian. "Vassil."

"Who is Vassil, and what do you want?"

"I have wood to sell, very cheap." And not waiting for the woman's reply, he goes into the house.

The Litvak steals in after him. In the gray light of early morning he sees a poor room with broken, miserable furnishings. A sick woman, wrapped in rags, lies on the bed. She complains bitterly, "Buy? How can I buy? Where will a poor widow get money?"

"I'll lend it to you," answers the supposed Vassil. "It's only six cents."

"And how will I ever pay you back?" asks the poor woman, groaning.

"Foolish one," says the rabbi reproachfully. "See, you are a poor, sick Jew, and I am ready to trust you with a little wood. I am sure you'll pay. While you, you have such a great and mighty God and you don't trust him for six cents."

"And who will kindle the fire?" asks the widow. "Have I the strength to get up? My son is at work."

"I'll kindle the fire," answers the rabbi.

As the rabbi put the wood into the oven he recited, in a groan, the first portion of the Penitential Prayers.

As he kindled the fire and the wood burned brightly, he recited, a bit more joyously, the second portion of the Penitential Prayers. When the fire was set, he recited the third portion, and then he shut the stove.

The Litvak who saw all this became a disciple of the rabbi.

And ever after, when another disciple tells how the rabbi of Nemirov ascends to heaven at the time of the Penitential Prayers, the Litvak does not laugh. He only adds quietly, "If not higher."

Those last three words embody a view of God, reason, and religion. If the Litvak believed in God and His heaven, he could conceive nothing higher. His comment thus signifies a skeptical attitude toward traditional theism. Yet he becomes a follower of the rabbi because of admiration for the rabbi's ethical commitments and the extraordinary manner in which he fulfills them.

The rabbi is not without guile. He acts surreptitiously, dons a disguise, and speaks misleadingly to the distressed woman. But the deceptions serve a moral purpose, and in striving to do good the rabbi is not bound by ordinary conventions. He does not slavishly follow the law but seeks to embody its spirit.

The rabbi thereby captures the essence of a religion that can be embraced even by those who do not adopt orthodox theistic beliefs. It has its rituals and prayers, but these are valuable only insofar as they lead to noble deeds. Whether to affirm the existence of God or Satan is a metaphysical question about which the rabbi and the Litvak may disagree. (Who knows what the cunning rabbi believes?) The rabbi's eminence, however, rests not on the profundity of his theology but on the deep concern he shows for the sick and the poor. His wondrous actions lead the Litvak to be in awe of the rabbi's holiness.

Belief in God, the divine will, and the promise of eternal life are important aspects of many religions, but not all. The Litvak is a doubter but becomes a disciple. He laughs at the Bible but eventually reveres the rabbi. The Litvak scoffs at talk of heaven, but as events unfold his understanding grows. In the end the Litvak realizes that without ever leaving this world the rabbi in his wisdom has found a way to deal with suffering and has attained a blessedness that lies beyond any celestial vision of which human beings may dream.

NOTES

1. *Four Films of Woody Allen: Annie Hall, Interiors, Manhattan, Stardust Memories* (New York: Random House, 1982), p. 366.
2. David Hume, *Dialogues Concerning Natural Religion* (New York: Oxford University Press, 1998), part XII.
3. *The Later Works of John Dewey, 1925–1953*, vol. 9, ed. Jo Ann Boydston (Carbondale: Southern Illinois University Press, 1988), p. 34.
4. My use of "His" is not intended to imply that God is masculine.
5. Hume, part VI.
6. Ibid., part V.
7. George Berkeley, *A Treatise Concerning the Principles of Human Knowledge* (Indianapolis: Hackett Publishing Company, 1982), sec. 146.
8. Hume, part X.
9. John Hick, *Philosophy of Religion*, 4th ed. (Englewood Cliffs, NJ: Prentice-Hall, 1990), pp. 39–48.
10. My use of "He" is not intended to imply that the Demon is masculine.
11. Arthur Conan Doyle, *The Complete Sherlock Holmes* (Garden City, NY: Doubleday, n.d.), pp. 471, 496, 769. The works cited are "The Final Problem," "The Adventure of the Norwood Builder," and "The Valley of Fear."
12. Doyle, "The Adventure of the Retired Colourman," p. 1113.
13. Hume, part X.
14. I Corinthians 13:12. The translation is from *The Holy Bible: New Revised Standard Version* (New York and Oxford: Oxford University Press, 1989).
15. Doyle, "The Final Problem," p. 471.
16. Ecclesiastes 4:2–3. The translation is from *Tanakh: The Holy Scriptures* (Philadelphia: Jewish Publication Society, 1988).
17. Anita Shreve, *All He Ever Wanted* (Boston: Little, Brown and Company, 2003), p. 79.
18. Devotees of Sherlock Holmes will recall that a dummy bell rope is a criti-

cal clue in Sir Arthur Conan Doyle's masterful story, "The Adventure of the Speckled Band."

19. Mortimer J. Cohen, *Pathways through the Bible* (Philadelphia: Jewish Publication Society of America, 1946), p. 460.
20. Jack J. Cohen, *The Case for Religious Naturalism* (New York: The Reconstructionist Press, 1958), p. 83.
21. David Trueblood, *The Logic of Belief* (New York: Harper & Brothers, 1942), pp. 293–294.
22. I take the term from Lewis Carroll's humorous poem "The Hunting of the Snark: An Agony, in Eight Fits," It concludes: "For the Snark *was* a Boojum, you see," thus explaining one unknown concept in terms of another and leaving both without sense.
23. Levi ben Gershom, *The Wars of the Lord*, trans. Seymour Feldman (Philadelphia: Jewish Publication Society, 1987), vol. 2, p. 111.
24. Janet Martin Soskice, *Metaphor and Religious Language* (Oxford: Clarendon Press, 1985), p. 57.
25. Ibid., pp. 57–58.
26. Ibid., p. 101.
27. Ibid., p. 140.
28. A fiery chariot takes Elijah to heaven. See II Kings 2:11.
29. David Hume, *An Enquiry Concerning Human Understanding* (New York: Oxford University Press, 1995), part X.
30. David Hume, *A Treatise of Human Nature* (New York: Oxford University Press, 1978), III, 1, 1.
31. Sidney Hook, *The Quest for Being* (New York: St. Martin's, 1961), pp. 130–131.
32. See Blaise Pascal, *Pensées and Other Writings*, trans. Honor Levi (New York: Oxford University Press, 1995), pp. 152–156.
33. Benjamin Franklin, *Poor Richard's Almanack*, 1736.
34. Amos 5:21–24.
35. I rely throughout this section on Ninian Smart, *The Religious Experience of Mankind* (New York: Charles Scribner's Sons, 1969).
36. Hume, *Dialogues Concerning Natural Religion*, part XII.
37. Jack J. Cohen, *The Case for Religious Naturalism*, p. 150.
38. Julian Huxley, *Religion without Revelation* (New York: New American Library, 1957), p. 141.
39. Baruch Spinoza, *Ethics*, ed. James Gutmann (New York: Hafner, 1957), part V, prop. 36, note.
40. See John H. T. Robinson, *Honest to God* (Philadelphia: Westminster, 1963).
41. See Mordecai M. Kaplan, *Judaism as a Civilization* (New York: Schocken, 1967).
42 Marc Scott Zicree, *The Twilight Zone Companion* (New York: Bantam Books, 1982), pp. 242–244.
43. William Blake, *Auguries of Innocence*, lines 119–124. "Endless Night" is the title of one of Agatha Christie's finest novels.
44. Matthew 7:12.
45. *The Babylonian Talmud* (London: Soncino Press, 1938), Shabbath, 31a.
46. Walter Kaufman, *The Faith of a Heretic* (New York: Doubleday, 1963), p. 212.
47. Exodus 20:5–6.
48. Ezekiel 18:20.
49. Exodus 20:10.
50. Exodus 20:14.

51. Matthew 5:30.
52. Matthew 5:32.
53. Matthew 6:25.
54. Matthew 5:39.
55. Matthew 21:12.
56. *The I. L. Peretz Reader*, ed. Ruth R. Wisse (New Haven and London: Yale University Press, 2002), xiii.
57. "If Not Higher" by I. L. Peretz, translated by Marie Syrkin, from *A Treasury of Yiddish Stories* by Irving Howe and Eliezer Greenberg, editors, copyright © 1953, 1954, 1989 by Viking Penguin, renewed © 1981, 1982 by Irving Howe and Eliezer Greenberg. Used by permission of Viking Penguin, a division of Penguin Group (USA), Inc. The accompanying notes are my own.
58. A type of liturgical poetry requesting forgiveness from sin.
59. A Ukrainian city with a flourishing Jewish community in the seventeenth century but the scene of a ghastly massacre of the Jews by the Cossacks in 1648.
60. A group of ten male adult Jews, the minimum required for a communal prayer.
61. The ten-day period from Rosh Hashonah, the Jewish New Year, to Yom Kippur, the Day of Atonement.
62. A Jew from Lithuania.
63. The multi-volume compilation of Jewish law and commentary, containing the Mishnah, the core of the Oral Law, and the Gemara, a supplement to the Mishnah.
64. Morning prayers.

Index